Inside the ARRB

Volume Two

Inside the Assassination Records Review Board:

The U.S. Government's Final Attempt

to Reconcile the Conflicting Medical Evidence

in the

Assassination of JFK

by

Douglas P. Horne

Chief Analyst for Military Records,
Assassination Records Review Board

(Volume Two of Five)

ISBN-13: 978-0-9843144-1-6

First Printing, November 2009
Second Printing, March 2010 (corrections entered)

Contents of Volume II

Knudsen revealed during his deposition that he had been a full-time White House photographer from 1958-1974. (His wife, Gloria, provided more details to the ARRB in 1996: she said he had been a part-time White House photographer from 1946-1953 before working there full-time starting in 1958.) He clarified that although he was officially assigned to the President's Naval Aide, he received his daily instructions from the President's secretary, Evelyn Lincoln. The reader may be interested to know that the black-and-white portrait of President Kennedy taken prior to his inauguration, and which ended up in the front of the Warren Commission report, was taken by Chief Knudsen.

Knudsen revealed a number of things at his deposition which were at variance with the then "known" chain-of-custody for the autopsy photographs. A summary of the more noteworthy revelations revealed in the course of his deposition is provided below:

	Information in Various Government Records Prior to the Knudsen Deposition (11-22-63 receipts, 11-01-66 inventory, James Fox memo of 2-16-67, and Feb 1967 Secret Service Joint Statement Re: Autopsy Photography)	Sworn Testimony of Navy Chief Robert L. Knudsen on August 11, 1978 to HSCA (His Personal Knowledge; Things He Either Did Himself or Witnessed Himself; No Hearsay)
Type of B & W Film Exposed at Autopsy	**18** sheets of 4"x5" B & W negatives, exposed in <u>duplex film holders</u>; images of body	**12** ea 4"x5" B & W negatives from a *film pack, or press pack*; images of JFK's body
Type and Quantity of Color Film Exposed at Autopsy	**20 sheets** of 4"x5" <u>color positive transparencies</u>, and two sheets of film with no image, one developed and one undeveloped; images of body	<u>Color *negatives*</u> (4" x5") exposed in duplex film holders; he remembered only 5 duplex holders, and **10 sheets** of film: either 9 with an image and one with no image, or possibly all ten sheets with an image present; all were pictures of the body

Date Out-of-Camera Film Products Developed; Quantities Developed; Where Developed; Who Was Present	B & W duplex negatives and color positive transparencies both developed on or about Nov 27th or 29th at NPC Anacostia; LT (jg) Vince Madonia listed as responsible for developing all film. Knudsen accompanied Fox to Anacostia with film.	On *November 23rd, 1963* Knudsen says he developed the *B & W press pack* at Anacostia, and Vince Madonia developed the *color negatives*. Knudsen says Fox accompanied him, but did not observe or participate in any developing work.
Date Color Prints Developed; How Many; Where Developed; Who Was Present	On or about December 9th, 1963; **one internegative and 2 color prints** made from each color positive transparency at NPC Anacostia; Knudsen accompanied Fox again; LT Madonia developed film.	On *November 24th*, 1963; ***seven (7) ea color prints*** produced *from each color negative*; LT Vince Madonia developed color prints at NPC Anacostia.
Who Ordered Photography to be Done?	USSS SAIC Robert Bouck ordered SA Fox to have both the out-of-camera originals developed, and color prints made.	*Dr. George Burkley* (RADM, USN) ordered Knudsen to develop the original films on November 23rd; on November 24th, Burkley, in the presence of CAPT Tazewell Shepherd (JFK's Naval Aide) and a USSS agent, ordered color prints made.
Who Made B & W Prints?	SA James K. Fox; in USSS lab, not at NPC Anacostia	*Unaware of any B & W prints*; never saw any.
Image Content	11–1-66 Military Inventory does not list photos of probes in body of President Kennedy	One B & W negative showed *2 probes in body of JFK* (in thorax); body 'sitting up.'

By now the reader should be fairly well acquainted with the format, or types of film, as well as the quantities of exposed film in each format, in the autopsy photograph collection in the National Archives—enough so that whenever Knudsen provides contrary information to the HSCA staff counsel, a sense of the skepticism, and occasionally even disbelief, on the part of the HSCA staff counsel, and the consequent tension in the room, is transmitted directly from the page to the reader of this book. You can almost sense the dilemma that confronted Andy Purdy: Knudsen was a long-time Federal employee (and military veteran) with much distinguished service under his belt, and yet he was providing *new evidence* that was contrary to almost everything the HSCA thought it knew about the autopsy photographs—he was 'upsetting the apple cart,' one month before House Select

Committee on Assassinations public hearings were scheduled in front of PBS television cameras, and near the end of the HSCA's life span, when much of its efforts were nearly concluded and its focus was shifting to wrapping things up and writing a quality report. In spite of the usefulness of study aids such as the comparative chart provided above, the only way to truly appreciate the impact of much of the Knudsen testimony, and to assess his credibility, is to sample it verbatim at key moments during the deposition.

There are numerous spelling errors of place names, surnames, and other words in the deposition which I attribute to the court reporter (not Mr. Knudsen); these I have corrected below to avoid confusion among readers. (I checked the audio recording of the deposition in the National Archives, and it was disappointing. One can only hear the voice of the court reporter, speaking into a mask as she repeats the testimony; the listener cannot hear the voices of Andy Purdy or Robert Knudsen.) The substantive questioning commenced as follows:

Purdy: When did you first become aware of the existence of photographs of the autopsy of President Kennedy?

Knudsen: The morning following the autopsy, Dr. Burkley had the film holders in a brown paper bag and handed them to me. Jim Fox, the Secret Service expert, was told to go over and develop them and see that they were secure at all times.

Purdy: Who gave you those orders?

Knudsen: I believe Dr. Burkley at that time. He said to develop them and to see that they were secure. Jim Fox was right there and the two of us went over to do the developing.

Purdy: Did Mr. Fox have some specific responsibilities relative to the White House photographer's office? Is that why he worked with you?

Knudsen: Jim Fox was the Secret Service photographer.

Purdy: Had you worked closely with him before?

Knudsen: On occasion, we had.

Purdy: Could you describe for us your involvement in the transfer of the films over to where they were going to be processed, and what role you played in the processing?

Knudsen: Jim and I got into the White House staff car to go over to the Naval Photographic Center. They [the films] were black-and-white, and color. I took the black-and-white in one dark room and gave the color—I believe it was Vince Madonia who took the color into the adjoining color dark room so we could process simultaneously. So, while Jim stood outside to see that we were not disturbed—

Purdy: You processed the black-and-whites?

Knudsen: Yes.

Purdy: You processed it at the Naval Photographic Center, or Processing Center?

Knudsen: Naval Photographic Center.

Purdy: Did anyone help you process those?

Knudsen: No.

Purdy: You were in the room completely by yourself?

Knudsen: That is right.

Purdy: Were you present during the processing of the color films?

Knudsen: No. I was in the black-and-white dark room processing and the color was in the next room being processed.

Purdy: Is it your recollection that LT Vince Madonia processed the color?

Knudsen: I believe Vince did. I will not swear to that.

Purdy: You believe—

Knudsen: Vince could have handed it to one of the technicians and had him do it. I do not know. I was in a hurry to get it done, so I went right in the dark room and started processing.

Purdy: To the best of your knowledge, James Fox stood outside and was in neither dark room?

Knudsen: That is right.

Purdy: You processed the black-and-white film holders, is that correct?

Knudsen: That is correct.

Purdy: Were any of the film holders blank on either or both sides?

Knudsen: No black-and-whites. I have been thinking about it. There could have been an unexposed sheet. In the back of my mind, there is something about an unexposed sheet of the color film. No empty holders.

Purdy: Unexposed sheet of color film?

Knudsen: In the back of my mind it seems there might have been one, but we accounted for that by bringing the blank sheet with us. In other words, we brought a sheet of film for—there are two sheets back for every holder.

Purdy: One of the sheets, was it overexposed or underexposed, the one that was blank? [Purdy has missed the boat here—Knudsen said "unexposed," not "underexposed."]

Knudsen: If it was blank, I would say it probably was not exposed. All of the other exposures were good exposures.

Purdy: It is your recollection that it was blank?

Knudsen: If there was a missing negative, it was a completely unexposed piece of film.

Purdy: That was among the color film holders?

Knudsen: That is a possibility. I would not say there was one. In the back of my mind there seems to be one piece of film that was without image.

Purdy: It is your specific recollection at this time that there were no empty black-and-white film holders?

Knudsen: That is correct.

Purdy: It is also your specific recollection that there were no blank images on any of the black-and-white film holders?

Knudsen: That is correct.

Purdy: It is also your recollection if there was a blank film in one of the color film holders, you retained it?

Knudsen: Very definitely. We would not destroy anything.

It's time to pause here. Knudsen has used the term "negatives" to describe the color film, but Purdy has not picked up on it yet. According to the paper trail, there were only color positive transparencies, and similarly there are only color positives in the Archives. Also, at this early stage of the deposition, Knudsen is referring to black-and-white film holders, and has not yet mentioned a film pack, or press pack.

Purdy: What did you do with these materials?

Knudsen: After they were dry, I took them back to the White House. Right offhand, I do not recall how long it was until a decision was made for seven sets of prints to be made.

Purdy: Approximately how long after the autopsy were these films developed? Was it the morning after, as you said before?

Knudsen: Yes.

Purdy: It was also—when that day did you return?

Knudsen: Developing them?

Purdy: Yes.

Knudsen: Developing takes—the film drying, and all, an hour and a half, two hours. I would say that we were gone less than two hours.

Purdy: Is it your recollection that you returned them in the morning, or the afternoon that day?

Knudsen: I could not tell you, because *I had been up all night. From the assassination right on, we worked right on through that night* through the following day and the next night. Hours, I could not tell you. [Author's emphasis.]

Knudsen's statement that he had been up all night does not make any sense to me, unless he was engaged in post mortem photography of President Kennedy after the autopsy ended about midnight; this testimony about having "been up all night," and that "we worked right on through that night" are entirely consistent with Knudsen telling his family that he "photographed the President's autopsy." If he was engaged in post mortem photography, it had to be after midnight when the formal autopsy ended, because neither Stringer nor Riebe ever recalled a third photographer in the morgue when they were working. Unfortunately, Purdy did not follow up by asking "what were you doing all night," and what did you mean by "we," i.e., whom were you working with?

Purdy: Where did you take the developed negatives?

Knudsen: The developed negatives went back, were retained by the Secret Service until we made prints.

Purdy: You returned them to the Secret Service?

Knudsen: Yes. After we developed them, we took them back to the West Wing of the White House to the Secret Service office.

—————————

Purdy: Under whose orders were you operating when you took the film to be processed and returned it?

Knudsen: Dr. Burkley, the one who gave me the film.

260

Purdy: You had processed black-and-white and color film that you turned over, is that correct?

Knudsen: That is correct.

Purdy: Were they black-and-white negatives, [color positive] transparencies, or both?

Knudsen: Black-and-white negatives, *color negatives*. [Author's emphasis.]

Purdy: They were color negatives. Were there color transparencies?

Knudsen: No.

Purdy: At that time, did you examine the black-and-white or color negatives to see what the images were on them?

Knudsen: I examined them for the purpose to see that we had good negatives. In the examination, I did see the images, but did not study them.

Purdy: Did you examine both the black-and-white and color negatives?

Knudsen: Right.

Purdy: When was your next contact, or the next time you had information about these autopsy negatives?

Knudsen: The next time was when they needed seven sets of prints.

Purdy: When was that?

Knudsen: I do not recall the exact time.

Purdy: Approximately when was that?

Knudsen: It seems to me that it would have been a day later; that four days is a complete jumble in my mind. I cannot remember the sequence of it.

_____

Purdy: Is it possible that you had the prints made several years later?

Knudsen: Oh, no.

Purdy: It is your recollection that it was within a very few days?

Knudsen: Oh, yes, definitely.

Purdy: Could you tell us the chain of events that led to the printing of the negatives, the printing of the photographic prints?

Knudsen: I was told that they needed seven sets of 8" x 10" prints.

Purdy: Who told you that?

Knudsen: To my recollection, Taz Shepherd, Burkley, and the Secret Service men were all present. I do not recall which one told me, the exact words. They apparently had been discussing what was required, and I was called in and told, here is what we need, and went back to the Photographic Center and made seven sets and brought them back to the White House. I have not seen the prints since.

—————

Purdy: Do you recall if Dr. Burkley asked that you make the prints?

Knudsen: As I say, to the best of my knowledge, Taz Shepherd, who was Naval Aide, Burkley, the Secret Service man—I do not recall who it was—the three of them were there.

Purdy: Was the Secret Service man James Fox?

Knudsen: No. Jim did not have authority for something of that nature.

Purdy: Was he present at the time?

Knudsen: To the best of my recollection, he went back over to the Photographic Center with us while the prints were being made, to ensure security.

Purdy: Do you recall whether he was there when you were told that you had to have the prints made?

Knudsen: No, I do not. I assume he was, because I took them immediately back to the Photographic Center to be printed, but I will not swear.

—————

Purdy: You went to the Naval Processing Center?

Knudsen: Naval Printing Center.

Purdy: Who actually made the prints?

Knudsen: Well, it is basically a mechanical operation. You put them in these trays and the machine just moves them from slot to slot. They are machine processed.

Purdy: Who supervised the machine?

Knudsen: Oh, Vince Madonia was there. I was there. I am sure Jim Fox was there with us.

Purdy: Do you remember there being some women technicians?

Knudsen: We had Sandy Spencer. [The ARRB staff would locate her in 1996 and take the deposition of Saundra K. Spencer in 1997.]

Purdy: Do you remember anyone reacting very strongly upon seeing the prints?

Knudsen: Well, it was a rather traumatic time for all of us. Right off the top of my head, I do not recall any outstanding event. Sandy was the type of gal that she could be upset over something like this. They definitely were not the type of pictures that a person would enjoy looking at.

Purdy: She worked at the Naval Photographic Center?

Knudsen: Yes. She was on detail from the White House.

Purdy: Did all of the people who were present there with you examine the prints, or did just some of them examine the prints?

Knudsen: Examine the prints—they were examined for quality but not for detail. In other words, as a photographer, I can take and make a print and examine it and make sure it is good quality and ten minutes later you can ask me what it was and I cannot even tell you who was in the picture. You are not looking for that sort of thing. You are looking for the quality, to make sure the print is technically correct. It was examined for technical purposes, but not for subject matter.

Purdy: Did you give the personnel present any special instructions about not talking about what they had done?

Knudsen: We were all told not to discuss the matter.

Purdy: Who told you that?

Knudsen: I was told by Dr. Burkley. I was told by the Secret Service. Taz Shepherd emphasized to make sure that everybody knows that they are not supposed to discuss any subject matter in these pictures.

Purdy: You passed that word on in the Naval Photographic Center?

Knudsen: Vince Madonia passed it on to anybody who was involved with the trays and like that. We had as few personnel as possible in the area. The area was cleared so that only those necessary to be there would see them. [The ARRB staff located Vince Madonia in 1996, and conducted a lengthy, unsworn in-person interview that was tape recorded.]

Purdy: After the prints were made, what happened?

Knudsen: I took them back to the White House.

Purdy: You and?

Knudsen: Jim Fox. He was with me. We took them back. There again, to the best of my recollection, we took it into the Secret Service office. I have never seen them since.

———————

Purdy: Did you do anything with the prints before you turned them over?

Knudsen: We were told to make seven sets so we laid out seven to make sure there were seven prints of each.

Purdy: Did you put them in folders or envelopes, or anything like that?

Knudsen: I believe we put each set in a separate envelope. We may just have flip-flopped, but to my recollection, we put them in separate envelopes.

Purdy: What did you consider a set?

Knudsen: One print of each view.

Purdy: Of each view of the black-and-white and color?

Knudsen: No, we printed only the color.

Purdy: You printed only seven sets of the color.

Knudsen: Yes.

Purdy: How many sets of the black-and-white did you print?

Knudsen: I do not recall print[ing] any. To the best of my knowledge, the black-and-whites were just a back-up in case there was anything wrong with the color, we had a back-up of the black-and-white.

———————

Purdy: You stated [to] me previously on the phone that you had a pretty good idea of where some of the sets of prints were going.

Knudsen: I was later told where some of the sets were going.

Purdy: Who told you that?

Knudsen: I do not recall.

Purdy: You also said to me on the phone that you believed that you had labeled the envelope [for each set] with some destination or a certain individual's name. Do you remember doing that?

Knudsen: It seems to me that, at the time, there were seven sets. It was either stated or written down that this one goes to Archives, this one goes to Attorney General, and we started through like that.

Purdy: What other destinations do you recall for the sets of prints?

Knudsen: Either at that time, or later, I was informed that Senator Ted Kennedy had a set.

Purdy: Do you remember a set being labeled for the Secret Service or FBI or any other government agencies?

Knudsen: I am sure that one was kept for the Secret Service...I do not recall the FBI being given any. I was told that the Warren Commission was offered a set and that they refused it.

Purdy: Who told you that the prints were sent to some of these various destinations?

Knudsen: As I say, I do not recall.

Purdy: Who might have told you?

Knudsen: It could have been the Secret Service personnel of the upper echelon. It could have been Dr. Burkley. I am not certain.

Purdy: Who could it have been in the Secret Service who might have told you where the prints were going?

Knudsen: It could have been Roy Kellerman, who had taken over handling everything at that point. It could have been any one of the upper echelon Secret Service. I talked with them every day.

———————

Purdy: Did you have a chance at any time to examine the prints closely enough that you now have a recollection of what they showed?

Knudsen: Oh, yes.

Purdy: When did you examine them that closely?

Knudsen: At the time that I was examining [them] for technical quality, a lot of those things were apparent.

Purdy: What things stick in your mind about those prints? What do you recall seeing?

Knudsen: Well, it was a close-up of a cavity in the head. *Probes through the body*— [Author's emphasis.]

Remember, neither Stinger nor Riebe recalled taking photographs of probes while they were inserted in the body, and yet Dr. Karnei *did* have a strong recollection of photographs being taken of probes in the body.

Purdy: Where did the probes go through the body?

Knudsen: [playing dumb—obfuscating] From the point where the projectile entered to the point where the projectile left.

Purdy: Where were those two points?

Knudsen: [Using a technical point to obfuscate again, and "stall"] I did not say there were two points.

Purdy: You said the projectile.

Knudsen: From the entry to the exit.

Purdy: Where were the entry and exit points?

Knudsen: Here again, I have a mental problem here that we were sworn not to disclose this to anybody. Being under oath, I cannot tell you I do not know, because I do know; but, at the same time, I do feel I have been sworn not to disclose this information and I would prefer very much that you get one of the sets of prints and view them. I am not trying to be hard to get along with. I was told not to disclose the area of the body, and I am at a loss right now as to whether—which is right.

Purdy: Was it a Naval order that you were operating under that you would not disclose?

Knudsen: This was Secret Service. To the best of my knowledge, Dr. Burkley also emphasized that this was not to be discussed.

Purdy: Do you remember seeing rulers in the photographs or anything other than the body itself?

Knudsen: Yes.

Purdy: What other things besides the body did you see, other than the rulers?

Knudsen: What appeared to be stainless steel probes.

Purdy: About how long were they?

Knudsen: The probes?

Purdy: Yes.

Knudsen: I would estimate about two foot.

Purdy: Was there one probe that you saw through the body, or were there more than one?

Knudsen: More than one. Here, we are getting into this grey area of what I was instructed not to discuss.

Purdy: I am sure you recognize this is a duly-authorized Congressional investigation?

Knudsen: That is right, I do. That is why I say this is where I have a problem. I realize this is a duly-authorized investigation of the United States government. Personally, my preference would be that you get a set of the prints and view the prints, and then there would be no question. That would get me off the hook on the fact that I am sworn not to discuss the subject matter.

Purdy: Do you know Robert Goff, the General Counsel of the Secret Service?

Knudsen: I do not know him personally.

Purdy: If he authorized you to discuss this information, would you be willing to discuss it? I should point out that we have the full cooperation of the Secret Service and the other government agencies in obtaining all other information and there were other orders that came down pertaining to this material on the autopsy that have been formally rescinded by government agencies so we could pursue the investigation. I am sympathetic to your concerns. I am not sure that you recognize the evidentiary significance of what you are saying here today and the importance of what you are not saying relative to other people's testimony relative to examinations of the prints that we have made.

Knudsen: I think this would clarify the whole situation. If the prints were examined, and then I would not be in the spot that I am, that I am sworn not to disclose it. It would give a very definite answer to you as to the number of probes.

Purdy and Knudsen were talking and thinking at cross purposes. Purdy thought that getting permission for Knudsen to speak openly about his recollections regarding probes in the body would "solve the problem;" Knudsen was again telling Purdy that if he would just look at the photographs himself, his questions would be answered, and Knudsen's "problem," about maintaining his silence, would be resolved. Knudsen did not realize that there were no photographs of probes in the body in the JFK autopsy collection at the National Archives.

Purdy: I should say that we have had access to the autopsy photographs and the questions that I am asking remain unanswered. So I would like to ask again, if either we could arrange, or you could arrange with the Secret Service to have this order lifted, if you then would be willing to cooperate with us?

Knudsen: I will cooperate as far as I can. As I say—

Purdy: If you are willing, we could take a short break and we could call the Secret Service, or I could give you the number and you can call them, or we can just ask a few other questions, have you gain a clearance and then reconvene on another day, if that is convenient with you.

Knudsen: Whichever you prefer.

Purdy: I think we will take a recess at this time.

While the HSCA staff attempted to contact the General Counsel of the Secret Service and obtain permission for Knudsen to speak about the President's wounds, the questioning continued:

Purdy: Were there other very sensitive photographs that you had to deal with that maybe were handled in a similar way as these with the Secret Service being involved in the transport of them...

Knudsen: I do not recall any other time Secret Service has ever escorted me for something that.

———————

Purdy: Could it have been seven prints [total]? Are you very sure it is seven sets of prints?

Knudsen: I know it could not have been [just] seven prints, because that would not have covered a print for each negative.

268

Purdy: How many negatives were you [sic]? How many prints were made?

Knudsen: I do not recall.

Purdy: Could you give me a rough idea? For example, were there a similar number of color and black-and-white prints, or were there a greater number of one than the other?

Knudsen: No black-and-white prints were made, to my knowledge.

Purdy: Were there similar numbers of black-and-white negatives as compared to color negatives?

Knudsen: It seems to me approximately ten negatives, color negatives. I do not recall. This is an approximate [sic].

Purdy: Do you think there were approximately ten [total] color prints made?

Knudsen: [not budging] No, approximately ten color negatives; seven prints of each of these.

Purdy: You made seven prints of each negative?

Knudsen: Yes.

Purdy: So that each set consisted of ten color prints?

Knudsen: Approximately. I do not recall the exact number. There again, what I am taking this from—it seems to me there were five holders that they took into the dark room. If there were five holders, ten negatives. If there were one [un]exposed sheet, there would have been nine negatives.

Purdy: Were there approximately ten black-and-white negatives, or a greater or lesser number?

Knudsen: *There was one total film pack. There would have been twelve negatives, black-and-white.* [Author's emphasis.]

The reader will notice here that Knudsen is no longer talking about the black-and-white negatives in terms of duplex holders, which was the manner in which Purdy framed that questioning at the beginning of the deposition. Knudsen shifts here to a recollection of a film pack—a cassette or "press pack" of 12 exposures of black-and-white negative film which is shot and developed as one intact roll, and then cut into individual frames after the film dries. My assumption is not that Knudsen is an unreliable witness, but rather, that Andy Purdy's constant probing and testing of Knudsen's memory regarding what *type* of film, and how *many* exposures were developed, has refreshed Knudsen's recollection here. Throughout the remainder of the deposition, on several occasions, Knudsen remembers developing a film pack, and never mentions duplex holders for black-and-white negatives again. I conclude, therefore, that he developed a film pack of 12 exposures.

Purdy: [Killing time, while waiting for permission for Knudsen to speak to come through from the Secret Service General Counsel] Did you ever have knowledge of, or were you ever told about, *autopsy x-rays*, for example? [Author's emphasis.]

Knudsen: No. *I do not know that any were ever taken.* [Author's emphasis.]

This is a highly significant response by Robert Knudsen. If he had photographed "the autopsy" as he believed, and as he later told his family, he would have been well aware of x-rays, since prior to midnight approximately 3 different rounds of x-rays were taken (at least one series of the head; a 'whole body set' prior to the Y-incision; and one of the torso after evisceration), and photographers had to leave the morgue to prevent their film from becoming fogged. This response by Knudsen—that to his knowledge no x-rays were ever taken—is further support for my contention that *if* Knudsen *did indeed* take post mortem photographs of President Kennedy, he was unknowingly photographing a charade choreographed by Humes, Boswell, Finck, and their superiors *after midnight and following conclusion of the autopsy*. The purpose of the charade by those misrepresenting it to Knudsen as "the autopsy" was probably to create false versions of the wounds for later substitution into the official collection of photographs. Following the conclusion of the (real) autopsy, sometime around midnight, there would have been no need for x-rays, which explains why x-ray technologists Jerrol Custer and Ed Reed had departed; furthermore, Dr. Ebersole, although present for some time well into the early morning hours, per his recollections to the HSCA medical panel, would simply not have even attempted to operate the portable x-ray machine; that was a technologist's function, not the function of the radiologist. In Naval medicine, with the radiologist an officer and the technicians enlisted men, this separation of functions would have been even more pronounced than in a civilian medical environment. Therefore, one can safely conclude that if Knudsen was present during post mortem photography, and was not aware of any x-rays ever having been taken, then he was *not* present at the autopsy, regardless of what he himself called the procedure he remembered photographing.

Initially, Purdy announced that Robert Goff had not returned their calls, and that they had only spoken to one of his assistants, John Mehan. While still awaiting Goff's return call, Purdy attempted to use Blakey's letter to Secretary of Defense Brown, requesting that the Navy orders silencing the JFK autopsy participants be rescinded, to get Knudsen to open up and discuss the wounds he saw in the photographs. (The irony here is that in utilizing this argument Andy Purdy was speaking to someone who considered himself an autopsy participant, and who was even quoted as saying so in a magazine article from the previous year—but that Purdy was unaware of this, and so failed to ask the biggest question of all to the deponent: "Did you take post mortem photographs of President Kennedy?")

Purdy: We have gone over quite a few of your recollections, and we are going to show you, in a second, the color autopsy prints that we have and ask you whether the prints that you are shown are consistent with your recollections of them when you saw them. The primary points that we are going to cover are the number and locations of wounds and the other details in the photographs that you described generally, such as the presence of metal probes in the photographs and the presence of rulers in the photographs, and what have you. Are you confident now that you saw metal probes in the photographs?

Knudsen: Yes.

Purdy: Are you confident that the metal probes were actually through the wounds when you saw them?

Knudsen: Yes, I am certain of that, because it showed the point of entry and exit with the probe.

Purdy: Were there ever photographs that you have seen, either before this incident or since that incident that you might be confusing with your recollection of these photographs?

Knudsen: To my knowledge, I have not seen anything regarding—I have never seen any photographs of it other than the ones taken there.

Purdy: Have you seen photographs of any other autopsies?

Knudsen: No.

Purdy: Have you seen photographs of any other dead bodies that may have [had] probes in them?

Knudsen: Yes, I have. I am certain on the Kennedy [photographs] there were the probes showing the point of entry and exit.

Purdy: How many probes were there that you saw in a given picture? What is the most probes that you saw in a given picture at one time?

Knudsen: I know there were two.

Purdy: Two metal probes that were through wounds when you saw them?

Knudsen: Yes.

At this point Purdy called another recess. Robert Goff, Secret Service General Counsel, spoke to Robert Knudsen on the phone and Knudsen's testimony then resumed.

Purdy: ...Mr. Knudsen and I have just spoken with Bob Goff on the phone and, Mr. Knudsen, if you just want to briefly state what Mr. Goff said to you about whether you could talk to us?

271

Knudsen: Well, Mr. Goff said that under the circumstances that, it being a legitimate government subcommittee, that he felt that it would be appropriate to cooperate to the fullest. He did not have any objection to my talking. The main thing that they felt [concern about] was continued silence towards any assassination buffs,[42] reporters or this sort of thing. But insofar as any [Congressional] Committee, they had no objection and thought that I should cooperate.

Purdy: Thank you. As I said previously, Mr. Goff is the General Counsel of the United States Secret Service. Now, before the break we were talking about the number of probes, and you had said that the most you saw in any one picture was two. I believe that is what you stated, is that correct?

Knudsen: I said the minimum was two.

Purdy: What was the most?

Knudsen: Over this period of time, I am not certain. It seems to me that there were three in one picture, but this I will not state for sure.

Purdy: Of the probes that you recall, where did they enter and where did they exit?

Knudsen: One was right near the neck and out the back.

Purdy: [In] The front of the neck and out the back of the neck?

Knudsen: The point of entry-exit.

I must interject here that for Knudsen to have known which site was an entry and which was an exit, he must have been present, listening to the conversation of the pathologists, when the probes were inserted and photographed; neither Knudsen, nor anyone else, could discern entry and exit points simply from looking at a photographic image that he only developed and cursorily examined. This

---

[42]I have always thought it sad, and unfair, that citizens who believe in educating themselves about their own country's history, and who are interested in studying, say, the JFK, or RFK, or Martin Luther King assassinations, simply because the evidence presented in the official accounts is not entirely persuasive, or is fraught with evidentiary conflicts, are denigrated and called 'assassination buffs' or 'conspiracy theorists,' as a way of trivializing their concerns. Perhaps the tables should be reversed, and those citizens who immerse themselves in the mass of original source material about one of these events in order to better make up their own minds about their nation's history—regardless of their conclusions—should be called 'responsible patriots;' and perhaps those citizens who don't read any serious non-fiction on their own initiative, and who want to go through life believing all government pronouncements on faith so that they can sleep well at night, and who believe it is unpatriotic to question authority, should be called *sheep,* or 'coincidence theorists.'

statement that the entry point for the probe was in the front of the neck is in agreement with Dr. Perry's observations at the Dallas press conference the afternoon of 11-22-63 that the bullet which struck President Kennedy in the anterior throat came from the front. This makes me wonder whether the procedures Knudsen witnessed and photographed in the morgue—for I do indeed believe he was in the morgue taking post mortem photography at some point in time the night of November 22-23, 1963—were perhaps *not only* for the purpose of creating false impressions of the condition of the rear of the head, but whether they were perhaps *also* for the purpose of preparing *a highly classified, restricted briefing of what actually happened in Dealey Plaza*. Otherwise, why photograph the purported path of a shot from the ***front*** which struck President Kennedy in the anterior throat, since it was in such bald disagreement with *the official story that Oswald did all of the shooting from above and behind?*

Purdy: The metal probe extended from the front of the neck to the back of the neck?

Knudsen: Right. One [meaning a different, or second probe] was through the chest cavity.

Purdy: Did it go all the way through?

Knudsen: Yes. It seems to me that the entry point was a little bit lower in the back than—well, the point in the back was a little bit lower than the point in front. Put it that way. So the probe was going diagonally from top to bottom, front to back.

Purdy: Approximately, regarding both probes, how high—you mentioned the one was from the front of the neck, the probe extended between points on the front of the neck and the back of the neck. How high on the back of the neck, and how high or low from the front of the neck would you say for that probe?

Knudsen: As I said, not studying them for technical purposes, it seemed to me that the point on the front was about this point, somewhere in this area here (indicating).

Purdy: Could you articulate?

Knudsen: What bone is this?

Purdy: You are pointing to a point right around the top—

Knudsen: Right about where the neck-tie is. That would be somewhere in that vicinity.

Here, Knudsen is unequivocally indicating that the entry point for a bullet designated by the first probe was at the necktie knot, which is precisely where Dr. Perry stated (3 times) on 11-22-63 that President Kennedy had a small entry wound. This further supports my speculation above that perhaps one of the multiple functions of the Knudsen photography session *was to document what really happened to President Kennedy.*

Purdy: Approximately how much lower than that would you say the other probe [was], which went through the chest cavity?

Knudsen: I would put it six, seven inches.

Purdy: Was it [the chest cavity] opened or closed in the photograph?

Knudsen: It was a side view. I just glanced at it to make sure.

If my assumption above is correct, Knudsen is playing 'dumb' here, staying within his role, pretending to have only developed some black-and-white negatives, and in doing so is concealing the fact that he was the photographer of the images in question. Is this the military man his widow spoke to me of, who would 'take secrets with him to the grave because he was told to by duly constituted authority?'

Purdy: From the side view, you saw both probes?

Knudsen: Right.

Purdy: Where would you place the points of the probes in the back? You say that one was in the neck, and one was in the back. Approximately how high up, or how low?

Knudsen: I would put in the back—it would seem to me it is probably around ten inches. There, again, I do not recall the length of time [sic]. I cannot say.

Purdy: You were kind of pointing to the middle of your back, about midway down, you would say?

Knudsen: Midway between the neck and the waist.

Purdy: Where was the other probe?

Knudsen: This one—

Purdy: You just indicated where the probe came out, on the lower—

Knudsen: Somewhere around the middle of the back. It seemed to me it was right around mid-chest.

Purdy: The probe that you said you could see coming out of the neck, the front of the neck, where was it out of the back of the neck? How high up would you say that one was?

Knudsen: About the base of the neck.

Purdy: Was the body lying flat, or sitting up, or lying on its front when you saw the probes through it?

274

Knudsen: It would have to be erected to put the probes through, because on the back there was no way.

Of course, another possibility that Purdy failed to mention was that the body (with probes inserted) could have been lying on its side and photographed from above. But Knudsen doesn't even consider this possibility. Once again, to me the certainty of his response here—as if to say "of course he was sitting up, I ought to know, I was there"—implies to me that Knudsen *was there*. I believe he is certain of the orientation because he took the photograph in question.

Purdy: Could you make out the faces of the people who were holding him or the faces of the people in the background?

Knudsen: To my knowledge, there were no faces.

Purdy: Could you see their hands?

Knudsen: There again, I did not study them.

Purdy: Was there, in any of the photographs, a photograph showing a metal probe through the head?

Knudsen: No, not to my knowledge. To my knowledge, the only photograph of the head was to show the wound in the right rear of the head there, a little right of center.

It is unclear here whether Knudsen is referring to the "white spot" down low near the hairline, or the "red spot" 4 inches higher near the tip of the ruler.

Purdy then commences showing Knudsen the HSCA 'working prints.'

Purdy: ...These are photographs of the autopsy prints. These are not the actual prints.

Knudsen: I was going to say, these are not the original prints. I can see that right off. The color is off. Did you want me to go through them?

Purdy: You can leaf through them and make comments where you feel that it is necessary. If you see photographs that you recognize, you might say that you recognize it.

Knudsen: I recall roughly—there again, I did not study them in detail, I just fanned through the negatives.

Knudsen then looks at several photos, and seeing a ruler in these images causes him to recall seeing a ruler in some of the photographs he saw in 1963.

Knudsen: I did not see these.

Purdy: The witness is referring to the color photographs of the brain. He said he had not seen those.

Examination of various photographs of the body continued.

Purdy: ...So it is your testimony here today that these photographs are not inconsistent with the ones that you saw?

Knudsen: No, not at all.

This seems to contradict what Knudsen told his family years later. Was he playing 'dumb' here to avoid getting involved in a major controversy? Was he playing it safe, even though his mind may have been racing a mile a minute? Possibly.

Purdy: Is there anything that you saw that is not represented by these photographs?

Knudsen: I feel certain that there was the one with the two probes.

Purdy: One photograph with two probes through the body?

Knudsen: That is correct.

Next, Purdy shows Knudsen a photograph showing the tracheostomy, almost certainly ARRB view no. 5, "right anterior view of head and upper torso, including tracheotomy wound (images 13, 14, 40, and 41)."

Purdy: ...do you see a point on the President which would correspond to one or more of the locations of the probe that you recall?

Knudsen: Right here (indicating).

Purdy: Could you articulate it?

Knudsen: Right here—the neck—where the necktie would be tied.

Purdy: Let the record show that the witness is pointing to the tracheotomy incision at the front of the President's neck. Is it your recollection, also, that there was a probe lower than that area? Is that correct?

Knudsen: That is correct.

Purdy: Looking at this photograph, approximately how much lower? Was it at a point that would not be visible in this photograph?

Knudsen: I am beginning to wonder now. I do not see anything here. But it is in the back of

276

my mind there was a probe through the body.

Purdy: Is it your present recollection that the body was not opened up in the chest area, or could you not tell whether it was opened up, or was it definitely not open in the picture that you recall but do not see here?

Knudsen: There again, I was looking quickly for quality. I did not study it. But I do not recall seeing any photograph of the chest being opened.

Sometimes I wonder if Knudsen photographed the body quite early after Stringer and Riebe had been ordered to leave the morgue for the taking of x-rays. This is theoretically possible: Stringer and Riebe would have been absent, and would therefore not have remembered Knudsen being there; and if Custer and Reed were still absent from the morgue, then Knudsen would not have remembered the taking of any x-rays.

Purdy: Do you think it is something you would remember, if the President's chest was cut and opened up?

Knudsen: Yes.

Purdy: Does this approximately correspond to the number of color prints that you recall?

Knudsen: That is correct.

Purdy: Is it just your recollection that there was one more, or at least one more, than is present in these?

Knudsen: It seems to me the one I saw with the probes was strictly a negative. I do not remember seeing a print of it. The first day, when we processed the film, we were just checking the negatives. I believe it was a black-and-white. I do not know. I believe it was the negative of the probe.

Purdy: You think it was black-and-white, or you think it might have been, or you are just not sure?

Knudsen: It was a negative. I do not recall ever having seen a print, but it seems to me that there was a negative, in checking the negatives.

Purdy then shows Knudsen some black-and-white autopsy prints, and they both notice a band of light across one of the images, but conclude it is an artifact of the printing process.

Knudsen: ...I do not see it.

Purdy: You are saying you do not see it?

Knudsen: I do not see it here, but in the back of my mind, it still seemed that there was one photograph, the body erect with two probes through it.

Purdy: Let me ask you—

Knudsen: [correcting himself] One negative.

Purdy: Is it your recollection that it was just one film pack of black-and-white film?

Knudsen: Yes.

Purdy: You say there are twelve exposures?

Knudsen: Twelve exposures.

Purdy: There definitely was not another pack?

Knudsen: I will not swear to that. I do not honestly remember.

Purdy: You personally developed the black-and-white film?

Knudsen: Right.

Purdy: No one else was in the room when you did it?

Knudsen: That is right.

Purdy: It is James Fox's recollection that he did the black-and-white developing at the Secret Service lab. That is inconsistent with your recollection.

Knudsen: He may have printed black-and-whites at his lab. The black-and-whites [i.e., the negatives] were developed at the [Anacostia] photographic center at the same time that the color was.

Purdy: You personally have a specific recollection of having developed the black-and-white negatives?

At this point the reader is probably wondering how many times the HSCA staff counsel is going to repeat this question.

Knudsen: Right. Jim [Fox] stood outside the darkroom door.

Purdy: It is also Mr. Fox's recollection that some of the black-and-white sides of the film holders either had no film in them or they were not exposed.

278

Knudsen: The black-and-white was film pack. The film holders were color. To the best of my knowledge, there was no black-and-whites in the holders. I know there was a pack.

Purdy: It is also your recollection that all of the exposures came up—well, of the black-and-whites?

Knudsen: Right.

Purdy: You said that maybe one of the colors either was underexposed or overexposed?

Purdy still doesn't get it. The answer previously given, in the way of clarification, was "unexposed."

Knudsen: It could not have been overexposed. There is no exposure. I do not recall for sure on this, but—

Purdy: If there was one like that—

Knudsen: There is something shady [in my memory] about the third piece of film we took with us.

Purdy: If there was one, it was color and not black-and-white?

Knudsen: Correct.

Purdy: Were you ever asked for a statement by any government body about the work that you did pertaining to the negatives of autopsy prints?

Knudsen: No.

Purdy: Do you recall that the orders to have the prints made up came to you from Fox?

Knudsen: No, I do not. At this point, I do not recall who gave the specific order.

Purdy: It is your sense that it was in a meeting with Taz Shepherd, Admiral Burkley, and possibly Jim Fox's being present. Is that correct?

Knudsen: It is my recollection that the prints [were ordered in the presence] of Dr. Burkley, the Secret Service and I do not recall who the agent was, possibly Fox and possibly Taz Shepherd.

Purdy: Mr. Fox has indicated that Dr. Burkley told him to have the prints made up, and then he went to Mr. Bouck of the Secret Service for his okay. Does that refresh your recollection?

Knudsen: It could have been Burkley. I know Burkley was definitely there when the prints—it seems to me that Burkley is the one who stated that the prints were to be made and, like I say, I do not recall who was there other than I know that Burkley was. It seems to me that Fox was, and it could have been other agents, and it could have been Taz Shepherd.

Purdy: You think that Taz Shepherd was aware of what was going on?

Knudsen: As an agent present in the field, he was aware of it.

Purdy: Do you have any personal knowledge about when and where the black-and-white prints were made?

Knudsen: No.

Purdy: Do you know that they were not made at the Naval Processing Center?

Knudsen: I do not know that for a fact. I assumed that the black-and-white prints were made by Jim Fox. He had black-and-white capabilities within the Secret Service. The reason we got involved was the color capability which he did not have.

Purdy: Was there anything else that you can add for us about the details of these incidents, or anything that you want to put in perspective or elaborate on at this time?

Knudsen: No. Like I say, it has been fifteen years and a lot of this is foggy. I do know that the best sequence of events that I can recall was the morning following the autopsy, Burkley handed me a paper bag with the black-and-white and color film and there was an agent—I do not recall who it was—and Jim Fox was there, and he said, "take this over to the Photographic Center, process it, bring the negatives back, don't let anybody see it." I said, somebody is going to have to in the color processing of it. "Don't let anybody see it who doesn't have to, and don't discuss it with anybody."

Purdy: Was there anyone else that you know of that may have seen the negative that you are talking about that showed the probes, anyone else that we [sic] might suggest we might talk to about that?

Knudsen: No. It is just in the back of my mind that I am certain that there is the one shot of the body erect, two probes through it, and I processed the black-and-white. I hung it up. I just quickly went down it to make sure I had everything there. I then closed the door. Jim and I stayed outside, had a cup of coffee or something while the film was drying. After it was dry, I put each negative in a four by five preserver, took it, took the color, which had also dried the same.

Purdy: Did Jim Fox look at those black-and-white negatives, to your knowledge?

Knudsen: Not in my presence.

Purdy: You were present when you and he turned them over?

Knudsen: We went back to—it seems to me it was W-16, I am not certain. We did go into W-16, but whenever it was we went with the negative. [sic] We turned them all back.

Purdy: The only reason you would have a feeling that he had reviewed them was the fact that you assumed that he made black-and-white prints?

Knudsen: I assume that Jim is the one that made the prints.

Purdy: Did Sandy Spencer or anyone else at Naval Photographic Center have an occasion to look at the black-and-white negatives, to your knowledge?

Knudsen: No. Sandy was basically color. As I say, I went into the dark room, processed it, went out the door, stayed outside the door. When it was dry, I went back and checked them. They were dry, and we departed.

Purdy: Have you had any discussion with any of the other people we have talked about today about what you saw in those photographs?

Knudsen: No, never. I never discussed anything on these photographs until today in detail.

Purdy: Have you had any previous experience seeing metal probes such as this so that you would know what it would look like on a negative?

Knudsen: The only reason I say I thought it was a metal probe, in my recollection, it was a rod. Twenty-four inches long, probably; three-eighths of an inch in diameter. It appeared to be aluminum, [or] stainless steel. There again, it was a negative this size, hanging like this to dry.

Purdy: You have had a lot of experience looking at negatives over the years?

Knudsen: Over the years.

Purdy: Could it have been some form of light shadow or a defect in the negative that you may have thought was a metal probe, or do you think there was actually an object, that there was a picture taken?

Knudsen: I thought that there had to be something in the negative that I do not believe could have been a defect, no.

Purdy: It did not look like an artifact of any kind?

Knudsen: It did not appear that way to me. Like I say, I did not take it down and study it over a view[er], or anything like that. I just glanced at it. The wall was approximately this color and the negatives were hanging like this (indicating). I just flipped them around like this (indicating).

I must interject here. If Knudsen photographed what was represented to him to be the autopsy, and took the black-and-white image in question, then he would not have had to do anything more than "glance at it" in the darkroom to gain an appreciation of whether or not it was of good photographic quality. In other words, if he took the image of probes in the body, then he knew very well what had been depicted by virtue of his having been there, and would have had no need to study the negative in detail "over a viewer" in order to remember its content with precision.

Purdy: Let the record show that the witness held up some papers from the top, as though it was a negative hanging from a line, and just turned them and glanced at the papers. How certain are you that seven prints, seven sets of prints, were made of the color negatives?

Knudsen: That is the number that sticks in the back of my mind. Why the number seven sticks there, I do not know.

Purdy: You have a specific recollection that there was a number, not just one or two, but there were number of sets of prints made. Is that correct?

Knudsen: Oh, yes. More than one or two.

Purdy: Does it refresh your recollection to know that no one else whom we have talked to recalls that there were more than one or two sets of prints made? I do not mean to imply that I am questioning your word. I just want to point out to you that there is a very significant discrepancy in people's recollections, and while yours seems very specific, I just wanted you to know that there were others who recall that it was otherwise.

Knudsen: Again, I repeat, it has been approximately 15 years. To the best of my recollection, there were more than one or two [sets of prints made]. Like I say, why the number—I will not swear to the number seven, but that number sticks in the back of my mind for some reason, and apparently there were more than seven negatives printed, therefore—

Purdy: Let me ask you this. If you were to be told that someone was absolutely certain, and had proof, that there were only one or two or three sets of prints made, what would your reaction to that be? Would your reaction be, well, I guess I just—

Knudsen: If they are absolutely certain, and have good reason to be certain of it, I would not argue with them.

Purdy: Would you be surprised to find that that was the case?

Knudsen: Like I say, this number seven—I do not know, but it sticks in the back of my mind. If you said, well, you can show me a document with the printers that there was to be two each or three each, I would say well, I will not argue with you.

Purdy: You would be surprised if you found that to be the case, that there were only one or two or three sets made, and not seven, is that correct?

Knudsen: I would not say I would be surprised.

Purdy: Is it not your present recollection?

Knudsen: My present recollection is there were more than one or two sets made.

Purdy: At this time, as we do with each witness, we will give you an opportunity to elaborate, or make any other comments that you would like to make, and I think we gave you that opportunity, but I asked a few more questions. If you would like to add anything, please do so at this time.

Knudsen: Like I say, It has been a long time. To the best of my recollection, it has been, as I said—on the number of prints, if you have reason to show that there were two or three, I would not argue with it. If, for some reason, this number seven sticks up in the back of my mind, I could well be wrong. But that number sticks in the back of my mind. As to that, I am certain the black-and-white negatives was one with the body sitting up with the probes through it. I do not know. I honestly do not know what to say now if that one is missing. It is in the back of my mind, in fact, *even to the point that it is the right profile. The body was sitting up, and looking at the right side profile.* [Author's emphasis]

Purdy: I should add that—

Knudsen: I will tell you one thing that would clarify it, if the negatives were available. The film pack is numbered right on the bottom at the factory, and you can go one through twelve.

Purdy: Also, there has not been previous evidence that there were either metal probes that were extended totally through the body, or that such probes were photographed through the body. So obviously, it would be significant if your recollection were correct, and it would be of evidentiary significance to us. I, in no way, mean to question your view, your recollection. I just want you to have it in historical perspective as to what some other[s] say, and you may be absolutely, completely correct.

Knudsen: I do not know why that one sticks in my mind. A right profile of the body. It would seem to me that if it were, as I am sure that it was, that there would have been something in the autopsy report as to the probes, and I cannot conceive in my mind why I would feel that this negative did have it. Like I said a couple of times, I did not study these things over a viewing glass like this (indicating). As you say, it was suspended from a clothespin on a wire, a hook on a wire, and I was just flipping them this way. I do not see any picture there that would confuse with the picture, the waist-up picture.

Purdy: If you should recall anything else, whether it is new things or elaboration or your opinions on anything change or someone should, someone's name should come to mind who might also be able to provide information, I hope you will feel free to contact us here.

Knudsen: You have talked to Jim Fox?

Purdy: Yes.

Knudsen: And he did not recall any black-and-white negative of that picture?

Purdy: I am not permitted to give out the substance of the investigation, but I think you can glean certain things form the nature of my questions.

Knudsen: Jim is the one who apparently printed the black-and-white [prints]. I know the black-and-white did not go into the Photo Center for printing, so I would assume that Jim did it. Why this sticks in my mind, that there was one with these two probes through the body that nobody else recalls, it puts a question in my mind, and yet—but I could not imagine where I could get the idea from, if I had not seen it. And yet it is starting to bother me now that there is nothing in the autopsy [report] about it. Certainly that would be in the autopsy [report], if it were true. At this point, I wish I had studied the negatives rather than glance at them. At this point, I am confused why it sticks in my mind so strongly that there was this photograph, yet nobody else recalls it, and it is apparently not in any report. If it is not in any report—I cannot conceive why it would not be in the [autopsy] report. If it were there—it is really bothering me as to why it does stick in my mind so much.

And so the Knudsen deposition concluded. As researchers John Newman and Peter Dale Scott have said, it is the things that are missing—and the instances in which things have been covered up, or suppressed, or lied about in the JFK assassination—that deserve special attention. Or, as I prefer to put it, wherever there is deception in the evidence, or suppressed evidence, you must ask yourself, "what is being hidden or covered up?" The implications of the suppressed Knudsen deposition, and its contents, will be discussed further in Part II of this book.

We will now turn to the third "lens" through which Robert Knudsen's involvement in post mortem photography in the Kennedy assassination can be viewed: the recollections of former USIA photographer Joe O'Donnell, the important lead provided to us by independent researchers Randy Robertson, Kathleen Cunningham, and Gary Aguilar.

JOE O'DONNELL DISCUSSES ROBERT KNUDSEN AND THE AUTOPSY PHOTOGRAPHS

Joe O'Donnell was a civilian government photographer working for the United States Information Agency (USIA) in 1963 who had been detailed to the White House from time to time. He had a professional association with Robert Knudsen and claimed that he had been shown autopsy photographs on two different occasions by Knudsen. O'Donnell's story about Knudsen and the autopsy photographs had been made known to Dr. Robertson via a common acquaintance in Nashville, Tennessee. Jeremy Gunn and I called Mr. O'Donnell on two different occasions; the first call was an assessment interview, and the second telephone call was recorded on audiotape.

The ARRB Staff Conducts Its First Interview of Joe O'Donnell on January 29, 1997

Mr. O'Donnell confirmed that he knew Robert L. Knudsen quite well, and had a close professional association with him circa 1963. He said he always called Knudsen "Knute," but never met his family.

O'Donnell claimed that during the week following the Kennedy assassination, on two occasions Robert Knudsen showed him autopsy photographs of President Kennedy.

On the first occasion, he said that Knudsen showed him approximately 12 ea 5" x 7" B & W prints. The views included the President lying on his back, on his stomach, and closeups of the back of the head. He said that the back-of-the-head photo(s) showed a hole in the back of the head, about 2" above the hairline, about the size of a grapefruit; the hole clearly penetrated the skull and was very deep. Another photo showed a hole in the forehead above the right eye which was a round wound about three eighths of an inch in diameter which he interpreted as a gunshot wound.

O'Donnell said the second such occasion occurred a few days later, when Knudsen showed him a second set of photographs, once again about 12 ea 5" x 7" B & W prints. On this second occasion, the back-of-the-head photograph(s) showed the head intact—there was no hole in the back of the head. Instead of a hole, he remembered seeing neatly combed hair which looked slightly wet, or damp in appearance. Another photograph he remembered showed President Kennedy lying on his back, with an aluminum probe emerging from his stomach or right side. (O'Donnell's recollections were vague about this probe photograph.)

O'Donnell said it was his impression that Knudsen had taken the photographs himself, but that he had never specifically asked him that question. He said he never discussed with Knudsen the apparent discrepancy between the two back-of-the-head photos.

The ARRB Staff Conducts Its Second Interview of Joe O'Donnell on February 28, 1997

This second interview was more in-depth, and was audiotaped. Anyone interested can listen to a copy of that tape at Archives II in College Park, Maryland, or can purchase a copy from the National Archives.

Mr. O'Donnell relayed to us various recollections of the highlights of his professional career in photography, which included being a combat photographer for the United States Marine Corps during World War II (in which he photographed wounded men and observed gunshot wounds). He said he photographed both Hiroshima and Nagasaki on the ground after their destruction by atomic bombs. O'Donnell recalled going to work for the USIA in approximately 1948, and relayed professional anecdotes to us about jobs he performed when detailed to the White House during the Eisenhower, Kennedy, and Johnson administrations.

Mr. O'Donnell relayed to us in some detail, and with some poignancy, the fact that he photographed President Kennedy's November 11, 1963 Veteran's Day visit to Arlington National Cemetery, in which, while viewing the city of Washington from the Custis-Lee mansion (directly above his present-day grave site), he personally heard the President say "I could live up here forever." Mr. O'Donnell also stated that he was responsible for setting up outdoor lighting at Andrews Air Force Base on November 22, 1963 following the assassination, as Air Force One was enroute from Love Field in Dallas, Texas with President Kennedy's body onboard. He claims to have personally relayed to Jacqueline Kennedy, after she had gotten into the Navy ambulance at Andrews AFB, the anecdote about President Kennedy saying "I could live up here forever" at Arlington National Cemetery on the previous Veteran's Day, just 11 days previously. O'Donnell told us that Mrs. Kennedy said to him on the spot, "then that is where we will put him."

He repeated to us that "Knute" Knudsen showed him post mortem photographs of President Kennedy on two occasions, sometime within a month after the assassination. Each time, he said that Mr. Knudsen produced the photographs from, and returned them to, a manila envelope, and that he had no idea what Knudsen subsequently did with the photographs. Two summaries of his recollections about each event are provided below.

Regarding the first viewing, he said Knudsen showed him about 12 ea B & W glossy prints, about 5" x 7" in size, which were post mortem images of the President. He said the images were quite clear and that he assumed they were first generation prints. He said some images were close-ups of the head, some were close-ups of the shoulders, and that some were views of the entire body. He said that in some images the President was lying on his back, and in some images he was lying on his stomach. O'Donnell said he remembered a photograph of a gaping wound in the back of the head which was big enough to put a fist through, in which the image clearly showed a total absence of hair and bone, and a cavity which was the result of a lot of interior matter missing from inside the cranium. He said that another image showed a small round hole above the President's right eye, which he interpreted as an entry wound made by the same bullet which exited from the large wound in the back of the head.

Regarding the second private viewing, he said Knudsen showed him approximately 6 to 8 (and no more than 10) additional glossy B & W prints of post mortem photographs of President Kennedy, in which the small round hole above the right eye was no longer visible, and in which the rear of President Kennedy's head now looked completely intact. He said the appearance of the hair in the intact back-of-the-head photo(s) was wet, clean, and freshly combed. His interpretation of the differences in the photographs of the President's head was attributed to the restorative work of the embalmers.

We asked Mr. O'Donnell whether he ever discussed the photographs with Mr. Knudsen, either during the viewings, or afterwards, and he said no. O'Donnell said he just felt privileged to see them, but that they were so disturbing that he didn't want to see them or think about them anymore.

O'Donnell further volunteered that he was asked to show Jacqueline Kennedy the Zapruder film in a private screening within a few weeks of the assassination. He said that no one was present at the screening but he and the President's widow, and that it was held at the USIA's projection room in the USIA building at 1776 Pennsylvania Avenue, in Washington D.C. He said that when he asked her why she tried to 'escape' from the limousine, she told him she was not trying to escape, but rather was trying to pick up pieces of the President's head from the top of the car's trunk lid, so that his head could be put back together. (O'Donnell had told us a more abbreviated version of this recollection during our first phone interview; the second account was entirely consistent with the first account.) He said that following her viewing of the head shot sequence in the film, JBK told him in a very forceful way, "I don't ever want to see that again." O'Donnell said that he interpreted this as an order to alter the film so as to remove the offending images of the head shot—namely, a halo of debris around the President's head. He told us he knows it was wrong, but that he removed about 10 feet of film from the Zapruder film. After we asked Mr. O'Donnell what format the Zapruder film was, he stated it was 16 mm film; when asked if he was sure it was a 16 mm film, he said that yes, it was 16 mm film. When asked to estimate how many frames he removed, O'Donnell simply repeated that he removed "about 10 feet of film." He said he has not seen the Zapruder film since that time. When he was asked whether he altered a copy of the film or the original, he said "I had the original."[43]

Mr. O'Donnell's memory was uneven. He sometimes had trouble remembering the names of Presidents. He also gave a different timing of his viewing of the two different showings of post mortem photographs at his second ARRB interview than he did at our first interview (i.e., at the first interview he said both viewings were within a week of the assassination, and at the second interview he said that both viewings occurred within a month of the assassination). On the other hand, he appeared to remember with precision some events from the 1940s through the 1960s.

Analysis of the O'Donnell Interviews

There are several important clues to the role of Robert Knudsen in the content of the O'Donnell interviews.

First, however, it must be admitted that neither interview sheds any definitive light on whether or not Knudsen did, or did not, photograph the body of President Kennedy himself.

If true, the content of the O'Donnell interviews strongly implies that Knudsen was involved in a very large and wide-ranging photographic operation, much larger than the one he revealed in his HSCA

---

[43]The Zapruder home movie identified as the 'original' that is in storage at the National Archives is an 8 mm format film, not 16 mm; and the *total* image content of the film is less than 7 feet long.

deposition. The reader will recall that when HSCA staff counsel Purdy asked Knudsen when he first became aware of photography related to the autopsy of President Kennedy, Knudsen answered that question promptly as November 23, 1963, and the remainder of the deposition revolved around the films associated with that first answer, and the subsequent making of prints from that first batch of out-of-camera film from 11-22-63. Purdy failed to ask broader questions such as, "were you involved in more wide-ranging photographic activities on subsequent dates," etc. He focused like a laser on the black-and-white negatives and color negatives Knudsen became aware of on November 23, 1963, and the making of subsequent prints from those initial films. In retrospect, his focus may have been too narrow.

O'Donnell's recollections, *if true,* mean that Knudsen perjured himself when he told Andy Purdy on two occasions that he never saw any black-and-white prints. Based upon the O'Donnell recollections, Knudsen either made black-and-white prints himself, or likely obtained them from Secret Service agent James K. Fox, who is known to have made them.

If O'Donnell's recollections are true, and *if Knudsen took post mortem photographs himself,* then the "before" and "after" nature of the images (i.e., before the autopsy and after completion of the reconstruction) indicate that Knudsen was probably present *both* at the earliest stages following the arrival of the President's body at Bethesda—perhaps when Stringer and Riebe were asked to leave the morgue, and before x-rays were taken—and at the reconstruction events following the autopsy. This timeline would explain what Knudsen meant in his HSCA deposition when he remarked that "we were up all night."

If O'Donnell's recollections are true, *but if Knudsen did not personally take post mortem photographs of President Kennedy,* then it is clear that Knudsen was in possession of both early (and truthful) photography showing the true condition of the body upon arrival at Bethesda, as well as photographs taken later in the evening, during post-autopsy manipulations of the scalp, or during reconstruction. The early photographs could have been taken by either Riebe, or Stringer, or both. However, this option leaves unanswered the key question: who took the photographs of the partially (or totally) reconstructed back-of-the-head? As I said earlier, I find it unlikely that John Stringer did this; if he had participated in such a cover-up, it is most unlikely that he would have told David Lifton in 1972 that the large cranial defect was occipital.

I personally am inclined toward the first option, since I am persuaded Knudsen *did* take post mortem images of the President. I am virtually certain that he was indeed the photographer of the "late" views taken during, or just prior to, reconstruction; if he did not *also* take the "early" photos described by O'Donnell, then he was in possession of "early" images taken by Riebe or Stringer, or by someone else. There can be no doubt that photographs continued to be taken during reconstruction; the sources for this conclusion are the recollections of Brigadier General Godfrey McHugh, President Kennedy's Air Force Aide, as recounted to David Lifton, the author of *Best Evidence,* in recorded telephone calls.[44] (The audio recordings of those telephone calls, along with

---

[44]On page 664 of the trade paperback (Carroll and Graf) edition of *Best Evidence,*
Lifton wrote: "McHugh said that photos were taken 'from the time they got the body...until it

numerous other witness interviews, were transferred to CD and donated to the National Archives' JFK Records Collection by David Lifton circa 1998.)

The most disturbing aspect of the O'Donnell recollections, if true, is that Robert Knudsen was probably *aware of* a photographic medico-legal coverup in the assassination of President Kennedy, at the very least, and chose not to reveal this to the HSCA during his deposition. Even if he did not take any post mortem images himself, he was, according to O'Donnell, in possession of "before" and "after" images taken by others that clearly implied a coverup. Any perusal of the Warren Report—its medical diagrams prepared by H.A. Rydberg, and its conclusions, as well as a reading of the formal autopsy protocol published in the Report—would have made it clear that the photographs he possessed in 1963 were proof of a cover-up. [The intact back-of-the-head in the "late" images is inconsistent with both the autopsy report, and the Rydberg diagrams; and the entry wound high above the right eye in the "early" images spoke of a shot from the front, which the Warren Report and the autopsy report never mention.] We know, from the ARRB staff interview with Knudsen's family, that he did discuss the Warren Report with his daughter, and did so in a manner expressing great skepticism about its conclusions. (See the audiotape of the meeting with Knudsen's family made by the ARRB for details.)

If Knudsen *did* take post mortem photography himself, but *only* immediately prior to, and during the *reconstruction* of the President's cranium, this social photographer, unaccustomed to any medical photography or medico-legal procedures, may legitimately have felt he was 'photographing the autopsy.' However, if Knudsen photographed *both* the "early" arrival of the body (with the Bethesda arrival condition accurately displayed) *and* the late reconstruction efforts (showing the back-of-the-head apparently intact and the small entry wound above the right eye covered up)*, then it is impossible to escape the conclusion that he knew he was an integral player in a cover-up,* and not just a possessor of someone else's mysterious pictures. If this was the case, no doubt he was given a national security cover story of a very serious nature, and took it to the grave with him, only revealing some aspects of the fraudulent nature of some images to his own family in private conversations. The likelihood that Knudsen was an integral player in a photographic coverup of the medical evidence in the Kennedy assassination seems even more likely, based upon what his widow Gloria told me about some military men being required to take some secrets with them to the grave, if they were ordered to do so by duly constituted authority. To me, this explanation best explains the Robert Knudsen in the HSCA deposition. Specifically, it would explain: (1) why he never volunteered that he took post mortem photographs—because he was ordered not to discuss that activity by the Secret Service in 1963; and (2) why he never exhibited surprise, or any objections, to the various autopsy images shown to him during the deposition, including those of the intact back-of-the-head.

There is one loose end that my hypothesis does not account for. Knudsen spoke to his family in private of at least one "badly altered photo" of the back of the head; and his son Bob said his father

---

was put into the new casket.'" Additionally, on page 658, Lifton makes the statement: "In my interviews with Godfrey McHugh in November 1967, he gave vivid descriptions of what seemed to be reconstruction, carried on in his presence while photographs were taken."

expressed the opinion that hair had been "drawn in" to alter the back-of-the-head image. If, as I believe, the autopsy photographs showing the back-of-the-head to be intact are *not* photographic alterations, but instead represent fraudulent (but authentic) images showing the result of major manipulation and relocation of scalp by the pathologists after the autopsy and immediately before the body was turned over to the embalmers, then *why would Knudsen complain about it* (if he took those pictures), and *why would he tell his wife and his son that the posterior head photos were altered*, if they were not photographic forgeries?

It could be that by 1978, when he was deposed, and perhaps because of his deposition, he was beginning to feel guilty about what he had done on the evening of November 22-23, 1963, no doubt out of a sense of duty, and patriotic obedience to higher authority in a time of severe national crisis. Perhaps by 1978 he privately realized he had been manipulated, and that in 1963 he had been an unsuspecting tool of conspirators who were simply covering up their own heinous act. If so, his private revelations to his family that some photos were missing, others were 'altered,' and that one had 'hair drawn in,' could have been his way of protecting his most precious possession, his integrity with his family, if the lid were to blow off the whole coverup as a result of the HSCA's investigation. Based upon how his deposition went, he may have felt that the coverup was about to unravel; he had no way of knowing that the HSCA would not only fail to seriously follow-up on the discrepancies he highlighted in the autopsy photograph paper trail, but that it would ignominiously bury his testimony. His revelations to his family may have been a kind of insurance policy with those he loved, a way to say "I told you I knew something was wrong!", in the event a photographic coverup were to become a finding of the HSCA's investigation, and a national news story.

Some readers will accept this speculation of mine about why he told his family what he did; others will not. How you interpret his statements to his family about autopsy photography depend upon: (1) whether or not you are persuaded that he took post mortem photographs of President Kennedy; and (2) whether you believe some of the more controversial autopsy photographs represent a fraudulent manipulation of the scalp to hide an exit defect in the rear of the head, or undetectable photographic alterations—i.e., forgeries.[45]

One thing is undeniable. One's opinion of Mr. Knudsen's role in JFK autopsy photography shifts markedly, and becomes more uncertain, as the reader progresses from lens 1 (his family's proud recollections), to lens 2 (the HSCA deposition), to lens 3 (Joe O'Donnell's recollections).

I have expressed my strong opinion in this book that the back of President Kennedy's head appears to be intact in Figures 63-65 because loose scalp from the upper left quadrant of the President's head was rearranged temporarily, after the FBI agents left the morgue, to obscure the exit defect seen in Dallas just long enough to fool the camera. (I write about this extensively in Chapter 12.) One

---

[45]My examination of magnified and enhanced images of the autopsy photographs of the intact back-of-the-head at the Kodak headquarters facility in Rochester in November 1997 persuaded me that these images, although very strange-looking, were not altered photographs, but rather, were images of real scalp and real hair—not artwork. I will discuss this subjective judgement further in Part II of this book.

alternative explanation, however, was proposed to me in 1999 by an independent assassination researcher with esteemed academic credentials whom I respect very much, Dr. David Mantik (who is a radiation oncologist, and who also has earned a Ph.D. in physics). On that occasion, he opined that when Knudsen said "he photographed the autopsy," he did not mean that he actually took post mortem photographs of the President's body in the morgue, but that instead *Knudsen probably meant he had rephotographed the original autopsy images after they had been photographically altered,* i.e., that he had taken photographs of the autopsy images after special effects work had been done, to create a new collection that was purported to be the original 'out of camera' images, but that really was not. This explanation would account nicely for the comments Knudsen made to his family about one photograph being 'badly altered,' and about one having 'hair drawn in' over the wound in the rear of the head.

I had another conversation with Dr. Mantik in 2009 in which he told me what his subjective impressions were when he viewed stereo pairs of the back-of-the-head images at the National Archives. (Dr. Mantik has made a total of 9 visits to the Archives to view either the autopsy photographs, the x-rays, or both.) He told me that when viewed stereoscopically, the area of the posterior scalp looks "two-dimensional," not three dimensional. He said that he conducted stereo viewing with multiple types of images of the back of the head, namely, color positive transparencies, color prints, and black and white prints. He said that they all yielded the same "bizarre" 2-D effect in the area of the posterior scalp. He also told me that he did not get this impression from stereo viewing of any of the other autopsy photographs.

I explained to Dr. Mantik that when I viewed magnified and enhanced images of the posterior scalp at the Kodak facility in Rochester, in November of 1997, that I could see no photographic 'matte' lines (the obvious signs of 1963-era special effects) anywhere on the back of the head, nor could I see any discontinuities between individual strands of hair or other anatomic features that would have been an obvious indicator that a 'matte insertion' had been performed to alter the back of the head images. I told him that when viewing the magnified and enhanced images at Kodak on their high-resolution computer screens, I could see individual pores of skin in the scalp on the back of the head, in between strands of hair, as well. His response was to suggest that if the intact posterior scalp was a very cleverly done matte insertion—a special effect—that his assumption was that the matte insertion itself was indeed a photograph of real human scalp. This would explain, he suggested, the fact that the posterior scalp I examined in closeup could look 'authentic' even if it were a matte insertion.

The problem that Mantik's subjective impressions present to me as a researcher is that the HSCA's photographic panel used stereoscopic viewing on the autopsy photos, and claimed not to detect any evidence of alteration or forgery. (I write about this in more detail in Chapter 12.) I have chosen, in this book, to take the professional opinion of the HSCA panel 'on faith' and to assume that because they could not detect any apparent signs of forgery or alteration, that the explanation for why the back of the head images look so strange, and contradict the Dallas observations (and even many of the Bethesda witnesses), lay elsewhere. But anyone can be wrong, so I have included Dr. Mantik's very strong impressions about stereoscopic viewing here, as an alternative hypothesis worthy of consideration.

VINCENT MADONIA AND AUTOPSY PHOTOGRAPHY

Vince Madonia's name appears in at least three critical assassination records related to autopsy photography: in paragraph nine of the RADM Burkley inventory and transfer receipt for autopsy materials from the Secret Service to Evelyn Lincoln[46]; in the February 1967 Joint Statement of Secret Service officials to Chief Rowley recounting their recollections of the circumstances surrounding the developing of President Kennedy's autopsy photographs; and in the HSCA deposition of Robert L. Knudsen. It was incumbent upon the ARRB, which was primarily concerned with records and their provenance, to find out what we could about Vince Madonia and his actual role in the developing of JFK's autopsy photographs.

After my colleague Dave Montague located him, I interviewed Vince Madonia twice: first on June 25, 1996 on the telephone in an assessment interview; and again on November 22, 1996 after we had flown him to Washington D.C. for an in-person, tape-recorded interview. I will recount below a summary of the two interviews.

Vincent Madonia served on active duty in the United States Navy from 1949-1974, and was the officer-in-charge of the color lab at the Naval Photographic Center in Anacostia in November 1963. He was a Limited Duty Officer (LDO) in the Navy, a Lieutenant (Junior Grade), or O-2, at that time; LDOs were highly qualified former enlisted personnel promoted to the officer ranks because of their useful and specialized skills in certain fields. LDOs were not 'unrestricted line officers' eligible to eventually command units, but they *were* highly specialized technicians whose leadership skills were needed within their areas of expertise. Madonia, for example, had been a Navy photographer's mate (a senior enlisted petty officer) prior to becoming an LDO; as his first assignment following his commissioning as an officer, he was assigned to NPC Anacostia, directly across the Anacostia river from Washington D.C., as the division officer in charge of the approximately 12 to 15 people working in the color lab.

He said that 3 or 4 of his people officially assigned to the color lab on paper were actually assigned full time to a separate "White House Lab" at NPC, which was separated from the remainder of the color lab behind locked doors, and that most of the work within the White House Lab was done at night, since the White House would routinely want photos taken during the day to be ready the next morning for distribution. When asked whether he recalled a Sandy Spencer, he said yes. Madonia said that Sandy Spencer (Saundra K. Spencer), a photographer's mate first class (i.e., an E-6), was the senior of the 3 people he had assigned to the separate White House Lab, and spoke very highly of her. Madonia praised her, saying she was a very reliable worker, an "excellent" worker, whom

---

[46]Paragraph 9 of the Burkley inventory of April 26, 1965—discussed earlier in this chapter—mentioned two photographic receipts with Madonia's name on them, indicating that services were performed by NPC Anacostia for the Secret Service. Those receipts have never been found by any assassination researchers, and the paragraph 9 materials were unaccounted for, and had been omitted from the Kennedy family Deed-of-Gift, when the JFK autopsy collection was transferred from the Kennedy family to the National Archives on October 31, 1966. (See Appendix 33.)

he had a lot of respect for.

During the first interview, when asked whether he had known a Robert Knudsen, Madonia had replied in the affirmative, and independently remembered that Knudsen was a White House photographer, volunteering "he may have been there [at NPC] that weekend [the weekend of the assassination]." As soon as he said this, however, he backed off, saying "take that out of your notes, I shouldn't have said that, I'm not sure." (During that interview he, like we at the ARRB, was using a speaker phone, and I wondered at the time, following this remark, whether there was someone in the room with him coaching him.) During the second interview five months later, which was tape recorded, Madonia seemed to remember much more about Knudsen than he did during the first interview—or rather, seemed more willing to reveal what he remembered about Knudsen. During the second interview, I showed Madonia a photograph from Richard Trask's book *Pictures of the Pain,* and he correctly identified the two individuals in the photograph as Robert Knudsen and Cecil Stoughton (the other military White House photographer, and the man who traveled to Dallas with President Kennedy onboard Air Force One.).

Vince Madonia identified the color lab's capabilities during my first interview with him, as follows:

- Could develop color negatives and color prints;

- Could develop B & W portrait pan film;

- Could *not* develop Kodachrome color positive transparencies (because this was a proprietary Kodak process);

- Could "probably" develop Ektachrome E3 color positive transparencies.

He said that the color lab almost exclusively did color prints. He said there was "no good system" for making prints from color positive transparencies; NPC had the *capability* to develop transparencies and then make internegatives, but he did not remember this happening following the JFK assassination. Madonia said that he was a supervisor while at NPC Anacostia and did no hands-on photography work while he was there.

Vince Madonia's Recollections of the Events at NPC Following the Assassination of President Kennedy

Madonia's recollections of the events at NPC the weekend of the assassination was remarkably consistent during the two interviews. He remembered 3 full days of intense photographic activity, which began the evening of the assassination prior to midnight. He said no one slept that first night because they were so busy working. He stated that Federal agents from both the FBI and Secret Service (he estimated 2 to 3 people) were present all 3 days of the weekend of the assassination to ensure tight control over films, and to prevent unauthorized reproduction. During the second interview he said he believed he saw Robert Knudsen sometime that weekend, but was not sure when. He did remember that some personnel in the White House Lab unit developed autopsy photography that weekend, as well as motorcade photography from about the time of the assassination, until and including arrival at a hospital in Texas and removal of President Kennedy from the limousine; however, he did not remember seeing any details of the President's wounds from any photography the weekend of the assassination. He did remember the development of *both color negatives* and *color prints* that weekend; he did *not* remember the development of color positive transparencies. *He did recall development of 35 mm film and 120 film, as well as a black-and-white film pack (consisting of 12 ea 4" x 5" frames) that weekend.* Madonia did not remember development of any other 4" x 5" photography that weekend, such as 4" x 5" color positive transparencies in duplex holders. He was reasonably sure that NPC developed *no* 4" x 5" color positive transparencies following the assassination.

Madonia said with some assurance that "tons" of photographs were produced that weekend; when asked to clarify, he said the numbers were literally in the hundreds. During the second interview he said that after 3 full days of activity developing photographs at NPC the weekend of the assassination, that assassination-related photography "dribbled in" for some time, but was not exactly sure how many days this continued. During the first interview, however, when I asked him whether he remembered photographic work related to the JFK autopsy being done after the weekend of the assassination, he said that yes, agents did come back for some more photos which "may have been about the autopsy" during subsequent weeks, during a couple of subsequent visits. Other than the subsequent visits having taken place, he could not remember any specific details about the work done.

Regarding the content of the autopsy photographs, Madonia emphasized that although he saw a lot of products being bundled up for delivery to the White House, he made a point of NOT being too curious about what the photographs showed. He summed up his attitude at the time by saying, "the less I knew about it, the better." All he could remember about wounds was a general impression that President Kennedy looked "pretty beat up," but when asked to expand upon or clarify this, he said that his memory of the specifics was poor and that he could not. I asked Madonia whether he remembered seeing any photographic images showing probes in the body of the President, and he said he could not remember one way or another. When Madonia was asked whether he remembered ever seeing photographs represented to be President Kennedy's brain, he immediately said "no." He said that it was his recollection that NPC did not keep any assassination-related material, and that therefore no logs would have been kept, since logs only recorded photographic materials kept on file.

Madonia, when asked, said that the names of Secret Service agents James K. Fox (with whom he apparently executed two receipts), Roy Kellerman, and Robert Bouck were all unfamiliar to him. He said he was not aware of any standing relationship between NPC Anacostia and the Secret Service.

I was not quite sure whether Madonia's extremely fuzzy recollections about the image content of the autopsy photos was genuine, or feigned. I got the impression that he might have been aware there was an existing controversy about the autopsy photographs held by the government, and perhaps made a conscious decision not to get involved in that controversy. This impression of mine was gained from subtle nuances in his tone of voice, and in the uncertain nature of his denials, about image content in the autopsy photos.

Madonia literally said "my mind is gone" during the first interview, and at that time said he could remember nothing about film formats, or quantities, or types of film developed the weekend of the assassination; however during the second interview he was able to answer my specific questions about 35 mm film, 120 film, and a B & W film pack. Perhaps our first interview, and the 5 months he had to think about his forthcoming second interview, aided and refreshed his recollection; it's possible. However, his recollections about the organization and set-up of the color lab; about working all weekend from November 22-24, 1963; about Federal agents from both the FBI and the Secret Service being present all 3 days; about many hundreds (or more) of photographs being developed the weekend of the assassination; about seeing Knudsen that weekend; and about the role of Sandy Spencer, were extremely consistent between the two interviews.

Analysis of Vince Madonia's Recollections During His ARRB Interviews

The recollections of Vince Madonia strongly support the sworn testimony of Robert Knudsen before the HSCA staff counsel. Here is why:

- He affirmed knowing Robert Knudsen, which was consistent with Robert Knudsen telling the HSCA that he knew Vince Madonia.

- He recalled seeing Robert Knudsen the weekend of the assassination, which agrees with Knudsen's testimony about visiting NPC and seeing Madonia on November 23rd.

- He recalled that Sandy Spencer was the senior person in the White House Lab unit, which explains why Knudsen remembered her during his deposition; Knudsen would have been one of her major customers, if not "the" major customer, because her White House Lab developed the social photography taken by White House photographers like Knudsen and Stoughton.

- He recalled the development of a B & W film pack, and color negatives, and color prints the weekend of the assassination; this is one hundred per cent consistent with the NPC photographic activity that Knudsen testified to having knowledge of.

The failure of Vince Madonia to recollect the developing of any color positive transparencies brings into some question the February 1967 USSS Joint Statement about the developing of color positive transparencies at NPC. The problem here is Madonia's spotty memory about some things, and the fact that the 2 memos between Fox and Madonia, listed in paragraph 9 of the Burkley inventory of April 1965, provide corroboration for the Secret Service report about photography sent to Chief Rowley in February 1967. Unless or until the two Fox-Madonia receipts (dated November 29, 1963) mentioned in paragraph 9 of the Burkley inventory are ever found, and we can examine their contents as to format and type and quantity of film processed, we can never know for sure whether or not the color positive transparencies and duplex B & W negatives in the paper trail were, or were not, developed at NPC Anacostia. My personal take on this is that they probably *were;* that is, that the document dated February 1967 is probably better evidence than Madonia's memory in 1996. (I believe Madonia when he says no color positives were developed *the weekend of the assassination,* since his recollections of that particular weekend seemed quite detailed during his second interview; but I believe that the USSS report is probably accurate when it says that color positives *were developed* at NPC on or about November 27th, because that assertion is backed up by the two receipts dated November 29th mentioned in the Burkley inventory.)

Madonia's recollection of 35 mm and 120 mm film being developed at NPC the weekend of the assassination supports Floyd Riebe on the one hand (35 mm), and the autopsy film paper trail on the other, which listed one roll of 120 film from the very beginning.

Summarizing, I conclude that NPC developed 35 mm film, 120 mm film, color negatives, color prints, and at least one black-and-white film pack (the one Knudsen referred to, at a minimum) the weekend of the assassination; and color positive transparencies and B & W negatives from duplex holders on November 29th.   If Floyd Reibe (who appears to have been telling the truth about the 35 mm film, providing Madonia's memory is correct) was correct about also shooting some color four by fives, and 2 black-and-white film packs, then NPC may have developed many more autopsy photographs than discussed in either the paper trail, or the Knudsen deposition.

VELMA VOGLER'S ACCOUNT OF THE DISPOSITION OF AUTOPSY PHOTOGRAPHS

Velma Reumann (nee Vogler) was a junior officer in the Navy who, in 1963 at the time of the JFK assassination, was the Personnel Officer at the Naval Photographic Center, Anacostia. Dave Montague and I telephoned her and conducted our interview on October 4, 1996. We had obtained a microfilm record of personnel serving at NPC in 1963; her name was on the list, and when we located her, we received quite an unexpected surprise.

She completed OCS in 1956, and then served at the following locations: Newport, Rhode Island; Naples, Italy: Bainbridge, Maryland; and then the Naval Photographic Center in Anacostia. Her tour of duty at NPC began in 1963 and ended in 1966. She recalled that approximately 300 people worked at NPC, and that there were 3 separate photographic departments, as follows: still photo lab, motion picture lab, and research and development.

Like most Americans, she went home from work after the assassination on November 22, 1963 and was therefore unaware of all of the photographic activity that weekend at her workplace. She had a vague recollection of some kind of photographic work related to the assassination being done at NPC within the 2 or 3 weeks period after the assassination, but does not know what kind of photography it was, or what the subject matter was.

Disposition of Assassination-Related Photographic Records

In 1996 Velma Reumann had a strong, independent recollection of NPC personnel boxing-up all photographic materials ("everything we—the film department—had") related to the assassination *on the orders of Robert Kennedy* and sending them to the Smithsonian Institution for permanent storage sometime within 6 months or so after the assassination. She cannot remember whether the orders from Robert Kennedy were in writing, or oral, but she was quite firmly of the impression in

1996 that the direction had come from Robert Kennedy, the President's brother, who at that time was still Attorney General of the United States, the chief law enforcement officer of the land.

My first reaction (to myself, in an internal aside) was to scoff at this. The National Archives is the normal repository for records of this nature, not the Smithsonian. In order to test the strength of her recollection about the Smithsonian, I asked her 'up front' whether she may have been confusing the Smithsonian with the National Archives or some other government body; she replied emphatically that she knew the difference between the National Archives and the Smithsonian, and reiterated that the boxed material went to the Smithsonian. She said she was certain of this because she, herself, was required to call an official at the Smithsonian to discuss the imminent transfer, and recalls that the individual to whom she spoke was as surprised by the selection of the Smithsonian as she was. Unfortunately, she did not remember the official's name or job description, nor does she remember the exact date of the transfer. When I asked her whether it was closer to six months after the assassination, or one month after the assassination, she said it was probably closer to six months after the assassination than one month.

I asked her if she was ever aware of the Zapruder film being shown, or present in the building at NPC, and she said no.

Ms. Reumann said that there was a general awareness during lunchroom conversations at NPC shortly after the assassination that the autopsy doctors had been silenced—that is, were forbidden to talk about the autopsy. Normally, photographers working at a facility completely disassociated from Bethesda NNMC should not have known anything whatsoever about the muzzling of pathologists who conducted an autopsy at Bethesda, whether rumor or not. This implies to me that the information (which as it turns out, was correct) was likely passed to someone in the White House Lab by Robert Knudsen himself, who almost certainly had intimate contact with all three pathologists on the evening of November 22-23, 1963, and may very well have witnessed an oral warning being administered to Humes, Boswell, and Finck inside the Bethesda morgue. This is admittedly speculative, but is, I think, reasonable speculation.

Can the Smithsonian Story Be True?

I am less skeptical now about this Smithsonian recollection than I initially was when I first heard it. The reason for this is that *Robert Knudsen's involvement with autopsy photography implies to me that he was picked for this assignment that night by Robert Kennedy.* Why do I believe this? Knudsen's son Bob told the ARRB staff that his father was close to both Robert and Jack Kennedy, and had very frequent contact with them in the course of his duties. It made no sense to pick a social photographer who was *unused* to doing detailed, 'macro' medical photography where lighting and focus were both so critical, and so *different* from portrait and social photography, unless your principal requirement was _loyalty and secrecy_. I now suspect that Robert Kennedy, the Attorney General of the United States (and essentially the 'Deputy President' in terms of real authority), was intimately involved with whatever medical cover-up took place in the assassination of his brother. Otherwise, many of those involved in the coverup likely would have balked and refused to cooperate. If asked to do so in the name of the man who was both the Attorney General and the President's brother, however, and if those orders from on high were accompanied by a convincing 'national security' cover story, then such orders may not only have persuaded those involved to 'put their country's security above the truth,' but may have compelled them to later *keep* the secrets of their involvement, and even 'take them to the grave,' in spite of being subpoenaed and deposed by various government bodies. If Robert Kennedy was personally engineering, or ordering others to engineer, a medical coverup, as the record suggests, it would not surprise me that he would order records of photography at NPC (which were no doubt inconsistent with the official paper trail of the autopsy photographs) to be deposited—buried—in some unexpected location, particularly if those records recorded evidence of unusual photographic activity.[47]

I awaited possible orders from Jeremy Gunn to begin 'stirring the pot' at the huge and labyrinthine Smithsonian Institution, but he never asked me to do so. I am not really surprised, nor do I blame him. Today the Smithsonian is comprised of 20 museums in total, and 13 of them are in the Washington D.C. metro area. We did not have the resources or time to conduct a search for this kind of needle in that kind of haystack. Besides, Velma Reumann mentioned *records,* not photographs; Madonia said NPC kept *no* autopsy photographs. Even without finding such records, we already had 'critical mass' in the area of extra photography beyond the official paper trail, since the recollections of Robert Knudsen and Vince Madonia were so consistent on this score.

SAUNDRA K. SPENCER AND AUTOPSY PHOTOGRAPHY

Both Robert Knudsen's HSCA deposition and Vince Madonia's ARRB interview led us to Saundra K. Spencer. This witness was so potentially important that we took the step of audiotaping the initial assessment interview on the telephone. We first interviewed Sandy Spencer on December 13, 1996—a little more than a month after we spoke to Velma Reumann and about three weeks after we interviewed Vince Madonia in person. A summary of the assessment interview is provided below:

- Saundra Spencer worked at NPC Anacostia from early 1960 until 6 months after the assassination.

------

[47]Other suggestions that Robert Kennedy was involved in a medical coverup (beyond his probable personal involvement in selecting Robert Knudsen to take 'off-the-record' post mortem photographs) include: (1) the attempts by RADM Burkley on 11-22-63 (who was relaying instructions from the Kennedy family—i.e., RFK—in the VIP suite on the 17th floor of the tower at Bethesda) to restrict the scope of the autopsy; (2) his documented personal involvement in April of 1965 in wresting possession of the 'official' autopsy photographs, and crucial paper records and biological materials, from the Secret Service and placing them under his personal control; (3) RFK's undoubted involvement in ensuring that the Kennedy family Deed-of-Gift drawn up by Burke Marshall barred public access to the photographs and x-rays for 5 years, kept public access to an extremely low level after that, and prevented publication of any of the images; (4) the HSCA's report (in volume 7) of Burke Marshall's conclusion that Robert Kennedy had likely disposed of the remains of the brain and all of the other biological specimens; and (5) his personal order to destroy the Dallas casket, the details and significance of which will be discussed at length in Part II.

- She was a PH1, an E-6 photographer's mate, and was in charge of the "White House Lab" which was a subset of the color division at NPC responsible for still photography. Officially, she said this White house Lab reported to the Naval Aide to the President, but in reality Chief Petty Officer Robert Knudsen, the Navy social photographer who worked at the White House, was the direct supervisor of the lab and its activities. He gave them all of their developing assignments, delivered exposed film to them, and took the developed product back to the White House. Representative of typical work performed by the White House Lab were prints of Presidential ceremonies, and family photographs.

- She said that on November 23, 1963, the day after the assassination, probably in the afternoon, a Federal agent named Fox (whom she believed was FBI) arrived at NPC; she went down to the quarterdeck to escort him up to the still color lab.

- Fox delivered to her 3 or 4 duplex film holders which contained 6 to 8 sheets of film; she said this film was *color negatives,* **not** color positive transparencies. [Her recollections thus corroborated Knudsen's and Madonia's.] The developing process she recalled using was called C-22 [which was entirely consistent with the process Earl McDonald had told us was used for color negatives].

- Test prints were made from each image, then filters were used for color correction, and then 8" x 10" color prints were made of each image.

- The agent took all of the materials with him when he left.

- The agent stuck with her "like glue" during the developing process.

- She was under the impression that the photographic images were classified material, but no one specifically, to her recollection, swore her to silence. She said they would not have had to, because the materials were considered to be classified by all concerned by their very nature.

- She said that in her division, color positive transparencies were never developed. She did not see any color positive transparencies on November 23, 1963, nor did she *subsequently* hear of any autopsy photography on color positive transparency film. [This is inconsistent with the Secret Service Joint Statement presented to Chief Rowley in February 1967, which indicated that such developing took place at NPC on or about November 27th.] When asked whether any other department at NPC had the capability of developing color positive transparencies, she said that the black-and-white section at NPC may possibly have had the capability of developing color positive transparencies, but that they could not have done so on November 23, 1963 because the whole building was secured that day, except for her section.[48]

- When asked, she said that Vince Madonia did not help with this processing job [i.e., the color negatives], and that as far as she knew, Chief Knudsen did not accompany agent Fox during Fox's visit[49]; she also said that this one visit on November 23rd was the only photographic event related to autopsy photography in which she participated.

- She said that none of the people working at NPC the weekend of the assassination got any sleep "for 4 days," because they were busy printing 10,000 copies of a "prayer card" on which was a photograph of the President which Jacqueline Kennedy had selected.[50] She also said that Fox's visit interrupted the production of the prayer cards.

- Image content of the color negatives and color prints Spencer remembered developing the weekend of the assassination is summarized below:

    - views were body shots, and were not like the normal autopsy photographs she had experience with from her previous duty at Pensacola Naval Air Station, in the sense that there was no one in the background, and she does not remember any instruments in the photographs;

    - the views were also unlike other autopsy photographs she had seen, in that the body of the President was "very clean," meaning there was "no blood and gore" visible;

    - she remembered that no measuring devices were visible;

---

[48]A possibility presents itself here. If the activity of November 27th (or 29th) mentioned in the February 1967 Secret Service photography report—the developing of out-of-camera B & W negatives exposed in duplex holders, and color positive transparencies exposed in duplex holders—was performed by the black-and-white section at NPC, that would explain how Madonia would know about it (and have his name affixed to receipts, per paragraph 9 of the Burkley inventory of April 1965), and Sandy Spencer would not know about it.

[49]My first reaction to this was that 'this presents no real problem.' People's recollections of events often differ slightly as to minor details, such as who was present at an event. Besides, if Knudsen was already developing his B & W film pack when Spencer went down to meet Fox, this could explain why Spencer did not remember seeing Knudsen that day. Later, I was to change my mind about this.

[50]Spencer subsequently produced one of these prayer cards at her ARRB deposition. It was printed on heavy, non-glossy photographic paper stock, and the photo referred to above was one taken by personal family photographer Jacques Lowe during JFK's visit to Nebraska in 1960 during his primary election campaign.

- she remembered no identification tags or cards visible in any of the photos;

- she did remember *a wound at the base of the front of the President's neck which was circular,* and about the size of the round end of a person's thumb;

- she did remember *a wound in the back of the President's head which she described as a "blown out chunk" about 2 to 2.5 inches wide located in about the center of the back of the President's head, about 3 or 4 inches above the hairline;*

- the top of the head was not visible in the photos, so she said she could therefore not tell us whether there was any damage to the top of President Kennedy's head;

- she remembered *no damage to the right side of the President's head.*

At the conclusion of this phone call the ARRB staff relayed its intent to have Saundra Spencer come to Washington for a more in-depth interview, and to view the autopsy photos in the National Archives. She agreed to come.

Needless to say, her recollections in this first interview were electrifying, a term I have used before this in regard to some other events involving eyewitness testimony about the medical evidence. This was a true 'epiphany,' one of those moments when you are *absolutely sure* that something is not only true, but highly significant—in this case, that *there was indeed a hole in the back of the President's head devoid of scalp and bone* just as everyone in Dallas had said there was. Her recollections also confirmed that some autopsy photographs were missing, and that therefore the official paper trail was incomplete; and that there was 'something' seriously wrong with the photographs of the intact back-of-the-head in the official collection in the National Archives.

Sandy Spencer's credibility in this first interview, on a scale of 1 to 10 (with 10 being the highest possible credibility), was assessed as a solid 10. Everyone present at the telephone interview (Executive Director David Marwell, General Counsel Jeremy Gunn, myself, and Dave Montague, who had located Ms. Spencer) agreed on that. However, the proof of the pudding would be in the eating—we had to await her deposition, in front of the autopsy photographs at the Archives, before we could take her recollections 'to the bank,' so to speak. After all, under oath, both John Stringer and Floyd Riebe had reversed previous unsworn statements they had made about what the autopsy photographs of President Kennedy depicted in the way of damage to the head. I couldn't wait for Saundra Spencer's deposition; if there ever was a rock-solid witness who would stand by her own recollections, 'no matter what,' it seemed like she was surely such a person.

The ARRB Deposition of Saundra K. Spencer

The ARRB staff deposed Saundra Spencer on June 5, 1997, about a month after our strange experience with Floyd Riebe. I wondered if this next witness, too, would reverse herself under oath and also deny—as Stringer and Riebe both had—her own previous statements that there was a substantial hole, a "blow-out," or probable exit wound, in the back of President Kennedy's head after his assassination. The issue is critical if you are a person who thinks as an attorney thinks about evidence—about the overriding importance of sworn testimony and the relative unimportance of unsworn testimony—and not as an oral historian thinks about evidence (namely, that the earliest statements a witness makes are likely the most accurate, whether they are made under oath or not). Knudsen's recollections to his family that at least one back-of-the-head image had been "badly" altered by "drawing in hair," no matter how convincing to us as 'oral history,' were hearsay, and furthermore, he never said that to the HSCA while testifying at his own deposition. In addition, O'Donnell's recollections to us that Knudsen showed him photographs of both a large occipital defect, and of an intact back-of-the-head image, were subject to challenge: a skeptic could claim that O'Donnell's credibility was in question because his memory about other events was sometimes poor, and because his story about alteration of the *original* Zapruder film (as opposed to a 16 mm copy) was too fantastic, and fraught with evidentiary contradictions, to believe.

As it turned out, Saundra Spencer did *not* recant under oath, as Stringer and Riebe had; she 'stuck by her guns,' and testified that on the weekend following the assassination she developed a color negative *and* a corresponding color print of a hole in the President Kennedy's head, through both scalp and bone, approximately 2 inches in diameter, in the upper occipital bone, or mid-region, of the back of the skull. Her testimony is a 'smoking gun' document in the Kennedy assassination, especially to those strongly oriented toward the primacy of sworn testimony, since it directly contradicts the recollections of Drs. Humes, Boswell, and Finck before both the HSCA Forensic Pathology Panel, and their testimony before the ARRB staff, that the images showing the rear of President Kennedy's head to be intact were indeed 'the way it looked that night.' [The only objections those three gentlemen ever posed to those photographs was to the interpretation of the likely site of the entry wound in the pictures, not to the intact nature of the rear of the skull.] It is not really significant that she also contradicted Stringer and Riebe, since they had clearly and undeniably *contradicted themselves,* and in doing so had lost all credibility on the issue of whether there was, or was not, a large occipital defect in the rear of the head at the autopsy. Further implications of Saundra Spencer's testimony to the ARRB will be discussed at the end of the excerpts of her testimony reproduced below. Significant portions of her testimony are reproduced here, because of the importance of her deposition to history.

Jeremy initially covered with her a brief history of her Naval career, and of the organization of the Naval Photographic Center. None of this testimony differed from our initial assessment interview with her, so it will not be repeated here. Jeremy did wish to clarify, on the record, her relationship with Chief Knudsen and his relationship with the NPC White House Lab, as well as NPC developing capabilities:

Gunn: What was your position in the White House Lab in 1963?

Spencer: I was Petty Officer-in-Charge.

Gunn: Did you have any supervisor who was also within the White House Lab?

Spencer: Chief Knudsen was our liaison and supervisor from the White House, but we fell also under the Officer-in-Charge of the color lab, but they pretty much left us alone, [and we] did our own thing. They gave us a cipher lock on our room and said 'do try to stay awake.' [This is clearly a reference to her earlier statement, in December 1996, to often having to work all night long to have photographs ready the next morning.]

Gunn: When you say "they" left you alone, you are referring to the color lab itself?

Spencer: The color lab and the Officer-in-Charge. They would ask periodically if we needed any support or anything, and if we needed anything we just asked them and we usually got what we needed.

Gunn: How many people worked under you in the White House Lab in November of '63?

Spencer: It averaged four to five at various times, people would come and go [and] as they transferred in and out, they were assigned to the Photographic Center, and they were then detailed to us.

Gunn: During the time that you worked in the White House Lab, did you ever develop color transparencies?

Spencer: No.

Gunn: Did you have the capability of developing color [positive] transparencies in the White House Lab?

Spencer: No.

Gunn: Did the color division, separate from the White House Lab, have any capability of developing color [positive] transparencies?

Spencer: Yes, they did.

Gunn: Was there a capacity to develop positive color transparencies by November of 1963?

Spencer: Yes.

Gunn: Do you know what kinds of film were capable of being developed, color transparencies in November of '63?

Spencer: It was the Ektachrome. Anything like the Kodachrome was sent out to Kodak directly.

Gunn: So Kodachrome would be sent to Kodak, but Ektachrome could be developed?

303

Spencer: Ektachrome could be in-house, and we were working with E3, E4s right around that time.

Gunn: You mentioned earlier a person by the name of Knudsen. How often did you see Mr. Knudsen?

Spencer: Not that often. When he needed a back-up photographer, we would go over [to the White House]. Usually, most of his film come [sic] by courier to us or we would go out to Andrews to pick up from the courier planes, and he would call us on the telephone, usually daily, and we would again courier or take his proof prints over and drop them off, and we would just get them back by courier circled with what he wanted.

Gunn: Do you remember who the supervisor of the color lab was in November of '63?

Spencer: Oh, I can picture his face, but I can't remember his name. It was a Lieutenant—

Gunn: Does the name Vince Madonia ring a bell?

Spencer: Yes, that's him.

Gunn: How often would you interact with Mr. Madonia around 1963?

Spencer: Oh, I would have seen him on a daily basis.

Gunn: Now, I would like to go to November 22nd of 1963, and ask you what you were doing when you first heard about the assassination of President Kennedy?

Spencer: I was sitting and color correcting a photo of John-John [taken] in President Kennedy's office, and it came over the NPC radio speaker that the President had been shot.

Gunn: After you heard that, what did you do?

Spencer: We just continued to work until we got word that they wanted to go ahead and close the NPC down and move all except our personnel out of the immediate areas...

Gunn: When you say they moved all the personnel out of NPC except "our area," do you mean the White House area or the color lab area?

Spencer: They secured the color lab crews and we [the White House Lab unit under Knudsen] stayed.

Gunn: So approximately, how many people stayed when the rest of NPC closed down?

Spencer: There was about three of us up there.

_____

Gunn: Ms. Spencer, did you have any work after November 22, 1963 that was related to the death of President Kennedy?

Spencer: Yes. We were requested to develop 4" by 5" color negatives and make prints of an autopsy that was—we were told it was shot at Bethesda after the President's body was brought back from Dallas.

Gunn: I would like to come to that in a minute. Prior to that, did you have any other work or responsibilities related to the death of President Kennedy?

Spencer: We were trying to put together the prayer cards. Mrs. Kennedy had selected a black-and-white photograph [taken by Jacques Lowe in 1960], and so we needed a number of them. What we did was take four prints, 4" by 5" prints, and do the vignetting on those, and then they were copied to a master negative, and we took it downstairs and put it on the automatic black-and-white printers to print out the required numbers. Then, we brought them back and we did not cut them here. We brought them to the White House. They took them to the printers and evidently they were printed and cut there.

Gunn: Did you bring with you today some examples of those prints that you made?

Spencer: Yes, I brought two on a half sheet.

Jeremy then marked the samples as Exhibit MD 146.

Gunn: Do you remember approximately how many of these prints you made?

Spencer: I think the count was supposed to be around 10,000, but I am sure we went over.

Gunn: What is your best recollection as to when you started working on the prints?

Spencer: It was after the President's body had been brought back [from Dallas] because Mrs. Kennedy personally selected the print. Chief Knudsen told us which one, and then we went ahead and pulled it, and started the process of producing the—

Gunn: President Kennedy's body arrived at approximately 6:00 P.M. in Washington D.C. Does that help you determine approximately the time when you began work on the black-and-white prints?

Spencer: No.

Gunn: Do you remember whether it was on the evening of November 22nd?

Spencer: It seems to me like we had gotten the word the following day, which would have been a Saturday.

Gunn: So on Friday, November 22nd, 1963, did you do any work related to either the funeral of President Kennedy or to autopsy photographs that you mentioned?

Spencer: No, we were primarily in a standby position.

Gunn: Approximately how long did it take for you to work on the black-and-white prints?

Spencer: It took most of the day. It seemed to me it was late, maybe 2 o'clock in the morning, by the time we got them over to the White House after we got the indication of which ones we needed to print.

Gunn: So this would be, then, you worked on them on Saturday, November 23rd, until approximately 2 o'clock in the morning on Sunday, November 24th, is that—

Spencer: I can't remember the day. All I remember is that it was after the President's body had been taken up to the Rotunda, because as we went to the White House, the lines were forming for the [ceremonial lying in state at the] Rotunda.[51]

Gunn: Just to make sure that I understand this correctly...you took prints over to the White House, the black-and-white prints, and at that time, you noticed lines forming to go [to] the Rotunda on Capitol Hill?

Spencer: Yes.

Gunn: And at the time that you took the prints to the White House, do you remember whether the body was at the White House or whether it was at Capitol Hill?

Spencer: It had to be up at the Capitol Rotunda at that time.

Gunn: Now, a few minutes ago you mentioned some work related to the autopsy photographs of President Kennedy. When did you first receive information that you would be doing some work on that issue?

---

[51]Actually, if Spencer commenced work on the prayer card photographs on Saturday, and finished about 2 o'clock in the morning on Sunday, then she witnessed lines forming in front of the U.S. Capitol building *prior to* the President's body being moved there after dawn on Sunday morning. The key recollection here is that the *lines were forming,* and the key time is that it was in the middle of the night, shortly after 2 A.M. The body was still lying in state in the East Room of the White House when Spencer and her colleagues delivered the 10,000 prayer card prints. The important thing here is not that she gets all historical details correct here, but that her testimony allows us to accurately reconstruct a timeline of events.

Spencer: We received a call from the quarterdeck, and they said an agent was there, and we were supposed to perform photographic work for him. They logged him in and brought him up. He had in his hand 4 by 5 film holders, so I am estimating—he was a large man—so he probably had four or five film holders. [This is consistent with the number recalled by Knudsen in his HSCA deposition.]

Gunn: Do you remember approximately when the telephone call happened, which day of the week?

Spencer: No, I don't.

Gunn: Do you remember what you were doing at the time that you heard about the telephone call from the quarterdeck?

Spencer: No, I don't. It seemed like it was in the morning.

Gunn: Were you working on the developing of the black-and-white prints, did it interrupt that, or was it before or after? [In our December 1996 telephone interview Spencer had told us that the Fox visit interrupted the work on the prayer cards.]

Spencer: No, it was after.

Gunn: So it was after you had finished the prints. Had you done any other work between the time that you worked on the black-and-white prints and that [sic] you received a call from the quarterdeck?

Spencer: We were finishing up job orders that we had, that had been requested from the White House.

Gunn: When Mr. Fox...came to the White House lab, approximately how many other people were working in the lab at that time?

Spencer: Two others.

Gunn: Now, when you say that the agent had 4 by 5 film holders, what do you mean by that?

Spencer: It means they either used a 4 by 5 [inch format] press camera or a view camera, and a film holder is two-sided container that holds two sheets of film, [and you] insert it in the camera, pull the dark slide, do your photograph, reinsert the dark slide, turn the holder over, and you are ready—and pull the dark slide, and you are ready for a

307

second shot. So there is [sic] two sheets of film in each of the holders.

Gunn: When you refer to a press camera or a press camera or a view camera, are those also known as large format cameras?

Spencer: Yes, large format cameras.

Gunn: Now, if I recall correctly, you said that your recollection was that he had four or five of these duplex film holders, is that correct?

Spencer: Correct.

Gunn: Did the agent speak to you directly or did he speak with somebody else?

Spencer: To me directly.

Gunn: What did he ask you to do?

Spencer: He said he needed the film processed and a print of each of them.

Gunn: What did you then do?

Spencer: We took them and then checked our film chemistry, brought it up to temperature, and processed the negatives. We put the negatives in the drying cabinet, and when they were completed, we brought them out. We went into the dark room and made a test print on them, which we processed and color corrected, and made the final print, at which time we took all the scraps and anything related to that job, and put it in an envelope and give it to the agent, returned his film holders to him.

Gunn: Did you keep any material at all related to the development of these photographs?

Spencer: Absolutely not. The agent was very specific that he wanted everything, any test scraps or anything that we might use.

Gunn: What type of film did you develop?

Spencer: It was a color negative C-22 process. [This is entirely consistent with what Earl McDonald told me about the process used to develop color negatives in that era.]

Gunn: Could you describe for me briefly what a C-22 process is?

Spencer: It is a standard color—well, it was a standard color negative at the time, and it's a three-layer image, reverse image of each of the three basic primary colors with a reddish yellow masking material that is incorporated into the negative to prevent bleedover of the various layers when printing.

Gunn: Did you develop those negatives in the White House Lab or did you go into the color lab to develop them?

Spencer: They were processed in the White House section in the Calumet Unit in the small off-room. We had the color negative processing facility capability plus the print processing.

Gunn: When you developed the first test print, what kind of paper did you put that onto?

Spencer: It's the standard color print material.

Gunn: Now, you brought with you today a photograph of President Kennedy that you said it was your understanding was taken approximately two weeks before the assassination, is that correct?

Spencer: Yes, the Black Watch[52] performed at the White House, and these were brought to us, so I would estimate this print was probably made about a week to 10 days prior to the printing of the autopsy material, so the chemical content within the paper should be fairly close to what the autopsy photo chemical content was.

Jeremy marked the Black Watch photo as Exhibit MD 147.

Gunn: Now, for MD 147, if I am understanding you correctly...the paper that Exhibit 147 was developed on is the same as you used for the test prints, is that correct?

Spencer: Yes, at the Photographic Center, when we ordered our paper, we ordered an entire run, and they cut it to the various sizes that we needed, so that we could make a 4 by 5, an 8 by 10, or a 16 by 20, all from the same color pack, and make them totally match, so that the paper should be the same batch that was used.

Gunn: When you said you made a test print, how many test prints did you make of each negative?

Spencer: The general rule was for us to make a test print of each [one], but I am not sure that we tested all of them, because, you know, they were all the same subject matter. It was general practice, though, to go ahead and prepare one test print of each.

Gunn: Do you know whether more than one test print was made of any of the negatives?

----

[52]The Black Watch was a ceremonial Scottish bagpipe marching unit that wore full kilt regalia, which was quite famous in the United Kingdom.

Spencer: No.

Gunn: That is, there were no prints—

Spencer: No, there were no—just one test print was made of each. [I think what Jeremy had
             in mind here was Knudsen's recollection to the HSCA that there were seven prints
             made of each negative; he was testing an internal hypothesis that perhaps several test
             prints of each negative could have provided an explanation for this recollection by
             Knudsen.]

Gunn: After the color correction, how many prints were made of each of each negative?

Spencer: One.

Gunn: So, would it be fair to say that, at maximum, there were two prints made of each
             negative?

Spencer: That is correct. [This event that Spencer is recalling, therefore, does *not* appear that
             it could be the same event at which Knudsen recalled 7 each prints being made from
             each negative, providing both his and Spencer's recollections were accurate. Not
             only was Knudsen apparently not present, but the numbers of prints made were not
             even close.]

Gunn: And were the final prints also developed on the same paper as Exhibit 147?

Spencer: Correct.

Gunn: And so would you expect that on the original test print, as well as the original color-
             corrected print, there would be the same type of markings that are on the back of
             Exhibit no. 147?

Spencer: Yes, it should have the same watermarks and markings plus the plus the same border
             pattern.

Gunn: When you say the "same watermarks," what do you mean?

Spencer: On the back of all Kodak paper, they print their Kodak label, and it changes from
             year to year, but it just says Kodak paper.

Gunn: So on the Exhibit no. 147, it appears that there is either a delta figure, or appears a
             delta figure, and then Kodak paper, is that what you are referring to?

Spencer: Yes.

Gunn: Do you know the difference between a negative and an internegative?

Spencer: Yes.

Gunn: What is the difference in just a very general way?

Spencer: A negative is an original piece of film. An inter-neg is an intermediate negative material designed to [facilitate] go[ing] from a transparency to a print.

Gunn: Would you have been able to tell, at the time that you developed the duplex films, whether the film was a negative or an inter-negative?

Spencer: Yes, because the inter-negative cannot be processed C-22.

Gunn: So that you are certain then that they were not inter-negatives that you developed?

Spencer: No, they were original.

Gunn: Approximately how much time did it take between the time that you first saw the 4 x 5 duplex holders and the time that the agent left?

Spencer: It takes—it was 30 minutes for the processing of the negative[s], approximately 45 minutes to dry the negatives, and then the printing, the other print process was 18 minutes, and then on the drying drums probably about 3 minutes, so less than two hours.

Gunn: Did the agent leave immediately after the final prints had been dried?

Spencer: Yes.

Gunn: So he did not stay around and talk at all or say anything?

Spencer: No.

Gunn: Did he talk to you at all about where he had obtained the photographs?

Spencer: No. When he gave us the material to process, he said they—had been shot at Bethesda and they were autopsy pictures, for us to process them and try to not observe too much, don't peruse.

Gunn: Did he say anything that you now recall other than what you have just mentioned?

Spencer: No. We did sign chain-of-evidence forms.

Gunn: Could you describe that form for me or what you recall about that?

Spencer: It was just a form that everybody that had handled the material signed.

Gunn: What happened to that form?

Spencer: The agent took it with him.

Gunn: Did you ever have a copy of that form?

Spencer: No.

Gunn: Do you remember whether it was typewritten or handwritten?

Spencer: It was on a regular printed form.

Gunn: Had you seen forms like that before or did it seem as though it was unique for that particular situation?

Spencer: It just was that—what the material, you know, film and paper, and he wrote down how many of each thing on it, and stuff, and I signed off on it.

Gunn: Did you use forms like that for your other work with the White House?

Spencer: No.

Gunn: Have you ever signed a form like that previously?

Spencer: It pretty much followed like for a classified piece of material.

Gunn: Did you develop photographs previously that had classified information in them?

Spencer: No, we just treated everything that we got as semi-classified and just kept it within the unit.

Gunn: Was there a reason of which you were aware for treating most of the material as if it were semi-classified?

Spencer: Because the only people that had the right to release it was the White House.

Gunn: After the agent left, did you do any additional work related to any autopsy photos?

Spencer: No.

Gunn: Did you do any other work related to the death of the President?

Spencer: No.

———————————

Gunn: Did you ever see any other photographic material related to the autopsy in addition to what you have already described?

Spencer: Just, you know, when they came out with some books and stuff later that showed autopsy pictures and stuff, and I assumed that they were done in—you know, down in Dallas or something, because they were not the ones that I had worked on. [Spencer could have been referring to *Best Evidence, High Treason, High Treason 2, Conspiracy of Silence,* or *The Killing of the President.*]

———————————

Gunn: ...did you ever hear of anyone else at NPC who had worked on any other autopsy photographs?

Spencer: No.

Gunn: Did you have any opportunity to observe the content of the negatives and the prints as you were working on them?

Spencer: Yes, I did.

Gunn: Can you describe for me what you saw as best you can recollect?

Spencer: Briefly, they were very, what I consider pristine for an autopsy. There was no blood or opening cavities, opening[s] or anything of that nature. It was quite reverent in how they handled it.

Gunn: If I can just ask for some clarification, do you mean that the body appeared to be clean, had been washed? Is that what you are suggesting?

Spencer: Yes.

Gunn: And that was different from what you had seen in other autopsy photographs, is that right?

Spencer: Yes. In other autopsies, they have the opening of the [body] cavity and the removing of vital organs for weighing and stuff of this nature. The only organ that I had seen

313

was a brain that was laid beside the body.[53]

Gunn: And that was in the photograph of President Kennedy?

Spencer: Yes.

Gunn: So there was a brain in the photograph beside the body, is that correct?

Spencer: Well, yes, by the side of the body, but it didn't appear that the skull had been cut, peeled back and the brain removed. None of that was shown. As to whose brain it was, I cannot say.

Gunn: But was it on a cloth or in a bucket or how was it—

Spencer: No, it was on the mat beside the table.

Gunn: Did you see any people in the pictures in addition to President Kennedy, such as bystanders or doctors?

Spencer: I don't remember anybody or any real measuring material, instruments, because normally, when you are photographing something like that, you have gauges in there, so that you can determine size and everything.

Gunn: Did you see any cards or identification markers that would identify an autopsy number or the victim, or something of that sort?

Spencer: I don't remember any.

Gunn: Were there any photographs that would show the entire body in one frame, do you recall?

Spencer: It seems there was a full-length one, kind of shot at a 45-degree angle, at a slightly high angle.

Gunn: Did you see any photographs that focused principally on the head of President Kennedy?

Spencer: Right. They had one showing the back of the head with the wound at the back of the head.

------

[53]Early in the deposition Spencer testified that she had personally photographed approximately 10 or 12 autopsies while she had been stationed at Pensacola Naval Air Station.

314

Gunn: Could you describe what you mean by the "wound at the back of the head?"

Spencer: It appeared to be a hole...two inches in diameter at the back of the skull here. [In her telephone interview with us the previous December, she had said 2 to 2.5 inches in diameter.]

Gunn: You pointed to the back of your head. When you point back there, let's suppose that you were lying down [with your head] on a pillow, where would the hole in the back of the head be in relationship to the part of the head that would be on the pillow if the body is lying flat?

Spencer: The top part of the head.

Gunn: When you say the "top of the head," now, is that the part that would be covered by a hat that would be covering the top of the head?

Spencer: Just about where the rim would hit.

Gunn: Are you acquainted with the term "external occipital protruberance?"

Spencer: No, I am not.

Gunn: What I would like to do is to give you a document or drawing, and ask you, if you would, on this document, make a mark of approximately where the wound was that you noticed.

After Saundra Spencer drew a sketch of the wound she recalled on an anatomical diagram from *Grant's Anatomy,* Jeremy marked her sketch as Exhibit no. MD 148.

Spencer: Probably about in there. [See Figure 32.]

Gunn: And you have put some hash marks in there and then drawn a circle around that, and the part that you have drawn, the circle that you have drawn on the diagram is labeled as being part of the occipital bone, is that correct?

Spencer: Yes.

Gunn: Did you see any biological tissue, such as brain matter, extruding from the hole that you saw in the back of the head?

Spencer: No.

Gunn: Was the scalp disturbed or can you describe that more than just the hole [sic]?

Spencer: It was just a ragged hole.

Gunn: And it was visible through the scalp, is that correct?

Spencer: Yes.

Gunn: Did you see any photographs with the scalp pulled back or reflected?

Spencer: No.

Gunn: Did you see any other wounds on the head in addition to the one that you have identified?

Spencer: I don't remember any additional.

Gunn: Did you see any photographs that would have shown the right profile of President Kennedy's head?

Spencer: I don't remember.

Gunn: Did you see any photographs that would have shown any wounds in either the neck or shoulders or back?

Spencer: It seems like I seen [sic]—there was at the base of the neck.

Gunn: When you are pointing, you are pointing to the front of your neck to the right side?

Spencer: Yes.

Gunn: Do you remember approximately how large that injury was?

Spencer: Just about the size of like your thumb pressed in.

Gunn: About how much time were you able to look at the photographs; did you get a good observation of them, [or] was it fleeting? How would you describe that?

Spencer: It was—they traveled. You placed them on the drum, they would travel around, so after you place it on, probably about 15 seconds or so, they start under the drum and it rotates around, and then they drop off, and you grab them and stack them. So probably just 10 or 15 seconds.

Gunn: Are your observations based upon the prints rather than the negatives?

Spencer: Yes. Like I said, the negatives have masking on them, and you don't see too much on a color negative when you are printing.

Gunn: And for the prints to dry, that takes approximately how long?

Spencer: Probably about two or three minutes by the time it goes on, it goes around the drum.

Gunn: And that is all entirely on the drum?

Spencer: Yes.

Gunn: So the prints themselves would not hang from a wire or anything?

Spencer: No, they have [an] electric drum, and it puts the ferrotype finish to it. That was before RC papers when you can air-dry them.

Gunn: What was your best recollection of the approximate size of the wound on the throat that you identified before?

Spencer: Just about like that, just like a finger, half-inch.

Gunn: Do you remember whether the wound was jagged or how that appeared?

Spencer: No, just—it appeared just indented. It was, again, clean, pristine, no—you know, it wasn't an immediate wound, it had some cleaning done to it or something.

Gunn: Were you able to observe any characteristics of the room in which the photographs were taken?

Spencer: No.

Gunn: Do you remember what the walls looked like or whether they—

Spencer: No, everything basically concentrated straight on the body. It didn't appear like the normal medical setting, you know. I don't know whether they did it in a separate room or they used special coverings on their tables or what, but I don't remember, you know, hospital stainless-steel gleaming or anything, or people running around in green scrubs or anything. It was just, like I said, it looked [like] a very reverent[ly] laid out arrangement.

Gunn: What is your best recollection as to how long after the autopsy you received the photographs? Let me try and put it in terms of some other events that happened. Do you remember whether you developed the photographs before or after the funeral, for example?

Spencer:	It was before.
Gunn:	Before the funeral. But your recollection also is that it was after the black-and-white [prayer] cards had been delivered to the White House?
Spencer:	Right.
Gunn:	Do you recall whether it was on a Sunday or a Monday?
Spencer:	It was sometime over the weekend. It was during the day...
Gunn:	What I would like to do is ask that the autopsy photographs be brought in and have [sic] you have an opportunity to take a look at those. We will take a short break.

The reader is encouraged during the testimony below to refer to the numbered autopsy photographs in the illustration section of this book.

First, Jeremy showed Saundra Spencer color positive transparency no. 29, representing the view titled "left side of head and shoulders."

Gunn:	...Ms. Spencer, could you go to the light box and tell me whether you can identify the color transparency of view no.1...image no. 29, as having seen that before?
Spencer:	No.
Gunn:	In what respect is the image no. 29 different from what you previously saw?
Spencer:	Like I said, there was none of the blood and matted hair.
Gunn:	Can you explain what you mean by that? Are you seeing blood and matted hair on image no. 29?
Spencer:	On the transparency.
Gunn:	But that was not present, the blood and matted hair was not present—
Spencer:	I don't remember.
Gunn:	—on the images you saw?
Spencer:	No.
Gunn:	Would you describe image no. 29 as a color positive transparency or a color negative?

Spencer: This is a color transparency.

Gunn: Ms. Spencer, could you again look at the color transparency and tell me whether, again, you are certain that you did not develop color transparencies of the autopsy of President Kennedy?

Spencer: No, I did not process any color transparencies.

Gunn: Let's turn to the print. Can you identify the print as being a print that you printed yourself at Naval Photographic Center?

Spencer: I don't believe it is.

Gunn: Can you look at the back—turn the light on, please—can you look at the back of the print and identify whether that is the same type of paper as the Exhibit no. 147, that you brought with you today?

Spencer: No, it's not.

Gunn: In what respect do you see it as being different?

Spencer: The Kodak logo is smaller.

Gunn: So based upon your experience, would it be safe to say that it is your best recollection, best understanding, that the print of the autopsy that is in the Archives does not correspond with the paper that you were using in November of 1963 at NPC?

Spencer: Correct.

Gunn: Could you look again at the image...in what respect is the image that you see in [no.] 29, in the color print, different from what you observed on the prints that you made at NPC?

Spencer: Like I said, the body was pristine, and this has dried blood on the [stirrup-shaped head] support, the ear, and the hair.

Gunn: Do you recall whether there was a metal holder for the head on the images that you developed?

Spencer: I don't remember a metal holder.

Gunn: Do you remember what kind of cloth or any other material was identifiable in the photograph in comparison to what you see in this image?

Spencer: As I remember it was a darker cloth. This [image no. 29] appears to be a towel over one of the trays, stainless-steel trays.

Gunn: Previously, you said that, if I recall correctly, that the background in the photograph looked different from what you had previously seen in terms of—I understood that you said that it didn't look like a hospital.

Spencer: Right.

Gunn: Could you describe the photograph that you see in front of you now, whether that is the same sort of background that you noticed in the photographs that you developed?

Spencer: Well, it would be the dark background, because normally, when you are doing the autopsies, the overhead lights and stuff are on. It appears that the lights have been turned off and that they were using a flash rather than just overall general lighting.

Gunn: Do you remember, in the photographs that you developed, whether the background was visible, such as the walls?

Spencer: No.

Gunn: You don't remember?

Spencer: I don't remember, but it appeared that it was darkened, the room was darkened.

Gunn: So, to that extent that the images would seem to correspond to what you recollect—

Spencer: Right.

Gunn: —the background would seem to, you don't notice any difference?

Spencer: No.

Next, Jeremy had one color positive transparency and one color print from view no. 2, titled "right side of head and right shoulder," placed in front of the witness.

Gunn: Do those two images [the color positive transparency and the print] correspond to the photographs that you developed at NPC in November of 1963?

Spencer: No.

Gunn: In what way are they different?

Spencer: There was no—the film that I seen [sic] or the prints that we printed did not have the massive head damages that is [sic] visible here. [As I recall, Saundra Spencer was becoming a bit fragile at this point, emotionally moved; President Kennedy was a vibrant, charismatic politician whom she had seen in person many times, and whose photographs she had developed almost daily for the better part of three years. The images she was looking at really were very hard to stomach, particularly since the ones she had developed looked much more 'cleaned up,' and in the images she remembered, the body was in much better condition.]

Gunn: Putting aside the question of the damage of the head, does the remainder of the body, the face, correspond with what you observed.

Spencer: No. [Spencer's eyes were moist.]

Gunn: In what way is it different?

Spencer: The face in the photographs that we did, did not have the stress that these photos—on the face that these photos show.

Gunn: Could you describe a little bit more what you mean by that?

Spencer: The face, the eyes were closed and the face, the mouth was closed, and it was more of a rest position than these show.

Gunn: Could you look at the back of the print and see whether that paper corresponds to the image that you brought with you today, please?

Spencer: No.

Gunn: It doesn't correspond. So, the paper that these prints are printed on is not the paper that you were using at NPC in November of 1963, is that correct?

Spencer: Correct.

Jeremy now had a representative color positive transparency and a color print from view no. 3, titled "superior view of head," placed in front of the witness.

Gunn: Do those two images, again when you are looking at a positive transparency and a print, do those correspond to the photographs that you developed in November of 1963?

Spencer: No.

Gunn: In what way are they different?

Spencer: Again, none of the heavy damage that shows in these photographs were [sic] visible in the photographs that we did.

Gunn: So, just to make sure that I am understanding you correctly, previously, in your deposition, you described a wound, a small, circular wound in the back of the head, approximately two inches or so as I recall that you stated, whereas, these show a much larger injury, is that correct?

Spencer: That is correct.

Gunn: Could you once again take a look at the paper on which the print is made and tell me whether that corresponds to the paper that you brought with you today?

Spencer: No.

Gunn: Just so the record is clear, the paper does not correspond to the paper that was used in November '63 at NPC?

Spencer: No.

Gunn: Is that correct?

Spencer: That's right.

Next, a color positive transparency and a color print from view no. 4, titled "posterior view of wound of entrance of missile high in shoulder," were placed before the witness.

Gunn: Can you tell me whether those photographs correspond to the photographs that you developed in November of 1963?

Spencer: No, it does not.

Gunn: In addition to what you have already said in describing the other photographs, is there anything additional in these photographs that appears to you to be different?

Spencer: They are using a measuring device, which I don't remember in any of the photographs that we produced, and I don't remember any hands on the President during any of the shots that we reproduced.

Gunn: Now, could you look at the place on the back of President Kennedy's head that corresponds to where you identified a wound in the back of the head. Do you see that wound present in these photographs?

Spencer: No, I do not.

322

Gunn: Would this view have shown the wound that you previously saw in the photographs of President Kennedy's head?

Spencer: Yes. The wound that I seen [sic] would have been approximately in this area [indicating].

Jeremy now had a color positive transparency and a color print representative of view no. 5, titled "right anterior view of head and upper torso, including tracheotomy wound," placed before the witness.

Gunn: ...Let me try the first question as being whether the paper on the print matches the paper that you brought with you to the deposition today.

Spencer: No, it does not.

Gunn: Ms. Spencer, could you look at the wound in the throat of President Kennedy and tell me whether that corresponds to the wound that you observed in the photographs you developed?

Spencer: No, it does not.

Gunn: In what way are they different?

Spencer: This is a large, gaping gash type.

Gunn: That is, in the fifth view, it's a large, gaping gash, is that correct?

Spencer: Yes. In the one that we had seen, it was on the right side, approximately half-inch [in diameter].[54]

Gunn: Is the wound in a different location or is it just a larger wound in the throat?

Spencer: It could be just a larger wound.

Gunn: Is there anything else that you can identify in these images that are different from what you observed in November of 1963, on the photographs you developed?

Spencer: Right. None of the flooring was showing or anything of that nature. I don't

---

[54]In his Warren Commission testimony, Dr. Carrico of Parkland hospital did testify that the small wound in the throat was just slightly to the right of the midline of the anterior neck. His description in 1964 was consistent with Saundra Spencer's similar description in 1996.

remember any floor. I don't remember any extremely high angles like this.

Next, Jeremy had two representative versions (a color positive transparency and a color print) of color images no. 42 and 43 (part of ARRB view no. 6) placed before the witness. This is the image titled, "wound of entrance in right posterior occipital region." Color images 42 and 43 were the ones that most resembled the anatomical template of the rear of the human skull from *Grant's Anatomy* upon which Saundra Spencer had drawn her sketch of the head wound she recalled seeing in a post mortem image.

Gunn: Ms. Spencer, is [sic] there any differences that you noticed between the sixth view that is now present before you, and those photographs that you saw in November of 1963?

Spencer: Yes. They are again using measuring devices that were not in the pictures that we did. The section that appears to be the skull weight [???], the side is not there, and again, there are hands in the background. This is not a photograph that was in the set that we produced. [Spencer seems to be saying that the flap of bone that sticks out from the right temporal area in photographs 42 and 43 was not present in the photograph of the rear of the head that she developed.]

Gunn: In terms of the location of the wound, do you see any differences or similarities with those that you developed in November 1963?

Spencer: No, there is no similarity. [The 2-inch diameter hole that Spencer sketched on the diagram from *Grant's Anatomy* should have been present smack in the middle of these photographs, if the two pictures represented the same condition of the body—but that is not the case. On photos 42 and 43 the scalp is completely intact in the area where Spencer had sketched the wound.]

Jeremy now had two representative views (a color positive transparency and a color print) of view no. 7, titled "missile wound of entrance in posterior skull, following reflection of scalp," placed before the witness.

Gunn: ...Ms. Spencer, in November of 1963, did you see any images corresponding to the seventh view that you have in front of you now?

Spencer: No.

Gunn: Could you look once again at the paper for the color print and tell me whether that is the paper that you were using in 1963 at the NPC?

Spencer: No, it is not.

Finally, Jeremy had two representative views (a color positive transparency and a color print) of view no 8, titled "basilar view of brain," placed before the witness.

Gunn: ...Ms. Spencer, during your testimony, you said that you had seen an image with the brain present next to the body. Is image [view] no. 8 the view that you saw previously?

Spencer: No.

Gunn: Did you see any [photographic] work in November of 1963 that resembled the view that you are being shown now?

Spencer: No, I did not.

Gunn: Could you look at the paper for the color print and tell me whether that is the paper that you were using in November of 1963?

Spencer: No, it is not.

Gunn: I think we don't need to take a look at the ninth [view] here, which is the superior area over the brain.[55]

Jeremy then launched into a summation:

Gunn: Ms. Spencer, you have now had an opportunity to view all of the colored images, both transparencies and prints, that are in the possession of the National Archives related to the autopsy of President Kennedy. Based upon your knowledge, are there any images of the autopsy of President Kennedy that are not included in those views that we saw?

Spencer: The views that we produced at the Photographic Center are not included.

Gunn: Ms. Spencer, how certain are you that there were other photographs of President Kennedy's autopsy that are not included in the set that you have just seen?

Spencer: I could personally say that they are not included. The only thing I can determine is that because of the pristine condition of the body and the reverence that the body was shown [sic], that—this is speculation on my part—that perhaps the family had the

---

[55] I think this was a mistake. Jeremy should have shown Spencer the view of the top surface of the brain to erase all doubt in the minds of "aggressive agnostics" and skeptics who may say that the ARRB staff failed to show the witness the one photograph that may have corresponded with the condition of the brain in the image she remembered seeing.

second set shot and developed as possible releases if autopsy pictures were demanded, because at that time, Mrs. Kennedy was attempting to keep all sensationalism out of the funeral and maintain the President's dignity and name.

Gunn: Are you able to —let's start with a conjecture as to whether the photographs that you developed, and the photographs that you observed today, could have been taken at different times?

Spencer: I would definitely say they were taken at different times.

Gunn: Is there any question in your mind whether the photographs that you saw today were photographs of President Kennedy?

Spencer: There is no doubt they are pictures of President Kennedy.

Gunn: Is there any doubt in your mind that the pictures you saw in November 1963 also were photographs of President Kennedy?

Spencer: No, that was President Kennedy, but between those photographs [that you showed me today] and the ones that we did, there had to be some massive cosmetic things done to the President's body.

Gunn: Do you have an opinion as to whether the photographs that you developed in 1963 were taken before or after the photographs you observed today?

Spencer: I would say probably afterwards.

Gunn: So you would think that the photographs that you developed were taken after reconstruction of the body?

Spencer: Yes.

Gunn: In the photograph that you saw in November of 1963, with the brain lying next to the body, were you able to observe whether there had been any damage to the brain?

Spencer: No, it was not [as] damaged as this brain, as the brain in these photographs were.

Gunn: When you say "these photographs," you mean [the ones] that we just saw today?

Spencer: The ones that we just viewed.

Jeremy and I were both surprised by this statement. Most of the damage to the brain specimen in question, based upon the photographs in the Archives, is seen in the *top* view, not the basilar view. Spencer had viewed only the *basilar,* or relatively undamaged *underside* of the specimen whose

326

photos are deposited in the Archives, and yet she said the brain image she had just viewed in the Archives in 1997 showed *more damage* than seen in the image she processed in November of 1963! This suggested that the brain imaged in the JFK post mortem photograph from 1963, the one she recalled developing and printing herself, may have been a substitute—a whole, or largely intact, brain—hurriedly obtained from the Naval Medical School at Bethesda.

It may be useful at this point to remind the reader that former FBI agent Frank O'Neill testified to the ARRB that JFK's brain was *more than half gone* when he observed it following its removal at the autopsy; and Dr. Robert McClelland, who stood at the head of the gurney in trauma room one at Parkland hospital in Dallas and examined the head wound closely, estimated in his Warren Commission testimony in 1964 that *at least one third of the brain—posterior cerebral tissue—was missing,* and recalled that part of the *cerebellum* had been "blasted out" also. FBI agent Frank O'Neill, and Gawler's funeral home mortician Tom Robinson, both told the ARRB staff that the *location* of missing brain tissue was in the extreme rear portion of the brain (which is obviously consistent with an exit wound, or blowout, in the back of the head). The recollections of O'Neill and McClelland indicate that *the brain photographs in the Archives cannot be of JFK's brain,* since **too much of the brain's mass is present in the photographs.** Furthermore, **the location of the damage in the Archives brain photographs is in the wrong part of the brain**. Specifically, the *right hemisphere of the cerebellum* is <u>undamaged</u> in the Archives photos; and *the right occipital lobe of the cerebrum,* although disrupted, is <u>partially present</u>. [The undamaged right cerebellar hemisphere, and the presence of a large amount of tissue in the posterior portion of the right cerebral hemisphere, are aspects of the brain photographs in the Archives which are *inconsistent* with the <u>location</u> of damage to President Kennedy's brain reported by O'Neill, Robinson, and Dr. McClelland.]

We have an ironic situation here: *two different switches* seem to have been made for the real brain specimen in post mortem photographs. The <u>first substitution</u> (after the conclusion of the mortician's work) appears to have been early on the morning of November 23, 1963, using an easily obtained, fixed specimen of an undamaged, i.e., 'whole' brain—probably from the Naval Medical School—photographed in place of the real brain (whose mass was more than fifty percent gone at autopsy). This first substitution was obviously conducted in order *not* to disclose the damage to the rear of the brain—evidence of exit—which was *consistent* with having been caused by a shot entering from the front, and *inconsistent* with damage from a shot fired from the Texas School Book Depository, and entering from the rear. [Bullets cause small punctures where they enter, and large, avulsive wounds where they exit.] Photographing the real brain would have been anathema to anyone attempting to cover-up evidence of frontal shots and blame the assassination on Lee Harvey Oswald, who was said to have been firing from above and behind. The <u>second substitution</u> (made later at the second brain examination—the photos now in the Archives) was undoubtedly made for the same basic reason—to suppress evidence of having been shot from the front—but it *also* had to present a pattern of damage consistent with the autopsy report's findings, so a more realistic specimen had to be found—or created—with a pattern of damage generally consistent with a shot that came from above and behind, on the sixth floor of the infamous Book Depository, since this series of photographs was to be placed in the autopsy collection for medico-legal purposes. The minimally damaged, or perhaps even completely undamaged brain in the photograph Spencer remembered was probably obtained in haste, *for the simple purpose of not revealing the actual damage to the brain,* and was likely intended only for a 'sanitized' and limited role, such as for the sole viewing of the Kennedy family, which is what the nature of the photographs Saundra Spencer described to us suggests—or for possible public release, should that have been forced upon the government by public pressure. In other words, those engaged in the coverup were *improvising* the night of the autopsy, and their main concern at that time was simply to *avoid* showing the authentic damage to the real brain. I suspect that one of the reasons the brain photograph Saundra Spencer developed has never surfaced, is because the relatively undamaged brain imaged in this photo is *inconsistent* with the brain photographed at the second brain exam, which exhibited severe disruption, and some missing mass, on the top and right side. The brain photographs taken at the second brain exam on or about November 29th were placed into the official record, so the brain photograph Saundra Spencer developed—showing little or no damage—could never be released.

Gunn: Ms. Spencer, before we started I said that I would give you an opportunity to add anything if you have any additional statement that you would like to make, and I will just give you that opportunity now.

Spencer: I had brought along a photograph that was reproduced approximately 10 days prior to the time that we printed the autopsy photographs that we produced at NPC, and because of [sic] the watermark and stuff on it does not match those I viewed, and NPC bought all [photographic paper] of a run, which meant every piece of paper within the house would have the same identical watermarking and logo on it, I can say that the paper was not a piece of paper that was processed or printed out of the Photographic Center within that period of time. Like I said, the only thing I can think of is that a second set of autopsy pictures was shot for public release if necessary.

Mr. Gunn: Ms. Spencer, thank you very much. We appreciate your time in coming all the way from Missouri. Thank you very much.

Spencer: I wish I could have identified them for you.

Gunn: Thank you.

Next, a discussion ensued off the record because we had forgotten to get Ms. Spencer to comment on the report about autopsy photography written by Secret Service Agent James K. Fox on February 16, 1967. I reminded Jeremy of this, and handed him the Exhibit of the Fox report.

Gunn: Ms. Spencer, there is one other question I would like to ask you about, and this is in reference to a document that is labeled Exhibit MD 121, that appears on its face to be a cover sheet and a memorandum signed by James Fox dated February 16, 1967. After we concluded the deposition, I showed you a copy of this document. Did you have an opportunity to read that?

Spencer: Yes, I did.

Gunn: Can you tell me, if you wouldn't mind, going through the document, and telling me anything that you perceive in the document either to be accurate, that is, as you recall, or inaccurate and different from what your own recollection is?

Spencer: Okay. During the time that I saw agent Fox, he did not have any black-and-white film with him. The only thing he had in his possession was color film, and he remained with us while we processed it and printed it. It was not printed on different days.

Gunn: Mr. Fox says that this happened on November 27th, 1963, which would be approximately five days after the assassination. Does that correspond with your recollection as to when he came to—or when an agent came to the NPC?

Spencer: No. My recollection was before the burial of President Kennedy.

Gunn: And in the statement by agent Fox, he refers to color positives. From what you have said before, that would not be—

Spencer: No.

Gunn: —correspond with what you yourself observed, is that correct?

Spencer: Right. The only thing that we processed was color negative material.

Gunn: Mr. Fox also refers to going with Chief Robert Knudsen. You knew Mr. Knudsen, is that correct?

Spencer: Yes. Chief Knudsen was our liaison boss between the White House and the Photographic Center, and he was not with the agent when the agent came, and if he was in the building, he would have come up.

Gunn: So to the extent that Mr. Fox is correct in what he makes on the statement, this is not the event that you yourself witnessed, would that be fair to say?

Spencer: That is correct.

Gunn: Thank you very much.

Major Implications of the Saundra Spencer Deposition

The first implication is of a compartmentalized operation, with multiple visits to NPC Anacostia on different dates, using different specialists at that facility each time to develop film. The film couriers apparently remained the same—either Knudsen, or Fox, or both of them at the same time—but the specialists doing the developing apparently changed for each visit. My tentative conclusions are as follows:

- The Saundra Spencer event clearly occurred on Sunday, November 24th; it involved developing *both* the color negatives and <u>one</u> color-corrected final print of each negative (following one test print of each negative); and Robert Knudsen did *not* accompany Fox on that occasion. I conclude that it was a separate event from the two consecutive events, on November 23rd and 24th, that Knudsen testified about to the HSCA in 1978.

- Knudsen's testimony has some things in common with the Spencer event, such as color negatives being developed, and the presence of 4 or 5 film holders. However, he testified to *two separate visits* on *consecutive days,* and he said Fox accompanied him on both occasions; the first visit—in which a B & W film pack and color negatives were developed—was definitely on Saturday the 23rd; and the second visit, on the next day (and therefore Sunday the 24th), was for the making of prints only, and *seven sets of prints* were produced from each color negative. In fact, Knudsen's belief, or assumption, was that Vince Madonia made the color prints; he never says it was Sandy Spencer, only that Madonia "may have" assigned someone else rather than exposing and developing the prints himself. Furthermore, although Spencer talked at length about how "good" the President looked in the sanitized post mortem photographs she developed, Vince Madonia told me at both of his ARRB interviews that the President looked "pretty beat up," or words to that effect. This is consistent with him having viewed images from the actual autopsy, not images after the conclusion of reconstruction and the application of restorative art to the body. After due consideration of all of the above, I conclude that Knudsen was speaking to the HSCA staff counsel about two <u>connected</u>, but entirely <u>different</u> events than the single event Spencer testified about to the ARRB.

- The other visits to NPC the two Secret Service photography memos of February 1967 refer to, on November 27th (for the developing of B & W negative film and color positive transparencies) and December 9th (for the making of one internegative and 2 color prints from each color positive), probably really took place as well. The two Fox-Madonia receipts mentioned in paragraph 9 of the Burkley inventory corrected the date of the first visit to November 29th, but in mentioning the name of Madonia they confirm that NPC was the site of the activity on that date. (Saundra Spencer's seeming certainty that the photographic paper upon which the Archives prints were made could not have come from NPC was seriously undercut when Kodak experts examined the 'Black Watch' print in November of 1997 at Rochester in my presence, and compared it to the Archives autopsy prints. The Kodak experts concluded that the Kodak logo and watermarks on the reverse side of Spencer's print, although a bit darker than those on the autopsy prints in the official collection, were actually the same size. They had no reason to believe in the validity of her claim that the autopsy prints in the Deed-of-Gift collection could be excluded from having been made at NPC. Their conclusion was that both the Black Watch photo and the sample Deed-

330

of-Gift color prints were both printed on paper manufactured in 1963, even though the markings on the reverse side of Spencer's print were darker.) The fact that Spencer was not aware of any photographic activity beyond her own on November 24th, whereas Vince Madonia did recall such activity within 2 to 3 weeks of the assassination, is simply further proof that a compartmented operation was taking place.

- Obviously, more photographs were being processed than were in the paper trail that commenced on 11-22-63. All that had to be done by those controlling what went into the 'final' autopsy collection was to ensure that the final totals of each type of film *did not exceed* the numbers established by both the 11-22-63 Stover-to-Kellerman receipt, and the Bouck-to-Stover letter of 12-05-63.[56] Those persons controlling the medical coverup were clearly creating a 'culled' collection, containing images that ranged from *early in the evening* on November 22nd prior to the official start of the autopsy, to others taken at various stages during the autopsy, and to other, intentionally fraudulent and misleading photographs, taken after the formal conclusion of the autopsy while the scalp was manipulated to make the back-of-the-head appear intact.

The second major implication of the Saundra Spencer deposition is that the Parkland hospital medical staff written treatment reports prepared the weekend of the assassination *were correct when they described an exit wound in the back of President Kennedy's head, and damage to the cerebellum.* If the post mortem images developed by Saundra Spencer were indeed taken following the *end* of reconstruction of the body and head, and after the application of restorative art by the undertakers, and there was <u>*still a 2-inch diameter hole in the occipital region*</u> (which was *not* in the location described by the HSCA as the entry wound), then not only are the Dallas doctors vindicated in the eyes of history, but the 'official' Deed-of-Gift images showing the back of the head intact—ARRB views no. 4 and 6—are fraudulent. I posit that they are not forged photographs, but rather *severely manipulated scalp rather crudely rearranged on the head of President Kennedy after*

---

[56] A pre-condition of this hypothesis is that at the autopsy, the Secret Service only put a limited number of films in the box that was to become the 'official count,' and in actuality took many more exposed films out of the morgue on the evening of November 22-23, 1963 than the receipts indicated. This may have led to the disagreement between Stringer and Stover over the receipt in which Stringer was simply ordered to "sign it" anyway. If Floyd Riebe really took photographs—and I believe he *did*—and if Knudsen really took post mortem photographs—and I believe *he did* also—then it is not difficult to believe that there were many more photographs that required developing than were recorded in the official receipt trail. My assumption here is also that FBI agents Sibert and O'Neill were either presented with a box of film to count by the Secret Service when they departed the Bethesda morgue, or were simply *told* what the totals for each type of film were by the Secret Service. I speculate that it is for this reason that the count of film in the Sibert-O'Neill FD-302 report matches what was in the Navy's receipt from Stover to Kellerman.

the conclusion of the formal autopsy to hide the very large occipital blowout that existed when the body arrived at Bethesda. Before the photograph that Saundra Spencer developed was exposed, a head-filler, a quick-drying material described in slightly different ways by two eyewitnesses to the reconstruction, undertaker Tom Robinson and Navy medical technician Paul O'Connor, was used to restore shape and structure to the severely damaged cranium; after a 'rubber dam' was obtained to help seal the large cranial defect and prevent body fluids from leaking from the cranium inside the casket, the remaining scalp was stretched back into place as much as possible and sutured together (as well as into the rubber dam material) outside the now-hardened and reconstructed skull. The two-inch diameter 'wound' that Saundra Spencer recalls seeing squarely in the middle of the back of the head in one photograph, high in the occipital bone, simply represented the small area that the undertakers could not repair and close; after all, missing scalp is missing scalp, and cannot be replaced.

The conclusion that is inevitable at this point is that Jeremy Gunn's suspicion was correct: the autopsy photographs of President John F. Kennedy, overall, constitute a collection whose primary intention *was to conceal, rather than reveal.* In any normal autopsy following a death by gunshot wounds, the autopsy photographs should be of such a nature that they leave no significant questions unanswered. In the case of President John F. Kennedy, the 35th President of the United States and the leader of the Free World at the height of the Cold War, his autopsy photographs in the collection assembled by the Secret Service leave the informed viewer with *nothing but* questions. Sadly, we now have some answers: many of the photographs are missing, the scalp in some photos seems arranged so as to reveal almost nothing about the head wounds, and other photographs appear to be crude attempts at misrepresentation, an extreme manipulation of scalp from elsewhere on the decedent's head moved to cover up a huge occipital defect—what in reality was an exit wound, and evidence of a fatal shot from the front. (A separate proof that there was an exit wound in the rear of the head, in the occipital region, will be provided in Part II, using the words of the pathologists themselves, rather than the eyewitness recollections of Ebersole, Sibert, O'Neill, Knudsen, O'Donnell, and Spencer.)

Most of the remainder of this chapter will focus in on the testimony of Drs. Humes, Boswell, and Finck in an attempt to complete the emerging picture of which autopsy photographs we may reliably say are missing from the collection. As the reader reads their testimony about the photographs, you will note a marked degree of discomfort from all three pathologists about what is shown in the photographs of the back of the head, and perhaps most telling, a marked degree of *disagreement* about what is shown, or not shown, in these mysterious images. I do not think this would be the case if the autopsy and its conclusions were the straightforward, simple, and cut-and-dried affair that they have insisted it was for so many years. Instead, I think they have failed to keep their stories straight, and the once-strong edifice of the medical coverup in which they were forced to participate, back in 1963, has crumbled over the years as bootleg autopsy photographs were released, as official investigations and fact-finding bodies chipped away at the inconsistencies in the evidence, and as researchers scrutinized the contradictory testimony of the pathologists. At the conclusion of the chapter I will present a table summarizing which autopsy photographs are likely *missing* from the collection that we know has existed since April 26, 1965.

DR. HUMES AND THE AUTOPSY PHOTOGRAPHS

Testimony About Photographs Missing from the Autopsy Collection in the National Archives

Dr. Humes testified before the Warren Commission on Monday, March 16, 1964, and in his testimony he described the taking of 3 photographic views of wounds which are not now in the autopsy photograph collection. The first two photographs were of the entrance wound in the skull near the external occipital protruberance (EOP), the first one showing the hole in the outer table of the skull after the scalp had been reflected, and the second one showing the corresponding damage to the inner table of the skull, namely, coning or beveling on the inside surface corresponding to that same entry hole. Excerpts from this testimony are reproduced below:

Humes: ...The scalp, I mentioned previously, there was a defect in the scalp and some scalp tissue was not available. However, the scalp was intact completely past this defect. In other words, this wound in the right posterior region was in a portion of scalp which had remained intact. So, we could see that it [the entrance wound in the back of the skull slightly to the right of the EOP] was the measurement which I gave before, 15 by 6 millimeters. When one reflected the scalp away from the skull in this region, there was a corresponding defect through both tables of the skull in this area.

Specter: Will you describe what you mean by both tables, Dr. Humes?

Humes: Yes sir. The skull is composed of two layers of bone. We will put the scalp in, in dotted lines [apparently making a sketch]. The two solid lines will represent the two layers of the skull bone, and in between these two layers is loose, somewhat irregular bone. When we reflected the scalp, there was a through and through defect corresponding with the wound in the scalp. This wound had to us the characteristics of a wound of entrance for the following reason: the defect in the outer table was oval in outline, quite similar to the defect in the skin.

Specter: You are referring there, doctor, to the wound on the lower part of the neck? [Was Arlen Specter woolgathering here? Why could he not understand something so straightforward? This could hardly have improved his standing with those Commissioners who were paying attention.]

Humes: No sir: I am speaking here of the wound in the occiput. The wound on the inner table, however, was larger and had what in the field of wound ballistics is described as a shelving or coning effect...Experience has shown and my associates and Colonel Finck, in particular, whose special field of interest is wound ballistics can give additional testimony about this scientifically observed fact. This wound then had the characteristics of [a] wound of entrance from this direction [indicating] through the two tables of the skull.

Specter: When you say "this direction," will you specify that direction in relationship to the skull?

Humes: At that point I mean only from without the skull to within.

Specter: Fine, proceed.

Humes: Having ascertained to our satisfaction *and incidentally photographs illustrating this*
phenomenon from both the external surface of the skull and internal surface were
prepared, we concluded that the large defect to the upper right side of the skull, in
fact, would represent a wound of exit. [Author's emphasis.]

No such photographs of an entry wound in the skull are in the collection at the Archives. (Humes
did not know these photographs were missing when he gave his testimony to Arlen Specter.) The
next excerpt is Humes' testimony that photographs were taken of the 5 cm wide bruise seen at the
upper apex of the right pleural cavity after the removal of the lungs:

Humes: ...In attempting to relate findings within the President's body to this wound which we
had observed low in his neck, we then opened his chest cavity, and we very carefully
examined the lining of his chest cavity and both of his lungs. We found that there
was, in fact, no defect in the pleural lining of the President's chest. It was completely
intact. However, over the apex of the right pleural cavity, and the pleura now has
two layers. It has a parietal or a layer which lines the chest cavity and it has a
visceral layer which intimately in association with the lung. As depicted in figure
385, in the apex of the right pleural cavity there was a bruise or contusion or
eccmymosis of the parietal pleura as well as a bruise of the upper portion, the most
apical portion, of the right lung. It, therefore, was our opinion that the missile while
not penetrating physically the pleural cavity, as it passed that point bruised either the
missile [sic] itself, or the force of its passage through the tissues, bruised both the
parietal and the visceral pleura. The area of discoloration on the apical portion of the
right upper lung measured five centimeters in greatest diameter, and was wedge
shaped in configuration, with its base toward the top of the chest and its apex down
towards the substance of the lung. *Once again Kodachrome photographs were made*
of this area in the interior of the President's chest. [Author's emphasis.]

No such photographs are in the collection in the National Archives. (In March of 1964, Humes did
not know they were missing.) About thirteen-and-one-half years after his Warren Commission
testimony, before the HSCA Forensic Pathology Panel in unsworn testimony on September 16, 1977,
Humes discussed the missing photographs of the bruise in the interior of the chest cavity again:

Humes: ...I think we described the irregular or jagged wound of the trachea, and then we
described a contusion in the apex of the lung and the inferior surface of the dome of
the right pleural cavity, and that's one photograph that we were distressed not to find
when we first went through and catalogued these photographs, because I distinctly
recall going to great lengths to try and get the interior upper portion of the right

thorax illuminated—you know the technical difficulties with that, getting the camera positioned and so forth, and what happened to that film, I don't know. There were a couple of films that apparently had been exposed to light or whatever and then not developed, but we never saw that photograph.

Baden: From the time you first examined them, that particular photograph was never seen?

Humes: Never available to us, but we thought it coincided very neatly with the path that ultimately we felt the missile took.

Testimony About the Location of the Entry Wound in the One Existing Close-Up View of the Skull, Photos No. 17, 18, 44, and 45

A long and confusing discussion took place among Humes, Boswell, and members of the HSCA Forensic Pathology Panel during this same session, in which various arguments were advanced as to whether the "high" red spot in the color back-of-the-head photos (numbers 42 and 43) near the end of the ruler, or the "low" so-called white spot, or 'droplet' near the hairline, represented the entry wound in the scalp. The Panel opted for the "high" red spot near the end of the ruler, and Humes and Boswell strongly disagreed, opting for the "lower" white spot near the hairline. This moved the discussion forward to what the ARRB came to call view no. 7, titled *"missile wound of entrance in posterior skull, following reflection of scalp"* (photos 17, 18, 44, and 45). One would think this would have resolved the dispute, since it was Humes and Boswell who drew up the descriptive listing, or inventory of the photographs, on November 1, 1966: they themselves came up with this description. However, to everyone's further consternation and confusion, this series of images *did not* clearly indicate where the entrance wound in the skull was, in spite of its labeling. An excerpt of the discussion follows:

Petty: Now, could you two possibly, thinking back 16 years, I know how difficult it is, but is there any way that you could show us where the entrance was in that wound [in photo 45]?

Boswell: I don't believe it's depicted in that picture.[57] (See Figure 66.)

Humes: How about here, "J"?

Boswell: Well, I don't believe so, because as I recall, the bone was intact at that point. There was a shelf and then a little hole, came up on the side and then one of the smaller of the two fragments in that x-ray [x-rays 4, 5, and 6 of the 3 loose bone fragments], when that arrived, we were able to fit that down there and complete the

---

[57]This was truly an incredible statement, given that Boswell, together with Humes, had generated the descriptive listing of the photographs, and had signed off on it on November 10, 1966.

Humes: circumference of that bone wound.

Humes: I don't remember that in that detail and I suspect—you see the background, there seems to be blue, with a blue towel placed beneath the head of the President, and I think that may be the wound right there [indicating].

Petty: Can you orient this for us, Dr. Humes? I am a little confused on exactly—now is this picture oriented like that, or is it like this? [A very confusing discussion follows.]

————————

Davis: Did the person who took the photographs ask you what to take or just took [sic] what he thought was—

Humes: No, no, he was directed.

Boswell: He was taking specific areas.

————————

Humes: I think that we were making an attempt, and of course, we didn't have a Polaroid in those days, like we might use now, to be sure that we had an image of what we wished, and its interesting how technology changes things. We were attempting in that photograph to demonstrate that wound [of entrance in the outer table of the skull], and I feel that we have failed to demonstrate that wound.

This was pretty lame. The real reason no one could agree on where the entrance wound was in the back of the head was because the two photographic views taken showing that damage in the skull (from both outside and inside the skull) are missing from the collection. Boswell even said so: "I don't believe it's depicted in that picture." If the picture of the entrance wound in the outer table of the skull is not in 'that picture,' numbers 17, 18, 44, and 45, then it is not in the collection. Period. These photos are the only closeups in the collection of the outer table of the skull that show scalp being reflected. The real question is: Why did Humes and Boswell label the picture the way they did in November of 1966? (More on this later, in Part II.)

During his ARRB deposition, Jeremy Gunn asked Dr. Humes about when most of the photographs were taken:

Gunn: Other than that series of photographs [17, 18, 44, and 45], were the remainder of the photographs all taken at the beginning of the autopsy, do you recall?

Humes: Virtually all of them were, yeah.

Gunn: Do you remember—

Humes: There's only basically two that weren't. One was the inside of the occipital region, which we interpreted as the wound of entrance, for obvious reasons, and one that never came—whatever happened to it, I was very disturbed by it. We took one of the interior of the right side of the thorax because there was a contusion of the right upper lobe of the lung. So the missile had passed across the dome of the parietal pleura and contused the right lobe. I wanted to have a picture of that, and I never saw it. It never—whether it was underexposed or overexposed or what happened to it, I don't know. And it's three years later when we were looking at it, of course. But we didn't see that photograph. So that was taken later, and the one of the inside of the skull was taken later. But all the rest of them were taken at the onset of examination.

Of course, there is no photo in the collection showing the internal aspect of the entrance wound in the skull in the collection.

Later in the deposition, Jeremy continued the questioning about photography of the skull entry wound, as follows [using view no. 7, photos 17, 18, 44, and 45]:

Gunn: The first question for you would be whether you can orient those photos so as to describe what is being represented in the photographs.

Humes: Boy, it's difficult. I can't. I just can't put them together. I can't tell you what—

Gunn: Can you identify whether that is even posterior or frontal or parietal?

Humes: Not with any certainty, no. Very disappointed.

Gunn: Previously in your deposition today, you said, if I recall correctly, that you had photographs taken with the scalp reflected that showed the entrance wound. Is that correct?

Humes: I thought I had, yes.

Gunn: Is it your understanding that these are photographs that—

Humes: They [17, 18, 44, and 45] could well be, but they're disappointingly confusing to me.

Gunn: What I would like to see if we can do the best that we can with [this] is to understand whether there was a photograph taken with the scalp reflected of the posterior portion of the head. Now, I understood from your testimony earlier today that you thought there was such a photograph taken. Whether the photograph you're looking at or not, whether that is that photograph or not isn't the question, but whether there was such a photograph taken.

Humes: I cannot recall specifically.

Jeremy then produced Exhibit 13, the Military Inventory dated November 10, 1966, which describes photos 17, 18, 44, and 45 as "missile wound of entrance in posterior skull, following reflection of scalp."

Gunn: Could you identify for me roughly the procedure that you followed in preparing the document that's now marked Exhibit 13? Just if you could explain the circumstances of how you came to prepare the document.

Humes: We came—we were told that it was necessary to have the photographs identified. We proceeded to the old building downtown, Archives building, where we met with Mr. Rhoads, I believe was the Archivist. And "J" and I—Pierre wasn't there, was he?—Jack Ebersole—no, Pierre was not there. "J" and I and Jack Ebersole and John Stringer, who actually took all the photographs, and they were brought to us one at a time, and we wrote a description of what we thought we were seeing.

Gunn: Okay. Could you look at the description that you created in 1966 that corresponds with the photos we're looking at now?

Humes: 44, for instance, this one.

Gunn: Does that document reference no. 17? That would be to one of the black-and-white photos [of the same image]. Does your description from 1966, three years after the autopsy, help you today identify or orient the photographs in view no. 7?

Humes: Well now, I guess now that I look at it, perhaps it does. The black-and-white one, down here opposite the edge of the rule, I presume that is what we're talking about right there [indicating].

A frustrating, confusing discussion ensued, which is almost impossible to understand when reading the transcript because Humes was pointing at the photograph. Concluding this discussion:

Gunn: So...if the ruler were [oriented] on the bottom of the—if the ruler were placed at the bottom of the drawing [sic], this [the presumed entry wound that Humes had been pointing at] would be slightly above the corner of the uppermost part of the ruler?

What Jeremy meant here, as he attempted to paint a word picture of the object in the photograph Humes had been pointing to, was that if the viewer reoriented the photo and placed the ruler at the bottom of the frame, an oblong dark spot slightly above the corner of the ruler, apparently a small hole in the bone immediately adjacent to the huge skull defect, was the object Humes was now claiming to be the entrance wound. (See Figure 66.)

Humes:	That's my belief, yes sir.
Gunn:	And that is what you believe to be, as best you can tell now—
Humes:	Yes.
Gunn:	—to have been the entrance wound—
Humes:	Yes sir.
Gunn:	—in the posterior skull?
Humes:	Yes sir. Without major conviction, but I believe that's the case.[58]

Humes appeared to be willing to say anything at this point just to get Jeremy off his back. Next, Jeremy showed Dr. Humes his Warren Commission testimony in which he discussed taking photographs of the entrance wound in the skull from both the outer and inner aspect of the skull, showing damage to both the outer and inner tables of the cranium.

Humes:	[reading aloud portions of his testimony on this matter to Arlen Specter] ...I don't—I have not yet been shown what I would construe to be the photograph of the wound of entrance from the internal surface [of the skull].
Gunn:	And at least it was your understanding as of March 1964 that a photograph of that sort had been taken?
Humes:	Yes. Yes.
Gunn:	Let's move to the bottom of the final paragraph of Exhibit 13 [The Military Inventory of 11-1-66], which is your report of November 1, 1966, signed November 10th.
Humes:	May I say [sic] what it says? We thought that we hadn't seen them all.
Gunn:	As of November 1966, were you of the opinion that there were any photographs of the autopsy that had been taken in addition to those that you were able to see at the Archives?
Humes:	The only one I recall specifically in that connection is the one I spoke to you about later [sic], was the interior of the thorax. I thought we had seen all the others. Maybe

---

[58]Boswell disagreed with Humes about this before the HSCA Forensic Pathology Panel, saying he did not see the entrance wound in this series of photographs. Here, after grueling questioning that goes on for several pages in the transcript, Humes thinks he has finally identified the entrance wound—but "without major conviction."

we hadn't. I don't know. You got to remember, this was three years after the fact. That's a part of the problem with all of this, temporal distortion of memory and what have you, accentuated when you get 35 years away.

_____

Humes: Am I led to believe that we have not found the photograph from inside of the posterior portion of the skull?

Gunn: You have now seen today all of the photographs of the skull we had.

Humes: I don't know how to explain it, because we didn't—I don't think we described in anywheres [sic] here [in our inventory, Exhibit no. 13] that photograph. I'd have to go through the whole list of photographs to see, but my recollection is that we took it from both the outside and from the inside after the brain was removed.

_____

Humes: [referring to photos 17, 18, 44, and 45]...Well, these are quite obviously from the outside of the skull. They're not from the inside. That's perfectly obvious. So I don't see one from the inside of the posterior cranial fossa where the defect was. And I'm disappointed because I thought we had such a photograph.

A long discussion ensued about the fact that the document which I call the "Military Review," dated January 26, 1967, and signed by Humes, Boswell, and Finck, says that photos 17, 18, 44, and 45 *depict the **exit wound** in the skull*, contradicting the Military Inventory of 11-1-66, prepared less than 3 months previously, which said these same photos depicted the ***entry wound*** *in the skull*.[59] Jeremy asked Humes about the implications of this, if it were true, for which photos were missing:

Gunn: If view no. 7, in fact, shows the exit wound [instead of the entrance wound, as the Military Inventory claims], would it then be fair to say that you now would recall three (3) photos that you believe were taken that are not now in the collection, one of them being a photograph of the posterior skull entry wound with the scalp reflect—

Humes: At least not recognizable as such.

Gunn: Sure.

Humes: It may be here, but not, to me, recognizable as such.

Humes has now recanted on his earlier ARRB testimony and is now saying he does **not see** an entrance wound in photos 17, 18, 44, and 45!

_____

[59]This issue will be discussed at great length in Part II.

Gunn: The second one being the interior of the skull—

Humes: Yeah. And that should have been sharp and clear because there was no blood by that time, you see. The brain had been removed, and it was a through-and-through hole, and I had every anticipation that you had no problem—you could tell the contour of the internal—you know, the internal portion of the posterior fossa, a child could recognize that. And we don't have that to see. And the chest.

Gunn: The chest being the third?

Humes: Yes.

Gunn: Okay. Thank you.

Joint Testimony (Unsworn) by Drs. Humes and Boswell on September 16, 1977 (In Closed Session) Before the HSCA Forensic Pathology Panel About the Location of the Entrance Wound in the Skull, As Shown in the Autopsy Photographs of the Rear of the Head

The reader will recall that Drs. Humes and Boswell met with the HSCA Forensic Pathology Panel on September 16, 1977 and provided unsworn testimony in a rather wide-ranging meeting that discussed many aspects of the medical evidence. Why they were not placed under oath is not specifically known to me, but it seems to me that the HSCA staff felt, perhaps, that Humes and Boswell might 'open up' and be more forthcoming in a 'working atmosphere' among their peers, fellow pathologists, if they were in a closed session and not under oath. This is hinted at by HSCA staff counsel Gary Cornwell during his opening remarks, in which he attempts to establish an atmosphere of voluntary cooperation and collegiality:

Cornwell: ...The only statement that I wish to make in advance is that Dr. Humes and Dr. Boswell have come here voluntarily, not by subpoena, and simply because the other doctors [the HSCA pathologists] thought there was some information that might be of assistance to them in their deliberations. We have decided that because of that fact, that it was the doctor's [HSCA pathologists'] request that they come, and Dr. Humes and Dr. Boswell have come voluntarily, the staff will ask no questions, and you all just proceed as you see fit.

Surely Cornwell, Blakey's principal staff assistant, knew that Blakey's plan was to take the sworn testimony of selected, high-profile witnesses during public hearings; yet I still find it hard to believe that Blakey and Cornwell, experienced attorneys, would not have Humes and Boswell placed under oath prior to speaking with the HSCA panel. (Perhaps they later decided this was an error, for when Drs. Ebersole and Finck appeared before the panel in March 1978, they were *both* placed under oath.)

What Drs. Humes and Boswell did not know prior to their appearance, was that Dr. Michael Baden, the Chair of the HSCA Forensic Pathology Panel, and other pathologists on the panel, *had already tentatively concluded,* on the basis of what they saw in the autopsy photographs and x-rays, and in concert with the written report of the panel of experts assembled by Attorney General Ramsey Clark (known as the so-called "Clark Panel" in the assassination literature), that all 3 government pathologists had *mislocated the entry wound by 100 millimeters, or approximately 4 inches, in the autopsy report.* This was to lead to some lively exchanges of questioning during the September 16th meeting, as the reader will see below.

Before we launch into the substance of that questioning, let me first summarize the circumstances in which the Clark Panel came to exist, and the ways in which it differed from the autopsy report signed by Humes, Boswell, and Finck, which was admitted into evidence by the Warren Commission in March 1964 as Commission Exhibit 387. (See Appendix 24.) Dr. Boswell testified during his ARRB deposition that the whole thing was a 'set-up.' Boswell was asked by Justice Department official Carl Eardley (the same official who was present at the Military Inventory on 11-1-66, and who later sent Boswell down to New Orleans during the Clay Shaw trial to assist the defense counsel, if necessary, because Pierre Finck was doing 'so badly' on the witness stand) to write a letter to the Justice Department, requesting an independent review of the autopsy report conclusions, based upon the autopsy photos and x-rays. Boswell told Jeremy Gunn during his deposition in February 1996 that Eardley had suggested to Boswell what he should put in the letter, and that he (Boswell) had gladly done so. (Boswell sent the letter to the Justice Department in February of 1968.) Boswell then testified that this was an "awfully good panel," and recalled that he, and Humes, and Ebersole had met with them for approximately half a day to discuss the case. The political atmosphere that prompted the formation of the Clark Panel appears to have been growing public doubt about the conclusions of the Warren Commission, as evidenced by:

- A *LIFE* magazine cover-story in November 1966 that challenged Arlen Specter's 'single bullet theory' (without which Lee Harvey Oswald could not have committed the assassination alone), using the recollections of Governor Connally, and startlingly clear blowups of individual frames from the Zapruder film;

- The long and detailed memo of November 08, 1966, written by former Warren Commission staff counsel Wesley Liebeler (with the assistance and urging of David Lifton) and sent to high officials within the government. It drew attention to the 'surgery of the head area' statement in the Sibert-O'Neill FD-302 report, as well as other evidentiary questions, and requested a fresh review of all of the medical evidence, this time including the autopsy photographs and x-rays, in the presence of the Warren Commissioners, the 3 pathologists, 3 outside forensic experts, and a responsible member of the critical research community. This powerhouse memo, although not made public, was essentially asking for a new Warren Commission, and surely created quite a stir within the Executive Branch of government, coming as it did within the same month that the Kennedy family had relinquished the autopsy photos and x-rays to the National Archives;[60]

---

[60]On January 20, 1967 officials of the Justice Department assembled Drs. Humes, Boswell, and Finck to review the autopsy photographs and x-rays in light of what they had

- Mark Lane's 1966 bestseller *Rush to Judgment* (essentially a defense brief for Lee Harvey Oswald) and the accompanying 1966 film, both highly critical of the Warren Commission's findings;

- Josiah Thompson's 1967 bestseller *Six Seconds in Dallas,* the first attempt at a scientific, evidence-based alternative hypothesis to the Warren Commission's findings; and its partial publication in the *Saturday Evening Post* magazine, with an attention-getting cover that declared "Three Assassins Killed Kennedy;" and

- Public awareness that the autopsy photographs and x-rays at the National Archives could *not* be viewed by the public.

I have always assumed that President Lyndon Baines Johnson, the biggest "hands-on" operator in U.S. Presidential history, was uncomfortable with the growing public doubts and pressed Ramsey Clark to do something in the way of 'damage control' by appointing a 'panel of experts' to conduct an independent review; this is the way the system works in Washington—politicians stall their critics, and attempt to outlast them, and to defend themselves, by appointing review panels considered likely to be favorable to their positions to study controversial issues. Since the assassination of the President was not a Federal crime in 1963, and the Federal government did not even have jurisdiction over the crime in the first place, it is hard for me to believe that the Justice Department, on its own, would have done anything of this nature unless directed to do so by the President. After all, the government already had an official position on the JFK assassination: it was called the Warren Report.

February of 1968, the month Boswell sent his letter to the Justice Department giving them a 'fig leaf' for the setting up of a panel of experts, was the month after the Tet Offensive by the Viet Cong in South Vietnam, a disastrous month for both American foreign policy, and American public opinion about the Vietnam war at home, for this was the month when it became clear that the South Vietnamese were losing the war, and were unlikely to ever win it, in spite of massive American logistic assistance and combat troop levels. The credibility gap between what Department of Defense civilian officials and U.S. Army generals had been saying about the war in public, and what Americans could see on their TV sets every night on the evening news, had seriously eroded faith in government credibility in general, and in the Johnson administration's credibility in particular. [As readers who are of the author's age (or older) will recall, what optimistic officials had been

---

written in their autopsy report, and to write a new report directly relating the autopsy findings to specific photographs and x-rays. The political purpose of this endeavor seemed clear: to attempt to prove that the autopsy photos and x-rays supported, and did not contradict, the autopsy report and its findings. (By the way, the ubiquitous Carl Eardley of the Justice Department was present yet again.) The report was signed out on January 26, 1967. I suspect that the Liebeler Memo of November 8, 1966 was probably a major stimulus to this event. The report is referred to as the "Military Review" in this book. (It will be discussed further in Part II.)

calling 'the light at the end of the tunnel' in Vietnam had begun to appear instead like 'the headlight of the oncoming train.'] The Tet Offensive was a pivotal moment domestically; January of 1968 was the month that public opinion 'flipped' on the Vietnam war issue, because after years of self-delusional, overly-optimistic reports, failure could no longer be disguised. Events on the ground had exposed the Johnson Administration's credibility gap. One would think that President Johnson had better things to do than worry about the Kennedy assassination, but apparently not. The Clark Panel met in secret on February 26-27, 1968, the very same month that Boswell had sent his letter! This was very fast action for anything of this nature within the U.S. government; clearly, the 'skids had been greased' ahead of time. Apparently, LBJ was looking to have some official 'damage control' in his hip pocket prior to the 1968 Presidential elections, in case the Kennedy assassination became a hot topic. (He had not yet firmly decided, or announced, that he would not run for President again.)

The public knew nothing about the Clark Panel until its report was publicly released on January 16, 1969, just four days prior to the end of the Johnson Administration. On that date it was released along with the January 26, 1967 Military Review Report (signed by Humes, Boswell and Finck) which had preceded it by 13 months. Both were essentially reviews of the photographs and x-rays to see whether anything in the collection changed the autopsy findings. The Clark Panel was comprised of 4 leading forensic specialists:

- William H. Carnes, M.D., Professor of Pathology at the University of Utah;

- Russell S. Fisher, M.D., Professor of Forensic Pathology at the University of Maryland and Chief Medical Examiner of the State of Maryland;

- Russell H. Morgan, M.D., Professor of Radiology, School of Medicine, and Professor of Radiological Science, School of Hygiene and Public Health, the Johns Hopkins University;

- Alan R. Moritz, M.D., Professor of Pathology, Case Western Reserve University.

In addition, an attorney named Bruce Bromley, a member from the New York Bar, was requested by Attorney General Clark to serve as legal counsel to the panel, was present throughout its deliberations, and collaborated with the panel in the preparation of its report. The Clark Panel report, a 16-page document, was signed in March and April of 1968 by the four forensic experts. With one major exception, its findings supported the Bethesda autopsy report. I will quote below from its concluding summary on the signature page:

> Examination of the clothing and of the photographs and x-rays taken at autopsy reveal that President Kennedy was struck by two bullets fired from above and behind him, one of which traversed the base of the neck on the right side without striking bone and the other of which entered the skull from behind and exploded its right side. The photographs and x-rays discussed herein support the above-quoted portions of the original autopsy report and the above-quoted medical conclusions of the Warren Commission Report.

On the surface, it sounded pretty good for Humes and Boswell and Finck, but beneath the surface, it was not so good. The Clark Panel concluded the fatal bullet to the head struck *much higher* than the autopsy pathologists had said in their report. The autopsy report stated the following about the location of the entrance wound to the skull:

> Situated in the posterior scalp *approximately 2.5 cm laterally to the right and slightly above the external occipital protruberance* is a lacerated wound measuring 15 x 6 mm. In the underlying bone is a corresponding wound through the skull which exhibits beveling of the margins of the bone when viewed from the inner aspect of the skull. [Author's emphasis]

The Clark Panel concluded in its closing discussion:

> One bullet struck the back of the decedent's head *well above* the external occipital protruberance" [Author's emphasis]

Earlier in the report, it specified the following about lateral skull x-ray film # 2:

> ...a hole measuring approximately 8 mm in diameter on the outer surface of the skull and as much as 20 mm on the internal surface can be seen in profile *approximately 100 mm above the external occipital protruberance*. [Author's emphasis] (See Appendix 42.)

Regarding the autopsy photographs of the back of the head, the Clark Panel specified:

> Photographs...42 and 43 [the basis for the HSCA's Ida Dox diagram] show the back of the head, *the contours of which have been grossly distorted* by extensive fragmentation of the underlying calvarium. There is an elliptical *penetrating wound of the scalp* situated near the midline and *high above the hairline*. The position of this wound corresponds to the hole in the skull seen in the lateral [skull] x-ray # 2...the wound was judged to be approximately six millimeters wide and 15 millimeters long. The margin of this wound shows an ill-defined zone of abrasion. [Author's emphasis]

In the quotation above the Clark Panel is referring to the "high" or "red spot" in photos 42 and 43 (see Figure 65), not to the "low" or "white spot," or "white mass" of apparent debris or tissue near the hairline.

The Clark Panel did not mention in its report that Humes, Boswell, and Ebersole had been present for approximately half a day of consultations; and it went out of its way to support their essential autopsy findings in its concluding paragraph on the signature page. But buried within the text were the statements quoted above that indicated the pathologists had erred by approximately 100 mm in locating the entry wound. The Bethesda autopsy pathologists, who had viewed the body for 4 to 5 hours, measured the size and location of the entry wound in the skull with a metric ruler, and palpated the entry wound with their fingers, had placed it low in the *occipital bone*; yet the Clark Panel, in spite of consulting with them for half a day in person, had concluded, based upon 4 autopsy photographs of the back-of-the-head (15, 16, 42, and 43) and one lateral head x-ray (# 2), that the entry wound was really *not* in the occipital bone at all, but *4 inches higher, in the <u>parietal bone</u>.*[61] (If one takes a skull model, locates the approximate position of the entry wound described in the autopsy report, and then moves it upward 10 centimeters, or 100 millimeters, it clearly lies within the parietal bone, and is not even an occipital wound anymore.)

What was going on here? Were all three autopsy pathologists that incompetent, or was there something wrong with the autopsy photographs of the back of the head? (In the case of the lateral skull x-rays, not all radiologists interpret them the way Dr. Morgan did. For example, ***all three ARRB independent forensic consultants,*** Forensic Anthropologist Dr. Douglas Ubelaker, Forensic Radiologist Dr. John Fitzpatrick, and Forensic Pathologist Dr. Robert Kirschner, told us they could see *<u>no bullet entry wounds in the lateral head x-rays</u>*. (See Appendices 43-45.) I find this most interesting. Experts often disagree, but the one radiologist on the Clark Panel was being outvoted here by three to one; remarkable! The questions is, *why* did Dr. Morgan come to the conclusion he did? I suspect he convinced himself that he "saw" an entrance wound in the skull in the lateral x-rays because he and his 3 colleagues *first thought they saw one in the scalp* in the back-of-the-head photos—the "high" red spot in color photos 42 and 43. (See Figure 65.)

Now that the reader is familiar with the essential preliminaries, namely, the Clark Panel's report and its effect upon the mind set of the HSCA Forensic Pathology Panel, we can proceed to the excerpts of the interplay between the panel members, and Drs. Humes and Boswell, on the subject of the location of the entry wound in President Kennedy's skull.

Relevant HSCA panel excerpts follow; the reader should reference Figure 65 (which represents photos 42 and 43), or Figure 64 (which represents black-and-white photos 15 and 16), throughout this testimony.

First, the discussion of where the Clark Panel located the entrance wound in the skull in the lateral skull x-ray, leads to a startling discussion of photograph 42:

Petty: I'm now looking at no. 2, x-ray no. 2. Is this the point [up high on the back of the head where there is a marked discontinuity in the bone in the rear of the skull] of entrance that I'm pointing to? [See Figure 37, the HSCA enhancement of this lateral head x-ray.]

Humes: *No.* [Author's emphasis.]

Petty: [incredulous] This is not?

Humes and Boswell: [speaking together] *No.* [Author's emphasis]

---

[61]The Forensic Pathology Panel's final conclusion about the location of the entrance wound concurred with the conclusion of the Clark Panel, and is shown in Figure 48, reproduced from volume 7 of the HSCA's 1979 report.

Petty: Where is the point of entrance [on the x-ray]? That doesn't show?

Humes: It doesn't show [in the x-ray]. *Below* the external occipital protruberance. [Author's emphasis]

Humes had just contradicted his location for the entrance wound written in the autopsy report: 2.5 centimeters to the right, *and slightly above,* the EOP.

Petty: [incredulous again] It's below it?

Humes: Right.

Petty: Not above it?

Boswell: No. It's to the right and *inferior to* the external occipital protruberance. [Author's emphasis]

What was going on here?

Petty: O.K. All right. Let me show you then color photograph no. 42, which then is the—

Humes: Precisely coincides with that wound on the scalp.

Humes is saying here that the low entry wound observed at autopsy, regardless of how it was described in the autopsy report, coincided precisely with the "low" object or "white spot," or "white mass" near the hairline at about the center of the head in photo no. 42. I think Humes and Boswell are modifying the description of the entrance wound—by now saying *it is below the EOP, rather than slightly above the EOP—in order to make this description match the lesion low in the scalp, near the hairline, that is present in photo 42.* They have conducted 'oral surgery' on their own description in the autopsy report, in order to match what they know is in a vital autopsy photograph. (Remember, they have seen that photograph previously on two occasions: November 1, 1966; and again on January 20, 1967, when they attempted to relate each photograph to the autopsy report written more than 3 years earlier. They had ample opportunity in January of 1967 to come to agreement on what was shown in photo no. 42.)

Klein: Could you describe that point that you just made?

Humes: That's an elliptical wound of the scalp which we described in our [autopsy] protocol. I'm quite confident. And it's just to the right and below by a centimeter and maybe a centimeter to the right and maybe two centimeters below the midpoint of the external occipital protruberance. And when the scalp was reflected from there, there was virtually an identical wound in the occipital bone.

_____

Petty: Then this is the entrance wound. The one down in the margin of the hair in the back?

Humes: Yes sir.

Petty: Then this ruler that is held in the photograph is simply to establish a scale and no more?

Humes: Exactly.

Petty: It is not intended to represent the ruler starting for something?

Humes: No way, no way.

Petty: What is this [red spot] opposite—oh, it must be, I can't read it—but up close to the tip of the ruler, there you are two centimeters down?

Boswell: It's the posterior-inferior margin of the lacerated scalp.

Boswell has told Dr. Petty that the "red spot" identified by the Clark Panel as a bullet entrance wound is *only the end of a large scalp laceration!* (Boswell gave the same testimony, under oath, at his ARRB deposition.)

Petty: [incredulous again] That's the posterior-inferior margin of the lacerated scalp?

Boswell: It tore right down to that point. And then we just folded that back and this back and an interior flap forward and that exposed almost the entire—I guess we did have to dissect a little bit to get to—

Humes: To get to this entrance, right?

Boswell: But not much, because this bone was all gone and actually the smaller fragment fit this piece down here—there was a hole here [pointing to the "white spot"], only half of which was present in the bone that was intact, and this small piece then fit right on there and the beveling on those [two halves of a circle] was on the interior surface [of the skull].

This testimony by Boswell in 1977 is *one hundred per cent consistent* with what he told the ARRB staff at his 1996 deposition: namely, that the skull bone was missing in the right rear of the head, in spite of the intact appearance of the scalp in photographs of the rear of the head; and that the entrance wound in the occiput was only part of a hole or circle immediately adjacent to the huge skull defect, and that its circumference could not be completed until a small fragment was inserted later in the autopsy.

The discussion of where the entrance wound in the skull was depicted in the autopsy photographs was resumed later during the panel session:

Petty: Joe Davis, you have questions, I think, about the inshoot area, don't you?

Davis: Well, in terms of the inshoot, my impression when I first looked at these films was that the inshoot was higher [then claimed in the autopsy report], and I equated that with the lesion in photograph, I believe it was...well, it's [no.] 43—and I interpreted—which one is this [before us now]?

Baden: This is no. 42.

Petty: We were wondering if that [the "high" lesion, or "red spot"] had been the inshoot.

The panel's members had already decided the Clark Panel was correct and was asking whether Humes and Boswell would verify this.

Humes: *No, no, that's no wound.*   [Author's emphasis.]

Davis: Because in no. 42 I interpreted that as a wound, and the other, lower down in the neck, as just being a contaminant, a piece of brain tissue.

Humes: *No, that was a wound* [the lower object in the hairline, the so-called "white spot"] *and the wound on the skull precisely coincided with it.* [Author's emphasis.]

Davis: Now it was a tunnel—

Humes: Yeah, tunnel for a way.

Boswell: Yeah, it's longer than it is wide, and tunneled along and actually under here, and then at the actual bone defect was above the—

Humes: And this photograph no. 45 [labeled as occipital wound of entry in the posterior skull with scalp reflected], I am quite convinced, is an attempt to demonstrate that wound, and not a very successful one I'm afraid, because I can't for sure pick it out.[62] This, I believe, was taken looking down at the inside—looking close to the posterior cranial fossa. [That is not what the Military Inventory description written by Humes and Boswell on 11-1-66 says; it says that this is a photo of the posterior skull with scalp reflected, meaning that it shows the entrance wound from the *outside* of the back of the head.]

Boswell: [Coming to the rescue, and seemingly agreeing with Humes' redescription of photo

---

[62]Humes recanted on this identification before the ARRB after lengthy questioning by Jeremy Gunn, and Boswell stated up-front that the photo was misidentified.

no. 45] And what we see here is a lot of red and fragments of bone. [Neither man seems to be troubled by, or even aware of the fact, that they are contradicting their own earlier description of photographs 17, 18, 44, and 45.]

Dr. Coe: Dr. Humes and Dr. Boswell, have you discussed these photographs [nos. 42 and 45] with the other pathologists who have previously gone over this with you [apparently referring to the Clark Panel]?

Humes: I have not. [Apparently the Clark Panel treated its peers with 'kid gloves,' in person, before slamming them in the body of its report.]

Boswell: I went over the photographs with Humes.

Coe: Because at least there's already one of them right—I had the impression that they apparently thought—I was just curious as to—

Humes: Our written description clearly, I think, indicates that point right there [clearly pointing at the "low" white spot in the hairline, in photo no. 42].

Coe: But they [the Clark Panel] describe, some of them, the entrance they feel being 10 centimeters above the occipital protuberance.

Petty: Well, there have been all sorts of changes from the original—I mean, right and left and up and down.

Coe: No. That's why I was interested in whether they had discussed it with the [Clark Panel] pathologists or whether the pathologists had been interpreting entirely from the photographs when they made the statement [about the entry wound really being 100 mm above the EOP].

Petty: So, on photograph no. 42, then, down right at the hairline, right at almost in the midline, is the inshoot wound, and this wound is centered in the photograph, but rather the posterior extension of the scalp tear is the subject of the photograph [at higher, or "red spot" near the tip of the ruler].

Humes: Again, to be sure that it [the framing of the photograph, no. 42] was related to the gentleman's [President Kennedy's] head rather than focusing specifically on a wound, no, I don't think we took the photograph specifically at that site [the "red spot" high in the scalp], do you, "J"?

Humes' syntax can often be tortuous, and extremely frustrating to read. He is asking Boswell for support here, saying "We didn't attempt to center the photograph on that "red spot," did we, "J"? We just took a picture of the head, and it turned out that the "red spot" simply *appears* to be the purpose for taking the picture, just because it happens to be centered in the frame of view!" Boswell, amazingly, agreed with the import of this statement by Humes.

Boswell: No. [!!!]

Petty: Can I go back to another interpretation which is very important to this committee? I don't really mean to belabor the point, but we need to be certain, as certain as we can be—and I'm showing you now photograph no. 15 [an HSCA enlargement of the "white spot" in the hairline], and here, to put it in the record, is the posterior hairline or margin of the hair of the late President, and there, near the midline, just a centimeter or two above the hairline, is an area that you refer to as the inshoot wound.

Humes: Yes sir.

Petty: Also, on the same photograph [apparently referring here to the color photos, 42 and 43, one of which was the source for the two enlargements] is a ruler, and approximately 2 centimeters or so down the ruler and just to the right of it is a second apparent area of defect, and this had been [photographically] enlarged [by the HSCA staff] and is shown to be an enlargement, I guess no. 16, which shows you, right opposite the 1 centimeter mark on the ruler, this defect, or what appears to be a defect. I don't see the connection with the lacerated scalp anywhere.

Baden: And no. 15 shows the enlargement of the lower area that's suggestive of an inshoot to you.[63]

Petty: And what we're trying to do is to satisfy ourselves that the bullet actually came in near the margin of the hair [down low] and not near the tip of the ruler [up high] as is shown in [enlarged] photograph no. 16.

Humes: This [the enlargement of the "high" red spot] is an enlargement from that other photograph [color no. 42], right? Dr. Boswell [earlier in the deposition] offered the interpretation that it might be an extension of a scalp wound. *I don't share his opinion about that.* I don't know what that is. Number one, I can assure you that as we reflected the scalp to get to this point, *there was no defect corresponding to this*

---

[63]A point of clarification is in order here. The two extreme enlargements of the "white spot" (HSCA photo no. 15) and the "red spot" (HSCA photo no. 16) discussed at this point in the HSCA panel transcript should not be confused with black-and-white autopsy photos no. 15 and 16 of the intact back-of-the-head, which were numbered on 11-1-66 at the Military Inventory. The HSCA panel never referred to black-and-white photos no. 15 and 16, which were so-numbered in November of 1966 and are reproduced in the illustration section of this book. The random congruence of numbers here is unfortunate, and possibly misleading.

in the skull at any point.[64] I don't know what that is. It could be to me clotted blood. I don't, I just don't know what it is, but it certainly was not any wound of entrance. [Author's emphasis.]

Humes: I would like to comment further, from our point of view, that these enlargements [of the "red spot" and the "white mass"] which you have shown us now of these other photographs is the first time I have seen these enlargements; I have not seen them before.

Humes, apparently, is attempting to wiggle out of the predicament he and Boswell find themselves in by soliciting sympathy, saying he is confused by enlargements because of their larger size, and because he has not had a chance to study them.

Davis: These were made up just 2 or 3 days ago. Two days ago.

Petty: May I make a comment on what you have just said, Dr. Davis? The problem, as I see it, is that this may be in fact a tunneling situation, with the bullet scooting along the skull here or somewhere, and not entering the skull down below [where it first struck the scalp]. Is that what you're saying now?

Davis: What I'm saying—what I'm inferring: in the absence of photographs and specific measurements, we could only conjecture as to how long the tunneling is, but I would envision this as a tunneling first and then entry into the skull.

Now, the real fireworks began.

Lovoquam: I don't think this discussion belongs in the record.

Petty: All right.

Humes: I agree.

Lovoquam: We have no business recording this. This is for us to decide between ourselves; I don't think this belongs on this record.

Petty: Well, we have to say something about our feeling as to why we're so interested in that one particular area.

---

[64] According to the drawing Boswell made on the skull model for the ARRB during his deposition, there was *no bone whatsoever under the scalp where the "red spot" is located in the autopsy photographs*.

Coe:	The reason we are so interested in this, Dr. Humes, is because other pathologists have interpreted the—
Lovoquam:	I don't think this belongs in the damn record.
Humes:	Well, it probably doesn't.
Lovoquam:	You guys are nuts. You guys are nuts writing this stuff. It doesn't belong in that damn record.
Baden:	I think the only purpose of its being in the record is to explain to Dr. Humes what—
Lovoquam:	Why not turn off the record and explain it to him and then go back and talk again.
Baden:	Well, our problem is not to get our opinions, but to get his opinions.
Lovoquam:	All right then, keep our opinions off. Here's Charles and Joe talking like mad in the damn record, and it doesn't belong in it. Sorry.

I think it's pretty easy to explain what is going on here. It's as if the high priesthood of an ancient religion were overheard by their illiterate and uneducated followers arguing about whether or not the Sun God really exists; Lovoquam was concerned that the degree of confusion and disagreement amongst the experts on the panel and the autopsy pathologists would undercut public confidence in its eventual conclusions. And of course, he was right to be concerned. Experts disagree all the time, as evidenced by the disagreement of *all three* ARRB forensic consultants with the Clark Panel about whether or not there is an entry wound depicted in the lateral skull x-rays. This emotional outburst by Dr. Lovoquam is "pure gold" to JFK assassination researchers, because it teaches us to study the primary evidence ourselves and make up our own minds, after taking into consideration the varying opinions of different 'experts,' and *not to defer to authority* in technical matters of evidence, because there is often no real consensus among experts; instead, the head of a panel or committee ultimately often 'pulls rank' and simply makes the final decision on a technical evidentiary issue, based on what he feels the consensus should be, when it is time to write a report. When this happens, the members within the group who disagree are forced either to "go along to get along," or to become dissenting "voices in the wilderness." (This is what happened on the Warren Commission in regard to Arlen Specter's extremely dubious 'single bullet theory.' Ultimately, Senator Richard Russell, who was not persuaded by Specter's theoretical construct, 'went along to get along,' and signed the Warren Report without writing a minority opinion—something he had threatened to do.) The transcript of the HSCA panel's discussions with Humes and Boswell about the location of the entry wound *does* undercut public confidence in where the entry wound was really located, but in my opinion this says more about the autopsy photographs of the rear of the head, and their validity, than it does about the qualifications of the experts.

Humes:	I think we're at a distinct disadvantage because, as I said, when we catalogued the

photographs and numbered them, and spent half a day or [a] day to do it, I'll confess to possibly even overlooking the area to which you gentlemen, and apparently someone else [the Clark Panel], has directed attention. I would not attempt to make an interpretation of what it [the "high" red spot in photos 42 and 43] represents because I can't at this point.

Davis: But at the time of the autopsy there was no defect in the scalp other than where the bone was gone.

Humes: Right.

Baden: When you say 'defect,' you're talking about a defect of the wound of entry?

Davis: Right.

Boswell: Now, I'm sure that our record describes the tunneling of that wound of entry pretty well, at least as to length and distance beneath the skin, doesn't it? I can't recall the description, but I'm sure it is there.

Humes: I'm looking for the color photograph that coincides with [HSCA enlargement] no. 15—which one is it?

Baden: 42 is the one.

Humes: Yeah. Whether this "defect" is a "defect," in my mind, I'm not sure. I'm not sure it's not some clotted blood that's lying on the scalp.

Baden: What we're trying to do is to have your best opinions and recollections to deal with.

Humes: Right.

_____

Baden: George [Lovoquam], is there anything further you'd like to add?

Lovoquam: No, I've said my piece. [Yes, you certainly did.]

Humes: [Can you] Show me the photograph where the external occipital protruberance is?

Davis: I can't show you where it is on this photograph to my satisfaction.

I will explain in Part II of this book *why* I believe *neither one of the two possible locations of the entry wound* in the autopsy photographs of the intact back-of-the-head matches the location described in the autopsy report, and *why* Humes and Boswell have *never* agreed with each other about what the "red spot" near the end of the ruler depicts.

Public, Sworn Testimony by Dr. Humes Before the House Select Committee on Assassinations on September 7, 1978 About the Location of the Entrance Wound in the Skull, As Shown in the Autopsy Photographs of the Rear of the Head

Humes was asked to appear one year later to give sworn public testimony to the full House Select Committee on Assassinations. He was warned in private by Dr. Petty, prior to his testimony, that if he did not 'recant' about what the "red spot" high in the photograph represented, he could suffer major embarrassment during his televised public testimony.[65] [I highly recommend that the reader familiarize himself with the rest of this story—exactly how Dr. Humes was persuaded to publicly recant about the location of the entrance wound—in Dr. Mantik's article, "The Medical Evidence Decoded," pages 287-288, in Jim Fetzer's anthology, *Murder in Dealey Plaza.*]

Relevant excerpts of Humes' testimony pertaining to the issue of where the entry wound in the skull was located are reproduced below. His malleability—his willingness to please authority when pressured to do so—was now in evidence. He was questioned by staff counsel Gary Cornwell:

Cornwell: I would like to show you what has been admitted into evidence as JFK exhibit F-48 during these hearings, a drawing of the back of the President's head. The committee has received evidence from Miss Ida Dox today that that drawing is an accurate representation of photographs taken during the autopsy and I believe the drawing represents photographs from the autopsy numbered 15, 16, 42, and 43, but apart from the testimony of Miss Dox, have you had an opportunity to compare that drawing with those photographs to determine if it fairly and accurately duplicates the photographs?

Humes: Yes, I have Mr. Cornwell, and I believe that it does. (See Figure 54.)

Cornwell: The particular photograph that this drawing represents, I take it, would have been taken as part of the normal procedure of the autopsy and for the same reasons that you previously described all the photographs were taken, is that correct?

Humes: Correct, to document the positioning and appearance of the wounds.

Cornwell, in an attempt to lay the foundation, and set the stage for Humes' recantation, now makes a major speech. He had to, really: the HSCA Forensic Pathology Panel had a serious problem in "the damn record."

Cornwell: In the process of examining that, among the other available documentary evidence in the case, our panel of forensic pathologists, of course, were not present during the autopsy, did not have access to the body and, therefore, you and your colleagues who were there are in a unique position to provide testimony as to the nature of the wounds to the President. In that connection, as you recall, the panel invited you, and

---

[65]Dr. Petty revealed this to a Fox News producer in 2006, who in turn relayed it to me.

you responded voluntarily, in fact, as I recall, on very short notice, you responded to an invitation to come speak to them informally. They, I guess, we could say, interviewed you as to your knowledge on the subject of the autopsy in the National Archives [where the actual photographs were located]. In pertinent part, the transcript which was made from the tape recording of that interview at pages 12 to 13 reflects that you reviewed not only that drawing, but an x-ray of the President's head and identified a small droplet in the lower portion of the photograph as a wound of entry and that that was the only wound of entry. Later in the transcript, at pages 39 to 40, the following colloquy occurred: Dr. Petty of the panel said, going back to the earlier discussion, "Can I go back to another interpretation which is very important to this committee? I don't really mean to belabor the point, but we need to be certain, as certain as we can be, and I am showing you now photograph 15—that, of course, was a photograph from which the drawing was made[66]—"and here to put it in the record is the posterior hairline or margin of hair of the late President and there near the hairline in just a centimeter or two above the hairline is an area that you refer to as the inshoot wound." That, in other words, was a verbalization of the description of the location of the small droplet near the bottom of the head. You replied, Dr. Humes, "Yes sir." Dr. Petty then continued, "Also on this same photograph is a ruler and approximately 2 centimeters or so down the ruler and just to the right of it is a second apparent area of defect, and this has been enlarged and is shown to you in an enlargement, I guess no. 16, which shows you right opposite the one centimeter mark on the ruler this defect or what appears to be a defect." Thereafter, skipping a small portion [of testimony] and going to the very next page, 40, you replied, "I don't know what that is. No. I, I can assure you that as we reflected the scalp to get to this point, there was no defect corresponding to this in the skull at any point. I just don't know what that is. It could be to me clotted blood. I don't, I just don't know what it is, but it certainly was not any wound of entrance."

Would it be accurate to state first, Dr. Humes, that at the point at which you made the statements we have just referred to, you were called rather unexpectedly from your normal occupation, came to Washington and with no preparation or no referral to prior notes immediately prior to that, were shown this and other evidence and made the statements that I have just referred to?

Humes: That is correct, and I comment that I was similarly summoned on Tuesday of this week, 48 hours ago, for this appearance likewise with no attempt or no chance for preparation and no idea of what questions were to be directed toward me.

---

[66]Cornwell blew it here; in that transcript, photo 15 referred to HSCA enlargement no. 15, an enlargement of the "white spot," or 'droplet' in the hairline. He was confusing his own committee's enlargement of an object in photo no. 42 with Military Inventory black-and-white photo no. 15, a closer view of no. 42 (without the ruler present in the field of view).

Cornwell: And we apologize for the short notice in both cases.

Humes: [A bit perturbed, knowing what is coming next] Fine. I hope we can straighten that out.

Cornwell: I would like to ask you if you would agree to various portions of what are reflected on this photograph. First, in the original photograph, there was shown, as in the drawing, a ruler; is that correct?

Humes: That's correct.

Cornwell: And in addition, there were the hands which are shown which appear to be holding the scalp so as to expose some portion of the back of the head.

Humes: That's correct.

Cornwell: Would you also agree that in the original photograph, the hair in the upper portion appears to be wet, [and] that in the lower portion appears to be relatively dry?

Humes: *I would indeed.* [Author's emphasis]

I wonder here if Humes was thinking about the fraudulent manipulation of *intact scalp from elsewhere on the head* that was manipulated to create this image by covering up the huge area of missing bone in the back of the head?

Cornwell: Would you also agree that the hair is spread apart in the upper portion of the photograph, exposing portions of the scalp and that in the lower portion, the hair is in a relatively natural position?

Humes: I would.

Cornwell: And finally, would you agree that the relative center portion of the photograph has what you, upon initially being shown this photograph in the Archives by our panel, could not identify, that's what you said might be a clot or some other item, and that is relatively off-center in the overall photograph the part you identified as being the wound of entry, the locations are as I described them? [sic]

Cornwell's syntax here is not any better than Humes' syntax, at his most convoluted.

Humes: Yes, apparently.

Cornwell: Now, I would like to ask you today if you have had at least a greater opportunity to look at the photographs along the lines that I have just indicated to you and if, after doing so, you have a more well-considered or a different opinion or whether your opinion is still the same, as to where the point of entry is?

This performance of Cornwell's is just as shameful as the "yanked-from-the-mouth" testimony Arlen Specter engaged in during March of 1964 with several of the Dallas treating physicians, when he got them to reverse themselves and testify that, hypothetically, under extreme (and false) conditions, the entry wound in the front of President Kennedy's neck could have been an exit wound, instead of an entry. Cornwell was only slightly more subtle than Specter, but was equally dishonorable in his behavior. Humes knew what he was expected to do here. He was expected to recant, to do the twentieth century equivalent of what Galileo Galilei had done before the Inquisition, when he was made to publicly swear before God that he had been in error—that the earth did not revolve around the sun—and to admit, contrary to his inner belief, that the earth was the stationary center of the universe, and that the sun revolved around the earth instead.

It was now Dr. Humes' turn, in 1978, before the PBS TV cameras, to make a speech:

Humes: Yes, I think that I do have a different opinion. Number one, it was a casual kind of discussion that we were having with the panel members, as I recall it. Number two, and I think before we comment about these photographs further, if I might comment, these photographs were made on the evening of November 22, 1963. I first saw any [sic] of these photographs on November 1, 1966, almost 3 years after the photographs were made, which was the first opportunity that I had to see those photographs. At that point, Drs. Boswell, Finck and I were asked to come to the National Archives[67] to categorize these photographs, label them, identify them and we spent many hours going through that. It was not the easiest thing to accomplish, I might say, after 3 weeks short of three years. But we identified them and I think in light of the very extensive opportunity that various panels of very qualified forensic pathologists have had to go over them, we did a reasonably accurate job in cataloguing these photographs. So, I saw them on that occasion. I saw them again on the 27th of January of 1967 when we again went to the Archives and made some summaries of our findings. [It was really the 20th of January; after typing, the report was signed on January 26th.] I go back further to the original autopsy report which we rendered, in the absence of any photographs, of course. We made certain physical observations and measurements of these wounds. *I state now that these measurements that we recorded then were accurate to the best of our ability to discern what we had before our eyes.* [Author's emphasis.] We described the wound of entrance in the posterior scalp as being above and to the right of the external occipital protruberance, a bony knob on the back of the head, you heard Dr. Baden describe to the committee

---

[67]Under the pressure of the public testimony Humes is conflating two different events here. He misspoke. On November 1, 1966, it was Humes, Boswell, Ebersole, and Stringer who met in the Archives to create a catalogue or descriptive listing of the photographs; Humes, Boswell, and Finck did not meet together until January 20, 1967, and the purpose of that meeting was not to make an inventory of the photographs, but rather to write a technical report relating the autopsy photographs to the autopsy report, CE 387.

members today. And it is obvious to me as I sit here how with this markedly enlarged drawing of the photograph that the upper defect to which you pointed or the upper object *is clearly in the location of where we said approximately where it was, above the external occipital protruberance;* therefore, I believe that is the wound of entry. It[s] relative position to boney structure underneath it is somewhat altered by the fact that there were fractures of the skull under this and the President's head had to be held in this position thus making some distortion of anatomic structures to produce this picture. By the same token, the object in the lower portion, which I apparently and I believe now erroneously previously identified before the most recent panel, is far below the external occipital protruberance and would not fit with the original autopsy findings. [Author's emphasis.]

So, Humes had recanted; *sort of.* He had stubbornly maintained that the measurements of the entrance wound made at the autopsy were correct at the time and were still valid, while giving Cornwell 'half a loaf,' by admitting that he had misidentified where the occipital entry wound he wrote of in the autopsy report was located in photographs 42 and 43 (see Figure 54, the Ida Dox drawing of these photos). Similarly, when Galileo recanted before the Inquisition, he reportedly whispered, "yet it still moves," referring to the fact that he knew the earth nevertheless still revolved around the sun, regardless of what the officials of the Church had made him say under duress. Unlike Galileo, at least Humes had not been placed under house arrest for the remainder of his natural life.

Cornwell did not even say thank you; he was probably ticked off that Humes had cheated him out of a total moral victory. He moved immediately on to discussion of the damage to the brain, without further ado. This performance by Humes tells me that not only was he willing to some extent to defer to authority, but that there was a limit beyond which he would not go; it also told me that it was a virtual certainty that the autopsy pathologists *really did find an entry wound on the skull exactly where they said they did in their report.* I think the reason Humes (and the other pathologists) have stood their ground on this issue is because if there is ever an *exhumation and a reexamination of the cadaver of the President*, that examination would indeed likely show a very low entry wound in the skull; in other words, we would be left with a mystery about why photographs looked strange, but the location of the entry wound in the autopsy report would be vindicated, as would the reputations of the pathologists (in this one regard, if nothing else). I conclude that there was *nothing* wrong with the description of the entrance wound in the autopsy report; but there *was* something very wrong indeed with the photographs of the back-of-the-head. Humes and Boswell knew this, I am sure, but were unwilling to disclose what it was. Better to endure harassment over the location of an entrance wound in a photograph, they probably reasoned, than admit that the entire series of photographs showing the back of the head intact was a fraud,[68] perpetrated by them to deceive history and cover-up the true facts of the assassination—that President Kennedy was shot in the head from the front, as well as from the rear, and had a massive exit defect in the back of the head, as well as an apparent rear entrance wound low in the occiput, adjacent to the edge of the posterior exit defect. In other words, it is my considered opinion that in the Bethesda morgue Humes and Boswell found physical

---

[68]Photographs 11, 12, 15, 16, 38, 39, 42, and 43.

359

evidence of crossfire immediately after the body arrived, and therefore indisputable evidence of conspiracy. This was the big secret that they were no doubt persuaded to cover up on the night of November 22-23, 1963 in the interests of national security.

They were trapped, I believe, by the state of the photographic record as it was recorded by them after midnight, on November 23, 1963, and sometime before the embalmers completed their work. Humes and Boswell couldn't quite get their stories straight, however, about what the lesion high in the photos (the "red spot") showed: whether it was the end of a laceration (as Boswell claimed), whether it was a spot of dried blood or a blood clot (as Humes first claimed to the HSCA panel), or whether it really was the entry wound they measured 2.5 cm to the right, and slightly above the EOP, as Humes said when he 'recanted.' That problem—of not getting their stories straight—remained to haunt them in 1996, at their ARRB depositions. [See Chapter 12 for more on the "red spot."]

Testimony of Dr. Humes to the ARRB Staff on February 13, 1996 About the Location of the Entrance Wound in the Skull, As Shown in the Autopsy Photographs of the Rear of the Head

Jeremy Gunn tried unsuccessfully to get Dr. Humes to draw the area of missing posterior skull bone on an anatomical diagram from *Grant's Anatomy* during his deposition. The exchange went as follows:

Gunn: Dr. Humes, I've put before you a drawing from *Grant's Anatomy* that shows the posterior portion of a human skull. Do you see that?

Humes: Yes.

Gunn: Where the occipital bone is identified?

Humes: Mm-hmm.

Gunn: [Gunn marked the document as Exhibit MD 72]...I'd like to ask you now, Dr. Humes, if you can tell me where there were any missing pieces of skull on the back of President Kennedy's head, if there were any, that can be seen within the—

Humes: I'm confused by this drawing. What is this? Is that the teeth?

Gunn: Yes. That's from the—

Humes: This is a funny—it's a strange way to depict the posterior portion of the skull, is all I can tell you. There was no [sic] [nothing missing of any] significance. It was just a hole. But it was further down, you see. It wasn't way up here.

Gunn: I note here is the external occipital protruberance.

Humes: Yes.

Gunn: Sir, could you show me first on Exhibit 72 where the wound was, approximately, in relationship to—

Humes: Not without referring to my notes. I don't have that number in my mind. Or [without] referring to the report that you have here, the autopsy report.

Gunn: Okay. Let me try another question. Can you describe generally where there was any missing bone from the posterior portion, to the best of your recollection?

Humes: There basically wasn't any. It [meaning the entry wound] was just a hole. Not a significant [amount of] missing bone.

Gunn: So a puncture hole—

Humes: Puncture hole.

Gunn: And no bone missing—

Humes: No.

Gunn: —anywhere in the occipital—

Humes: No, no. Unless maybe—you know, these drawings are always strange. Unless the part of this wound [indicating] extended that far back. I don't think it did, really. Most of it was parietal temporal.

Humes was contradicting his own autopsy report, where he wrote that the exit defect was largely parietal, but extended somewhat into the *occipital* and temporal areas.

Gunn: So on the scalp of President Kennedy...underneath the scalp the bone was all intact with the exception of the puncture wound—

Humes: Yeah.

Gunn: —and perhaps some fragment—

Humes: In the back of the skull, back, yes sir.

Boswell, of course, was to contradict this in no uncertain terms two weeks later, with both his oral testimony and with the diagram he executed on the ARRB skull model, showing the location of missing bone in the skull. He (Boswell) had already told the HSCA staff and the HSCA Forensic Pathology Panel that the entry wound in the occiput was not a simple hole in a solid plate of bone, but that it was a *portion* of an entry wound at the very edge, or border of the huge exit defect, which had to be completed by inserting a fragment of skull bone brought to the morgue well after the autopsy was in progress. And of course Boswell confirmed at his own ARRB deposition, through his skull diagram, that significant portions of the occipital bone were missing down through, and including, the lower right rear of the skull, and in the upper left rear of the skull also. (See Figure 12.)

If my hypothesis is correct, Humes was stonewalling here, and prevaricating, in order to backstop the fraudulent images of intact scalp in the rear of President Kennedy's head. My interpretation of Boswell's testimony is that interestingly enough, he was being more honest about how much posterior bone was missing—while freely admitting during his deposition that he was holding scalp in place for the rear-of-the-head photos. In the event of an exhumation, Boswell's reputation was going to fare much better than that of James Joseph Humes.

When Jeremy presented the autopsy photos showing the back-of-the-head to be intact (view no. 6, photos 15, 16, 42, and 43) the following exchange took place:

Gunn: Dr. Humes, are you able to identify what you have described previously as an entrance wound in the posterior skull of President Kennedy in view no. 6?

Humes: This is the same problem I had at the Committee Hearings.

Gunn: Referring to the House Select Committee on Assassinations?

Humes: Yeah. I had big difficulty trying to see which was which among these things, between here and here [gesturing back and forth between the "high" red spot and the "low" white spot].

Gunn: When you say "here and here," the first one you were pointing to [was] something that appears roughly sightly below the ruler, and the second "here" was referring to the object that is quite near the bottom of the frame?

Humes: Right. I mean, they threw these up on a great big screen and said which is what, and I really had difficulty. I couldn't be sure. I'm disappointed. I was disappointed in that regard. I still have trouble with it.

Gunn: Are you able to identify on view 6 the entrance wound?

Humes: Not with certainty, I'm sorry to tell you.

Gunn: Are you aware of where the House Select Committee on Assassinations panel of experts identified what they believed to be the entrance wound?

Humes: No. No.

Gunn: Do you see the gloved hand?

Humes: Mm-hmm.

Gunn: Are you able to identify whose arm that is holding the President's head?

Humes: No.

Gunn: When that photograph was being taken, was the scalp being pulled forward, that is, towards the eyes of the President, in order for that photograph to be taken?

Humes: It's possible. I'm not sure. It looks like that's what's happening. The edge of the defect is adjacent to where the fingers and thumb of the person appear on the photograph.

Jeremy steered the discussion on to the subject of where the HSCA had placed the entry wound, namely, the upper of the two lesions in the Ida Dox diagram, the "red spot."

Gunn: And based upon your recollection and examination of the photos, is that ["red spot" up high near the tip of the ruler] where you now would identify what you believe to be the entrance wound in the skull?

Humes: I cannot flat-footedly say that. I have trouble with it. The head is turned toward one side. I don't know. It's very difficult. Very difficult. It's an educated guess, to be perfectly honest.

Gunn: For the marking [i.e., lesion or apparent piece of debris] that is towards the bottom near the hairline, what is your best understanding of what that designates?

Humes: I don't have the foggiest idea. See, what's important is where the wound is in the bone. You can't tell that from these pictures.

This sounds pretty lame to me, if none of the posterior skull bone is missing and the entry wound was a simple puncture in a plate of bone, as Humes claimed earlier in the deposition.

Gunn: What is your understanding of the correlation, if any, between a puncture wound in the scalp and the puncture wound in the bone?

Humes: They're directly over align—directly aligned.

Gunn: So there was not a penetration of the scalp with the bullet going along the cranium and then going in at some—

Humes: My impression was it went right through from the site of the skin wound, when you looked at the wound from the inside and matched them up with the scalp wound.

Gunn:	Did you have any difficulty identifying the scalp entry wound during the time of the autopsy?
Humes:	No, I didn't at the time of the autopsy, but the photographs I think create ambiguity. For me they do, much to my displeasure and dismay. I thought they would erase ambiguity rather than create it.
Gunn:	Would you have expected the marking that you took to be the entry wound in the scalp to have been better represented in the photos than what you were seeing—
Humes:	Yes, I would have hoped that it would have been. Yes sir.

Had this had been an aggressive cross-examination in a court of law, it would have been appropriate at this point to spring the big question on Humes: "Dr. Humes, did you participate in a cover-up of the medical evidence by manipulating loose scalp to cover an exit defect in the posterior skull, and by simulating a higher entry wound (more consistent with being shot from the Book Depository) by puncturing the scalp in the cowlick area?" But that is 20-20 hindsight, 10 years after the event, as I write this chapter in the year 2006. We were not conducting an aggressive cross-examination, but rather a carefully neutral fact-finding deposition. Furthermore, if Humes was involved in such a national security exercise in 1963, he had plenty of chances to 'fess up,' and never did so; therefore, springing an 'ambush question' on him like that probably wouldn't have made any difference.

He did give us one clue, however, after his deposition was over and we were walking him down the hall toward the elevator to the lobby at Archives II, where "J" Thornton Boswell was waiting to pick him up. Humes was intellectually, emotionally, and physically exhausted by his day-long deposition, but the pressure was now off and he was loosening up; his guard was down. His parting words to us as we got on the elevator was *"I sure hope you people can figure this thing out."* To me, this sounded like the James J. Humes that David Lifton had sensed over the years as he interviewed Humes on the phone (in 1966), and repeatedly read between the lines in Humes' autopsy report—the person with forbidden, or secret knowledge, who reveals hints to you from time to time in his statements and writings, but who will never reveal the whole truth of what he was involved in outright. Dr. Humes really did seem to have an "I've Got A Secret" type personality, with regard to the Kennedy assassination.

DR. BOSWELL AND THE AUTOPSY PHOTOGRAPHS

Testimony About Photographs Missing from the Autopsy Collection in the National Archives

Dr. Boswell said nothing of importance—in fact, almost nothing at all—in his testimony before the Warren Commission. Arlen Specter clearly wanted Humes to be his star pathology witness.

About one month *prior* to the tape-recorded, unsworn testimony of Humes and Boswell before the HSCA Forensic Pathology Panel, Boswell was interviewed by three HSCA staff members. One of them, Andy Purdy, wrote an OCR about the Boswell interview on August 17, 1977, the day of the interview. I have reproduced short verbatim passages from that OCR below which pertain to photographs Boswell remembered being taken that are not in the Archives today:

- "Dr. Boswell indicated that in the area of the neck wound there was a '...contusion along the inner margin of the apex of his lung' which was '...the only way we could trace the entire path of the bullet.' He said the bullet passed through the upper thorax; he said he thought they photographed '...the exposed thoracic cavity and lung...' but doesn't remember ever seeing those photographs."

- "Dr. Boswell couldn't recall if there was more than one interior chest photograph taken...he '...thought a photograph was taken of the lung.'"

This was the first time that anyone had mentioned that a photograph was taken of the bruise *on the apical portion of the lung itself.* Humes had testified to Specter before the Warren Commission that both the dome at the top of the pleural cavity, and the top portion of the lung, were bruised—but he only mentioned taking a photograph of the bruise in the pleural dome of the eviscerated chest. In order to photograph the bruise on top of the right lung—a bruise that corresponded with the bruise at the top of the pleural dome—the lung must have been illuminated outside the body, after its removal. There is no such photograph (nor are their photographs of *any* removed organs) in the collection in the Archives.

After showing Dr. Boswell all of the representative views of the body of President Kennedy, Jeremy Gunn, ARRB General Counsel, launched into his questioning about missing photographs:

Gunn: ...are there any other photographs that you remember having taken during the time of the autopsy that you don't see here?

Boswell: The only one I have a faint memory of was the anterior [sic] of the right thorax. I don't see it, and haven't when we tried to find it on previous occasions, because that was very important because it did show the extra-pleural blood clot and was very important to our positioning that wound.

Gunn: There are additional descriptions of photographs showing—described as showing the entrance wound in the skull from both the interior and the exterior with the scalp reflected. Do you remember any photographs with the scalp reflected showing the wound of entrance in the skull?

Boswell: Well, I seem to remember a couple of photographs. That might be one [meaning unclear here], and particularly one showing the beveling of that same wound—or not beveling, but the tunneling. [Boswell is talking about the entry wound in the rear of the head when he mentions tunneling.] But I can't imagine that there are any photographs missing. Numerical-wise, are they all here?

Gunn: I am not aware of any photos that are missing since the 1966 inventory. The question would be whether there were other photographs taken that were not in the 1966—

Boswell: Yeah, well, we've always looked for the one of the chest cavity, and then I seem to remember photographs, color photographs of the tunneling [of the entrance wound in the scalp].

Gunn: Do you remember seeing the photographs themselves or do you remember taking the photographs?

Boswell: I've never seen the one of inside the chest. The one of the skull wound, I thought I remembered seeing it, but I—now, I've seen an awful lot of pictures like in Livingstone's books. Where those came from, I don't know. And whether they're fabricated, some of them, or not—and I may be confusing pictures I've seen that are alleged to be autopsy photographs.[69]

Jeremy then asked Boswell to read the pathologists' description of 'tunneling' associated with the entrance wound in the Military Autopsy Review report of 1-26-67.

Gunn: ...for the record, the portion of the document that we are looking at says "The scalp wound shown in the photographs appears to be a laceration and a tunnel, with the actual penetration of the skin obscured by the top of the tunnel." That's referring to view no. 6, photographs number 15, 16, 42, and 43, if we could see one of those [gesturing to Steve Tilley of the National Archives].

Boswell: That's the same one.

Gunn: Dr. Boswell is now looking at the sixth view [of autopsy photos].

Boswell: I guess maybe that's the one I remember. It looks different to me today as I see this. I don't appreciate the tunnel as much as I have in past examinations, and the position is different. You see, the problem is, though, that this scalp is all loose, and this might not be—as we're viewing this, this might not be the [real] position of this wound.

---

[69]The bootleg autopsy photographs in Harrison Livingstone's books all originate from either the B & W James K. Fox set, or the color Robert Groden set, and all are degraded representations of the actual photographs in the Archives that Boswell had just looked at minutes before. I do not understand the basis of his comment here. There are no photographs in Livingstone's books, or Lifton's book, or Groden's book, or Crenshaw's book, that are not in the National Archives. They are identical, except that the versions published in books suffer from contrast buildup and accompanying loss of detail, and are cropped somewhat and therefore show a smaller field of view in some cases than the color transparencies and B & W negatives in the Archives.

Gunn:	Again, you're referring to the mark down near the hairline—
Boswell:	Right, on—
Gunn:	—on view 6?
Boswell:	Photograph 42. This scalp may fit differently, and this might easily be closer to the underlying bony wound of entrance. When I look at this again, it sounds very much like we've described it here.
Gunn:	Okay. In other words, this photograph of view 6 corresponds with the language [about tunneling] used in Exhibit no. 14 [the Military Autopsy Review] on the bottom of page 3?
Boswell:	Exactly.

In summary, then, Boswell told both the HSCA staff and the ARRB staff that he recalled *the chest photograph (of the bruise at the top of the right pleural cavity)* was missing, and he told the HSCA (but not the ARRB) that he thought *the bruise on the lung itself* had also been photographed. He also expressed an opinion to Jeremy during his deposition that the description in the 11-1-66 Military Inventory of photographs 17, 18, 44, and 45 as "missile wound of entrance in posterior skull, following reflection of scalp," was an incorrect description. Doing so, of course, implies that the real photograph taken that would have matched that description is therefore missing also—that is, the pathologists attempted to match that description with a skull photograph in 1966 because they remembered that such a photograph had been taken. If photos 17, 18, 44, and 45 do not match that description, then that photograph is therefore missing also.

Testimony Before the HSCA Forensic Pathology Panel on September 16, 1977 About the Location of the Entrance Wound in the Skull, As Shown in Autopsy Photographs of the Rear of the Head

Boswell (in concert with Humes) did express opinions on this critical matter before the HSCA Forensic Pathology Panel, and the exchanges between Humes and Boswell on the one hand, and the HSCA panel on the other, about where the entrance wound in the skull was located in photos 42 and 43 were reproduced above in considerable detail in the subsection on Dr. Humes.

Testimony to the ARRB Staff on February 26, 1996 About the Location of the Entrance Wound in the Skull, As Shown in the Autopsy Photographs of the Rear of the Head

Jeremy Gunn first discussed the entry wound in the back-of-the-head photos with Dr. Boswell using view no. 4, photos no. 11, 12, 38, and 39, titled "posterior view of wound of entrance of missile high in shoulder."

Gunn:	I'd like to ask you a question first about the scalp, although that's not the center of

the photograph, and ask you whether the scalp had been pulled up in any way in order to keep any flaps from hanging down over the back [of the neck]. I don't know if that question was—

Boswell: Yes, I understand.

Gunn: Maybe if we could look at that photograph [view 4] in conjunction with the one from the third view ["superior view of head"].

Boswell: Where the flap is coming down.

Gunn: Yes.

Boswell: I know this—the flap is stretched forward here, because if this fell back down—with him in this sort of recumbent position, yes, this scalp would fold down and cover this wound.

Gunn: So you're saying that on the fourth view...the scalp has been pulled back and folded back over the top of the head in a way different from the way that they appeared in the third view, the superior view of the head?

Boswell: Yes.

Gunn: Is that fair?

Boswell: In the previous one, it was permitted just to drop. In this one, it's pulled forward up over the forehead, toward the forehead.

Gunn: Who, if you recall, pulled up the scalp for the photograph to be taken?

Boswell: There are about three of us involved here, because there are two right hands on that centimeter scale. I think that I probably was pulling the scalp up.

Gunn: I'd like you to notice in that photograph—and again, we're still talking about the fourth view [photos no. 15, 16, 38, 39]—that there is a little white marking—I don't know what that is—that is very near the hairline.

Boswell: Here? [pointing at the "white spot"]

Gunn: Yes. Do you see that either matter of tissue or something [sic]---

Boswell: I have seen that and worried and wondered about it for all these many years. Some people—many people have alleged that to be the wound. I don't think it is.

368

Gunn: In relationship with that white marking, whatever it is, could you say or describe approximately where the entrance wound was, where the entrance wound would be in relationship to that?

Boswell: Well, I think that the entrance wound is up in here someplace. I'm talking like a couple of centimeters above the hairline and 4 centimeters to the left of the ear. But I can't argue with that. I don't know what that is. I've seen this in other photographs. In some areas, it's a little translucent bubble. I think that the wound of entrance is up in here [indicating].

Gunn: Okay. What I'd like to ask you to do is measure with the centimeter measure here. Maybe if we can—

Boswell and Jeremy discussed a way of denoting where Boswell thought the entrance wound *should* appear in the photograph, in a "word picture" that readers of the transcript could understand. Jeremy then tried to sum up Boswell's comments:

Gunn: Okay. So if President Kennedy [in photos 11, 12, 38, and 39] were standing erect, then—and we're talking about the measurements corresponding to the photograph [the 8 x 10 print in the Archives, not the transparency] and not to real life. But from what I was understanding, you were saying that the measurement would be approximately 3.5 centimeters at approximately a 45-degree angle from that white spot, that is, if President Kennedy were standing erect? Is that fair?

Boswell: Yes.

Gunn: And it's in the direction towards the right ear?

Boswell: Toward the ear. That's maybe like 30 degrees.

Gunn: And the point that you are estimating that the entrance wound was located, is that the location that was previously recorded as approximately 2.5 centimeters to the right and slightly above the external occipital—

Boswell: Right.

Gunn: Okay.

Gunn: Okay. Could we turn to the sixth view, which is described as "wound of entrance in right posterior occipital region?" That corresponds to black-and-white photos no. 15 and 16, and color photos no. 42 and 43. Do these photographs appear to you, Dr. Boswell, to be accurate representations of photographs taken during the autopsy of President Kennedy?

Boswell: Yes.

Gunn: In that photograph, is the scalp of President Kennedy being pulled forward?

Boswell: Yes.

Gunn: For what purpose is it being pulled forward?

Boswell: In order to take the photograph, because if it wasn't pulled forward, this would just—the scalp would come down and cover the wound of entrance here. And this was necessary to demonstrate the wound here.

Gunn: Okay. Now, as you're looking at the photograph of President Kennedy, if you're looking at it as if President Kennedy were standing erect—of course, he's lying on his side, but we'll look at it from the perspective of the ruler being vertical, pointing upwards, and the head pointing upwards. Could you identify where on the photograph the wound of entrance was located, please—the wound of entrance in the skull?

Boswell: This is the one that I have—photograph that I have had a dilemma about for so many years. This is the white spot that you showed me in the other photograph.

Gunn: Yes, down near the hairline.

Boswell: Yeah. And that is not where I thought that the wound of entrance was. This *must* be the wound of entrance. [Boswell's own emphasis.]

Gunn: You're pointing down to the white marking near the hairline?

Boswell: Yeah. I'm trying to find anything up in here, and obviously the photographer was taking this in such a manner to show that [indicating the "red spot"]. I can't find anything else. This [the "white spot"] is in disagreement with this [one of the three Rydberg drawings used by the Warren Commission, CE 386], obviously.

Gunn: When you say it's in disagreement, you're referring to Exhibit MI 13—

Boswell: Yes.

Gunn: —the Rydberg drawing [CE 386]?   [See Figure 43.]

Boswell: Right. Because this [the "white spot"] is more in the midline and lower.

Gunn: I'd like to draw your attention to [the object] in the color photograph the round, reddish marking just to the right of the ruler, very near the top of the ruler.

Boswell: Yes.

Gunn: Could that round or ovular-shaped marking be the entrance wound?

Gunn was referring here to the "red spot" high in the scalp identified by both the Clark Panel and the HSCA Forensic Pathology Panel as the entrance wound in the skull.

Boswell: *No.* [Author's emphasis.]

Now Boswell has said it under oath; his HSCA testimony was unsworn.

Gunn: What is that, if anything, that round or ovular-shaped marking?

Boswell: I think it's the—this is awfully near the front of the scalp fragment here, and here is a laceration up here with complete separation. And when—

Gunn: You're referring there to the very top of the scalp—

Boswell: Just under the fingers that's holding the scalp up. And if you let—when you let this fall down, in one of the previous photographs—

Gunn: I'm sorry. Just for the record, you're letting the scalp fall down towards the back and cover where the ruler would be?

Boswell: Yes. If you let that fall down, then this would be right in the midline and that line that you asked me about where the tissue was separated but not completely separated. And I think this is probably the other side of that traumatic disfigurement of the scalp.

Jeremy did his best to clarify this 'Humes-speech;' it was obvious at this point that Humes and Boswell were indeed spending a lot of time together.

Gunn: If I understood you correctly, were you saying that that marking [the "red spot"] that we've been pointing to that is near the top of the ruler and somewhat to the right might be the beginning or at least part of the laceration of the scalp?

Boswell: Yes. That's occurring from beneath with the explosion of the bullet.

Gunn: I'd like to point out the parting of the hair that goes at approximately a 45-degree angle irregularly out to the right. Is that hair that is being pulled to the left covering part of the laceration?

Boswell: Probably. I can see it; probably up in here, at least.

Gunn: Is there any question in your mind about whether that photograph may have been changed or altered in any way?

Boswell: Oh, I don't know how they would—how anybody could have done that. I mean, all the other things that I see here, my hairy arm, everything else looks normal.

Gunn: Holding aside the question of how someone might have done that, is there anything in that photograph that appears to be different from how you remember seeing it on the night of the autopsy?

Boswell: No, and I've seen it many times since then, and it's—I think this was the photograph that was taken there. It's just that my memory of this apparent lesion—

Gunn: Down at the bottom towards the hairline?

Boswell: —was in a different location. But everything else fits.

Gunn: In looking at that photograph, do you have any reason to re-evaluate the location of the wound of entrance in the skull from being 2.5 centimeters to the right and slightly above the EOP?

Boswell: Well, these figures are more important to me than this [photo], because I—this I'm not sure of. These [numerical measurements on the Autopsy Descriptive Sheet] I am sure of. These I am sure of.

Gunn: When you say "these figures," you're referring to the autopsy face sheet, Exhibit 1?

Boswell: The measurements on the face sheet.

—————————

Gunn: ...Now I'd like to ask you a question about what is underneath the scalp of what we are looking at now. Let's take the marking that appears toward the hairline right at the base of the neck, or where the hairline meets the neck. If we take the point above that, where would you say that the scalp [sic] is or that the skull will be missing underneath the scalp that we can view there?

Boswell: Probably right about here.

Gunn: So you're—

Boswell: Just about the base of the ear.

Gunn: So you're pointing to approximately halfway up the ruler that we can observe and to the right of that small fragment [the "white spot"], so the skull is missing—

Boswell:	Right.

Gunn:	—underneath there?

Boswell:	Yes.

———————

Gunn:	Just to try a different description, because we're trying to put this into words where we're looking at photographs, would it be fair to say—again, we are imagining President Kennedy [in photos 15, 16, 42, and 43] is standing erect [instead of lying on his left side, as he actually is], although he's lying down in this photograph. *So with the ruler pointing up, would the portion as it would appear on this photograph to the left of his right ear all be the portion of the skull that was missing?* [Author's emphasis]

Boswell:	Yes.

For a diagram of what Boswell means here, see Figure 12, my drawing of the posterior of the 'Boswell skull,' the model he marked up at his deposition.

DR. FINCK AND THE AUTOPSY PHOTOGRAPHS

Testimony About Photographs Missing from the Autopsy Collection in the National Archives

Dr. Finck's sworn testimony was taken before the HSCA Forensic Pathology Panel on February 11, 1978. Although they did not ask him whether the bruise in the right pleural cavity was photographed, he did testify to the fact that both photographic views taken of the entry wound in the skull (outer table and inner table) were not in the collection of autopsy photos in the Archives.

Finck:	*...I remember positively that a Navy photographer took pictures* and I wanted pictures *of the crater* [on the inner table of the skull] *in particular* because this is a positive finding for a wound of entry in the back of the head. *So I wanted a picture showing no crater from the outside and a clear cut crater from the inside,* but I don't know. [Author's emphasis.]

———————

Petty:	May I ask one other question, perhaps two. If I understand you correctly, Dr. Finck, you wanted particularly to have a photograph made of the external aspect of the skull from the back to show that there was no cratering to the outside of the skull.

Finck:	Absolutely.

Petty:	Did you ever see such a photograph?

Finck: I don't think so and I brought with me [the] memorandum referring to the examination of photographs in 1967 when I was recalled from Vietnam. I was asked to look at photographs and as I recall there were two blank 4 by 5 transparencies; in other words, two photographs that had been exposed but with no image and as I can recall *I never saw pictures of the outer aspect of the wound of entry in the back of the head and inner aspect in the skull in order to show a crater* although I was there asking for these photographs. *I don't remember seeing these photographs.* [Author's emphasis.]

Petty: All right. Let me ask you one other question. In order to expose that area where the wound was present in the bone, did you have to or did someone have to dissect the scalp off of the bone in order to show you this?

Finck: Yes.

It is clear from this testimony that Dr. Finck, the wound ballistics expert, is the person who directed the taking of the 2 photographic views of the entry wound in the skull; if he says they are not in the collection, then I believe his is the definitive judgement. This testimony makes clear that Humes, in his tortuous, meandering testimony before the ARRB staff on the location of the entry wound in view no. 7, which runs on and on for several pages in the transcript before he finally settles upon a tentative location in the photo for a 'possible' entry wound, was simply trying to mollify his questioner, to please Jeremy on this issue, so that his torment on this question would end. (This is the frustratingly compliant, somewhat 'malleable' Dr. Humes that we also saw in his HSCA public testimony—willing to bend just enough to make his inquisitors happy, so they would hear what they wanted to hear and 'go away and leave him alone.') Clearly, ARRB view no. 7 (photos 17, 18, 44, and 45) is *not* what it is labeled to be—it does *not* depict the missile wound of *entrance* in the posterior skull. It may show the posterior skull, and depict evidence of a wound in the skull bone, but it does *not* depict an *entrance* wound. That photograph (of the entry wound) is not in the collection.

Relevant testimony by Dr. Finck about missing photographs during his ARRB deposition is not worth repeating below; he claimed not to remember anything anymore, about specific photographs taken of the skull. Jeremy read to Dr. Finck an excerpt from his own text in the report he submitted to his Commanding Officer at the AFIP, General Blumberg, in February of 1965, indicating that he had directed the taking of exterior and interior photographs of the entrance wound in the skull, but Finck, in spite of this, claimed to have no independent recollection of doing so. Whether or not his ARRB testimony claiming to have no recollections about this event was truthful, the real facts here were established by Finck's own report to General Blumberg in 1965, and his testimony under oath before the HSCA panel in 1978. The record was clear.

Testimony Before the HSCA Forensic Pathology Panel on March 11, 1978 About the Location of the Entrance Wound in the Skull, As Shown in the Autopsy Photographs of the Rear of the Head

Finck's testimony about the autopsy photographs showing the back-of-the-head began as follows:

Petty: This is the photograph that seems best to show the back of the head. This seems to be photograph no. 42. Now where is the wound of entrance on the back of the scalp that you see in no. 42?

Finck: It is probably this wound [indicating the "white spot"]. Probably. I can't, I don't—

Petty: Dr. Finck has pointed to a mass right at the junction of the hair with the neck.

Finck: This is not too clear so I can't tell if it is this or that, honestly.

Petty: Say it again. You say this or not?

Finck: Is it that or is it something else? I don't know.

_____

Petty: ...Would you like to look at the color transparency which is probably better?

Finck: Yes. No. 42...Well, I would say that this was the wound of entry to the right of the external occipital protruberance. It is more accurate to determine an anatomic location when you have the wound itself on the dead body. On the photographs it is embarrassing, it is distorted as far as the angle of shooting is concerned, so you feel much more at ease when you have the dead body and the wounds to establish a location than when you have photographs.

_____

Baden: Were you present when these color photographs were taken of the head?

Finck: I was at least for some of them.

_____

Petty: Well, what we are trying to say is which in your recollection, maybe—which in your recollection, Dr. Finck, is the gunshot wound of entrance [in photo 42], this ["white spot"] at the hairline from which we have this enhanced photograph or this ["red spot"] toward the end of the ruler just above the level of the ears?

Finck: This one [pointing at the "white spot" near the hairline].

Petty: Which one are you pointing to?

375

Finck: The wound of entry.

Petty: And that is near the hairline or that is up toward the upper portion of the ear?

——————————

Finck: In the lower half of the photograph. Would that be good enough identification for the record?

Petty: This is the one by the hairline.

Wecht: By the hairline.

——————————

Petty: ...I just want to be sure that this is what you feel is the inshoot wound and that is near the hairline and not the—I hate to use any term to describe it but not the object near the central portion of the film near the end of the ruler.

Purdy: The red spot in the cowlick area. Dr. Finck, upon examining these two areas, what opinion do you have as to what, if anything, that red spot in the upper portion is?

Finck: I don't know what it is.

Pierre Finck was so agitated by what he saw, and by the repeated questioning about the location of the entrance wound in photo no. 42, that he asked to appear again before the panel the next day, on March 12, 1978. Only a portion of that audiotape was transcribed, but researchers may obtain a copy of the entire audiotape from Archives II at College Park, Maryland.

Reproduced below is some of his testimony from the very next day, when he reappeared before the panel at his own request.

Finck: ...I'd like to refer to the photographs shown to me, not seen in 1964, taken in 1963, at the time of the autopsy, not seen at the time of the Warren Commission hearings, and seen for the first time [by me] in January 1967. I think that the doubts and the controversies now arise from the fact that the people used these photographs as a basis for interpretation, saying they don't fit the autopsy report. And that's what bothers people and that's why I came back—to try to clarify that situation as well as I can after all that time. At the time of the autopsy, I palpated the scalp of President Kennedy, I examined it. Outer and inner surfaces of the scalp in the back of the head. That is, and I would like the photograph to put a number down because I didn't do that yesterday. [This is Finck the compulsive note-taker.]

Purdy: Forty-two.

Finck: I would like to see that one, this one.

_____

Finck: ...I was asked several questions regarding two areas in this 8 x 10 color print, and going back to the questioning, going back to my answers, try to summarize my opinion about this photograph, having examined the scalp myself, I don't think there is much any point in arguing about the so-called wound seen high in the scalp, above the level of the right ear, on the, above the upper end of the right ear on the photograph. There is not much point in arguing about this, when asked the question, "could that be a wound of entry, is that the penetrating, or a perforating wound?" for the good reason that, at that level I did not see in the scalp of President Kennedy, a perforating wound of the scalp. Again, there was only one perforating of the wound—perforating wound of entry of the scalp in the back of the President's head, and that was the wound low in the photograph with a white center in contrast to the previously described area which has a red center on the photograph. What I'm referring to now is the wound in the lower, lower portion of the photograph, near the hairline, and this is what corresponds to the perforating wound of the scalp, a wound of entry in the back of the head, unequivocally being a wound of entry because it corresponds to the hole in the bone I have described with no beveling on the outer aspect of the skull and with beveling on the inner aspect of the skull. Again, here we have to remember the difference between what you palpate with your fingers at the time of autopsy and what you see on a flat photograph. The external occipital protruberance is not clearly seen on a photograph like this, so I have to trust my measurements, my locations at the time of autopsy.

This went on at some considerable length, with Finck emphasizing the primacy of what the pathologist observes and palpates and measures at autopsy, over photographs.

There was a long discussion about whether or not Finck had claimed there was brain tissue coming out of what he said was the entrance wound in photo 42. In other words, was the "white spot" just debris lying on the surface of the hair near the base of the neck, or did the "white spot" represent brain tissue *extruding from a perforating wound through the cerebellum?* This was an important question asked by Dr. Rose, but he did not get very far with Finck because Pierre played "hard to get," quite slippery and evasive, as the ARRB found out he could be in 1996.

Rose: What you have interpreted as brain tissue extruding from a wound...

Finck: Oh, I didn't say brain tissue, did I? I said tissue.

Rose: Tissue. What we talked about as brain tissue...

Finck: I said the white area, apparently tissue, I don't...I think it's very dangerous to, to make positive identifications on the basis of a photograph. The only value of a photograph is to, it's the best record we have after all these years. The dead body is no longer there. But we should not make the photographs say more than what they can say.

Rose: Would you say beneath that wound, or that white tissue is, that there would be injury into the deep tissue beneath that area as well? So that it would extrude back out through the hole?

Finck: Probably. Yes. That wound being a perforating wound of the scalp, there was soft tissue coming out of that wound, if it's your question.

Rose: Which most likely would be brain, probably?

Finck: I don't know if I can answer that by yes or no.

Rose: Uh...

Finck: How can I, I am always trying to give an honest, sincere answer, and I hesitate to give answers which I cannot strongly defend, so some of the questions I have answered by [saying] definitely, by yes or no, but at times I don't think I can be that specific.

This went on and on. The session did nothing to calm Dr. Finck or to resolve whether brain tissue was extruding from the apparent entry wound near the hairline in photo no. 42.

There was one moment of comic relief at this second session, which is on the tape but does not appear in the abbreviated, partial transcript of the session. Finck, engaged in a running argument all day with panel members about where the external occipital protruberance was located on the back of the average person's skull, finally summed up the futility of the discussion by saying, in his pronounced Swiss accent, "It's not the Matterhorn, you know!" When Jeremy Gunn, Tom Samoluk, David Marwell and I heard Finck make this profound exclamation while listening to the tape at the ARRB offices, we all "fell out."

Testimony to the ARRB Staff on May 24, 1996 About the Location of the Entrance Wound in the Skull, As Shown in the Autopsy Photographs of the Rear of the Head

Jeremy Gunn presented Dr. Finck with color transparency no. 38, titled "posterior view of wound of entrance of missile high in shoulder," and the following exchange occurred about the location of the entrance wound in the rear of the head:

Gunn: Could you look at the skull in the photograph, particularly the portion in the top of the skull, and could you describe what you see at the top of the photograph?

Finck: Very close to the margin?

Gunn: Yes.

Finck: —of the photograph?

Gunn: Yes.

Finck: There is part of the scalp and, above that, red tissue, yes.

Gunn: Did you ever see President Kennedy's body in a condition such as you can observe it here now in this photograph, or had the body already been changed before you arrived at the autopsy?

Finck: I can't answer.

Gunn: It appears to me that there is something like a straight line that goes onto the right side of President Kennedy's head, quite straight. Can you tell me what that depicts from your own observations?

Finck: Parallel to the upper edge of the transparency?

Gunn: Yes.

Finck: The edge of the scalp.

Gunn: So, for example, were you able to tell whether that is a laceration from a bullet wound, *or whether that would have been a surgical incision, for example?* [Author's emphasis]

Finck: You are referring to the edge of the scalp?

Gunn: Yes.

Finck: That is not the bullet wound. It is the edge of the scalp. The bullet wound's much lower.

Gunn: Does it appear to you that there is a straight line in the scalp, or line that appears somewhat straight in the scalp, on the right of the mid [sic] to the right of the midline?

Finck: Yes. Not made by a bullet though.

Gunn: Can you tell me how it would come to be?

Finck: It is an incision.[70]

Breakthrough! Humes and Boswell had denied seeing any evidence of surgery in the head area. Was this incision in photo no. 38 evidence of post mortem surgery to gain access to the skull and remove evidence from the brain?

Gunn: Did you yourself see an incision during the time of the autopsy that would have resulted in that sort of cut?

Finck: I don't remember.

Gunn: Dr. Finck, if I could ask you to look just once more to see if you can see any evidence in this photograph of where the bullet entry wound was in the head of President Kennedy, if you can see any evidence of that in this photograph?

Finck: It is very difficult to do with preciseness in a photograph. I examined the wounds themselves. To look at a photograph is not like the examination of the wound itself.

Jeremy: Okay.

And that was it. Jeremy moved on to some very important questions about x-rays, which will be covered in the next chapter.

Although in many ways the most slippery and obstinate of the three pathologists, Finck had confirmed that there was an artificial, man-made straight cut in the scalp in photograph no. 38 that could *not* be attributed to damage from a bullet—a surgical incision. There were obviously several possibilities that could explain this; but it was indeed possible corroboration for the explosive statement in the Sibert-O'Neill report quoting Humes' oral utterance that there had been "surgery of the head area, namely in the top of the skull."

DENNIS DAVID'S RECOLLECTIONS OF WILLIAM PITZER'S DISPLAY OF POST MORTEM PHOTOGRAPHY OF PRESIDENT KENNEDY

Earlier, in a long footnote, I explained the context of any remarks in the assassination literature about LCDR William Pitzer's death at Bethesda NNMC. John Stringer testified to the ARRB that Pitzer was not present at the autopsy—and then left the door open just a tad by clarifying, saying that at least he did not *recall* him being there. In contrast to Stringer's testimony are the unsworn, but nevertheless strong recollections of former Navy hospital corpsman first class (E-6) Dennis David, "Chief of the Day" on 11-22-63, who today says that he was actually shown autopsy images of President Kennedy taken inside the Bethesda morgue. I truly can come to no firm conclusion on this matter, and I think it is a debate that will never end. Some researchers are of the belief that Dennis

---

[70]This incision is not visible in the cropped bootleg version of this autopsy photograph. It can only be seen in the color positive transparency in the National Archives.

David, and others like him who claim Pitzer was in the possession of autopsy images following the death of President Kennedy, are trying to imbue Mr. Pitzer's violent death at Bethesda with special meaning by claiming that instead of committing suicide, as his autopsy report concludes, that he was murdered as the ultimate penalty for possessing forbidden knowledge about the Kennedy assassination. Others note that his recollections are rock-solid and consistent,[71] and that just because he did not tell David Lifton about these recollections when he was interviewed on film in 1980, it does not mean that they are untrue. Without prejudice one way or the other, I will present below, as a kind of post script to this lengthy chapter on autopsy photography, the recollections passed on to me by Dennis David on February 14, 1997 in a telephone interview. I was told *not* to tape record the interview by Jeremy Gunn after I requested permission to do so; therefore, I will be as precise as possible below in summarizing what Dennis David said. To avoid this issue simply because I cannot resolve it in my own mind would be to repeat the mistake of the HSCA with the Knudsen deposition, and that I will not do.

Mr. David said that 3 or 4 days after the autopsy, a good friend of his, LCDR William Bruce Pitzer, who was in charge of all Bethesda audio-visual services, showed him photographic images of President Kennedy's autopsy inside Pitzer's office. Dennis David told me he was shown the following:

- A portion of a B & W 16 mm movie film, displayed using a viewer with two reels on it and a hand-crank. David estimated the size of the reel of film was probably 10" in diameter, and that the reel was about half full of film. He said he witnessed only a short section of the film, which appeared to show the President's body during initial examinations, and before any incisions. He said the film was clearly shot in the morgue at Bethesda, but not from immediately adjacent to the autopsy examination table; instead, it was shot from a distance—either from the gallery, or from well back in the room. He said that other person's torsos, from the waist down, and some gloved hands examining the body, could be seen in the film. He said that the motion picture film, although somewhat grainy, clearly showed a gaping wound in the back of the President's head, and that the top of the head looked intact.

- Six or seven 35 mm color slides of post mortem images of the President; like the movie film, these were also pre-incision, post mortem images of JFK. He said the slides were viewed by holding them up by hand in front of a lamp.

- Four or five black-and-white prints, approximately 3" by 5" in size, of post mortem, pre-incision images of President Kennedy.

---

[71]The account he gave to me, for example, was very, very consistent with what he told British documentary producer Nigel Turner on video; that account can be seen in episode 6 of *The Men Who Killed Kennedy,* a lengthy oral history of the Kennedy assassination that focuses on evidence supporting the conclusion that JFK was *not* killed by a lone gunman firing from behind.

The image content of the color slides and B & W prints, said David, "made it very clear that President Kennedy was hit from the front as well as the rear." When I asked him to clarify this, he said that first, he could see in these images a round or oval wound, about one quarter to three eighths of an inch in diameter, in the right front temporal area of President Kennedy's head, just below the hairline on the front of the head, which he immediately interpreted as a bullet entry wound. He also said that, just as in the B & W movie film, there was a gaping hole in the back of the head. When I asked him about the condition of the top of the head in these photographs, he replied that the top of the head looked intact in these photographs as well. He further specified that the orientation of the print and color slide images were straight on, profile, and oblique images of the upper torso and head of President Kennedy, and was quite certain that there was no evidence of any "Y-incision" in the chest, in any of the images he viewed. When asked to specify on the telephone, through as precise a use of language as possible, exactly where, to the best of his recollection, the entry wound in the front of the head was located, he estimated it was *about three inches forward of the right ear, and just below the hairline near the top of the forehead."*[72] He also said that the images of the tracheostomy in the anterior neck depicted what in his opinion was much larger, and sloppier, than most "trachs" he had seen throughout his career. When asked, he replied that he did not see any photographs of the back of the body, so he could not answer any of my questions about the wound the pathologists noted in the upper right posterior thorax.

In response to follow-up questions by myself, Tim Wray (who was then head of the Military Records Team, and my immediate supervisor), and Dr. Joan Zimmerman (a very accomplished and industrious Ph.D. in history with insatiable curiosity, who was a Senior Analyst on the ARRB's Secret Service Records Team), Mr. David said that he only viewed these films on this one occasion with LCDR Pitzer, and never subsequently discussed the images with Pitzer in any way. He said that by the time he viewed the images, he and others were aware that various people directly involved in the autopsy had received letters directing them not to talk about the events the night of the autopsy, under threat of court-martial. The resulting sense of fear and sadness, he said, kept him from discussing the events of November 22-23, 1963 with anyone at Bethesda after he viewed the autopsy film in LCDR Pitzer's office. Mr. David verified that he himself had never received a letter directing him to be silent, but the knowledge that others had received them made him very reluctant

---

[72]Interestingly, the reader will note that this is the location of the "incised wound" present in some autopsy photographs (view no. 2, photos number 5, 6, 26, 27, and 28), that Boswell testified about in his ARRB deposition. (See Figure 62.) Dennis David's description of this apparent entry wound also sounds very consistent with what Joe O'Donnell recalled seeing in the first set of autopsy photos shown to him by Robert Knudsen in 1963, and is furthermore also the same apparent location for an entry wound to which assistant White House Press Secretary Malcolm Kilduff pointed with the index finger of his right hand when he was on television at Parkland hospital the day of the assassination. Dr. Charles Crenshaw, suggestively, also pointed to this area high on the right forehead above the right eye when describing the likely entry site for a bullet in his April 1993 interview for ABC's *20/20* news magazine. Was an entry wound in the front of the head, high above the right eye and very near the hairline, obliterated by post mortem surgery at Bethesda NNMC? This will be discussed further in Part II, in Chapter 12.

to talk about the subject for many years; he said he did not speak about the events he was involved in publicly until he granted a newspaper interview to a reporter in 1975.[73] He clarified that LCDR Pitzer *never actually said that he was at the autopsy,* but that while viewing the films in Pitzer's office he assumed that Pitzer had been there, based on his possession of the film, and the context of their conversation. He said that the last time he saw Bill Pitzer was approximately December 3 or 4, 1965, when Pitzer attended Dennis David's swearing-in as an LDO Ensign (an O-1 Limited Duty Officer) in Captain Stover's office at Bethesda. Subsequently, in early 1967, a female occupational therapist named Murray at Great Lakes Naval Station told him of Pitzer's death, and indicated to him that the death had been ruled a suicide.

When asked, Mr. David said that he was familiar with David Lifton's book *Best Evidence,* as well as other assassination books that he did not name. He volunteered that in 1992 he went to Pittsburgh and attended a videotaped group interview about the Kennedy assassination along with former Navy medical technicians (and autopsy participants) Paul O'Connor and James Jenkins; Floyd Riebe (John Stringer's photography assistant at the autopsy); and Jerrol Custer (one of the two former Navy enlisted x-ray technicians who together shot the JFK x-rays). He said that pathologist Cyril Wecht was present at, and participated in, the interview, which was set up by a private company called GNC Communications. Mr. David also volunteered that in 1994, someone at GNC communications had arranged and funded the videotaping of a hypnosis session in which he was hypnotized and his memories of events surrounding his involvement with the assassination were probed. Mr. David volunteered that what he thought had been about 10-15 minutes under hypnosis had actually turned out to be about 1.5 hours, and that on a scale of 1 to 10 (with ten being the highest rating possible), the hypnotist/interviewer had rated his veracity as "an 11," meaning that he considered Mr. David to be very credible. Mr. David said he had personal copies of videotapes made of both the group interview in 1992 and his hypnosis session in 1994, but seemed uncertain about whether he would be allowed by the company that filmed them to share them with us, because of copyright considerations.

Inevitable Questions About Dennis David's Pitzer Recollections

All autopsy witnesses who recall photography in the morgue remember how extremely tightly the Secret Service controlled all film exposed during the autopsy, so the inevitable question arises: "How could William Pitzer or anyone else who worked at Bethesda end up with so many autopsy photographs?" It seems that unless he had a 'secret source' on the inside who was authorized to shoot exposures very early after arrival of the President's body, such as a Chief Knudsen, it would not be possible for him to have the color slides and black-and-white prints that Dennis David claims

---

[73]Dennis David spoke first to the newspaper reporter in 1975, and then to David Lifton in 1979-80, about how Navy enlisted personnel, under his direct supervision, carried a simple, gray-colored, metal shipping casket into the morgue on 11-22-63 from a black hearse that arrived at the morgue loading dock about 6:40 or 6:45 P.M., accompanied by civilians wearing suits. David claims that later that evening, after the conclusion of the autopsy, Dr. Boswell told him that the casket his Navy personnel had carried into the anteroom outside the morgue contained the body of the President. (This will be discussed further in Part II.)

to have seen. The reader will recall, however, that Knudsen reportedly told his son Bob that he was present early in the autopsy, as soon as the body arrived. If Knudsen was personally selected by Robert Kennedy and given a clandestine role in autopsy photography, it is *just possible* that he could have taken photography of the body early that evening immediately after its arrival, prior to any manipulations were performed on the body, and briefly recorded the true nature of the wounds prior to any incisions or alterations. (We do know that both autopsy photographers, Stringer and Riebe, were asked to leave the morgue early that evening prior to the taking of x-rays, and that the x-ray technologists, Custer and Reed, were also asked to leave the morgue for a brief period of time early in the evening before taking the first set of skull x-rays.) If Robert Kennedy, as the evidence suggests, was compliant in the execution of a medical coverup, and if he let it be known that Knudsen was his special, personal photographer at the autopsy—perhaps for the purpose of recording the true nature of the wounds before the facts were covered up—then it would theoretically have been possible for Knudsen to escape the Secret Service dragnet on film: he would have had 'special status' under this scenario. Since FBI agents Sibert and O'Neill implied in their report that they were barred from the morgue for some period of time early that evening because of the taking of x-rays, this could explain why they made no mention in their FD-302 report of Knudsen, or any of the photographic products mentioned by Dennis David—they simply may not have been aware of these events. The unanswered question remains: Did Robert Knudsen shoot the 16 mm motion picture film that LCDR Pitzer later showed to Dennis David?

The B & W 16 mm movie film that Dennis David recalls viewing is truly problematic. Even if Pitzer (or someone else) sneaked a movie camera into the morgue (under, say, an article of clothing such as a jacket or coat) and sat in the gallery early in the evening prior to the "Y-incision" being made at 8:15 P.M., it is hard to imagine anyone operating a movie camera of that era without someone noticing; the mechanical drives in cameras, and the motion of the film past the shutter, made a certain amount of noise when the camera was operated—movie cameras were not totally silent like today's video cameras. Under the speculative hypothesis developed above, one would think that the Secret Service would have immediately confiscated any such film, *unless* it had been shot by Knudsen, or someone else identified as Robert Kennedy's personal representative. I know of no link between William Pitzer and Robert Kennedy, and Knudsen was a still photographer by trade, not a person who specialized in taking motion pictures. So I have doubts. But Knudsen's colleague at the White House, Air Force photographer Cecil Stoughton, shot movie film on occasion, and surely anyone who was a photographer by trade in the early 1960s would be capable of operating a motion picture camera—it was a very popular hobby in that era. So while Stringer testified that Pitzer was not present in the morgue, and may have told the truth about that, his absence does not preclude some motion picture film having been shot by Knudsen, if he was present representing Robert Kennedy's interests with special permission to record events. The images that Dennis David said were shown to him by Pitzer might have been exposed by Robert Knudsen, and later obtained from him by Pitzer.

This controversy will never be definitively resolved unless film evidence is produced that backs up the recollections of Dennis David. My 'gut feeling' on this, however, is that Dennis David *did* view post mortem photos of President Kennedy in Bill Pitzer's office. Dennis David has been both consistent, and (in my view) credible on this account, even if we cannot determine the source of the images he recalls seeing.

SUMMARY OF MISSING PHOTOGRAPHS

The following chart should prove useful in summarizing for the reader, in a very succinct format, a catalogue of how many different photographic views taken at the autopsy on President John F. Kennedy on November 22-23, 1963 may be missing from the official collection of autopsy photographs in the National Archives:

Cumulative Count of Total Number of Missing Photos	Description of Photographic Image Taken at Autopsy Which Cannot Be Found in National Archives (i.e., not present when Military Inventory drawn up on 11-1-1966)	Sources for Allegation (Name and Venue)
1.	Entry wound in occipital bone of skull (outer table of skull, with scalp reflected)	Humes: W.C. testimony, HSCA panel, ARRB deposition; Boswell: ARRB deposition; Finck: Blumberg Report, HSCA panel
2.	Entry wound in occipital bone of skull (inner table of skull, taken after brain removed, to show beveling)	Humes: W.C. testimony, ARRB deposition; Finck: Blumberg Report, HSCA panel
3.	5 cm bruise in the top of the dome of the right pleural cavity, taken after right lung removed (i.e., "chest photograph")	Humes: W.C. testimony, HSCA panel, ARRB deposition; Boswell: HSCA OCR, ARRB deposition; Stringer: HSCA OCR, ARRB deposition
4.	Bruise on apical portion of the right lung itself	Boswell: HSCA OCR

5.	Photographs of probes in body	Knudsen: HSCA deposition; Karnei: ARRB interview
6.	Elevated view of whole body	Stringer: ARRB interview, ARRB deposition
7.	President lying 'face-down,' on stomach	Riebe: 1979 Lifton interview; Stringer: ARRB deposition; O'Donnell: ARRB interview
8.	President's body (torso), in sitting position (while held up by pathologists)	Riebe: 1989 Lifton interview; Stringer: ARRB deposition; Knudsen: HSCA deposition
9.	"Scene" photographs in morgue	Riebe: 1989 Lifton interview, and ARRB deposition
10.	Internal organs (presumably after removal)	Riebe: 1979 Lifton interview
11.	Brain, outside body after removal, being placed into metal pail	Riebe: ARRB deposition
12.	Body cavity, in the area of the adrenals	Stringer: ARRB deposition
13.	Brain inside cranium, prior to removal	Stringer: ARRB deposition
14.	Large, gaping occipital wound in rear of skull	Riebe: 1988 KRON-TV interview, and 1989 Lifton interview
15.	Small (2" diameter) occipital defect ("blow-out") in middle of posterior head	Spencer: ARRB interview, ARRB deposition
16.	Round hole (puncture wound) in anterior neck	Spencer: ARRB interview, ARRB deposition

17.	A brain after removal, photographed beside body	Spencer: ARRB deposition
18.	Round hole (puncture wound) high in forehead above right eye, near hairline	O'Donnell: ARRB interview; David: ARRB interview and Nigel Turner filmed interview; Malcolm Kilduff: reporting hearsay from Admiral Burkley at Parkland hospital

Each reader will make his or her own assessment of the degree of confidence to ascribe to each particular allegation in the above chart, based upon the credibility they assign to the witnesses mentioned, and the number of independent recollections of each event. One thing is certain, however—one possibly missing 4" x 5" color positive transparency, agonized over by Justice Department official Carl Belcher in 1966, cannot possibly account for all of these missing photographs.

TENTATIVE CONCLUSIONS

Within the collection of autopsy photographs alone, there is overwhelming evidence of a coverup in the assassination of President John F. Kennedy.

- More film was exposed in terms of both quantity, and in terms of different formats, than are in the paper trail of official receipts. The numbers are not even close.

- As many as 18 different post mortem views known to have been taken of the body of President Kennedy are missing from the collection in the Archives, if the eyewitnesses who made these claims are all correct. Even if only half of the claims are correct, this is a considerable number of different views to be missing, and too great to call a 'loose end.'

- Humes, Boswell, Ebersole, and Stringer all signed an inventory on November 10, 1966 which *falsely stated* that all photographs taken at the autopsy were present, and that they had no reason to believe any were missing—and they did so knowingly.

- Reliable witnesses at both Parkland hospital in Dallas, and at the autopsy at Bethesda NNMC, have claimed that a substantial portion of the back of the President's head was missing after he was shot on November 22, 1963. There are so many reliable witnesses who have said this, and said so under oath, that there is 'critical mass' here. Yet the photographs of the back-of-the-head do not show such damage. When the witnesses who say otherwise include experienced trauma room physicians; Secret Service agents; FBI agents; Navy doctors present at the autopsy (other than the pathologists); at one time or another, and to varying degrees, all three of the pathologists; embalmers; Navy photographers; and the Navy radiologist at the autopsy—and their observations are consistent about the fact that there was a large defect in the rear of the head devoid of scalp and bone—then there is *something* wrong with the photographs showing the back-of-the-head intact. This could account for the *real reason* why the existing autopsy photographs were not introduced into evidence by the Warren Commission. They may have been privately used to persuade many in government that President Kennedy was shot only from above and behind, in order to combat rumors of crossfire and conspiracy—but then kept 'officially sequestered' to prevent Parkland and Bethesda witnesses, who would have known they presented a false depiction of the wounds, from contradicting them—from impugning their authenticity—after the assassination. That effort succeeded initially, but it has now failed, thanks to the HSCA and its Ida Dox drawings, and the two collections of bootleg photographs; and Americans are left with unacceptable evidence of having been lied to about a crucial event in their country's history, at a crucial *time* in their country's history—at the height of the Cold War.

- All three autopsy pathologists have admitted to confusion and doubt regarding the back-of-the-head photos—specifically, because they cannot locate, with any confidence, the entrance wound in the rear of the skull which they examined at the autopsy and wrote about in the autopsy report. While their recollections about where they saw it located with their own eyes, how they palpated the wound with their own fingers, and how they measured it at the autopsy were remarkably consistent, their individual explanations for the anomalies in the back-of-the-head images have varied greatly. Something is wrong here. The responses of these 3 men when questioned over the years about this topic suggest that they knew more than they were admitting to, but that they could not get their stories straight. It is the biggest evidentiary mess of the Twentieth Century.

In Part II of this book, I will explain the 'big picture'—how a false brain specimen introduced into the photographic record, a rewritten autopsy report, intentionally deceptive autopsy photographs, and fraudulent skull x-rays all complemented each other, and constituted the means by which "the big lie" was introduced into American society and politics.

Chapter 5: The Autopsy X-Rays

There were only fourteen (14) autopsy x-rays placed in the Archives on October 31, 1966 when the Kennedy family Deed-of-Gift was executed. Of these, 3 are skull x-rays; 8 are views of various portions of the body; and three are repeats of views of loose skull fragments brought into the morgue by Secret Service agents at different times during the latter portions of the autopsy.[1] These fourteen x-rays are described as follows in the Military Inventory signed on November 10, 1966:

No.	Description from Inventory Conducted on 11-1-1966 and Signed on 11-10-1966
1.	Anterior-Posterior ["A-P"] View of the Skull, Slightly Heat Damaged (8" x 10" Film)
2.	Right Lateral View of the Skull, With Two Angle Lines Overdrawn on the Film (8" x 10" Film) [the "right lateral" skull x-ray in the literature]
3.	Lateral View of the Skull (8" x 10" Film) [the "left lateral" skull x-ray in the literature]
4.	X-Ray of 3 Fragments of Bone With the Larger Fragment Containing Metallic Fragments (8" x 10" Film)
5.	[Same as above]
6.	[Same as above]
7.	Anterior-Posterior View of the Abdomen (14" x 17" Film)
8.	Anterior-Posterior View of the Right Shoulder and Right Chest (14" x 17" Film)
9.	Anterior-Posterior View of the Chest (14" x 17" Film)
10.	Anterior-Posterior View of the Left Shoulder and Left Chest (14" x 17" Film)
11.	Anterior-Posterior View of the Abdomen and Lower Chest (14" x 17" Film)
12.	Anterior-Posterior View of Both Femurs Including Both Knee Joints (14" x 17" Film)

---

[1] Each one of these x-rays is labeled in the Military Inventory as depicting 3 fragments of bone, and they are consistently described in this way throughout the literature on the JFK assassination. Indeed, the photographic reproduction of one of these x-rays published by the HSCA shows only three fragments in the photograph. (See Figure 39.) However, when the x-rays were viewed in conjunction with a "hot light" in the Kodak lab at Rochester in November of 1997, it was discovered that there are actually four (4) fragments in each of the three x-rays. The fourth fragment is very, very small. Participants at the autopsy talk and write of the Secret Service introducing three (3) fragments from Dallas, not four. I conclude, therefore, that perhaps a small piece of bone broke off of, or became detached from, one of the 3 fragments during, or following, its examination by the pathologists.

13.	Anterior-Posterior View of the Pelvis. There Is A Small Round Density of Myelogram Media Projected Over the Sacral Canal (14" x 17" Film)
14.	Anterior-Posterior View of Lower Pelvis, Hips, and Upper Femurs (14" x 17" Film)

With the exception of the three x-rays of the loose fragments of skull bone, all others were taken in the Bethesda morgue, during the autopsy, with a portable x-ray machine for the sole purpose of finding bullets, or bullet fragments, in the body. The three x-rays of loose skull fragments were taken on the 4th floor of Bethesda, within the main x-ray department, on an installed machine which yielded an image superior to those produced by a portable unit.

In this chapter we will first examine the paper trail of the autopsy x-rays (which is not nearly as convoluted as that of the autopsy photographs), and will then study both the sworn testimony and unsworn interview responses of the radiologist at the JFK autopsy, CDR John H. Ebersole, M.D.; and of the two Navy enlisted x-ray technicians, Jerrol F. Custer and Edward F. Reed.[2] The reasons for studying their recollections is to determine whether there are any missing x-rays of the skull or the body; how many different rounds of x-rays were taken during the autopsy and for what reasons; and to attempt to establish a relative timeline of when x-rays where taken compared to other events—for example, were any x-rays taken before photographs, or vice-a-versa; and how soon after the arrival of the body were the first x-rays taken, and which ones were taken first? The 'big question,' of course, as in the case of the autopsy photographs, is whether or not the skull x-rays in the Archives today represent what eyewitnesses saw at the autopsy (and in Dallas); and if not, why not? In attempting to answer this question, we will revisit, in much more detail, the groundbreaking work of independent researcher David Mantik, M.D., Ph.D., which was first introduced to the reader in Chapter 1. He has visited the National Archives on nine occasions, with the permission of the Kennedy family's legal representative, and examined both the autopsy photographs and x-rays. We will again study his work with the skull x-rays, using optical densitometry, and the startling implications of this analysis to our ability to make sense out of the conflicting medical evidence in the Kennedy assassination. We will also compare how both Dr. Mantik, and Dr. John Fitzpatrick (the forensic radiologist who served as the ARRB's outside consultant on the JFK x-rays) have interpreted the head x-rays of President Kennedy at the National Archives, and what their interpretations tell us about damage to the brain at the time the x-rays were taken at Bethesda on November 22, 1963. Finally, we will review the testimony of Drs. Humes, Boswell, and Finck to the ARRB about certain aspects of the skull x-rays which are of particular interest to Dr. Mantik; their responses to the ARRB staff's questions bear heavily upon Dr. Mantik's hypothesis that the 3 skull x-rays are forged composite copy films. Also explored in this chapter will be the allegations that high-ranking members of the U.S. military may have been exercising control over the

---

[2]The testimony and unsworn comments of all 3 individuals—Ebersole, Custer, and Reed—provided extremely important information about the autopsy *unrelated* to the x-rays themselves. Those recollections will be revealed and assessed in this chapter as well, so this chapter is about much more than 'merely x-rays'—it is also about vital information concerning the autopsy revealed by the radiologist and the two x-ray technologists who were present.

autopsy—and the possible identity of two of these individuals.

THE PAPER TRAIL

The last 5 pages (pages 50-54) of the research memo I signed out on May 9, 1996 about the chain-of-custody study of the autopsy materials dealt with the x-rays. The content of those 5 pages is summarized below; I have added some additional, important background information about the Harper Fragment, the piece of skull bone found in Dealey Plaza which was later photographed and x-rayed.

The Ebersole-Kellerman Receipts, and the Contents of the Sibert-O'Neill Report

Just as in the case of the receipts for photographs exposed at the autopsy of President Kennedy on November 22-23, 1963, there are two versions of a receipt for x-ray film prepared by the Navy at Bethesda NNMC: first, a signed and annotated version (that is, with hand written emendations) containing the signatures of both CDR Ebersole and Roy Kellerman; and second, a retyped version incorporating the hand written changes, which is unsigned by either Ebersole or Kellerman. Both receipts for x-rays are addressed *from* CDR John H. Ebersole (the consulting radiologist at the JFK autopsy), *to* ASAIC Roy H. Kellerman of the U.S. Secret Service, and are dated November 22, 1963.

They are described below:

-First version. It states that the following number and types of x-ray films were taken this date:

- eight (8) 14 x 17 inch x-ray films; and
- three (3) 10 x 12 inch x-ray films. [The typed word and number "three (3)" preceding the measurement 10 x 12 have been lined out and replaced by hand with the quantities "six (6);" the initials "JHE" are written by hand next to this change.]

-Second version. The same receipt cited above has been retyped (on an unknown date), incorporating the pen-and-ink changes in quantity which were made in the line referring to 10 x 12 inch format x-ray film. The pen-and-ink changes to the original document are the only changes noted in the retyped document. It is not signed by either Ebersole or Kellerman, but the phrase "CERTIFIED TO BE A TRUE COPY" is typed above each of the undated signatures of CAPT J. H. Stover and RADM C. B. Galloway. If the reader counts the total number of x-rays listed on this document, the total is 14; this is the same total in the National Archives today. The contents of the retyped receipt are summarized below:

- eight (8) 14 x 17 inch x-ray films; and
- six (6) 10 x 12 inch x-ray films.

The Sibert-O'Neill Report, signed by those two FBI agents on November 26, 1963—but based upon the notes they independently took at the autopsy prior to leaving—lists only "11 x-rays" in its text. The obvious implication, at first glance, is that they must have departed before the series of 3 x-ray exposures of loose skull fragments from Dallas was exposed in the main x-ray laboratory later on the evening of November 22-23, 1963. But there is a problem with this assumption: Sibert and O'Neill actually *write* of the x-raying of the largest bone fragment from Dallas in their report, yet their total of eleven (11) x-rays does *not* match the total of fourteen (14) in the two Ebersole-to-Kellerman receipts. If they were aware of the critical x-rays taken of the 3 bone fragments—and of the significance of these x-rays—and in fact went to the trouble to write a special paragraph about that event, then why would they not boost their total of x-rays to reflect the new total following this event? Mere carelessness? We will never know, and are therefore left with an unexplained discrepancy between the Navy's receipt trail and the FBI report emanating from the autopsy.

The Harper Fragment

The Harper fragment is a key piece of evidence in the assassination, whose import will be discussed again in Part II. A summary of its origins would be in order here, since the FBI took x-rays of the bone fragment.

Andy Purdy's HSCA staff OCR, dated August 17, 1977, is the source for this summary information. (See Appendix 10.) A pre-med student named Billy Harper found a piece of bone in the grass of Dealey Plaza (on the south side of Elm Street) on November 23, 1963, and turned over the fragment that day to his uncle, Dr. Jack C. Harper. Dr. Harper took the fragment to Methodist Hospital on Monday, November 25th, at which time he contacted the FBI. *Dr. Harper told Andy Purdy that the consensus of the doctors who viewed the skull fragment was that it was a part of the **occipital** region of the skull.* Dr. Harper said the fragment was photographed at Methodist Hospital, and that he retained a photo of the skull fragment for about a year, at which time the FBI took it from him. Dr. Harper said the skull fragment had relatively fresh blood on it.

Purdy spoke to Dr. A. B. Cairns, former Chief of Pathology at Methodist Hospital, about the so-called Harper Fragment. Dr. Cairns told Purdy that the piece of skull fragment came from an area approximately 2.5 to 3 inches above the spine area in the back of the head. Cairns told Purdy that it had the markings of a piece of skull fragment from the ***lower occipital area,*** specifically: suture and inner markings where blood vessels run around the base of the skull. Dr. Cairns remembered a small area of the skull fragment showing grayish discoloration suggesting metal had stained the bone. He said he had experience with damage caused to bone fragments by lead in the past, which looked similar to this discoloration. Cairns told Purdy that he could see blood markings which indicated that the skull fragment had been dislodged recently. Cairns told Purdy that there were no markings on the bone specifying whether the skull fragment was either an entrance or an exit wound, but he expressed an opinion that he thought it came from an area close to the entry wound by virtue of the way the tables [of the skull] were broken.

Fortunately for history, those at Methodist Hospital who examined the skull fragment took color photographs of its external surface and its internal surface next to a ruler, for scale, and honest civil servants at the FBI preserved those photographs for history by placing them in the National

Archives.[3] (See Figures 41 and 42, reproduced from the HSCA report.) I say 'fortunately for history,' because the Harper Fragment, like the brain and tissue sections and tissue slides from President Kennedy's autopsy, has disappeared. The last person known for sure to have his hands on it was RADM George G. Burkley, MC, USN, Military Physician to the President. A two-part typewritten receipt for the delivery of what is surely the Harper fragment was signed by Dr. Burkley on 11/27/1963, and reads as follows:

11/27/63 5:15 p.m. Just received a small Neman Markus [sic] box about 2.5" x 3.5" containing material which had been discussed previously with them [meaning the FBI]. A letter of the full report will be made. This material will be deposited with the Commanding Officer of the Bethesda Naval Hospital for subsequent retention with other material of similar nature. Material was received in the presence of Dr. James M. Young and me. The contact with the FBI was Roy Jevous at Code 175 x 353. (Signature, above typewritten name) G. G. Burkley, M.D.

Received from Robert I. Bouck, Special Agent in Charge, U. S. Secret Service, specimen of bone that appears to be from a skull, turned over to Secret Service by David Burros. It was apparently found on the parkway near the scene of the assassination (marked fragment No. 2 for identification).

Both above described specimens to be turned over to Naval Hospital by Dr. Burkley for examination, analysis, and retention until other disposition is directed. (Signature, above typewritten name) G. G. Burkley, M.D.

Comments follow. There is no known receipt in the JFK Records Collection *to* Burkley *from* any senior Naval officer at the Bethesda complex—not from CAPT Stover, or CAPT Canada, or from RADM Galloway—for these two bone fragments. The Naval mind set on 11-22-63 seems to have been extremely careful to record receipts for items known to have been relinquished to the Secret Service. Since there are no extant receipts for the delivery to Bethesda of either the Harper or Burros fragments, I wonder whether Burkley ever turned them over at all. If he did, and receipts were executed, it now appears that these receipts were later 'deep-sixed.' When Burkley says above that the Harper and Burros Fragments will be turned over to Bethesda for "subsequent retention with *other material of a similar nature*," he is probably referring to the 3 skull fragments x-rayed after

---

[3]Neither the Secret Service nor Dr. Burkley got their hands on these photographs, so the photos of the Harper fragment didn't disappear like the fragment itself did. I should make clear to the reader at this point that *all of the bone fragments* that appear on x-rays no. 4, 5, and 6, *as well as* the Harper fragment, and an additional fragment found on Elm Street by a person named David Burros, are *missing*. We know from the ARRB depositions that the 3 bone fragments brought into the morgue late in the autopsy by the Secret Service were *not* placed back into the body during reconstruction. Although it is *possible* that the Secret Service got rid of the bone fragments of President Kennedy's skull, I think that the prime suspect is either Dr. George Burkley—or Robert Kennedy, if Burkley secretly transferred them to RFK.

the autopsy on JFK, which were *not* placed back into the body by the embalmers from the Gawler's funeral home. As we shall see later in this book, Burkley orally invoked the authority of Robert F. Kennedy, the President's brother and Attorney General, to obtain the brain of President Kennedy from Drs. Humes and Stover, and almost certainly did so prior to the President's funeral on the afternoon of November 25th; he likely later used similar pressure to obtain from the officials at Bethesda the 3 skull fragments the Secret Service introduced into the morgue late in the autopsy—as well as the Harper and Burros Fragments, if he ever turned them over to RADM Galloway or CAPT Stover in the first place.

Since no other person in the President's limousine suffered a head wound, and since the Harper Fragment was observed by at least two doctors to exhibit traces of fresh blood, the Harper Fragment *must* have come from President Kennedy. This cannot be reasonably questioned by anyone. If it was indeed occipital bone, as it was identified to be in Dallas by competent and disinterested physicians with 'no axe to grind' who held it in their own hands and examined it close-up with their own eyes, then the autopsy photographs showing the scalp in the back-of-the-head to be intact *cannot be authentic.* A fragment approximately 2.5" by 2.25" in its largest dimensions cannot possibly have exited the occipital region of the skull without lacerating the scalp in the rear of the head. Similarly, the recollections of those such as the numerous Parkland hospital doctors and nurses on the treatment staff; Navy photographer Saundra Spencer; Gawler's funeral home embalmer Tom Robinson; FBI agents Sibert and O'Neill; and Secret Service Agents Roy Kellerman and Clint Hill, who have described missing scalp and bone in the back of President Kennedy's head, tend to be corroborated by, and are entirely consistent with, a Harper fragment that represented part of President Kennedy's occipital bone. Thus, the provenance and potential importance of the Harper fragment have now been amply demonstrated, and need not be covered again in detail later in this book.

Now, on to the evidence related to the FBI's x-rays of the Harper Fragment.

An FBI internal memorandum from Mr. R. H. Jevons to Mr. Conrad, dated 11/27/63, states in part "...we x-rayed the bone [the Harper fragment] and examined it microscopically for the presence of bullet metal but none was found...". I personally sighted these 3 x-rays of the Harper Fragment in the National Archives in May of 1996, in the presence of Steve Tilley. *However, they are not listed in the paper trail of JFK post mortem x-rays discussed earlier in this chapter.* This indicates to me that they were never in the possession of the Secret Service, and therefore never ended up on the Burkley Inventory and Receipt dated April 26, 1965 when all of the autopsy materials in the possession of the Secret Service were transferred to Evelyn Lincoln in her private office in the National Archives. Clearly, the FBI held onto them until they were deposited directly into the National Archives.

A second FBI document, a letter from the FBI to Rear Admiral George Burkley, dated November 29, 1963, formally notifies RADM Burkley that "...this piece of bone was x-rayed." The letter simply transmits to Burkley the information discussed in the internal FBI memo of November 27th, from Jevons to Conrad, mentioned above.

Dr. Burkley's April 26, 1965 Inventory and Receipt of Materials Transferred to Mrs. Evelyn Lincoln at the National Archives

This document lists the following items pertaining to x-rays:

> Envelope containing 8 x-ray negatives 14" x 17"; 6 x-ray negatives 10" x 12"; 12 black-and-white prints 11" x 14"; 17 black-and-white prints 14" x 17"; all negatives and prints pertaining to x-rays that were taken at the autopsy.

I do not know who made the black-and-white prints of the x-rays—that is , whether it was James K. Fox of the Secret Service (who had a black-and-white photography lab of his own), or Vincent Madonia of NPC Anacostia (at the request of Fox), or someone else. The prints of the x-rays may just possibly have been used to brief selected Warren Commission staff members, since a June 14, 1966 memo from the Secret Service to the Treasury Department about the forthcoming Kennedy family Deed-of-Gift states, in an aside, that the x-rays were used to brief the Warren Commission staff on the autopsy procedure and results. (It would be much safer and more convenient to display black-and-white prints of the x-rays for this purpose, than the actual x-rays themselves. Prints of the x-rays could have been carried to the site where the staff members worked, whereas likely the staff members would have had to come to Mr. Bouck's office at the Old Executive Office building to review the actual x-rays. When briefing lay persons, prints of x-rays are generally just as useful as the actual x-rays.)

Neither the Harper fragment, the Burros fragment, nor any of the loose skull fragments x-rayed at Bethesda the night of the autopsy are mentioned anywhere in the Burkley Inventory and Receipt. If they had been, they would likely have been mentioned in paragraph 9 with the other biological materials. Presumably, therefore, these skull fragments were all disposed of long before the April 25, 1966 inventory was conducted. The inventory conducted that day seems to have been very, very accurate and was witnessed by numerous persons; if any of the loose bone fragments from the skull of President Kennedy had been present that day, they would have been noted on the inventory.

The Kennedy Family Deed-of-Gift

The wording pertaining to the autopsy x-rays in the Deed-of-Gift letter is identical to that in the Burkley Inventory and Receipt of April 26, 1965.

The Military Inventory Signed on November 10, 1966

This inventory, conducted by Humes, Boswell, Ebersole, and Stringer, was discussed at length in Chapter 4. Presumably it was Dr. Ebersole who provided the anatomical descriptions of each x-ray for this inventory, for which a draft was prepared on November 1st, and the smooth version was signed on November 10th, 1966. The descriptions provided are reproduced essentially verbatim in the descriptive chart at the beginning of this chapter. There has been no change whatsoever to the contents of the x-ray collection since it was received by the National Archives on October 31, 1966.

DR. FINCK'S HSCA TESTIMONY PROVIDES A BASELINE REFERENCE FOR WHEN AND WHY CERTAIN X-RAYS WERE TAKEN

When he testified before the HSCA Forensic Pathology Panel on March 11, 1978, Dr. Finck discussed the sequence and timing of the taking of head x-rays and what he called the 'whole body survey.'

Petty: ...When did you arrive first in the autopsy room?

Finck: It was approximately 2030 hours, 8:30 P.M.

Petty: Was the autopsy in progress at that time?

Finck: Yes, it was. I arrived after the start of the autopsy. Dr. Humes called me at home, asking that I come to the National Naval Medical Center.

_____

Baden: Dr. Finck, just so I understand, when you arrived the brain had already been removed from the cranial cavity?

Finck: As far as I remember, yes.

Baden: And at that point when you arrived, did a decision have to be made as to whether to proceed further or not in the autopsy?

Finck: *Having only x-ray films of the head,* I am the one who suggested the whole body x-ray survey before going further, as far as I remember, to rule out the presence of an intact bullet in that cadaver...[Author's emphasis]

_____

Petty: All right. Now let me recapitulate as I understand what you have said here. One, you arrived at about 8:30 in the evening, give or take a little bit. Two, at the time you arrived you believed the brain had already been removed.

Finck: Yes.

Petty: What was the situation that was verbally presented to you at the time you got there?...What was your briefing, in other words?

Finck: I don't remember...I remember, however, that on the phone Dr. Humes told me he had good x-ray films of the head. That I remember.

Summarizing, Finck's testimony means that *skull x-rays* had been taken, developed, and interpreted *before* Dr. Humes called him on the telephone and invited him to participate in the autopsy; and, if his memory was correct, that when he arrived at the morgue at about 8:30 P.M., *no other x-rays had yet been taken,* but the brain had been removed. Finck testified that the whole body x-ray survey had been his own idea, and that it was carried out after 8:30 P.M.

The reader has by now become amply familiar with the exacting nature of Dr. Finck's "anally retentive" personality. He would not have made the statements quoted above, under oath, unless he were *quite certain* about his recollections. Another reason I tend to have confidence in his recollections here is because they were tied to specific events: a "before" event (before he arrived at the morgue, when he took Humes' phone call and was told Humes had good x-rays of the head), and an "after" event (the lack of any x-rays of the body when he arrived, and the corresponding need for a whole body survey).

DR. JOHN H. EBERSOLE TESTIFIES BEFORE THE HSCA FORENSIC PATHOLOGY PANEL ON MARCH 11, 1978

Most of the questions for Dr. Ebersole naturally revolved around the taking of x-rays; the few questions about autopsy photography were covered previously in Chapter 4. But interspersed among his testimony about the x-rays are several revealing comments about the autopsy, as reproduced below.

Since the head of his department (a CAPT Brown) was out of town on 11-22-63, circumstances placed CDR John H. Ebersole in a position where he was asked to interpret the x-rays taken at President Kennedy's autopsy, even though he was only the acting chief of the radiology department at Bethesda NNMC, and was not yet board-certified as a radiologist. His deposition transcript reveals that he had served onboard the first two U.S. nuclear-powered submarines, and he became a board-certified radiologist in December 1963, the month after the assassination. He indirectly downplayed the significance of this when he reminded the HSCA panel that the only purpose for taking the x-rays on November 22, 1963 was to locate bullets or bullet fragments in the cadaver of the President, not to perform any diagnostics. He testified to the HSCA panel that the portable x-ray machine, although not the best tool for diagnostic analysis, was more than adequate for the purpose of looking for bullets or bullet fragments in the cadaver.

Dr. Ebersole Testifies That the Throat Wound Was Sutured Upon Arrival of the Body at Bethesda, and That the Back of the Head Was Missing

When his deposition began, Dr. Ebersole was asked to describe the condition of the body of President Kennedy when he first saw it. He made two noteworthy responses—noteworthy in that they are contrary to other indicators in the record:

Baden: ...Could you give us any recollections that you have now of the condition of the President's body when you first saw it...

Ebersole: ...upon removing the body from the coffin, the anterior aspect, the only things noticeable were a small irregular ecumonic [ecchymotic?] area above the super ecolobular [supraorbital?] ridge *and a neatly sutured transverse surgical wound across the low neck.*[4] [Author's emphasis]...as we turned the body [over] on the autopsy table there was a textbook classical wound of entrance [in the] upper right back to the right of the midline three or four centimeters to the right of the midline just perhaps inside the medical board [medial border?] to the upper scapula...*The back of the head was missing* and the regular messy wound. [Author's emphasis]

This observation that the back of the head was missing did not seem to cause any stir among the HSCA panel members. Not one of them asked any follow-on questions about this crucial statement. It was a remarkable failure on their part to exhibit curiosity about whether or not the autopsy photographs showing the back-of-the-head to be intact did, or did not, represent the authentic condition of the body at the autopsy.

Dr. Ebersole Discusses the Sequence of X-Rays Taken and His Own Role

His testimony continued:

Ebersole: ...So prior to starting the autopsy we were asked to x-ray the body to determine the presence of a bullet. We took several x-rays of the skull, chest, trunk. These were taken in the autopsy room on the autopsy table. They were hand carried by me in their cassettes to what we designate as Tower Four, the fourth floor of the hospital, handled by a dark room technician, given back to me and hand carried by me to the autopsy room.

Comments follow. **First**, upon initial review I believed Dr. Finck's testimony regarding the timing and sequence of the first two major rounds of x-rays (namely, first of the head, prior to Humes calling him at home; followed after Finck's arrival by a whole body survey) was more believable, and more precise, than Ebersole's. Ebersole appears to have *conflated* the taking of the head x-rays and body x-rays—what Finck testified to as being separate events—into *one event* in his testimony. **Second**, Ebersole is placing himself here 'at the center of the action' by claiming that *he himself* hand carried all x-rays to the fourth floor, and then hand carried them all back to the morgue. This 'illusion of centrality' by some eyewitnesses to events was discussed previously in this book. Ebersole is not believable here because *both* Ed Reed *and* Jerrol Custer, the two enlisted x-ray technicians assisting Dr. Ebersole in the morgue, testified to the ARRB that they had *each exposed* the x-rays all by themselves; had *each hand carried* the x-ray cassettes up to the x-ray department laboratory on the fourth floor; had *each developed* the x-rays themselves; and then had *each hand carried them* back to the morgue. (Their testimony will be covered later in this chapter.) The reader should view with skepticism here any claim by Ebersole that he carried the x-ray cassettes to the fourth floor himself, not just because Custer and Reed disagreed with him, but also because a

_____

[4]Neither Humes, Boswell, Finck, nor any of the enlisted assistants in the morgue on 11-22-63 recalled that the tracheostomy had been sutured when the body was received. This is no reason, in-and-of-itself, to disregard Ebersole's testimony here. If the sutures were quickly removed, or if other viewers were preoccupied with studying the enormous size of the President's head wound, this could explain why they did not recall the sutured tracheostomy.

photograph taken at Bethesda by a photojournalist on 11-22-63 shows Jerrol Custer, the young Navy petty officer who was Reed's instructor, carrying x-ray cassettes in a hallway at Bethesda.[5]

Ebersole: [continuing] The initial films showed the usual metallic fragments in the skull but no evidence of a slug, a bullet. This was a little bit disconcerting. *We were asked by the Secret Service agents present to repeat the films and did so.* Once again there was no evidence of a bullet. [Author's emphasis]

It is not clear from this testimony whether Ebersole means that *both head and body x-rays* were repeated, or that *only the body x-rays were repeated.* We will return later in this section to an examination of Ebersole's recollections about the sequencing and content of different sessions of x-rays, and will compare his recollections to Dr. Finck's, in further detail.

Dr. Ebersole Testifies to 'Early' Knowledge of a Bullet Wound in the Front of the Neck

Next comes one of the most intriguing recollections in Ebersole's testimony:

Ebersole: I believe by ten or ten thirty approximately *a communication had been established with Dallas and it was learned that there had been a wound of exit in the lower neck that had been surgically repaired.* I don't know if this was post mortem or pre mortem but at that point the confusion as far as we were concerned stopped. [Author's emphasis]

Later in his deposition, the head of the HSCA panel, Dr. Michael Baden, questioned Ebersole about this recollection:

Baden: ...Now you have mentioned that the tracheostomy was sutured when you first saw it.

Ebersole: There was a sutured wound, a transverse wound at the base of the neck.

Baden: Do you remember any other sutured wounds?

Ebersole: No, I do not.

Baden: Sutured incisions that might have been—

Ebersole: No.

---

[5]The photograph is published in David Lifton's book *Best Evidence,* and was used by Custer at his ARRB deposition to back up his claim that he was the person who carried the cassettes to the fourth floor lab. Custer verified, during his ARRB deposition, that it was he and Reed in the photo, and that he was carrying the x-ray cassettes, while Reed (his student) was carrying his (Custer's) heavy, lead-lined apron.

Comments follow. **First**, if true, Ebersole's testimony about learning there was an *exit wound* in the front of the President's neck *during the autopsy* means that Humes perjured himself before both the Warren Commission and the ARRB about not learning there was a bullet wound in the front of the throat until early Saturday morning when he spoke to Dr. Perry in Dallas. **Second**, Boswell testified to the ARRB that the pathologists *did know on 11-22-63 at the autopsy that there was an exit wound in the front of the President's neck,* thus contradicting Humes and corroborating what Ebersole testified to here. **Third**, no one at Parkland hospital on 11-22-63 described the President's throat wound, orally or in written treatment reports, as anything but an entrance wound. **Fourth**, no one at Parkland hospital did any surgical repair of the anterior neck bullet wound, or the tracheotomy, whatsoever.

So what does this mean? **First**, we know that Federal agents were using the telephone inside the morgue 'all night long,' based upon the accounts of several autopsy eyewitnesses. **Second**, Nurse Audrey Bell volunteered to Jeremy Gunn and me when we interviewed her in March 1997 at her home in Texas, that Dr. Perry complained to her on Saturday morning, November 23, 1963 that 'people from Bethesda' had been bothering him on the phone all night long, trying to get him to change his professional opinion about having seen an *entry* wound in the front of President Kennedy's neck, to one of having seen an *exit* wound instead. (This important hearsay evidence will be discussed again later in Part I, in my chapter about the short trip Jeremy and I took to Texas in 1997.) I don't know what Dr. Perry told his tormentors on the evening of November 22-23, 1963, but I do know that he straddled the fence rather nicely during his March 1964 testimony before the Warren Commission, testifying to Arlen Specter that the wound in the front of the neck "could have been either" an entrance wound or an exit wound. By then, Perry was already compromising with the truth as he had first expressed it on the day the President died, when he stated unequivocally, 3 different times at the Parkland press conference while standing next to Dr. Clark, that the bullet that pierced the President's neck was coming <u>from the front</u>. **Third**, since we know for a certainty that *no one* at Parkland tried to 'surgically repair' or suture either the bullet wound in the throat or the tracheostomy, I conclude that David Lifton was correct when he speculated in *Best Evidence* that conspirators had retrieved the bullet from a frontal shot that impacted the anterior neck just below the larynx to the right of the midline, by probing deep inside the tracheostomy incision (which they knew had been made through the bullet wound) with forceps, and that in doing so they had greatly enlarged that wound—from the neat, 2 to 3 centimeter wide incision Dr. Perry remembered making, to the large wound 7 to 8 centimeters in width that Humes testified about to Arlen Specter, and which he described in the autopsy report as having "widely gaping, irregular edges." Suturing the enlarged tracheostomy may have been an attempt to disguise the amount of damage inflicted by the clandestine probing. **Fourth**, and finally, I conclude that in announcing that "Dallas" said there was an "exit wound" in the front of the neck, and that it had been "<u>surgically repaired</u>" in Dallas, the agent using the telephone, or one of his superiors in the morgue, was attempting to both cover up the tracks of those who had been involved in removing evidence from the body—evidence that a wound had been *enlarged* during an evidence-tampering operation—as well as *provide an excuse for why it was sutured* when the body arrived at Bethesda. **Fifth**, if this hypothesis is correct, the frontal shot that hit the anterior neck may have *lodged on top of the pleural dome, directly above the right lung,* after lacerating the right side of the trachea. [A .22 cal. round fired from a silenced rifle would have been an underpowered round.] This location would have allowed its surreptitious removal prior to autopsy (through the hastily and crudely enlarged tracheostomy wound). If true, it also provides an alternative explanation for the bruise on top of the right lung and the corresponding one at the top of the right pleural dome: that damage, rather than representing the mid-point of a transiting bullet's purported track through the body from rear to front, *may very well have actually represented where the bullet from a frontal shot lodged after it stopped,* consistent with Dr. Kemp Clark's opinion, expressed to the *New York Times* on the weekend of the assassination, that the frontal bullet 'ranged downward in the President's chest and did not exit.' I suspect Dr. Ebersole's recollection of a sutured tracheostomy wound **is correct,** *because he remembers the explanation coming from Dallas, via telephone, that the wound had been "surgically repaired."* Even if his recollection of suturing is *not correct,* the bruise atop the right lung could still very well represent *where a frontal bullet lodged in the body,* with the crudely enlarged tracheostomy that Humes described to the ARRB as a gaping wound that "obliterated" the bullet wound, serving as evidence of its surreptitious removal after the body left Parkland hospital, and before the Bethesda autopsy began.

Dr. Ebersole Drops A Bombshell: The Large Bone Fragment from Dallas Was <u>Occipital</u> Bone

The deposition continued:

Ebersole: The only function that I had was later in the evening, early in the morning, perhaps about twelve thirty *a large fragment of **occipital** bone* was received from Dallas and at Dr. Finck's request I x-rayed these [sic]. These were the last x-rays I took. [Author's emphasis]

I commented in the previous chapter on my amazement that no one on the HSCA panel asked Ebersole why he characterized this fragment of bone as occipital. Every time I reread the Ebersole deposition transcript, I am amazed anew. This *largest* of the three late-arriving Dallas fragments that were x-rayed as a group, *according to the autopsy report,* showed *external* evidence of beveling interpreted by the autopsy pathologists as an *exit wound,* and the x-ray of the fragment revealed minute particles of metal in the margin of the semi-circular exit wound in this bone. (The autopsy report does not address from what part of the skull the bone came.) If the bone fragment <u>was occipital bone,</u> as Ebersole claimed in his HSCA testimony, **then it was evidence of exit in the rear of President Kennedy's head, based upon the unambiguous statement about beveling of the outer surface of that bone fragment in the autopsy report.** (And evidence of exit in the *rear* of President Kennedy's head would be proof of a fatal shot from the *front*—and therefore the simplest, most basic proof of conspiracy, since the Warren Commission conclusively established that *other shots* definitely came from the rear, from at least one site: the Texas School Book Depository.) The implications of Ebersole's statement here were "off-scale," and should have been readily apparent to anyone paying attention (who had an open mind), and yet <u>not one member</u> of the HSCA Forensic Pathology Panel asked Ebersole ***why*** he testified that the bone was occipital. The Sibert-O'Neill report states its dimensions were 10 x 6.5 centimeters. The exact passage in the Sibert-O'Neill report reads as follows:

Also during the latter stages of the autopsy, a piece of the skull measuring 10 x 6.5 centimeters *was brought to Dr. Humes who was instructed that this had been removed from the President's skull.* Immediately this section of skull was x-rayed, at which time it was determined by Dr. Humes that one corner of this section revealed minute metal particles and inspection of this same area disclosed a chipping of the top portion of this piece, both of which indicated that this had been the point of exit of the bullet entering the skull region. [Author's emphasis]

Clearly, Sibert and O'Neill are talking about the same fragment testified to by Ebersole, and written about in the autopsy report. But what about the wording used when the fragment was presented to Dr. Humes? "Dr. Humes...was instructed that this had been removed from the President's skull." Dr. Boswell testified to the ARRB that the Secret Service had also brought a smaller fragment into the morgue that completed the circumference of the *entry wound low in the occipital region;* now, even later in the autopsy, the Secret Service provided the largest of the three fragments they introduced into the morgue, providing evidence of *exit.* Was the Secret Service introducing evidence of desired results into the morgue whenever confusion or uncertainty predominated? Was the autopsy being 'stage-managed?' Was the word "removed" a Freudian slip by those who had personally been engaged in, or who had knowledge of, surreptitious alteration of the President's body?[6] ASAIC Roy Kellerman also used the word "removed" twice in his sworn Warren Commission testimony before Arlen Specter:

Specter: I would like to develop your understanding and your observations of the four wounds on President Kennedy.

Kellerman: O.K. This all transpired in the morgue of the Naval hospital in Bethesda, sir. He had a large wound this size [indicating].

Specter: Indicating a circle with your finger of the diameter of 5 inches; would that be approximately correct?

Kellerman: Yes, circular; yes, on this part of the head [indicating].

Specter: Indicating *the rear portion* of the head.[7] [Author's emphasis]

Kellerman: Yes. [See Figure 82.]

Specter: More to the right side of the head?

---

[6]David Lifton makes clear in *Best Evidence* his conclusion that something akin to a crude craniotomy had been performed on the President prior to his arrival at Bethesda: the avulsed defect in the right rear of the skull and been greatly enlarged, to a wound about 5 times its original size, so that it extended well into the parietal and temporal regions, and what was left of the brain had been severely disrupted, presumably for the purpose of removing bullets or bullet fragments—key evidence—from the brain.

[7]Incidentally, this verifies Ebersole's HSCA testimony (discussed above) that the back of the head was missing when the President's body was first examined at autopsy.

Kellerman: Right. *This was removed.* [Author's emphasis]

Specter: When you say, "This was removed," what do you mean by this?

Kellerman: *The skull part was removed.* [Author's emphasis]

Specter: All right.

Ford: Above the ear and back?

Kellerman: To the left of the ear, sir, and a little high; yes. About right in here [indicating].

It's clear to me at this point that Kellerman is saying the large skull defect was in the right rear of the skull, posterior to the right ear.

Specter: When you say "removed," by that do you mean that it was absent when you saw him, or taken off by the doctor?

Kellerman: It was absent when I saw him.

Had Kellerman slipped up here and revealed more than he had intended? Possibly. Although Specter had given him an "out" by asking a leading question and suggesting that perhaps a Bethesda pathologist had removed missing skull bone, Kellerman did not take advantage of it. He couldn't, because Dr. Humes had publicly made an oral utterance shortly after 8:00 PM, when the Dallas casket was opened, that there had been "surgery of the head area, namely, in the top of the skull"—implying that someone *other than himself* was responsible for said surgery—and the two FBI agents present had dutifully recorded this statement in their official report about the autopsy prepared on November 26, 1963. (As I will reveal later in Chapter 6, I now suspect that if Kellerman had been honest enough—and foolish enough—to attribute the removal of the bone fragments to the Navy pathologists, he would in all likelihood have been compromising his own covert operation, which he was trying so hard to stage-manage that evening.) So I conclude that Roy Kellerman took the easy way out of the pickle he had placed himself in with his Freudian slip, and chose the safest of the two responses offered to him by Specter's leading question, saying: "It was absent when I saw him." Kellerman's answer did not address the *causation* for the bone that was missing, and I find this significant. His use of the term "removed" was extremely suggestive of post mortem surgery, and when asked to explain his use of this term under oath, *he never mentioned damage by a bullet* as the explanation for the missing bone, or as the reason why he had used the term "removed."

Later in his testimony, Kellerman used the term "removed" again:

Kellerman: Just for the record, I wish to have this down. While the President is in the morgue, he is lying flat. And with the part of the skull *removed,* and the hole in the throat, nobody was aware until they lifted him up that there was a hole in his shoulder. [Author's emphasis]

This time Specter didn't even bat an eye.

Ebersole is Questioned About the Number of X-Rays Taken, Views Shot, and Sequence of Exposures

Baden: A couple of questions relative to the x-rays. We have with us the x-rays numbered 1 to 4.[8] Do you recall that those are the numbers of x-rays that you had placed in the Archives?

Ebersole: Yes.

Baden: When you placed the x-rays in the Archives were you satisfied that they were each and every x-ray that you took? Is there a possibility that there were additional x-rays that you did not see when you put the x-rays in the Archives?

Ebersole: No. Those were the numbers we took of which there were images.

Baden: Did you take x-rays on which there were not images?

Ebersole: That may be possible. One film had no image and it was destroyed.[9]

Baden: But there were no x-rays other than the ones that were put into the Archives?

Ebersole: That is right.

Baden: Do you recall when you took the x-rays in the sequence of taking x-rays and you took the x-rays initially before any incision was made in the body [sic]?

Ebersole: That is right.

Baden: You took the head, chest, abdomin [sic], extremities?

---

[8]The transcript reads "1 to 4," but I am sure it is a typo by the court reporter; Baden must surely have spoken "1 to 14," otherwise Ebersole would have corrected him.

[9]Ebersole here probably meant photographic film—autopsy photographs, not x-ray film. This claim of his that one piece of photographic film was destroyed because it contained no image was contradicted by Knudsen, who testified to Purdy later in 1978 (in August) that even if there had been no image on a piece of photographic film of the President's autopsy, it would nevertheless *not* have been destroyed. I do not put much credence in this statement by Ebersole about photographic film, since he was not present when any film was developed, and was witness only to a speculative discussion between Humes, Boswell, and Stringer on 11-1-66.

Ebersole: The order was skull first, then chest, then trunk.

Baden: I see. When Colonel Finck came in *these had already been taken?*   [Author's emphasis]

Ebersole: Yes, *and repeated once.*   [Author's emphasis]

I initially found this extremely doubtful, as explained above earlier in this chapter, based upon Finck's testimony.

Baden: Now when you say repeated, were x-rays repeated after the autopsy had started? Do you have an independent recollection of that?

Ebersole: The second group of x-rays were taken either before the incision was made or very shortly thereafter.

Baden: Maybe your memory will be refreshed as we go through the x-rays.

Ebersole: Yes.

Baden: ...Number one, what is this long rectangular object at the lower portion of the x-rays of the head?...Was that a measuring device or a radial [radio?] opaque?

Ebersole: It is a rectangular metal object. It looks *as if it could have been used as a measuring device,* yes. [Author's emphasis]

The object being referred to here is either a personal marker used by the x-ray technicians, or the rectangular metal tag upon which was imprinted the five digit *unit identification code (or UIC)* for the Bethesda NNMC, "21296."   In the Navy the UIC is a reference number assigned to each command which is used for logistics, personnel record keeping, and financial tracking purposes, and is unique to the command to which it is assigned, to the exclusion of all other commands. This metal tag is found in all of the JFK x-rays *except for* 2 taken of the body, and those taken of the loose skull fragments, and identifies the x-rays bearing its image as having been taken at Bethesda NNMC. If the size of the actual metal tag were precisely known, then *measuring its dimensions on the x-ray* and comparing those dimensions to the *actual dimensions* of the tag could also be used to determine the "magnification factor" of the x-ray. The "magnification factor" is expressed as the ratio of the real size of a known object divided by the size of its x-ray image. (Because the x-ray beam expands as it exits the machine, x-ray images recorded on the x-ray film are always slightly larger than the object in real life that was x-rayed. A magnification factor is expressed as a decimal fraction of some value less than 1.0; that is, if the radiologist multiplies the size of the anatomical area of interest on the x-ray by the magnification factor—say .89, for example—then he can obtain the actual size of the object in the body that is depicted on the x-ray.) Regardless of what Ebersole was referring to, the principle is the same.

The reason Dr. Ebersole did not give Dr. Baden a better answer as to what the metal rectangular object was—he did not seem to realize it was also an identification device, and seemed to be guessing that it was a measuring device—is because it was not something he himself placed in the x-ray cassette. It was placed there by one of the x-ray technicians, either Custer or Reed, prior to taking each x-ray—it was something they routinely placed in the cassette prior to exposing each image. Its absence in the three x-rays of the loose fragments taken in the main laboratory later that evening is another indicator that Ebersole (or someone else) may have taken those x-rays, and not the x-ray technicians.

Purdy:	Dr. Baden, which x-ray?
Baden:	X-rays 1 and 2 and it is also present on x-ray no. 3. Now, number one, do you recognize the three skull x-rays, 1, 2, and 3, as the ones you had taken?
Ebersole:	When I last saw these I personally affixed some metal tape to them. Was that on these at any time?
Baden:	The red metal tape numbered 1, 2, and 3.
Ebersole:	These are the films.
Baden:	These are the films that you took?
Ebersole:	Yes.
Baden:	And that you put into the Archives later?
Ebersole:	Right.

Baden:	On looking at film no. 1 you see there are two artifact points. Could [you] describe those and indicate what you think they are?
Ebersole:	These are raised blisters, rounded areas on the x-ray film due to overheating the emulsion and probably coming about [as a result of] placing it on what we call a hot light...
Baden:	Do you have any knowledge when and how they occurred?
Ebersole:	I don't know. It may have happened that night and I may have been the guilty party as well as under standard view boxes [sic].

I seriously doubt that the burn marks on the A-P x-ray happened on the night of the autopsy, since it is extremely doubtful that there was a "hot light" in the morgue, which Ebersole seemed to have realized in mid-answer above. (A hot light is something that was likely present only in the main x-ray department on the fourth floor; only standard viewing boxes would likely have been present in the morgue.) If this x-ray is a forged composite copy film, as Dr. Mantik suspects, then the burn marks definitely *did not occur on the night of the autopsy,* and could only have occurred after the copy film was manufactured. The ARRB's consulting forensic radiologist, Dr. Fitzpatrick, told us that he had *never seen* burn marks like the two artifacts on the A-P x-ray, and stated that someone was very careless with a hot light. (More on this later in this chapter.)

Dr. Ebersole Drops Yet Another Bombshell: In His Opinion, President Kennedy Was Shot in the Side of the Head (Not in the Back of the Head)

Baden: Do you on examination of these films [the 3 head x-rays] have an opinion as to where the gunshot *wound of entrance* was in the head radiologically? [Author's emphasis]

Ebersole: In my opinion ***it would have come from the side*** and [sic] the basis of the films. I guess that is all that can be said about the films at this time. [Author's emphasis]

In the statement immediately above, Ebersole, who had already testified to the HSCA panel that *the back of the head was missing* when the body arrived at Bethesda, and that a large bone fragment 'from Dallas' was *occipital bone,* has just said that the head x-rays indicated to him that the bullet entry wound came *from the side.* If the reader connects all of those dots with the known location of the limousine on Elm Street at the time of the fatal shot, then one can infer a fatal shot originating from the Grassy Knoll, to the exclusion of all other locations, which (when one marries together Ebersole's sworn testimony and the description of the large bone fragment in the autopsy report) entered the right side of the head, and exited the occipital bone in the back of the skull, leaving the back of the head '*missing*' when he first observed it at autopsy. Ebersole was either inadvertently, or very cleverly and intentionally, telling the HSCA panel quite a lot about the murder of President Kennedy during his testimony.

It's pretty clear that this didn't sit too well with Dr. Baden, who tried immediately to take some of the import out of Ebersole's testimony:

Baden: Have you had occasion in the past to review the films for the purpose of determining—

Ebersole: No, sir. Again I would like to emphasize my purpose of taking the films, and my interpretation that night was solely to locate a bullet that at that time we thought was still in the body.

Baden: And your subsequent exposures to the film[s] were in no way related to trying to identify or to interpret the films?

Ebersole: That is correct. They were to identify the films for insertion into the Archives...

Because Dr. Baden did not get the answer he apparently wanted from Ebersole about where the x-ray films showed the entry wound in the skull to be, he immediately tried to discount the importance of

Ebersole's testimony in response to that question. No wonder Ebersole's deposition was 'buried' (sequestered for 50 years) by Michael Baden and Robert Blakey: it cast doubt upon all of the principal conclusions of the HSCA Forensic Pathology Panel. They had bet all of their chips upon the authenticity of the autopsy photographs of the back-of-the-head, and the interpretation of a rear entry wound on the right lateral skull x-ray by *one radiologist* on the Clark Panel; Dr. Ebersole's testimony about what he recalled seeing on the body, of what type of bone the large fragment 'from Dallas' represented, his interpretation of the location of the entry wound from study of the head x-rays, and his opinions about the accuracy of the photographs of the large head wound, *all* seriously challenged the foundations of the HSCA panel's conclusions. I am unaware of any text in volume 7 of the HSCA's report which discusses the fact that Dr. Ebersole's testimony was at variance with the HSCA panel's conclusions; I hold Michael Baden responsible for this intellectual legerdemain. I hold Robert Blakey responsible for classifying Ebersole's testimony for fifty years, and attempting to keep it under wraps until the year 2029, by which time Blakey, Baden, and all others on the staff of the HSCA who were covering up the fact that they were, in reality, faced with a huge evidentiary *mess,* would be six feet under the grass. We owe film maker Oliver Stone, and the honest, bipartisan response of many members of Congress to the resulting controversy over the allegations of conspiracy and coverup in his film *JFK,* a large debt of gratitude for the resulting JFK Records Act, which forced the release of internal HSCA documents like the Knudsen and Ebersole depositions in the summer of 1993.

Further Testimony About the Skull Films and the X-Rayed Skull Fragments

Baden: These three films in particular [the 3 skull x-rays], were they all taken before the autopsy was begun?

Ebersole: Yes. The skull films were definitely taken before the autopsy.

Baden: Did you repeat the skull films?   [Ebersole had already implied, twice, that he did.]

Ebersole: To my knowledge. [Apparently meaning "yes."]

Wecht: What are the numbers?

I think that Wecht, here, meant to clarify "how many skull x-rays are there?" or perhaps "how many total did you take?" But Baden (not Ebersole!) gave a deflective answer to Wecht. His 'non-answer' below worked. No one on the HSCA panel followed up with the obvious questions about how many total skull x-rays had been taken, if they were indeed repeated, as Ebersole, three different times, seems to have indicated they were.

Baden: [Apparently deflecting Wecht's question] One, two and three are the skull. [Quickly moving on] Now if anybody has any subsequent questions or comments, please do not hesitate to raise them. The x-rays labeled 4, 5, and 6 are the fragments. Who assigned the numbering to the film?

Wait a minute! This was the time for any first-year law student, or any interested party on the HSCA panel who was paying attention, to stop and say, "Dr. Ebersole, if you took more than one set of x-rays of the skull, why are there only 3 skull x-rays in the collection?" It is a great shame that Dr. Ebersole died in 1993, prior to the establishment of the ARRB; if Jeremy Gunn, the ARRB General Counsel, had been able to take his deposition, I suspect that Jeremy—with his remarkable skill in questioning witnesses, and his patience and tenacity—would have verified whether Ebersole took one or two series of head x-rays, and would have tried very hard to elicit from him exactly how many were taken, and which views.

Ebersole: I think I probably did at the time they were put in the Archives but temporally speaking this was the last to be taken, no. 4. [Ebersole is referring here to the series of x-rays of loose skull fragments, nos. 4, 5, and 6]

Baden: To rephrase the question, does the numbering in any way indicate the sequence in which they were taken?

Ebersole: No, it is not the time sequence.

Baden: So 4, 5, and 6 which are x-rays of bone fragments were the last films that you took?

Ebersole: Yes.

Baden: Now the response to that was yes?

Ebersole: Yes.

Baden: Do you recall seeing those fragments and x-raying the bones?

Ebersole: Yes. This was maybe midnight to one o'clock when these fragments arrived from Dallas.

Baden: After the autopsy [was completed]?

Ebersole: The autopsy was still going on during that period.

Baden: And it is your impression that before the autopsy was finished [that] at ten thirty at night contact had been made between Dr. Humes and—

Ebersole: I must say these times are approximate but I would say in the range of ten to eleven P.M. Dr. Humes had determined that a procedure had been carried out in the anterior neck covering the wound of exit. Subsequent to that the fragments arrived. At the time the fragments were x-rayed Dr. Finck was present.

Baden: Do you have any idea, what did you do with the fragments after you finished x-raying them?

409

Ebersole: Returned [them] to the autopsy room. They were kept in the autopsy room.

Baden: Do you have any independent recollection as to whether or not they were retained or interred with the body?

Ebersole: No recollection after giving them back to Dr.—

Lovoquam: Were these taken with the portable?

Ebersole: No, I believe these were taken in the main x-ray department. If you notice, the bone detail on these is really much better than on the other films and I think these I carried to the x-ray department and took them in the x-ray department.

Baden: All three x-rays?

Ebersole: Yes.

Baden: Four, five, and six?

Ebersole: Yes. *I would particularly like to call your attention to 6 as being a finer quality film than you see in the other ones.* That is more typical of the type of film that you obtain with a stationary or regular diagnostic equipment rather than portable. [Author's emphasis]

This statement—that x-ray number 6 is of better quality than numbers 4 and 5—is of great potential significance, and will be discussed later in this chapter.

Baden: Now do you recall also when you took the x-rays 4, 5, and 6 whether you turned the bones or were they all taken at three different exposures in the same position?

Ebersole: I cannot recall that. I think the repeated films were necessary because we didn't feel that these early ones [4 and 5] were properly exposed.

_____

I viewed these x-rays at the National Archives on numerous occasions, and to the best of my recollection, the bone fragments are in identical positions on the three x-rays.

Baden: Do you recall discussion as to the significance of the radio opaque material in the one margin of the largest fragment?

Ebersole: I felt they were metallic fragments from the bullet.

Baden: Entrance or exit?

Ebersole: I don't believe I could tell.

This was the perfect point for Baden to revisit with Dr. Ebersole why he identified this large bone fragment that they are discussing here as *occipital bone* earlier in his testimony. Baden didn't do it. This speaks of a certain arrogance, of a certainty that he, Dr. Baden, knew more than someone who was at the autopsy and who held this bone fragment in his hands and examined it with his own eyes. (Dr. Angel of the HSCA panel, in 1977, in front of Humes and Boswell and without much certainty, had tentatively identified this bone fragment as coming from the forward-top portion of the head on the right-hand side, *either directly forward of or directly behind* the coronal suture—that is, it was either frontal bone, or parietal bone, and he tentatively identified the suture seen on the bone in the x-ray as probably being the coronal suture. But he did this in an atmosphere in which the autopsy photographs of the apparently intact back-of-the-head were being freely discussed before him, and this no doubt steered him away from considering that the fragment could have been occipital bone.[10] If Dr. Angel had heard Dr. Ebersole's testimony about this bone being occipital bone, I'm sure he would have shown much more interest in that statement than Michael Baden did.)

Baden: Do you recall discussing that with the other doctors in the autopsy room?

Ebersole: No.

Baden: Now do you recall discussing them specifically with Dr. Finck?

Ebersole: We discussed it, yes. *I don't know that there was any conclusion reached.* [Author's emphasis]

The autopsy report certainly says that there was a conclusion reached, and so does the Sibert-O'Neill report. The conclusion reported in those documents is that this particular bone fragment displayed beveling, or shelving on the outer aspect of the skull—evidence of *exit*. However, neither report identifies the anatomical location of the large fragment—whether it was occipital, parietal, temporal, or frontal bone.

Baden: On the largest fragment with the metal fragments present, the radio opaque fragment[s] present, would you have any comment on that serrated margin on that fragment?

I believe that Baden here is trying to avoid using the word 'occipital' which Ebersole used earlier to describe this bone fragment. By asking about the *serrated edge* of the bone fragment, Baden is attempting to find out whether Ebersole can identify a particular cranial suture (the 'knit line' where the different bones in the skull are joined together); if Ebersole could have identified a particular suture, it may have either confirmed, or ruled out, his previous identification of this bone fragment

---

[10]No doubt this is also the reason Dr. Angel tentatively interpreted the Harper Fragment, from its photographs, as parietal bone—because the back-of-the-head appeared intact in the autopsy photographs.

as 'occipital.'[11]

Ebersole:	No, not from that angle.

Baden: Do you have any independent recollection of what the fragments looked like apart from the x-rays?

Ebersole: No, except that I was rather surprised on the x-rays to see the metallic fragments because I could not see them by naked eye. The piece that I remember [the 10 x 6.5 cm fragment mentioned in the Sibert-O'Neill report] was a larger piece, it was handed to me in the Commanding Officer's office and was wrapped in gauze. It looked like ordinary fresh bone. They were then taken to the main x-ray department from [sic] the fourth floor and x-rayed there and then taken to the autopsy room.

Baden: Do you recall, were you told from whence they had been obtained?

Ebersole: I think Dr. Finck had told me they had just arrived from Dallas.

Baden: Where?

Ebersole: No, just arrived from Dallas, period.

Baden: Do you recall seeing beveling on the bone on the largest fragment?

Ebersole: No.

Baden: No, you don't see [sic] it or no, you don't recall?

Ebersole: I don't recall the degree of beveling we had. This would have been something that Dr. Finck would have been very interested in and they were turned over to him.

And this ended Michael Baden's questioning of Ebersole about the large bone fragment from Dallas, the one Ebersole identified as *"occipital"* earlier in his testimony. Baden had very carefully danced around the big question, without actually using the word "occipital," and without directly asking Ebersole "why did you earlier call this bone fragment occipital?" It would have been most useful from a historical standpoint if Baden had simply asked the question. It was clearly on his mind, but he didn't ask. It was a major failure on the part of the entire HSCA Forensic Pathology Panel that *no one* on the panel asked this direct question.

---

[11]Per Figures 9 and 16, the *lamboid suture* in the back of the skull separates the roughly triangular occipital bone from the right and left parietal bones; the *sagittal suture* running fore-and-aft on the top of the skull separates the left and right parietal bones from each other at the top of the head; and the *coronal suture,* running left-to-right in a transverse direction across the top of the head, separates the two parietal bones from the frontal bone.

Additional Testimony About the X-Rays of the Body

Later during the deposition Dr. Baden notes that the metallic marker with the Bethesda UIC code of 21296 on it is not present on either x-ray numbers 10 or 11 (even though the Military Inventory says that it is). Dr. Ebersole speculated that either the x-ray technician forgot to put the marker in the cassette, or the x-ray beam did not capture the image because of the positioning of the cassette.

A considerable amount of discussion was dedicated to trying to determine which x-rays of the body were taken after evisceration. This, of course, was an important clue as to whether the body x-rays in question were taken very early in the autopsy, or much later, after the Y-incision and the removal of internal organs. These questions bore directly upon the credibility of Dr. Finck's recollections, vs. Dr. Ebersole's, regarding timeline considerations. The table below compares the joint opinions of the panel and Dr. Ebersole, with those of the ARRB's forensic radiologist consultant, Dr. Fitzpatrick.

X-Ray #	Part of Anatomy Depicted	HSCA Panel/Ebersole Opinions	Dr. Fitzpatrick's Opinions
7.	Abdomen and lower chest	<u>Viscera present</u> (and many dirt artifacts on x-ray which appear to be metal but are not)	Post-incision, <u>but prior to the removal of organs</u>
8.	Right shoulder and chest	<u>After evisceration of chest: lungs and heart removed</u>. Also, although one piece of metal noted near C-7 by Dr. Ebersole, his opinion was that all other objects in the neck area were dirt/artifacts. Dr. Ebersole saw a possible fracture of the transverse process of either C-7 or T-1.	Post-incision, <u>organs removed</u>
9.	Chest	Many dirt artifacts present on x-ray	<u>Lungs present and thyroid cartilage present</u>.
10.	Left shoulder and chest	<u>After evisceration of chest; lungs and heart have been removed</u>	(no comments made)
11.	Abdomen and lower chest	<u>After evisceration; lungs and heart not present</u>	Post-incision, <u>organs removed</u>
12.	Both femurs & knees	(no comments made)	(no comments made)

13.	Pelvis	Prior to evisceration	(no comments made)
14.	Lower Pelvis, hips, and upper femurs	Prior to evisceration	(no comments made)

As the above chart shows, 3 of the x-rays in the Archives show images of the body taken <u>after the organs have been removed</u>: x-rays number 8, 10, and 11. These are images are of the eviscerated right and left lungs, and eviscerated abdomen, and support Finck's recollection of a whole body survey done after his arrival. (Remember, when Finck arrived the lungs and heart had already been removed.)[12] We also know that permission to extend the Y-incision into the abdominal area and remove the organs below the diaphragm (i.e., the liver, stomach, spleen, pancreas, kidneys, intestines, etc.) was obtained from RADM Burkley *after* he gave belated approval to remove the lungs, so these 3 x-rays could have been taken well into the autopsy. The x-ray of the femurs, number 12, could have been taken later in the autopsy also, but there is no way to tell.

Dr. Ebersole's memory is also vindicated, however, for 4 of the x-rays (nos. 7, 9, 13, and 14) were taken <u>prior to evisceration</u>; and two of these, nos. 7 and 9, views of the abdomen *and* lower chest, and of the chest *only,* must have been taken <u>before Finck's arrival</u>, because we know that Finck arrived after the lungs had been removed.

So each man—Finck and Ebersole—was *partially correct.* The reader must be wondering at this point why he or she should be concerned with when x-rays of the body were taken. The reason is because there are crucial inconsistencies within the testimony of the x-ray technicians regarding *what* happened *when,* in regard to the taking of various x-rays, as we shall see later in this chapter. The conclusions that the data table above allows us to reach will assist us in unraveling some of the timeline problems inherent in the testimony of Custer and Reed regarding *what* happened, and *when,* <u>during the autopsy.</u> How important this is will be revealed in Part II.

The analysis conducted above reveals that there were at least 3 rounds of x-rays taken during the autopsy, and that there were no doubt significant delays in between each round, delays that will become significant later when we conduct our timeline analysis of events during the autopsy.

The minimum of 3 rounds of x-rays appear to have been as follows:

1. Head only (based upon Humes' phone call to Finck)
2. Body prior to evisceration (and possibly, additional head x-rays, based upon uncertainties in Ebersole's testimony)
3. Body after evisceration

Regarding gaps in time between different rounds of x-rays, Ebersole testified as follows in reply to

---

[12]In the so-called "Blumberg Report" signed by Finck on February 1, 1965 he wrote that the lungs, heart, and brain had all been removed by the time he arrived at the Bethesda morgue.

Dr. Weston after the HSCA panel had reviewed with him the condition of the body portrayed in the various body views: "My recollection is that we took most of these pictures before the autopsy started but the film shows that my recollection is not very good in that respect and I would have to state that there might have been quite a time gap between the first films and the later ones that showed the viscera removed." The importance of this realization by Dr. Ebersole will become evident later in this chapter when we discuss the testimony of Jerrol Custer.

The HSCA Panel Revisits Dr. Ebersole's Opinion About an Entrance Wound in the Side of the Head

Drs. Weston and Baden, later in the deposition, chose to question Dr. Ebersole's competence to interpret x-rays of gunshot wounds with regard to entry and exit, and to specifically question his opinion about an entrance wound in the side of the head (which was, after all, at variance with the autopsy report and the sworn testimony before the Warren Commission of Drs. Humes and Finck). Excerpts of these two exchanges follow:

Weston: Before you go on with this, for the record I would like to have a little better handle on what you feel that you are qualified to testify about based on those x-ray films and your expertise. In other words, I don't want to pose questions to you which—

Ebersole: I think your question is a very good one. Although I was trained in diagnostic radiology, I am not a diagnostic radiologist and have not been since 1963 at which time I started doing radiation therapy and have engaged in that full time since. As far as my expertise that night, I don't think it should be questioned because what was being asked of my expertise was, is there a slug in the body?

Weston: I understand that. I am coming back to your expertise now. Looking at those skull films, would you feel comfortable in saying there were fractures there?

Ebersole: Yes.

Weston: And yet I understood you to say that I think, would you not, and yet I understood you to say that you felt like there had been a bullet wound on the right side of the head, is that correct?

Ebersole: No. I would say *on the basis of those x-rays and x-rays only* one might say one would have to estimate there that the wound of entrance was somewhere to the side or to the posterior quadrant. [Author's emphasis]

Weston: To the side or the posterior quadrant.

Ebersole: This is 180 degree [meaning unclear here].

Weston: Okay. Fine. That is all I have.

Dr. Ebersole appears to contradict himself here, but I would say "not really." His answer to Dr. Weston employs the caveat "on the basis of those x-rays and x-rays only." It is my firm impression that Dr. Ebersole's first answer to this question, earlier in the deposition, when he stated that it was his opinion that the head x-rays showed an entrance wound in the side of the head, took into account his overall impressions at the time of the autopsy: his visual recollection of the body (i.e., with the back of the head missing), and his recollection that the large fragment of bone from Dallas was occipital bone, as well as his personal opinion about what the pattern of general damage on the President's head, as seen in the morgue, implied about the direction of the fatal shot. (Numerous autopsy witnesses, when asked what their opinion about the direction of the fatal shot was *at the time of the autopsy,* said they had the firm impression at the time that President Kennedy had been shot from the front.) I think that in his initial answer, even though he was specifically asked about *the head x-rays* and what they depicted about an entry wound, he was recalling his overall impressions of the general pattern of damage that he saw *at the time of the autopsy, based upon all of the evidence before him.* He *appeared* to back off when questioned again about his opinion that there was an entry wound in the side of the head, because the questioner forced him to restrict his answer to interpretation of the x-rays alone, and not to consider other evidence that he had before him at the autopsy (such as the appearance of the President's body). I think Ebersole here realized his competence was being directly challenged, and furthermore, may have been well aware that his earlier statement had challenged the orthodox view of what had happened in Dealey Plaza, so he slightly changed his answer, and justified this change by denoting a major caveat, and in doing so appeared to back off, in an attempt to 'get the monkey off of his back.'

But the panel wasn't finished with him yet on this issue:

Baden: I take it also from your initial responses pursuant to Dr. Weston's comment just a few minutes ago to the evaluation of the injury to the head that you had not evaluated the skull films for points of entrance or entry at the time of the autopsy or subsequently.

Ebersole: That is correct, sir.

Baden: And that you were hesitant to give us an opinion as to entrance and I am also bringing up exit now from your background training and expertise.[13]

Ebersole: That is correct.

The implication here was really not so subtle: 'if you continue to insist that there was an entry wound in the side of the head, or even that there could have been such a wound, we will savage you and destroy your credibility.' I get the impression, though, that if Dr. Ebersole had answered the original question about where the entry wound was by saying "the rear of the head," he would not have had to endure further questioning about his qualifications or expertise from either Dr. Weston or Dr.

---

[13]When asked during the deposition how many gunshot wound cases he had evaluated as a radiologist, Dr. Ebersole had said about 20 to 25, during the course of his career. This is not a high number, as I am sure he was well aware.

Baden.

The problem for the HSCA Forensic Pathology Panel, though, was that he _did_ say it—his first answer to their question about where he thought the entry wound was depicted by the head x-rays was, **_"in the side of the head."_** And he had also said that the large bone fragment 'from Dallas'—the fragment identified _in the autopsy report and the Sibert-O'Neill report_ as bearing evidence of <u>exit</u>—was **occipital bone.** And he had also testified that **_the back of the President's head was missing_** when the body arrived at autopsy. Furthermore, when shown photograph no. 42 of the intact back-of-the-head by the HSCA panel, he recalled that the large defect in the head was **_"more of a gaping occipital wound than this"_** and that **_the autopsy photographs depicted a wound "more superior and lateral" than what he remembered on the body._** And all of these statements were in 'the damn record,' as Dr. Lovoquam might have put it. No wonder the HSCA staff director buried his deposition for 50 years. Blakey wanted to broadcast successful public hearings, and publish a good-looking report; these were his main criteria for defining a successful investigation of the assassination, as former HSCA staff investigator Gaeton Fonzi has written in his book, _The Final Investigation._ You could not have successful hearings unless you got Dr. Humes to recant about where the entrance wound was located in the autopsy photographs of the back-of-the-head; and you could not have a good-looking report unless you had apparent unanimity of opinion within the Forensic Pathology Panel about all the essentials of President Kennedy's wounds. It was bad enough that Humes and Boswell had both contradicted the Clark Panel and the HSCA panel on where the entrance wound in the head was depicted in the autopsy photographs; Humes' public recantation was necessary to get over this hurdle. If Ebersole's deposition had also been published in volume 7, _along with_ the Humes and Boswell testimony before the panel (which was ultimately published), then the HSCA Forensic Pathology Panel, I think, would have been exposed as the close-minded body it really was, a panel that was trying to impose an interpretation upon evidence that too many witnesses to the events in question vehemently disagreed with. As a result, both the Ebersole and Knudsen depositions, and the staff interview reports of many of the autopsy witnesses, were sealed for 50 years. The HSCA staff leadership's decisions about which evidence was 'good evidence' and which evidence was 'bad evidence' could be the subject of a major study of what lawyers consider the "best evidence." That career attorneys opted to go with photographs and x-rays over eyewitness testimony and personal recollections is really not that surprising. What is surprising, and what is unforgivable, is that Robert Blakey tried to hide many of these serious evidentiary conflicts, and make it appear as though they did not exist, rather than openly acknowledging them in volume 7 of his staff report .

DR. MANTIK INTERVIEWS DR. EBERSOLE

Less than one year before Dr. Ebersole's death, he was interviewed by independent JFK assassination researcher Dr. David Mantik, who like Dr. Ebersole, was also a radiation oncologist. The tape recorded telephone interview was conducted on December 2, 1992, and all of the summary information below was obtained by me directly from the audiotape of that interview, which Dr. Mantik donated to the ARRB to assist us with our preparations for the depositions of various autopsy participants.

Dr. Ebersole was not nearly as cooperative with Dr. Mantik as he had been with the HSCA panel, but nevertheless Dr. Mantik did manage to glean some particularly useful information from Ebersole before the end of the telephone call. That information is summarized below:

- In reference to a previous phone call from Dr. Mantik, Dr. Ebersole answered in the affirmative, saying "yes," when Mantik asked him to confirm whether it was still his recollection that there were **5 or 6** skull x-rays taken.

- Dr. Ebersole, in response to a question about the location of the upper back wound, placed its location at approximately **"T-4,"** which is the fourth thoracic vertebra.

- Ebersole stated that the tracheostomy was open, and **not sutured.**

- Ebersole denied that there were any big metallic fragments on the skull x-rays.

- Ebersole recalled that the fragment trail in the lateral x-rays went from the occiput toward the right forehead.

- Ebersole stated that the large exit defect in the skull was located very close to the entry wound, approximately 2 to 2.5 cm lateral to the entry wound.

- In this phone call, Ebersole had attempted not to talk about the subject at all, and had stated early in the phone call that he didn't know why so many people were interested in a subject in which the facts were so well established, or words to that effect. Initially he referred Mantik to the two articles published in *JAMA* in 1992, in which first Humes and Boswell, and then Finck, had defended the autopsy report and its conclusions, saying that everything anyone needed to know was in those articles.

- When Dr. Mantik brought up the subject of the large, extremely radio-opaque 6.5 mm diameter object present in the A-P x-ray, Dr. Ebersole immediately terminated the telephone call. (See Figure 38.)

Comments follow: **First,** Dr. Ebersole's confirmation that there were a total of 5 or 6 head x-rays taken at the autopsy, *if true,* would mean that *2 or 3 head x-rays are now missing,* since there are only 3 in the collection. The reader should keep this possible discrepancy in mind while reviewing the unsworn recollections and ARRB testimony of enlisted x-ray technicians Jerrol Custer and Ed Reed later in this chapter. **Second,** his recollection that the back wound was located approximately parallel to the fourth thoracic vertebra, T-4, is *consistent* with the relatively "low" clothing holes in the President's shirt and suit coat, the "dot" representing this wound placed on the body chart at the autopsy by Dr. Boswell, and with the location Dr. Burkley placed in the White House Death Certificate on Saturday, November 23, 1963, before the autopsy report was finalized: namely, T-3. Ebersole's T-4 location for the entry wound in the back is *inconsistent* with the apparently "high" position of the upper posterior thorax wound shown in autopsy photographs, and the 1977 revision Dr. Boswell made to his own body chart diagram when he was interviewed by the HSCA staff (see Figure 56). **Third,** the fragment trail from the occiput toward the right forehead that Ebersole remembered in his conversation with Mantik is consistent with the autopsy report, but *not* with what is shown on the lateral x-rays in the National Archives: namely, a fragment trail from the right forehead to the upper parietal region, and large, outwardly displaced bone fragments in the upper posterior skull.

Finally, Ebersole's termination of the telephone call when Dr. Mantik brought up the subject of the large 6.5 mm radio-opaque object on the A-P x-ray was, in my view, highly significant. Mantik's eventual conclusion that this object on the A-P x-ray was an artifact intentionally superimposed on a composite copy film of the original A-P skull x-ray—evidence of forgery used to implicate Lee Harvey Oswald, who had supposedly purchased a 6.5 mm Mannlicher-Carcano mail order rifle—was only tentative at this point in time, because his research was not yet finalized, much less published. To my knowledge Dr. Mantik's first lecture on this subject was given at the "ASK" JFK assassination symposium in Dallas in November of 1993, more than 11 months after this phone call, and after Dr. Ebersole's death. For Ebersole to terminate the conversation so abruptly when this question was raised tells me that he was very much aware of the 6.5 mm object's significance; namely, that nothing anywhere near its size had been removed at the autopsy from the cranium of President Kennedy, and that the HSCA had concluded in its 1979 report that the object on the x-ray represented a shaved off section from the tail of the bullet that entered the rear of President Kennedy's head. [The latter conclusion is—incidentally—an impossibility, because the tail of the purported 'skull bullet' was found in the front seat of the limousine, and nothing was shaved off of the tail!] The fact that the whole subject was "radioactive" to him may indicate that he was aware the 'radio-opaque' object was not present in the original, authentic A-P x-ray that he reviewed the night of the autopsy. His sole function the night of the autopsy, according to Dr. Ebersole himself, was to look for bullets and bullet fragments in x-rays, not to attempt diagnostic work such as attempting to determine evidence of a bullet's entry or exit in any of the x-rays. Stated a little bit differently, the 6.5 mm object is the brightest area on the A-P x-ray, is the most "radio-opaque" or lucent object in the entire skull image, and clearly appears to represent a relatively large and very dense piece of metal. If it *was* present in the A-P x-ray the night if the autopsy, then Dr. Ebersole and the 3 pathologists *all* failed miserably to perform their primary functions, which according to Dr. Burkley that night, was to remove bullets or bullet fragments from the cadaver. (Two *smaller* fragments, much *less* bright on the A-P x-ray than the 6.5 mm object, *were* removed from President Kennedy's cranium at the autopsy based upon Ebersole's on-site interpretation of the A-P and right lateral head x-rays. This strongly suggests that neither Ebersole, nor Dr. Humes, was incompetent in this regard.) If the 6.5 mm object was *not* present in the A-P x-ray the night of the autopsy, then Dr. Ebersole was either knowingly part of a medical coverup, or was guilty of *dereliction of duty* at his HSCA deposition, *for not bringing up that important discrepancy.* He must have been aware of the issues involved here, for him to react the way he did when Dr. Mantik asked the question. We will return to the subject of the 6.5 mm diameter object on the A-P x-ray later in this chapter.

NAVY ENLISTED X-RAY TECHNOLOGISTS JERROL CUSTER AND EDWARD REED

As best can be determined, Dr. Ebersole interpreted the x-rays at the Bethesda autopsy, but did not operate the portable x-ray machine in the morgue; and Navy enlisted x-ray technicians Jerrol Francis Custer and Edward Francis Reed, Jr. teamed up to operate the portable x-ray machine in the morgue, and together developed the x-rays on the fourth floor of Bethesda NNMC in the main x-ray department laboratory. The researcher who reads their respective depositions in their entirety will note that in his ARRB testimony, each man exhibited what I have called the 'illusion of centrality' regarding his own specific role at the JFK autopsy. Both Custer and Reed essentially told Jeremy Gunn that they had each operated the portable x-ray machine all by themselves, and that they each developed the x-ray films that night all by themselves. It is not the purpose of this chapter to resolve that issue, but rather to examine: (1) whether photographs were taken before the initial x-rays, or vice-a-versa; (2) how many x-rays were taken, particularly of the head, in an attempt to determine whether any x-rays may be missing today; and (3) exactly when the taking of x-rays began, and what delays may have occurred, or how long the intervals of time were, between different rounds of x-rays. The responses received to questions about items (1) and (3) above will assist us in creating a timeline of various autopsy events in Part II of this book. Both Custer and Reed were Navy corpsmen at the time whose specialty was x-ray technology. Custer was an instructor for the 24 different Navy corpsmen enrolled in a one-year-long training program in x-ray technology at the Bethesda Medical School; Reed was one of his students in the year-long class. Jerrol Custer was also the supervisor of the three x-ray technicians on duty the night of the autopsy, and was responsible for directing Reed in his work that evening. We will now study the recollections of Ed Reed and Jerrol Custer as they pertain to the x-rays they took and to the wounds they observed; other recollections pertaining to the casket in which the President's body arrived, the body wrappings around the President's cadaver, and other issues pertaining to the chain-of-custody of the body will be covered in Part II of this book. After we cover the content of David Lifton's interviews with each man, and their ARRB testimony, the reader will be presented with a comparative table so that the essentials of their recollections about x-rays may be compared.

Edward F. Reed, Jr.

David Lifton interviewed Ed Reed on the telephone on November 25, 1979; the information reported below is obtained directly from that audiotape.

David Lifton Interviews Ed Reed on November 25, 1979

Reed recalled taking x-rays of the skull, neck, and body; he told Lifton he only remembered taking 2 x-rays of the head: one A-P x-ray, and one lateral. (There are 3 head x-rays in the official collection in the Archives.) Reed also said that although Custer was senior to him, that Custer did not know how to use the portable General Electric (G.E.) x-ray machine. He said that Custer did not do anything while he, Reed, was taking the x-rays, except sit "in the podium" (i.e., in the gallery). Reed said that he loaded 2 pieces of film in each x-ray cassette as 'insurance' in case the automatic processor did not work properly that night, and that therefore there were two simultaneous images exposed when each x-ray was taken. He said he intended to manually develop the second film of each view, if the first film of each view was not properly developed by the automatic processor. Reed said that because the automatic processor worked fine that night, he later destroyed the second (undeveloped) x-ray of each view that had been exposed. Reed told Lifton that his own impression the night of the autopsy was that President Kennedy had been shot from the front. During the time he was in the morgue the night of the autopsy, Reed did not recall the autopsy pathologists reaching any real conclusions about what had happened to the President; he simply had a general impression of confusion and uncertainty on their part. Reed recalled a wound that was right parietal, but 'more posterior,' toward the back of the parietal area; his personal impression the night of the autopsy was that President Kennedy had been shot in the throat from the front, and that the bullet had exited the back of his head.

Edward Francis Reed, Jr. Testifies Before the ARRB Staff on October 21, 1997

Neither Ed Reed nor Jerrol Custer wanted to be questioned by the ARRB staff, and both men had to be subpoenaed before they would agree to appear. During the preliminaries, early in the deposition, Jeremy Gunn established who was in charge the night of the autopsy.

Gunn: And who is Mr. Custer?

Reed: He was the supervisor on duty that evening at National—at the Bethesda National Medical Center.

Gunn: Did he have any responsibility for x-rays?

Reed: Yes, he did. He supervised the three students that were on call that evening.

Early in the deposition Jeremy asked questions to ascertain Reed's knowledge base, and the extent to which some of his answers might be tainted by the opinions of others.

Gunn: Mr. Reed, did you do anything to prepare for the deposition today?

Reed: I re-read some articles, the ones that were just presented in front of me. [Reed had brought copies of two published articles with him about the JFK x-rays, one written by him for a professional x-ray journal, and the other one written for a similar journal by Jerrol Custer.]

Gunn: Exhibits no. 199 and 200?

Reed: Yes.

Gunn: Did you read anything else?

Reed: No.

Gunn: Did you talk to anyone else about the deposition?

Reed: My wife, some close friends.

Gunn: Did anyone offer you any advice as to what you should say during the course of the deposition?

Reed: Yes, they did.

Gunn: What was the advice that you were given?

Reed: Tell the truth.

Gunn: And was there anything else?

Reed: No.

Gunn: Have you read the Warren Report on the assassination of President Kennedy?

Reed: Thirty years ago.

I wasn't sure I believed this; many people own a copy of the Warren Report, but few people have read it.

Gunn: But not since then?

Reed: No.

Gunn: Are you aware of the House Select Committee on Assassinations that made an inquiry into the assassination of President Kennedy?

Reed: Yes, I am.

Gunn: Did you ever read the report issued by the House Select Committee?

Reed: In brief.

I found this even harder to believe.

Gunn: After reading the Warren Report and the report of the House Select Committee on Assassinations, did you have any reaction to the accuracy of what was contained in those reports, as far as you knew—information related to the autopsy?

Reed: At that time, no.

———————————

Gunn: Have you ever seen the original autopsy photographs or x-rays since the time of the autopsy?

Reed: No.

Gunn: Have you ever had the opportunity of reading the deposition transcript of Dr. John Ebersole that he gave to the House Select Committee on Assassinations?

Reed:	A long time ago. *Probably around when it first was written*. *What is the date on that?* [Author's emphasis]

Gunn:	1978.

Reed:	*I looked at it briefly.* [Author's emphasis]

At this point I began to get a sinking feeling. I knew, as well as Jeremy did, that Ebersole's deposition transcript had been sealed for 50 years by Robert Blakey and that it had only been released by Congress in August of 1993 in response to the JFK Records Act. The HSCA had not even mentioned taking Ebersole's deposition in its report. Reed could not possibly have read the Ebersole transcript "around when it was first written." This response by Reed immediately led to Jeremy's next question:

Gunn:	Mr. Reed, how would you characterize your memory of the events of November 22, 1963 with regard to how clear they seem to you and how good your recollection is of those events?

Reed:	I'd say about 95 per cent correct.

I wondered at this point whether we had a "know it all" in front of us—someone who wanted to avoid appearing stupid and wanted to appear very smart, and was not above stretching the truth or prevaricating in order to achieve that impression. This is not the kind of witness you want to have before you at a neutral, fact-finding deposition where you are not going to aggressively confront the witness.

Reed is Questioned About the Wounds on President Kennedy

Jeremy's questioning of Reed about his independent recollections of the President's wounds went as follows:

Gunn:	Did you see any scars or wounds anywhere on his [President Kennedy's] forehead or face?

Reed:	Not on his forehead or his face.

Gunn:	Did you see any wounds at all on his head?

Reed:	Yes, I did.

Gunn:	Could you describe where those wounds were?

Reed:	It was in the temporal-parietal region, right side. I could—it was large enough that I could probably put four fingers in it.

Gunn:	Now—
Reed:	Not my whole fist, but four fingers.
Gunn:	And you're putting your fingers up on your head right now?
Reed:	That's correct.
Gunn:	And would it be fair to say that the part—portion of your head that you're touching would be right above the ear?
Reed:	That's correct.
Gunn:	Straight above your ear.
Reed:	And anterior. Slightly anterior. Slightly forward. As we say in the medical field, anteriorly forward.

When Reed had been interviewed by David Lifton in November of 1979, he had said that the head wound was "right parietal, but posterior, toward the back part." In 1979 Reed could not have seen any of the autopsy photographs, since the bootleg photos were not published until 1988. (If he had gone to the library prior to Lifton's interview and looked through volume 7 of the HSCA report, then his answer to Lifton that the right parietal wound was "posterior, toward the back part" was in contradiction to what he had seen in the Ida Dox illustration of photos 42 and 43. I conclude that his response to Lifton was his best recollection 16 years after the event, without having seen images *of any kind,* and that it was not 'tainted' or influenced by the HSCA report. It seems to me that if anyone had seen the Ida Dox drawing of the intact back-of-the-head, he could not have said that a right parietal wound was "posterior, toward the back part" without remarking that his memory was in opposition to the drawing he had seen published in the HSCA's report.) Ed Reed brought with him to the deposition a trade paperback copy of *Best Evidence* containing the B & W Fox set of bootleg autopsy photos. It is my opinion that his (presumably) more accurate memory in 1979 had been modified by looking at the autopsy photos widely published since 1988.

Gunn:	Did you have an opportunity at the beginning to see the back of President Kennedy's head?
Reed:	Yes.
Gunn:	Did you see any wounds in the back of his head?
Reed:	No.
Gunn:	Was the scalp intact, as far as you could observe, on the back of his head?
Reed:	Yes.

Gunn: Did you see any wounds on President Kennedy's throat—

Reed: Yes, I did.

Gunn: —in the front?

Reed: Yes, I did.

Gunn: Anterior throat. What—could you describe what you saw?

Reed: A large, gaping wound. Approximately seven centimeters in width—in length. Excuse me, in length. And about two centimeters in width.

Gunn: In addition to that wound, did you see any other wounds on President Kennedy's body?

Reed: Not at that time.

Gunn: Did you subsequently see additional wounds?

Reed: Later, when we lifted him up to put a[n] x-ray plate under his thorax—under his back, I saw a small, gaping wound [sic]. Approximately seven millimeters in circumference.

Gunn: Did you see any other wounds in the course of the autopsy?

Reed: None.

Gunn: Was the wound on the anterior neck sutured?

Reed: No.

Gunn: Could you describe the general appearance of President Kennedy's hair? That is, is there blood on it? Is it clotty? [sic] Is it messy, clean? What would be your description of that?

Reed: It was—appearance—from my past experience as a Navy corpsman, it was dry blood. Small fragments of bone externally, dry blood on the skin surrounding the wound...

Gunn: Do you recall at all whether the hair seemed particularly bloody, or was it relatively—did it appear as if it had been cleaned, or what was your impression?

Reed: It was—it wasn't cleaned thoroughly. It looked like somebody might have taken a rag and wiped it—you know, the back of his neck—from the blood. *But it was dry blood throughout the hair.* [Author's emphasis]

Photos 42 and 43 (of the intact back-of-the-head) appear to show clean, washed hair that is not covered by dry or matted blood, and that has possibly been combed to better show the "red spot," or apparent entrance wound.

Timeline Questions: What Happened, and in What Order?

Jeremy began to cover timeline questions next:

Gunn: ...I'd like to go back to the point where you have described your—the view that you had when you first saw the body, and ask you: what was the next procedure or next event that happened at the autopsy?

Reed: We were asked—Jerry Custer and myself <u>were asked at the time to sit in the podium</u> [sic], and wait until—let me, let me eliminate that last statement. I'm trying to—we <u>were asked at that time to go back to the main [x-ray] department</u>, the fourth floor—Jerry Custer and myself. *We were asked to leave after—you know, after we lifted the body onto the table, we were asked to leave, and go up to the fourth floor, and wait for a telephone call for us to come down.* [Author's emphasis]

Gunn: Do you know why you were asked why to go to the fourth floor?

Reed: Just to be ready to take x-rays.

Gunn: Okay. Did you at some point get a call saying to come back to the—

Reed: Yes, we did.

Gunn: *About how long was that?* [Author's emphasis]

Reed: *Maybe 15 minutes after that.* [Author's emphasis]

Gunn: Did you then go immediately back to the morgue?

Reed: We went—we went down through the hallway. We took the elevator. We went down to the back hallway, past the military guard—Marine guard, and then into the room. And then they asked me to take a lateral skull of President Kennedy's head—lateral view of President Kennedy's skull. Side view.

Gunn: Who was it that asked you to take the lateral view?

Reed: It was a combination of CDR Humes, Dr. Ebersole. Those two.

Gunn: Did you notice any difference in the placement of the body or anything that had been done to the body between the time that you left the morgue and the time you came back to take the x-ray?

Reed: None.

Gunn: In addition to Dr. Ebersole, you, and Jerry Custer, was there anyone else who was involved in preparing the x-rays?

Reed: No.

Gunn: What did you do, in order to take the lateral x-ray?

Reed: First, I discussed it with Dr. Ebersole. And he said, "Take a lateral view of the skull." I suggested at that time that we take a small metallic fragment for magnification purposes, and put it—attach it to the side of the head closest to the film. This is just something that was a suggestion of mine, since Dr. Brown [the head of the Bethesda x-ray department] wasn't there. And I was trying to make sure that we had good radiographs and a good way of measuring different little fragments, if there were any. I set—I did that. Put the—taped it to the back part of the mastoid [bone on the jaw] on the left, and placed the cassette against his left side of his head. And at that time, we didn't have cassette holders as we do now. We just taped it to the side of his head. I might have placed a sandbag beside it, also. And I proceeded to take the portable x-ray machine and place it on his right side, align—align it with the lateral—his skull cross hairs. Align it to the—one inch above and anterior to the skull on his right side. And then I collimated—what we call collimation. You take the light of the x-ray machine—there's no x-ray involved. It's just the collimation. And you cone down to enhance the x-ray, and not have any scatter radiation. I was the only one at that time that had a lead apron on, also, in the room. Everyone else was asked to stand clear of the area, at least 20 feet. I took the—I measured his skull. And we have a chart attached to the side of the machine, and you for centimeter size [sic]. And you measure that, and it gives you the kilovoltage, which is the penetrating power of the x-ray. And I utilized the technique chart. I'd like to back up just a little bit. At that time, up—when we were upstairs waiting to go, I put two films in each cassette. That means that I'm only using one side of the screen of the cassette vs. two. That means I have to increase my technique. So, when I —after I measured President Kennedy's head and put the—put all the ingredients into the—you know, final ingredients—all the factors—all the factors into the machine, I increased the kilovoltage 10—10 kvs. Ten kilovolts. The reason for that is because of the loss of radiation because of the two films in the cassettes.

Gunn: Why did you have two films in the cassette?

Reed: The reason I did that was in case the films were either overexposed or underexposed. That I could eyesight in a darkroom—in the manual darkroom on the fourth floor of

427

radiology. There was no darkroom in the morgue on the ground floor. Each film had to be hand-carried up as we proceeded through the whole procedure, and hand developed upstairs. I mean, if it had to be hand-developed, I had two films in each cassette. I put one film into the M3 processor, and waited 5 minutes, 5 or 6 minutes. It took approximately 5 minutes. And it came out dry at the other end. At that time, I looked at a view box—put it up to the view box, saw that it was technically satisfactory. The film was technically satisfactory. At that time, I took the other film that was in the cassette, and put it in a film bin in the darkroom. We had 3 film bins. Not all of them were filled with film. One was empty. The reason it was empty was because during cleaning out on Thursday, we took all the films out of the cassettes, and put them into a film bin—an empty film bin, and cleaned all the cassettes. And then we took all the film out of the film bin, and put them back in the cassettes. That's why we had an empty film bin. And during the evening [of the autopsy], every film that I took—every one of them was perfect. Not one had to be hand-developed. And I stuck every [extra] film in the film bin. I did that for—only to—because I didn't want to waste film. It sounds kind of ridiculous, but that's why I did it. Not to waste the film.

Gunn: There was no exposure on the films that you put in the film—

Reed: There was—yeah. Every film we took down in the morgue had—whenever you use a cassette that there was two films inside, and there was a[n] image on both films. The latent image. A latent image is a[n] image you can't see. If you took it out and hold it up to the light—in the light, it would all be green. We call that a latent, l-a-t-e-n-t image. Both films had a latent image on the film from each cassette. But whenever you develop a film, that latent image becomes a stationary image—a realistic image that you can see...[continuing]

Reed continued to go on and on here, making no sense whatsoever. He couldn't talk his way out of this one. If two films were in each cassette when each body view was exposed to the x-ray beam, then each film was obviously exposed to light by the illumination screens within the cassette and could not be reused, whether it was developed or not. Reed was talking nonsense, and Jeremy and I knew it. There was no way for him to "save film" that was exposed to an x-ray image but not developed. Using it again would create a double-exposure, of no use to anyone.

Gunn: What happened to the latent images after you were—after you put them in the film bin?

Reed: I didn't do anything until the—about 1:00 o'clock in the morning, whenever we were done with the autopsy. Maybe it was earlier than that. Maybe it was around 10 o'clock in the evening. I found no need—because every x-ray was so good. So, I—I said "What am I going to do?" I said to myself, "What am I going to do with these films?" If I'd known then—now what I knew then, I would have kept them for the—for Dr. Brown. But I just turned the light on. I just turned the—flipped the light, took them out of the film bin, and threw them into the trash.

Gunn: So, by putting the light on, does that have an effect—

Reed: That completely exposes the film. *It makes them unusable again.* There is still silver on the film, but there is no latent image. The latent image is destroyed as soon as that is hit by white light. [Author's emphasis]

The second film from each cassette was unusable anyway, whether it was exposed to ambient light in the room or not. I wondered whether Reed briefly considered whether to develop the extra copies of each x-ray and keep them for himself, but then changed his mind and exposed them to light before throwing them away. If so, he could have felt guilty about it and this could account for the nonsensical explanation he had given to us about 'putting them into the film bin to try to save film.' In view of Dr. Mantik's hypothesis that the A-P head x-ray and the 2 laterals in the collection are not the originals, but are really forged composite copy films with artifacts imposed upon them to alter the images, it's a great shame that Reed did not develop and retain the second original of each x-ray. If they had been developed and retained, they could have been used as scientific 'controls' to definitively test Mantik's hypothesis.

Gunn: Now, you described, a few moments ago, taking the first lateral image. How many images did you take?

Reed: Numerically?

Gunn: Numerically.

Reed: We took an A-P [anterior-posterior view of the head] and lateral skull.

Gunn: That makes two of the skull?

There are 3 skull x-rays in the collection, an A-P and *two* laterals.

Reed: That's correct. A-P and lateral neck [Reed meant to say 'skull']; two of the neck. Then we did a chest x-ray on a 14 x 17, a large film. The other films were 10 by 12—10 inches by 12 inches. Now we proceeded to take the larger film, 14 by 17. Now, this time frame is about an hour. We didn't take them all at one time.

Gunn: Let's—I would like to get all of them.

Reed: Okay.

Gunn: Those that you took, let's—

Reed: Let's go through the—

Gunn: —let's do what you took first.

Reed:	Then we took an A-P abdomen, from his nipple line down to his pubic bone.
Gunn:	If you could—
Reed:	That's one.
Gunn:	I'm sorry. If you could hold it.
Reed:	Okay, I'm sorry.
Gunn:	Is this still in the very first round of—
Reed:	No, no. The first round was just the lateral skull.
Gunn:	Just—
Reed:	The lateral skull was the only film I—that I took upstairs and developed it. That was the only film [in the first round]. Then, when I came back down with the film, they said, "Do an A-P skull."
Gunn:	Okay.
Reed:	And I did a[n] A-P skull. Then I ran it up the steps again—past the guards, up the steps, into the darkroom, developed the film. Jerry Custer stayed downstairs on the podium, watching, while I was upstairs developing the film. So, then I went back upstairs, developed the A-P skull, ran it down. And then they were—the doctors were—looking at it. And I was fairly close to them, and they asked me to step back. So, then—there was like a little reading room, just a little alcove. And then they asked me to step back. So, I had to step back about 10, 12 feet.
Gunn:	Why did they ask you to step back?
Reed:	I don't know. I—I think I mentioned maybe in my—you know, it's been a while. But in my—I might have heard something about a conspiracy. The word. Not that they were conspiring themselves, but there might have been mention of a conspiracy. And maybe—maybe—whether I heard that or not, that—maybe that's why they asked me to step back.
Gunn:	Let me make sure that I understand correctly the sequence. The first exposure that you made was a lateral x-ray. You then—
Reed:	Lateral skull.
Gunn:	Lateral skull. And you then take that upstairs—

Reed: That's correct.

Gunn: —develop it, and bring it back.

Reed: That's correct.

Gunn: You're then asked to take an A-P skull—

Reed: After they saw that lateral, then they asked me to do an A-P skull. They didn't ask me to do both at the same time.

Gunn: So, you then took that up, and you came back.

Reed: That's correct.

Gunn: What was the next thing that you were asked to do?

Reed: Lateral cervical spine. Lateral neck.

Gunn: And did you then develop that one, or did you—

Reed: Yes, I did. I ran that back upstairs.

Gunn: So, this is now three separate trips—

Reed: That's correct.

Gunn: —trips for three separate x-rays?

Reed: That's correct.

Gunn: Okay. And the next thing that you did?

Reed: Was a[n] A-P cervical spine. A-P neck.

Gunn: Okay.

Reed: And once again, I ran that upstairs, developed it, and brought it back down.

This was not the picture of 'major rounds' of x-rays being taken that Dr. Finck and Dr. Ebersole testified to. Reed was describing piecemeal, incremental activity.

Gunn: What was the approximate amount of time between the development—between the exposure of the first lateral x-ray and the fourth cervical—the fourth x-ray, that of the cervical x-ray?

Reed: About 25 to 28 minutes.

Gunn: When you took the films up for developing, did you go alone; or was there someone with you?

Reed: I went alone.

Jerrol Custer contradicted this, as the reader will see later in this chapter. He has always spoken of a very close security escort by a Federal agent when he went upstairs to develop x-rays, and also spoke of using an elevator.

Gunn: Do you know whether any x-rays were taken while you were not present in the room?

Reed: Not that I'm aware of. I'd have to say no, because Mr. Custer was still in the same position when I came back each time.

Gunn: After the fourth x-ray was taken, what were you then asked to do?

Reed: Then we were asked to do—to sit in the podium for a short period of time, approximately 20 minutes, while they were just discussing—the doctors were discussing the x-rays. And some of the technologists—the lab technologists were doing what they usually do. They weren't opening anything up. There was [sic] no saws or anything at that time that I was aware of—anything that was going on medically at that time. There were just more discussions. Then, after 20 minutes—15, 20 minutes, I was asked to do A-P chest—anterior-posterior chest. We call it A-P chest...then the A-P abdomen...the abdomen [x-ray] is from the nipple line to the pubic bone. And then we did a pelvis x-ray...I didn't have to take any of these films upstairs. I stayed in the morgue. And then I did his humeri, which are—we consider arms. And his forearms.

Gunn: So, how many x-rays of each arm?

Reed: One of each. I mean, one of the up—This is the arm. This is forearm. From the shoulder to elbow is arm.

Gunn: So, two x-rays—

Reed: One.

Gunn: —of the right arm—

Reed: One.

Gunn: —and two x-rays of the left arm. The whole arm.

Reed: That's correct.

Gunn: Okay.

Reed: What we call the entire upper extremity. Two films of each.

Gunn: Okay. So, for President Kennedy's entire arms, there were a total of four x-rays?

Reed: That's correct.

Gunn: Okay. And did you take any of the legs, the femurs?

Reed: Yes, we did. Again, the medical terminology. The femur is the thigh...and the leg is actually from the knee to the ankle. That is actually leg. Not from the hip to the ankle.

Gunn: Okay.

Reed: I proceeded to take two of the lower extremity, the leg and the thigh. A-P,. One of each. And then I proceeded to take the left, one of each, the leg and the thigh.

Gunn: So there was—

Reed: And that was the end of the radiographs.

Gunn: So, then, there were effectively two x-rays of each of President Kennedy's four extremities?

Reed: That's —two—one, two, three, four, Eight [total].

The Military Inventory listing of x-rays describes only two A-P x-rays showing the arms (nos. 8 and 10, of the right and left shoulders-and-chests); one A-P x-ray showing both femurs and knees (no. 12), and one A-P x-ray of the lower pelvis, hips, and upper femurs (no. 14). In summary, then, only *four* x-rays in the collection in the Archives show the extremities of President Kennedy, not the *eight* that Reed recalled above.

Gunn: Right. Did you take any other x-rays?

Reed: No.

Gunn: What did you do with these last two, three—I have 11 x-rays?

Reed: We took them upstairs, and we developed them.

Gunn: When you say "we," who else went with you?

Reed: Jerry Custer.

Gunn: Did you take any x-rays at any subsequent point during the evening?

Reed: No.

Gunn: Were you told the purpose of taking any of the x-rays? Let's start with the lateral skull x-ray.

Reed: No.

Gunn: For example, were you told that the purpose of the x-rays was diagnostic versus attempting to locate any bullet fragments?

Reed: No.

Reed then discussed overhearing the doctors speculate about bullets possibly hitting bone and then traveling down the extremities or into the body cavity.

Gunn: So, although you were not told why, it was your understanding that the purpose of taking the body x-rays was to locate a bullet. Would that be fair?

Reed: Well, from what I overheard in the conversation, yes.

_____

Gunn: Were you the person principally responsible for developing each of the x-rays?

Reed: That's correct.

Gunn: And were you the person principally responsible for taking each of the x-rays?

Reed: Yes, I was.

Gunn: What type of x-ray film was used?

Reed: Kodak.

Gunn: Do you remember the name of the Kodak film?

Reed: At that time, there was only one type of film—x-ray film.

Gunn: Okay.

Reed: Compared to 20 different types of films today.

_____

Gunn: Do you recall whether the name of Kodak was on the edge of the film?

Reed: Yes, it was.

Gunn: Was that true for both the smaller films that you mentioned, as well as the larger film?

Reed: That's correct, yes.

Gunn: Did you, at any point, see photographers in the morgue?

Reed: Yes, I did. But they didn't have their equipment. There was no equipment at that time with them.

Gunn: Do you know when the photography was taken?

Reed: I assumed, after the initial x-rays. I assume, after all the x-rays. Let me cancel that "initial." After all the x-rays. I was not there when there was any photography taken—any photographs. We were asked to leave after 15 minutes in the beginning. And they could have taken the photographs at that time, but I can't say whether they did or did not.

Gunn: You're referring to the time that you and Jerrol Custer were upstairs, waiting for the call to come back and take the x-rays?

Reed: That's—that's correct.

Gunn: They could have been taken, but you just don't know.

Reed: Absolutely.

Gunn: Did you see any tripods, or—

Reed: Yes, I did.

Gunn: —any kinds of ladders?

Reed: Yes, I did.

Gunn: What did you see?

Reed: I saw a tripod when they were setting up for photographs.

Gunn: And when was it that you saw them setting up for photographs? Again, was that before the first x-ray, or—

Reed: Yes.

Gunn: Before the first x-ray?

Reed: That's correct.

Gunn: Had you ever seen any of the photographers before?

Reed: Yes.

Gunn: Did you know them by name?

Reed: No. I saw them at the NCO club.

_____

Gunn: Okay. You've described the sequence of the taking of the x-ray films. Can you tell me whether there were any incisions that were performed on the body between the time of the first x-ray and the time of the last x-ray you took?

Reed: As far as I know, no.

Gunn: When you brought the last of the x-rays that you had developed back to the morgue, had there been any incisions performed on the body at that time?

Reed: No.

Of the 14 x-rays in the National Archives, there are *four* taken after the Y-incision in the body, according to the HSCA Forensic Pathology Panel (nos. 7, 8, 10, and 11); in three of these (nos. 8, 10, and 11), the organs have been removed prior to taking the x-ray.

Gunn: *Were you present during the time of the first incision?* [Author's emphasis]

Reed: ***Yes.*** [Author's emphasis]

Gunn: *What was the first incision?* [Author's emphasis]

Reed: ***The cranium. The scalp, right here.*** [i.e., the frontal bone behind the hairline]

Gunn: And can you describe how that procedure—

Reed: CDR Humes made an incision. After we brought all the x-rays back, we were all allowed to sit up in the podium and observe. And CDR Humes made an incision—that I could see from my vantage point—***an incision in the forehead, and brought back the scalp.*** [Author's emphasis]

436

Gunn: Okay.

Reed: Like this [indicating].

Gunn: *And you were making a line first across the top of your forehead, roughly along the hairline—*   [Author's emphasis]

Reed: ***With a scalpel.***   [Author's emphasis]

Gunn: *—and then pulling the scalp back.*   [Author's emphasis]

Reed: ***That's correct, just like this*** [indicating].   [Author's emphasis]

Gunn: And were you able to see the size of the wound when the scalp—

Reed: Not from my—not from where I was, no. The podium was a good 20 feet away.

Gunn: What else did you observe from where you were with regard to any incisions or operations on the head?

Reed: ***Well, after about 20 minutes, Dr. Humes took out a saw, and began to cut the forehead with the bone—with the saw. Mechanical saw. Circular, small, mechanical—almost like a cast saw, but it's made—***   [Author's emphasis]

Gunn: Sure.

Reed: —specifically for bone.

Gunn: And what did you see next?

Reed: We were asked to leave at that time. Jerry Custer and myself were asked to leave.

Gunn: Did you see the brain removed?

Reed: No.

Gunn: Did you go back into the morgue at any time that evening?

Reed: No, I did not.

Gunn: Did you see any incisions on the chest at all?

Reed: None.

Gunn: Did you ever see President Kennedy's body again?

Reed: No, I did not.

Gunn: Other than the times that you mentioned that you went upstairs to develop the first set of x-rays, were you with Jerrol Custer for the remainder of the evening?

Reed: At the return—at the completion of all the x-rays?

Gunn: Yes.

Reed: Yes.

Gunn: Did Dr. Ebersole know how to take x-rays; do you know that?

Reed: I can't answer that.

Gunn: Why are you unable to answer that?

Reed: Most physicians, radiologists or radiation therapists—he was a radiation therapist. That was his speciality. That's why I had to assist him originally—are not really trained to take radiographs, other than barium enemas and upper GIs. Upper gastric and lower gastric—lower colon. Other than that, they're not trained. They know what views to take. They know what views to take for them to read the films, but they do not know how to take a radiograph, unless they come up through the ranks.

Gunn: Did you ever hear of any x-rays that had been taken after a Y-incision had been performed on President Kennedy?

Reed: No.

Gunn: Later in the evening, did you ever hear about bone fragments arriving at Bethesda?

Reed: No.

Gunn: Did you, yourself, take any x-rays of any skull fragments at Bethesda later that evening?

Reed: No, I did not.

Gunn: After you were asked to leave the morgue, which room did you go to—or where at Bethesda?

Reed: We went to the on-call room on the fourth floor of the main building, in main radiology.

Gunn: And did you stay there for the rest of the evening?

Reed: Yes, I did.

Gunn: How far is the on-call room from the developing lab?

Reed: Approximately 50 feet. Fifty or 75 feet.

Gunn: Would you have known if someone had gone into the developing lab?

Reed: Absolutely.

Gunn: Did anyone go into the developing lab—

Reed: No.

Gunn: —later that evening?

Reed: No. Radiology was secured.

_____

Gunn: Did your hear any discussion at Bethesda about the autopsy or what happened during the autopsy within the next few weeks?

Reed: The only discussion I had was in the morning. At approximately 8:00 o'clock, I was called—all of us were called individually—down to the Master-at-Arms on the ground floor in the main atrium. At that time, we were asked to sign a statement, just to assure that we would not release information, other than under military situation.

Gunn: I'd like to show you a document marked Exhibit 192, and ask you whether this is the document you signed—or a photocopy of the document you signed?

Reed: That's my signature, and that's the form that I signed.

_____

Gunn: Mr. Reed, you said that you and Mr. Custer went up to the on-call room; is that correct?

Reed: That's correct.

Gunn: Did Dr. Ebersole go with you to the on-call room?

Reed: No.

Gunn: I would like to show you a document that is marked Exhibit no. 60 for this

439

deposition, which is the testimony of Dr. Ebersole before the House Select Committee on Assassinations.

Reed: Okay.

Gunn: And I'd like to ask you some questions about—

Reed: Sure.

Jeremy asked Reed to read a passage on page three (lines 7 through 13).

Gunn: Do you see the portion in line seven and eight, where he [Ebersole] refers to carrying the [x-ray] cassettes containing the x-rays?

Reed: That's—yes.

Gunn: Did he do that?

Reed: No.

Gunn: Are you certain that he didn't do that?

Reed: I'm 110 per cent certain that he did not do that.

Gunn: And the reason you're certain that he did not do it is because...?

Reed: I did it. Four flights of stairs, running four floors. And I was 20 years old. I was in great shape. I don't think Dr. Ebersole could have crawled up those steps as many times as we did, and carry the cassettes. Four or five at a time at the end—at the end, you know.

Gunn: Could you turn to page number 4, and look at the paragraph on lines 11 through 15, please?

Reed: I read it.

Gunn: Did you, at any time, hear any Secret Service agents make requests with respect to taking x-rays?

Reed: No.

Gunn: During the time that the doctors were examining the x-rays in the morgue, was Dr. Ebersole present with them, discussing findings with them?

Reed: Yes, he was.

Gunn:	Was Dr. Ebersole privy to communications with the autopsy doctors that you were not able to hear?
Reed:	Yes.

More Questioning About the Location of the Exit Wound in the Head

Gunn next asked Reed to read another passage on page 62 of the HSCA's Ebersole transcript (lines 15 through the end of the page and including the first line on the next page).

Gunn:	...have you had an opportunity to read the portion that refers to the occipital wound?
Reed:	Yes.
Gunn:	Do you know which part of the skull is the occiput?
Reed:	Yes, I do.
Gunn:	Do you recall the wound on President Kennedy's head as having been occipital?
Reed:	No.

Gunn:	Do you recall ever having been contacted by a staff investigator of the House Select Committee on Assassinations?
Reed:	Yes, I do.
Gunn:	Can you tell me what happened when you were contacted?
Reed:	Well, we had a discussion, maybe 15, 20 minutes [of] discussion.
Gunn:	Was this on the telephone, or in person?
Reed:	It was on the telephone.
Gunn:	Do you recall, by chance, who the person was?
Reed:	No, I don't.

Gunn:	...what do you recall about that conversation?
Reed:	Oh, geez...a gentleman calls up. I wasn't short with him; but, you know, my mind wasn't 100 per cent into it...I explained to him over the phone...somewhat in detail,

441

what I explained to you gentlemen today and what I've written in an article...

Reed then started to dance around the meaning of the word 'occipital' after perusing the next document Jeremy handed him, Exhibit 194 (HSCA staffer Mark Flanagan's OCR of his telephone interview with Reed). He complained that it was often used imprecisely, and could mean almost anything, since the temporal, parietal, and occipital bones all come together near the mastoid bone (the rear of the jaw). Reed had seen the text before him and he knew what was coming.

Gunn: In Exhibit 194, Mr. Flanagan reports you as having identified the wound in the head [as being located] in the occipital region. Is it your best understanding now that you said "occipital region" to Mr. Flanagan, or that Mr. Flanagan misunderstood what you had said?

Reed: No, I probably said that. Because this is such a vague area. This area [indicating]. When you put your fist up there—talking over the phone, you know, without precise measurements—I mean, a layman wouldn't—you know, someone not—not related to the—someone that knows the medical terminology would know the general area. Let me say it that way.

In my view Reed was still talking nonsense; he *was* medically trained, and the word 'occipital' coming from him should have had a relatively precise meaning. Mark Flanagan may not have been medically trained, but as a young attorney I am confident he was an accurate recorder of what a witness said on the telephone about something as important as the location of the President's head wound. Reed was hoisted on his own petard, as Stringer and Riebe had been. Why were these people changing their descriptions of the head wound over time? I wondered if it were a simple demonstration of the <u>psychological power of photographs</u> (which we have all grown up thinking of as *accurate representations of 'reality'*) to cause a person to inwardly challenge, and then even modify his own recollections? Or were these people knowingly (and cynically) changing their stories because they were afraid of the 'government,' the same government that had been able to produce real-looking photographs that they knew were fraudulent, i.e., somehow at odds with what they knew to be true?

Jeremy was not ready to let Reed go on this issue yet.

Gunn: Okay. Could you turn back to page 62 [of the Ebersole HSCA transcript, in which he looks at photo 42, and says that he remembered "more of a gaping occipital wound" then the intact back-of-the-head before him at that moment] of—

Reed: Okay.

Gunn: —Mr. Ebersole's testimony, and look once again. He also describes the wound as occipital.

Reed: Mm-hmmm.

Gunn: Is Dr. Ebersole correct in describing the wound as occipital?

Reed: It's more—it's more anterior than occipital. [This contradicted what Reed had told David Lifton in 1979, when he said the wound was in the *posterior* part of the parietal region.] If a—it's such a small part of the occipital bone, that it's an overlap. See—see this? Right here. When I say I originally saw the wound—the occiput is down here. Okay? But a little bit of occiput protrudes into my fist right now, and the parietal and temporal bone. It's like a—it's a[n] area that encompasses other areas.

Reed was squirming like a worm on a hook, but it gave me an insight. *Now* I thought I knew why he would not come to testify unless we subpoenaed him: he was very uncomfortable talking about the location of the exit wound in the head, because of the internal conflict in his mind between his actual recollections, and the image content of the bootleg autopsy photos that had been in the public domain since 1988. In 1978 he hadn't had any compunction about describing the exit wound in the head as 'occipital' to Mark Flanagan because he had not yet seen the autopsy photographs that contradicted that recollection.

Gunn: Sure. I understand what you're saying. Although, both Dr. Ebersole and yourself referred to that in 1978 as occipital, and neither of you referred to it as parietal or temporal.

Reed: Well—

Gunn: Isn't that correct?

Reed: Yes.

Gunn: Was the wound principally occipital, extending into parietal and temporal?

Reed: Yes, I'll—

Gunn: But principally occipital?

Reed: I'll say—I'd say you could use that terminology, yes.

Jeremy continued to question Reed about things Flanagan had written in the OCR recording the highlights of his phone call with Reed in 1978.

Gunn: Were you aware of a bullet being found in Dallas during the night of the autopsy, or did you learn about that at a subsequent time?

Reed: I heard it during the autopsy...but I'm almost 100 per cent positive during the autopsy I heard someone mention that they found a bullet. And in fact, I think it was about the time we were lifting the body out of the casket earlier in the evening...

443

Next, Jeremy quoted a statement attributed to Reed by Flanagan in the OCR about the doctors searching for a bullet in the femur and lower abdomen.

Gunn: What I understand Mr. Flanagan to be saying is that there was a bullet that entered the upper back, and that it was searched for in the femur and lower abdomen.

Reed: I'll agree with that.

_____

Gunn: On page 2, there is a reference that says that the doctors removed the brain, and retained it for future examination.

Reed: That is what I was told.

Gunn: So, that is not accurate?

Reed: I never saw that done.

Gunn: Okay.

Reed Examines the Autopsy X-Rays and Photographs

Jeremy concluded the deposition by showing Mr. Reed all 14 x-rays in the collection, and selected autopsy photographs of the body. Reed recognized two types of markers on each head x-ray that he said he had positioned himself: the metallic marker that he taped over the left mandible for magnification purposes, and a metallic marker placed inside the x-ray cassette, showing the Bethesda UIC of 21296, and the date 11/22/63. Here are excerpts from Reed's testimony regarding x-ray no. 1, the A-P head x-ray:

Gunn: Mr. Reed is being shown an x-ray that is identified as no. 1 from November 22nd—

Reed: Here it is right here, guys.

Gunn: —from the inventory.

Reed: The piece of metal that we put on the side of his head—here it is, right here.

Gunn: You are looking at the autopsy x-ray no. 1?

Reed: Right.

Gunn: And you are seeing a metal thing right down by what would be the left jaw, but on the right side of the—

Jeremy was attempting to explain here that the marker was on the anatomical left of the President's jaw, but was on the right hand side of the A-P x-ray image as it is viewed, since the x-ray beam traveled through the skull from front to rear; viewing an A-P x-ray over a light box was equivalent to looking at a photograph of someone's face taken directly from the front. That is, anything on the anatomical left of the decedent would be on the right-hand side of an A-P image.

Reed: This is the marker that we pasted on the side for magnification purposes.

———————

Gunn: Let's start with what you have described as a marker down by the left jaw. Again, the marker here is up on the right side of the film in looking at it. Can you describe what that marker is, please?

Reed: This marker is a piece of aluminum with a small hole in the middle, in the distal third. As soon as I saw that, I recognized that is the piece of metal that I put on the left side of President Kennedy's skull. Actually, on the left side of his mandible.

Gunn: And that was to help you measure the proportions of the skull?

Reed: That's correct. For magnification purposes [after developing].

Gunn: Now, you have referred to another—what I believe you called a marker. That is over on the right side, written at an angle; correct?

Reed: That is correct...this is the correct marker. This is the type of marker that we used [inside the cassette] at this time.

Gunn: Can you read what the marker says? Now, this is the second marker that we are talking about. Those appear to be numbers and letters, correct?

Reed: Yes. Let me turn this [the x-ray] over, so I can visualize it better. This is the correct way of reading it. Here is the date, 11/22/63.

Gunn: And to the left of the date, what is that? It looks to me as if it is an upside down "F." Does it look that way to you?

Reed: It does.

Gunn: Do you know what that would signify?

Reed: No, other than it shouldn't have been there. It probably was underneath. We had these sliding in little metal tracks at that time. In rushing, we might have put—November 22nd is the date. But what that "F" is, I can't explain. And this 21296 [referring to the unit identification code unique to Bethesda NNMC]...is a number that we just arbitrarily gave to the next patient who arrives.

This was an incorrect explanation. The 21296 is the Bethesda UIC code; I thought Reed should have remembered that this number did not vary from patient to patient, and remained the same in each x-ray cassette, regardless of who the patient was. (Only the date changed.) Reed was spinning tales about something he did not understand. But he was certainly animated about recognizing the two familiar metal markers in each x-ray of the skull; his enthusiasm was unfeigned—he recognized familiar markers confirming these x-rays as work that he had been involved in at the President's autopsy.

Jeremy then moved on to the extremely bright object in the A-P x-ray that was interpreted by the Clark Panel and the HSCA Forensic Pathology Panel as a bullet fragment 6.5 mm in diameter, located high on the rear of the skull. Jeremy asked Reed, who was 'only' an x-ray technologist (and who was *not* a trained radiologist), to interpret this object in the x-ray:

Gunn: Okay...there is a semi-circular white dot there [on the A-P head x-ray]. Do you see that?

Reed: Yes, I do.

Gunn: Do you recall seeing that on the night of the autopsy?

Reed: Yes, I did. [In contrast, Humes, Boswell, and Finck did *not* recall seeing that bright object in the x-ray the night of the autopsy.]

Gunn: What was your understanding of what that was?

Reed: That is a metallic fragment from the bullet.

Gunn: Did you see that metallic fragment removed from the body?

Reed: No, I did not.

Gunn: Is there anything else on the x-ray that appears either different from what you observed on the night of the autopsy—

Reed: No, there is not.

Gunn: There is no doubt in your mind that this is the authentic x-ray that you took on the night of the autopsy?

Reed: This is the authentic x-ray taken that evening.

Jeremy then questioned Reed about x-ray no. 2, the right lateral head x-ray. After asking Reed whether he could authenticate it, Jeremy asked Reed if he could locate the position in the right lateral x-ray of the extremely bright (i.e., radio-opaque) object that had just been discussed on the A-P head x-ray:

446

Gunn: ...Are you able to identify x-ray no. 2 as having been taken by yourself on the night of the autopsy?

Reed: Yes, I can, and this is the radiograph I took that evening.

Gunn: How are you able to identify that as the radiograph you took that evening?

Reed: In two ways. One, by—again, the metallic piece of metal placed on the side of his mandible. And two, by the position of the cassette. I put it vertically, rather than horizontally, that evening. In other words, normally, I would put it straight up and down; but I put the film this way to get some of the cervical spine on the film.

Gunn: Are there any other identifying marks that help you identify whether that is the x-ray film that you took on the night of the autopsy?

Reed: Again, the specific date is on the film. And the same number, 21296, with the logo of the United States Naval Hospital, National Naval Medical Center, Bethesda, Maryland, was attached.

Gunn: If you recall, in the first x-ray you looked at, we discussed a semi-circular item...I think you identified it as a bullet fragment. Are you able to identify that fragment in the lateral view?

Reed: Yes, I can.

Gunn: Where is that?

Reed: In the frontal lobe of the skull.

Wrong answer. If this had been a game show, the buzzer would have gone off and Reed would have been told to sit down. Reed was pointing to the elongated 7 x 2 mm fragment in the lateral x-ray (near a sinus above the eye, behind the forehead) that Humes had removed at autopsy and described in the autopsy report. The actual location on the lateral head x-ray of the object corresponding to the very bright object on the A-P head x-ray was <u>high on the rear of the skull</u>—except that on the rear of the skull, it was a *much smaller* object and was *not nearly as bright*. Jeremy was asking an x-ray technician to interpret an x-ray, with predictable results. (David Lifton fell into the same quagmire in 1989 when he asked Jerrol Custer, in a videotaped interview, to interpret photographs of x-rays published in the HSCA report.) I felt some sympathy for Reed, since he was not a radiologist; but Reed was not the kind of witness who wanted to admit ignorance, and unfortunately he once again invented an answer rather than saying "I don't know," or "I am not qualified and I would only be guessing."

Jeremy: And you are pointing to—

Reed: The front. Right above the supraorbital ridge of the right occiput—of his right orbit.

Gunn: You don't mean "occiput"—

Reed: No, scratch that. Of the orbit. Supraorbital rim. It is right impregnated in there [sic].

Gunn: And, once again, you did not see that removed during the—

Reed: No, I did not.

Gunn: —the autopsy? There appears to be some white fragments that go along the top of the skull. [Jeremy was describing what is an apparent bullet fragment trail leading from the forehead to the rear of the skull.]

Reed: Yes.

Gunn: Do you see those?

Reed: Yes, I do.

Gunn: Are you able to identify whether those are artifacts, or whether those were present on the night of the autopsy?

Jeremy meant to say: "Were they present in the x-ray image on the night of the autopsy, and if so, do you think they are artifacts (caused by dirt in the x-ray cassette) or do you believe they represent bullet fragments?"

Reed: They were present in the same area [of the x-ray] that evening.

Gunn: Did you have an understanding as to what those white fragments represent?

Reed: Yes, I did.

Gunn: What was that?

Reed: Metallic fragments from a bullet.

Next, while questioning Reed about x-ray no. 3, the other lateral head x-ray, the following exchange took place:

Gunn: Mr. Reed...is this an image that was taken by you on the night of the autopsy, and then subsequently developed by you?

Reed: Yes.

448

Gunn: Can you describe very briefly what that view is?

Reed: This is again the lateral skull, with the same identifying marker as the previous lateral skull. I wasn't sure if I took 2 lateral skulls, but I must have...

Gunn: Let me ask you this question. Is there any question in your mind as to whether image no. 3 is a copy or—

Reed: No. It is the original.

Reed went on to explain that if it were a copy film, one would see the outlined border of the overlapping original film around portions of the edges of the x-ray. (Interestingly, however, when Jeremy had asked Reed to measure skull x-ray no. 2, that was supposedly 10 x 12 inches, the measurement of its width was one eighth of an inch less than 10 inches, and the height was one quarter inch short of 12 inches.)

Gunn: Do you remember in the first x-ray that you looked at, we identified a semi-circular object that you identified as a bullet fragment?

Reed: Yes.

Gunn: Can you identify that fragment on x-ray no. 3?

Reed: Yes. It's anterior again. It's right there [pointing to the 7 x 2 mm fragment which on the x-ray appears to the layman to be behind the forehead].

Wrong answer—again.

Gunn: Can you explain why it does not appear as bright on x-ray no. 3 as on x-ray no. 1?

Reed: No, I can't.

Gunn: Should it be just as bright—

Reed: I mean, really—it should be.

Gunn: —though smaller?

Reed: It should be. It should be. It should be. That could be bone fragment, but—It looks more white than metallic on the other x-ray [no. 1].

Gunn: On the first one.

_____

Gunn: Well, let me try—Is it possible that that bullet fragment was, in fact, on the back of

449

the skull near the occiput, rather than the frontal bone? And that would be the reason it would not be appearing on this?

Jeremy was feeding Reed the interpretation of those radiologists who had compared x-rays no. 1 and no. 2, and had interpreted the large, bright, 6.5 mm object on the A-P skull x-ray as being the same object that looked like a very small fragment on the outer table of the rear of the skull in the right lateral skull x-ray, x-ray no. 2.

Reed gave a meandering, evasive answer that didn't mean much of anything.

Gunn: ...the part that we've been talking about, where the—where you've identified the larger metal fragment, is in the frontal bone. Near—what we would say in lay terms, on the forehead—

Reed: That's correct.

Gunn: —right above the nose.

Reed: That's correct.

Next, Jeremy showed Reed the three x-rays of loose bone fragments, x-rays no. 4, 5, and 6. Reed said he definitely did not take them, and had never seen the fragments depicted before. Reed noted that none of the three x-rays of skull fragments had any identifying markings such as he had described previously in connection with x-rays no. 1, 2, and 3: no metal left/right markers, no UIC code tags reading 21296, and no date taken.

Gunn: And previously in your testimony, you said that you were within 50 feet of the developing lab [in the main x-ray department] at Bethesda Naval Hospital, is that correct?

Reed: I'd have to say yes.

Gunn: So, as far as you know, it would be unlikely that this x-ray was taken and developed at Bethesda on the night of November 22nd/23rd?

Reed: That's correct.

A curious thing happened when Jeremy showed Reed the various x-rays of the body, nos. 7 through 14. Reed recognized the metal left/right markings familiar to him in the x-rays taken of the body with none of the organs removed, but he saw no metal markings familiar to him in two of the three x-rays taken of the body after evisceration (nos. 10 and 11). This was of great interest to Jeremy:

Gunn: Based upon what you've said thus far, it appears to me that there are identifying markers on those films where the organs are present. The markings are not, at least, visible with this particular light on those where the organs have been removed.

Reed: I agree.

Jeremy had overstated his case a bit; one of the 3 x-ray films showing the eviscerated body (no. 8) *did* have a metallic marker visible in the x-ray, according to Reed. Unaccountably, Reed promptly agreed with Jeremy, even though he had *just stated* that he was confident he had taken x-ray no. 8, because he saw a "right marker" made out of lead depicted in the x-ray.

Later in the deposition, after all of the x-rays had been viewed, Jeremy revisited the issue:

Gunn: So, once again, consistently from what we have observed, those [x-rays] where internal organs have been removed but did not have the—

Reed: Right. Right.

Gunn: —numerical identifier [the UIC code for Bethesda, 21296].

Reed: That's correct. That's correct.

Gunn: And those [x-rays] that do have the organs [present in the image], do have the identifier.

Reed: That's correct.

This wrapped up the questioning on x-rays:

Gunn: In addition to the 14 films that we have seen, do you remember taking any additional x-rays?

Reed: I thought I took his forearms and his legs. But again, I knew I didn't take his—I remember recalling not taking hands and feet. That's the only x-ray I can actually say—I know I didn't take his hands and feet. But I thought I took his legs and his forearms, but probably I didn't.

Jeremy Gunn wrapped up the deposition of Ed Reed by asking him some limited questions about selected autopsy photographs:

Gunn: Could you tell me whether the view that you're seeing right now...[photo no. 26]...is consistent with your recollections from the autopsy of President Kennedy?

Reed: No. [See Figure 62.]

Gunn: In what way is that different?

Reed: This flap here.

Gunn: You're referring to the portion just above the—

Reed: Just above the ear. This flap seems to be projected outwards, and I don't remember that—recall that being like that. And as far as this area here—

Gunn: You're referring to—

Reed: —from the brain, the brain itself was not exposed that much.

Gunn: So, whereas it appears that brain tissue is extruding from the wound, that's not consistent with what you recall seeing?

Reed: No.

Jeremy next brought out the color transparencies of the intact back-of-the-head, photos 42 and 43.

Gunn: Mr. Reed, is that photograph consistent with what you viewed during the autopsy of President Kennedy?

Reed: No, it's not. [See Figure 65.]

Gunn: In what way is that different?

Reed: The head was never projected that way. And the hair was not matted back. And there was no scale, measuring—this was done when I was not present.

Gunn: Now, let's state we're—the presumption that we have is not that you were present when this photograph was taken, but whether the head itself appears—and the wounds on the head are consistent with what you observed at the time of autopsy.

Reed: I can't answer that in this projection, because everything I was doing was from the front to the back.

Gunn: And if you didn't see it, then that's fine.

Reed: Okay.

Gunn: You should just say that you didn't see that view.

Reed: I did not see that view. I did not see that entrance—or exit wound, whatever that wound is.

Jeremy next presented the autopsy photos of the superior view of the head.

Gunn: Mr. Reed, is that view of President Kennedy consistent with what you saw the night of the autopsy?

Reed: No. [See Figure 61.]

Gunn: In what way is it different?

Reed: It's more gaping, more open.

Gunn: That is, the photograph is more open, or what you observed—

Reed: The wound. The wound is more open, more gaping than I observed.

Gunn: So, the photo—with the photograph, the wound appears to be larger than what you observed on the night of the autopsy?

Reed: That's correct.

Gunn: Is there any question in your mind whether that is, in fact, a photograph of President Kennedy on the night of the autopsy?

Reed: That's a photograph of President Kennedy that night of that evening, but it's just—the wound is opened up a little bit more.

The final view Jeremy showed Reed was view no. 4, color photos 38 and 39.

Gunn: Now, previously, Mr. Reed, if I recall correctly, you said that you had seen a bullet wound in President Kennedy's back; is that correct?

Reed: That's correct.

Gunn: Is that view you're looking at now consistent with the wound that you saw during the night of the autopsy?

Reed: Yes, it is. [See Figure 63.]

Gunn: And could you now look also at the back-of-the-head, and see whether the head appears to be consistent with what you saw at the time of the autopsy?

Reed: Yes, it is. Yes, it is. But again, the—everything is not hanging back as much as it was on the other views. This is more consistent with what—when he arrived and we laid him up on the table. This is more consistent with the view that I saw.

Gunn: Let me try to rephrase that, and tell me if I'm saying this correctly. In the view that you saw that was number 3, the superior view of the head, it appeared as if there was matter that was extruding from the head. Whereas, in this particular view, that does not seem to be the case.

Reed: Oh. Extruding. But not as prominent. There's still a fragment of the bone on the left side. [I believe Reed meant to say "right side."] And there's still matting, and blood, and bone, and brain; but it's—in the projection this is in, it's more erect.

Gunn: So, the view that you have now in front of you, which is the fourth view, appears to be more consistent with your observations than the one that showed much greater matter extruding from the—

Reed: That's correct.

Gunn: —wound; is that correct?

Reed: Yes.

Ed Reed concluded his own deposition with some closing remarks:

Reed: ...Looking at the x-radiographs [sic] brought back some memories. And I'd have to say [now] that I didn't take his tibia and his forearm. And the general statement, when I said hands and feet, is a wider area than I recollect. And the time frame between—I—there could have been some x-rays taken between the initial set and the chest x-ray and the abdomen. And then they might have had me come back later on and then do the abdomen, and the pelvis, and the legs. That's why they're missing lung markings. Because those definitely are x-rays that I took...some statements I made over the phone, in 1978, were made in haste and possibly I erred. And as far as the occiput, as far as the radiographs, it really is more anterior and [sic] posterior. [Reed meant to say "more anterior *than* posterior."] It really didn't—the occiput was only minimally involved.

Jerrol Francis Custer

We probably had more JFK researcher interview material on Jerrol Custer than on any other autopsy witness, and yet he really did *not* want to talk to the U.S. government about his role in the President's autopsy following the Kennedy assassination. He had talked numerous times with JFK assassination researchers David Lifton, Harry Livingstone, and Tom Wilson over the years, and like Floyd Riebe, had been interviewed in 1988 for a television documentary by Sylvia Chase of KRON-TV in San Francisco—but had hung up the phone on the HSCA staff member who contacted him, per his own admission. (In Custer's defense, the prohibition against speaking about the assassination was still in effect at that time, as far as he knew, so he was only complying with the 'letter of silence' delivered to him in November of 1963.) By the time I was permitted to call him in 1997, I had assumed that he would be much more forthcoming about speaking with the ARRB than he had been with the HSCA, since he had subsequently spoken with so many researchers—in some cases, on film or video. I was wrong. He hung up on me, too, and in a rather unceremonious manner, after telling me in particularly strong and colorful language that he was not going to cooperate with the ARRB.

(I couldn't ascertain at the time whether he was 'afraid of the government,' as many witnesses to the JFK assassination and its aftermath are, or whether he was simply exhibiting an overabundant disrespect for authority so common in many ex-enlisted military service members. Ultimately, the reasons for his refusal to cooperate really didn't matter; it was unacceptable, period. If the ARRB had done nothing about this, it would have been an admission of weakness and lack of resolve.) I didn't think the ARRB should take this lying down, and fortunately Jeremy agreed, so Custer was subpoenaed along with Reed, and appeared before us one week after Reed's deposition.

Before I launch into Jerrol Custer's ARRB deposition, it is very important that we review what he told David Lifton on audiotape in October 1979, on film in 1980, and on videotape in1989. We will be focusing here on consistencies in his recollections, for it is those recollections that are *consistent* over the years that are more likely to be correct, in my judgment.

Custer's Audiotaped Interview with David Lifton on October 7, 1979

Lifton had first interviewed Custer on September 30, 1979, but since the tape I have of that interview is almost inaudible, and only about half of the conversation can be made out, I have not used that source. All of the summary points below were obtained by me from the audiotape of the second Lifton-Custer interview, on October 7, 1979, which, like the Ed Reed interview from November of 1979, can also be obtained from the National Archives:[14]

- Custer told Lifton he remembered taking *at least five* (5) skull x-rays:

  1. An A-P;
  2. A "Townes" view [a 45 degree angle projection, in which he said the x-ray beam is projected from top-to-bottom of the skull, toward the foramen magnum—the hole in the bottom of the skull through which the neck and spinal cord pass—which should have shown the blowout in the back of the head];
  3. Two (2) laterals; and
  4. One tangential view [with the x-ray beam passing along the right side of the head, from rear to front, and the x-ray cassette placed under the right eye, so as to record the missing skull in the right posterior region of the skull].

- When informed by Lifton that none of the head x-rays showed a blow-out in the rear of the skull, Custer was astounded. He then reiterated that he was sure he had taken an x-ray showing a blowout in the back of the head, with the film cassette under the defect on the right side, and the x-ray beam going from the anatomical upper left to the lower right of the skull. (He appears to me to be describing the "Townes" view here.)

---

[14]David Lifton donated to the JFK Collection many of his audiotaped witness interviews, after they had been "cleaned up" by removing background hiss and transferred to CD by his friend and fellow researcher, Pat Valentino.

- He said the tracheostomy wound was ragged, as if the skin had been "torn up."

- He said he remembered a possible entry wound above the right eye.

- He said he remembered a Secret Service agent opening up a camera and exposing the film to light.

- Custer recalled a "king-sized hole" in the occipital region, and another in the region of the "right temple."

- He said President Kennedy's skull was "cracked like a hard-boiled egg" that had been smashed by rolling it between your hands and applying too much pressure, and that the right-rear portion was "gone."

- Custer remembered "taking a set of skull x-rays," and in association with that "set," making 3 or 4 trips upstairs to develop them in the main x-ray laboratory.

- He said he was ordered not to identify the x-rays: to use no tags, to fill out no logs, and not to specify name, date, or autopsy number in the images.

- Custer vividly recalled seeing Jacqueline Kennedy enter the lobby of Bethesda when he was going upstairs with a Federal agent as escort to develop x-rays of President Kennedy that had already been exposed. (Initially, he told Lifton that this occurred during his 2nd or 3rd trip upstairs; later in the interview, he recalled it may have been his 1st or 2nd trip upstairs.)

- Custer told Lifton that at about 9 A.M. the day after the autopsy, that a Naval officer—he believed it had been Dr. Ebersole—had asked him to x-ray loose skull bone fragments. He said that in association with this event, he had been awakened by four Naval Officers, each of them a senior officer, a Captain (an O-6), that they had congratulated him on his work and had told him that the x-rays of the fragments were to be used for a "head reconstruction for a bust of the President."

Custer's Filmed Interview with David Lifton in 1980

Excerpts from this filmed interview were released commercially on David Lifton's *Best Evidence* research videotape, which sold approximately 50,000 copies during the 1980s. Two key elements of Custer's audiotaped interview in October of 1979 were repeated:

- The head wound in the right rear of the skull was enormous, big enough to have put both of his hands into the defect; and

- He again vividly recalled seeing Jacqueline Kennedy enter the lobby of Bethesda NNMC as he was heading upstairs to develop exposed x-ray film of the deceased 35th

President. [This has serious implications for the autopsy timeline that will be discussed in Part II, because we know that Jacqueline Kennedy entered Bethesda immediately after the motorcade from Andrews AFB containing the bronze Dallas casket stopped in front of the hospital at about five minutes to seven on November 22nd.]

Custer's Two-Hour Long Videotaped Interview with David Lifton on July 14, 1989

This is an extremely lengthy interview, and like the videotape of Lifton's 1989 interview of assistant autopsy photographer Floyd Riebe, it allows the viewer a very good opportunity to assess Custer's credibility on a number of issues. In this sense both videotaped interviews (of Riebe and Custer) are even more useful than the ARRB depositions, since behavioral scientists tell us that at least 70 per cent of all communication is non-verbal; the viewer of these tapes can assess by facial expression, tone of voice, and body language how credible the answers appear to be.[15] (Custer's answers to some questions, such as the taking of specific x-rays, appear to me to be much more credible than others, in which Lifton unfortunately asked him to interpret the head x-rays, something an x-ray technologist is not formally trained to do.) A textual deposition transcript reveals nothing about these subjective, but critical clues to witness credibility. Furthermore, the videotaped interviews of Riebe and Custer were made in 1989, about 8 years prior to taking their ARRB depositions, so presumably their memories of the events of November 1963 were of better quality in 1989, than in 1997.

A summary of the major points related to x-rays and wounds in Custer's 1989 videotaped interview is provided below, using my personal copy of the videotaped interview provided to me by David Lifton:

- Custer *again* remembered taking *at least five (5) head x-rays*, as follows:

  1. One A-P head x-ray;
  2. Two (2) laterals (which he said depicted the exit wound in the right rear of the head);
  3. A "Townes" view (which he said depicted the exit wound in the rear of the head); and
  4. An "oblique/tangential" view of the exit wound in the right-rear of the skull.

- He remembered the head being more fragmented than the x-rays show it to be. [The

---

[15]Both videotapes, obtained from David Lifton by the ARRB and used to help us prepare for our depositions, were placed by the ARRB in the JFK Collection at the National Archives, and presumably they could be viewed today within Archives II in College Park, Maryland upon special request. David Lifton requested that they not be copied for public distribution because of copyright considerations—portions of both interviews may end up in a research video one day—but this should not prevent an interested citizen from viewing them at the Archives.

reader should recall at this point Dr. Humes' ARRB testimony that working with the loose skull fragments in the cranium was like "working with clouds," because their position was so imprecise and subject to movement.]

- Custer said the photographic images of the cranial x-rays published by the HSCA in volume 7 of its report do *not* depict the condition of the skull as he remembers it, because none of them show the posterior skull defect he remembers.

- He said he recalled at one point during the evening being told to "go upstairs," and staying upstairs about *three quarters of an hour to one hour*, before being called down to the morgue to take x-rays. At another point in the interview, Custer said that he and Reed were told to leave *immediately after the President's cadaver was placed upon the autopsy table*, and that approximately *one to two hours passed* before x-rays were taken.

- Custer repeated his recollection about seeing Jacqueline Kennedy enter the lobby while a Secret Service agent was escorting him up to the main x-ray laboratory to develop exposed x-rays already taken of President Kennedy's cadaver.

- Custer, for the first time I am aware of, talked about a metal fragment dropping out of President Kennedy's back, when the body was lifted up after he had taken a thoracic x-ray; he said that Dr. Ebersole "grabbed" the metal fragment when it fell out of the body onto the autopsy table. There were no details provided in the interview about the size of the fragment or where it might have come from in the President's back.

- Custer remembered double-loading the cassettes with x-ray film (i.e., two films per cassette instead of one), but says he destroyed the extras later because he was afraid of getting in hot water.

- Custer said that Dr. Humes and Dr. Boswell were both on the telephone a lot during the autopsy.

- Custer said that the throat wound looked like a bullet entry hole, not like a transverse gash, when shown the bootleg autopsy photograph depicting the tracheostomy. [This contradicted his 1979 recollection that it was an ugly gash with torn skin.]

- Custer said the Ida Dox illustration of autopsy photos 42 and 43 made for the HSCA was not an accurate representation of how the body looked the night of the autopsy, because he recalled that when he looked at the back of President Kennedy's head, there was "nothing there." (See Figure 54.)

- Custer said he never saw the flap of temporal bone (seen in the Ida Dox diagram) at the autopsy.

458

- He said all that Dr. Ebersole was interested in was bullet fragments; that he had no interest in diagnostics of the head wounds.

- He said that Dr. Ebersole told him and Reed to "take whatever x-rays you need," and that he and Reed positioned the body on the table prior to each x-ray. Custer also recalled that Reed was "my student" at the time. Custer said that Reed assisted him, but that he (Custer) chose the techniques and made the exposures.

- Custer, unfortunately, attempted to interpret the head x-rays at Lifton's request, and made two incorrect radiological interpretations that I am aware of: first, he claimed that the A-P and right lateral head x-rays show the forehead to be missing on the right side (which according to Dr. Fitzpatrick and Dr. Mantik and the HSCA panel, it does not); and second, he claimed to see an exit wound in the rear of the skull when Lifton showed him a *pre mortem* head x-ray of President Kennedy from the HSCA report. [In my opinion, this does *not* make the remainder of his recollections worthless; it simply reminds us that he is not a radiologist, and therefore should not be asked to diagnostically interpret x-rays. The recollections of the x-ray technician at an event should 'trump' the recollections of a radiologist, however, in regard to how many x-rays, and which views, were taken, for example, since the x-ray technologist performed these actions himself, and they relate directly to his areas of professional expertise.]

- At the end of the interview, Lifton challenged Custer about the obvious inconsistencies in two aspects of his testimony: namely, that on the one hand, he recalled seeing Jackie Kennedy enter the lobby as he was transporting x-rays taken of her deceased husband up to the x-ray laboratory—whereas, in other portions of his interview, he recalled a substantial delay occurring after the arrival of the President's body before the first x-rays were taken by Reed and him. When asked which of these two recollections he was the most confident of, Custer said it would have to be the recollection of seeing Jackie Kennedy in the lobby while the Secret Service agent was escorting Reed and him up to the lab.

- Custer told Lifton he had been a hunter for many years, and that based upon his personal knowledge of what entrance wounds and exit wounds from rifle bullets looked like, it was his opinion on the night of the autopsy that President Kennedy had been shot from the front.

Jerrol Francis Custer Testifies Before the ARRB Staff on October 28, 1997

The reader should be painfully aware by now of the many major inconsistencies between the recollections of Ed Reed and Jerrol Custer regarding not only their individual roles at the autopsy, but much more importantly, how many x-rays were taken of the head. Reed had independently recalled only 2 head x-rays when questioned by both Lifton and the ARRB staff, and Custer had consistently recalled at least 5 head x-rays when interviewed on two different occasions, 10 years apart, by David Lifton. Attempting to resolve this matter—to determine whether or not it could reasonably be concluded that any head x-rays were missing, and whether or not the x-rays in the collection did, or did not, accurately represent the condition of the head at the autopsy, were the major goals of our deposition. Custer had had a lot to say over the years, and it was time to test his recollections in a formal setting, under oath.

Gunn: Have you ever read the Warren Report on the assassination?

Custer: Never had the chance. I never could get a copy of it.

Gunn: Did you ever read the report of the House Select Committee on Assassinations?

Custer: That's another copy I couldn't get.

Gunn: Okay. Are there any books or articles that you now recall that you read that pertained to the autopsy or the assassination?

Custer: "Best Evidence."

Gunn: That's a book by David Lifton?

Custer: David Lifton. [continuing...] "High Treason."

Gunn: And that's by Harry Livingstone?

Custer: Right. And let's see, what else? [Custer looked to me for assistance; I had met Custer at the airport and had taken him to his hotel room, as was our usual procedure with medical deposition witnesses who were unfamiliar with Washington D.C. In his hotel room, at Jeremy's request, I had examined the materials he had brought with him in response to the *Subpoena Deuces Tecum*.]

Horne: He has the manuscript of "Treachery in Dallas;" and I told him it's been published. [The author is Walt Brown.]

Custer: Right. I have the original manuscript.

Gunn: And have you read "Treachery in Dallas?"

Custer: I read the manuscript, now [sic].

Gunn: Okay, sure.

Custer: I'm not sure about the book.

Gunn: Sure, that's fine. Are there any other books that you recall that you have read on the assassination or autopsy?

460

Custer: No, that's it.

_____

Gunn: Was there ever a time at which you were asked or requested not to speak about the autopsy of President Kennedy?

Custer: Well, there was [sic] two different situations. The next day [i.e., November 23, 1963], when Dr. Ebersole came back to Bethesda with the bone fragments and the bullet fragments—that time; and the time in the morgue—there's three, actually—and in [Rear Admiral] Galloway's office.

Gunn: Maybe if we could go through those three events in order. The first time that you were asked not to discuss the autopsy was which time?

Custer: In the morgue.

Gunn: Okay, in the morgue. And that was when in the morgue? On the night of November 22nd or 23rd?

Custer: On that night.

Gunn: Okay. And who was it that asked you not to speak of—

Custer: Dr. Ebersole. He made it perfectly clear that I was not to speak about this.

Gunn: If you could convey the sense of the words that he gave you as best you can, what—

Custer: "Keep your mouth shut."

Gunn: Okay. That's perfectly blunt.

Custer: Plain and simple.

Gunn: Okay. And the second time you were asked, or requested, or instructed not to talk about the autopsy was when?

Custer: That was the next day, after he had come back from the White House from being debriefed.

Gunn: And that was, again, Dr. Ebersole who—

Custer: Dr. Ebersole.

Gunn: —who had said it to you. Then, the third time was—

Custer: Let's back up one thing.

Gunn: Sure.

Custer: At that time, he made it quite clear, this came from [a] high level that I was not to say anything. And he reiterated "anything." If I did, I would be quite sorry.

Gunn: Did he tell you whom he—you mentioned a moment ago that he had been to the White House.

Custer: Right.

Gunn: Did he tell you whom he had spoken with at the White House?

Custer: Yes, he did.

Gunn: Whom did he say he spoke with?

Custer: The head of the Secret Service.

Gunn: When he said that high-level people—

Custer: Right.

Gunn: —did not want anything to be discussed, did he tell you who those high-level people were?

Custer: No. He just said high-level people.

Gunn: Was Mr. Reed with you—let me withdraw that. You're acquainted with the name Edward Reed?

Custer: Yes.

Gunn: He was the one who was the [x-ray technology] student whom you identified in the photograph [from *Best Evidence*].

Custer: Correct.

Gunn: Was Mr. Reed with you, either during the first time that you received the instructions from Dr. Ebersole or the second time?

Custer: No. He was with me the third time, when we were both in Dr.—well, actually Vice Admiral Galloway's office. [Galloway, the Commanding Officer of the National Naval Medical Center, was actually a Rear Admiral. The only person the Medical

Corps of the U.S. Navy who was a Vice Admiral in 1963 was the Surgeon General of the Navy, VADM Kenney.]

Gunn: Okay. Could you tell me about the third time that you received instructions not to speak about the—

Custer: Well, that was the most traumatic. After I signed the gag order, I was told if anything—no matter what—got out, it would be the sorriest day of my life. I'd spend most of my life behind prison walls.

Gunn: And did that sound—that threat sound credible to you?

Custer: Very credible.

Gunn: Let me show you a document marked Exhibit no. 195 [the 'letter of silence' addressed to Custer], and ask you whether you have previously seen that before?

Custer: Yep, this is it.

Gunn: Now, I note that the document that does not appear to have a signature on that. Do you see any signature on it?

Custer: No, I don't.

Gunn: Is that the document—obviously, without the signature that—

Custer: Correct.

Gunn: —that you ended up signing?

Custer: Correct. I would not get out of that office unless I signed that signature, because there were armed guards. They were right behind me. And I know for a fact, if I did not sign that, I would have been gone. It was made quite clear.

Gunn: Who else was—who else received instructions about not speaking about the autopsy at the time that you did?

Custer: The only two people that were there was myself and Mr. Reed.

Gunn: So, Dr. Ebersole was not there at that time?

Custer: No, he wasn't.

Gunn: Did you see Mr. Reed sign a statement similar to the one I just handed you?

Custer:	Yes, I did. He's another one that wouldn't have got [sic] out of the office, unless—
Gunn:	Okay.
Custer:	They didn't have armed MPs [Military Police] standing there for nothing.
Gunn:	Is it your understanding now that the order of secrecy has been lifted?
Custer:	Yes, it is.
Gunn:	Do you have any hesitancy now about talking candidly about what you witnessed—
Custer:	Absolutely not.
Gunn:	I'd like to ask you for your own individual sense and judgment of the quality of your memory of the events from November 22nd and 23rd. How good do you think your memory is of those events?
Custer:	Unfortunately, too good.

Timeline Questions: What Happened, and in What Order?

Gunn:	Approximately when did you take the first x-rays of President Kennedy?
Custer:	Approximately, I would say, it would have to—the first thing I remember—it would have to be after the Y-incision was made, so the autopsy was already in progress.
Gunn:	Okay. Let me try and get a little bit of timing.
Custer:	Sure.
Gunn:	And I understand this won't be entirely certain. Approximately how much time passed between the time that you first saw President Kennedy's body and the time that you took the first post Y-incision x-ray photo—x-ray?
Custer:	I would safely say within an hour. Maybe a little less. Maybe a little more, but it wasn't any more than that.
Gunn:	Okay. We'll come back and go through the—
Custer:	Sure.
Gunn:	—through these things. Did you take x-rays in different series? And by that I mean, for example, did you take some x-rays of the head, leave and develop them, and then come back and take other x-rays?

Custer:	Correct.
Gunn:	So, you took different x-rays, developed them, came back—
Custer:	Right.
Gunn:	—and took others?
Custer:	Okay. And can I reiterate on this a little bit?
Gunn:	Sure.
Custer:	Basically, because we didn't have enough film there at the time. So, we had to take things in series, run back, develop them, and then bring them back.
Gunn:	What is your best recollection of the number of series of x-rays that you took on the night of November 22nd/23rd?
Custer:	You mean numbers of—pertaining to the head?
Gunn:	Just how many—
Custer:	Pertaining to the neck?
Gunn:	How many times did you take a series of x-rays, then go and develop them, and come back?
Custer:	Figure—Well, let's see. One, two, three, four, five; one. That would be one. Took one, two, three; two. About three or four times.
Gunn:	Okay.
Custer:	Maybe five, at the most.
Gunn:	Did you, at any point during the evening, see anyone from what I would call the Presidential entourage or the Presidential party?
Custer:	The first round of x-rays. I was coming up the main hall—Like I explained to you—
Gunn:	You're referring to the main hall at Bethesda?
Custer:	Well, the—
Gunn:	—Bethesda hospital?

Custer:	The picture that we had here. Coming up the main hall towards the rotunda as they were coming in. And this is where I was stopped by the Secret Service.
Gunn:	So, you're referring—stopped just before you entered into the rotunda?
Custer:	Right. They did not even want them to see me, because there was all the press here coming in. And they didn't want them to know that that was there.
Gunn:	Okay. So, the Presidential party passed through the rotunda in front of you.
Custer:	Correct.
Gunn:	And then what happened to the Presidential party?
Custer:	They got onto the elevators, and went up to the towers.
Gunn:	And after they had done that, what did you do?
Custer:	I was allowed to go past, go to the back hall, and up to the x-ray department.
Gunn:	Okay. How were you able to determine that there were—the people you saw were from the Presidential entourage?
Custer:	I saw Jacqueline Kennedy in the bloody dress that she still had on.
Gunn:	Did you see anyone else you recognized?
Custer:	If I'm not mistaken, I think I saw Bobby Kennedy that night, too. It was either Bobby or Teddy. I'm not sure right off the—I saw one of the brothers. I remember seeing them.
Gunn:	Did you, at that time—or were you, at that time, able to identify the Secretary of Defense, Robert McNamara?
Custer:	No.
Gunn:	If you had seen Robert McNamara, would you have known who he was?
Custer:	At that time?
Gunn:	At that time, 1963.
Custer:	Probably not.
Gunn:	Okay. What was the last series of x-rays that you took on the night of November 22nd

or 23rd?

Custer: The lower portion of the body.

Gunn: And about how long after the first x-rays that you took did you take the last series of x-rays?

Custer: Well, that's going to be kind of difficult, because every time we brought x-rays back—every time we brought x-rays back, they were placed on the viewing box. There was a conversation between Ebersole and the two gentlemen who were doing the autopsy. And, of course, the gallery had to stick their two cents in, and—it had to be most of the night.

Jeremy tried asking the same question in a different way:

Gunn: What was, in a very general way, the condition of the body at the last time that you saw it on the night of November 22nd/23rd?

Custer: Do you want me to be blunt?

Gunn: Yes.

Custer: A mess. There was body fluid everywhere. The body was literally butchered.

This was a melodramatic answer, but it didn't help Jeremy with establishing a timeline for the taking of x-rays. Jeremy tried again:

Gunn: Did you see reconstruction of the body at all by morticians?

Custer: I remember when I looked into the skull—I remember seeing an apparatus in there. I wasn't sure of what it was. I just remembered this.

Gunn: When was it that you saw what you've described as "an apparatus" in the skull?

Custer: This was in the first series of films. The only reason why this [memory] clicked is, because I remember I was told by the duty officer that the corpse was taken to Walter Reed hospital first—compound—Walter Reed compound first, and then brought to Bethesda.

Gunn: Could you describe the apparatus that was in the skull?

Custer: It was non-human. It had—I'm not sure if it was metallic or plastic. There was so much going on at that time. I just happened to see it. It registered. And that was it.

Gunn: Did anyone besides the duty officer make any reference to Walter Reed?

Custer: Yes, that one gentleman who was in the [free lance photographer's] picture with Reed and myself, that was at the end there. [Indicating, gesturing to the photograph in *Best Evidence*.]

Gunn: On the far—the one on the far left?

Custer: Far left; right. He was the duty officer. No, not there. The other picture.

Gunn: Yeah. In addition to the duty officer, was there anyone else?

Custer: The chief on duty that night. There was two.

Gunn: Okay.

Custer: There was a duty officer and a duty chief.

Gunn: Okay. And they both said that the body had been to Walter Reed?

Custer: Right; Walter Reed compound. They didn't say "hospital." They said "compound."

Gunn: Did you hear anyone else make any statements about Walter Reed, other than the duty officer and the duty chief?

Custer: That's the only two.

I really didn't know what to make of all this then, and I don't know what to make of it now. But I am skeptical. The reason is because all of this—the "apparatus" in the head, and the rumors of JFK's body coming from Walter Reed—were discussed in one form or another in Lifton's book *Best Evidence*. For example, Lifton speculated in the illustration section of his book about what he thought looked like "a clip in the head" in one of the bootleg autopsy photographs (of the superior view of the head while the body was lying supine on the examination table), and in his text he reported in detail the consideration of Walter Reed hospital as a potential site for the autopsy by those aboard Air Force One. I was skeptical because Custer had not mentioned these things during either his 1979 audiotaped interview with David Lifton, or his 1989 videotaped Lifton interview. Was he making this up to make himself look more important? Had his memory become modified after reading assassination books, so that he now really believed what he was saying here? I do not have a firm opinion, to this day. But I am skeptical.

Gunn: Did you ever have occasion to make x-rays of any bone fragments from the head of President Kennedy?

Custer: That was the next day, in a private room up on the fourth floor, with a portable x-ray unit. And at—Do you want me to reiterate a little bit?

Gunn: Okay.

Custer: I was told to place bone fragments on these—or not bone fragments—metal fragments that were given to me on these portions of the skull, and [to] take different exposures.

Gunn: Okay. We'll get back to that later.

Jeremy and I had previously discussed the claims of various autopsy participants as reported in different assassination books, particularly the books written by Lifton and Livingstone, which both concentrated largely upon the medical evidence. I knew Jeremy well enough to sense that he was extremely skeptical about this claim of Custer's, which had been reported in one of Harry Livingstone's books, *High Treason 2*. Jeremy had been interested in talking about x-rays no. 4, 5, and 6 of the loose skull fragments referenced in the autopsy report, not about Custer's claims that Ebersole wanted him to take x-rays of metal fragments taped to bone, which had been written about in *High Treason 2*. Jeremy was skeptical about this claim of Custer's because it was relatively recent. He had given Custer the "brush off."

Custer: Okay.

Gunn: Were you present in the autopsy [room] during the time that any photographs were taken?

Custer: Photographs were being taken all the time. When I'd finish a set of films, Floyd [Riebe] would come in and shoot his films. He'd run through a complete roll of films, and take them out of his camera. This is a couple of times—what struck me funny [is that] a couple of them were taken away from him. Then he'd take another camera and place it in like, little containers. A couple of the Secret Service come over, and took them away from him for some reason. I—I couldn't figure that out. And Floyd kind of got to the point where he got upset about it and said, "Hey."

Gunn: When you say "Floyd," you're referring to Floyd Riebe?

Custer: Right. Correct.

Gunn: Did you see any agent, yourself, take film away from him?

Custer: Yes, I did.

Gunn: Did you see any agent actually expose film to light?

Custer: Not at that time.

Gunn: Did you at any point during the autopsy—

Custer: No.

Gunn: —actually see it?

Custer: No. I was too busy. I just remember seeing that particular incident.

Gunn: In addition to seeing Floyd Riebe take photographs, did you see anyone else take photographs?

Custer: There was a chief there that night that was taking movies. Remember how I had stated [earlier in the deposition] that he was the gentleman that had committed suicide, supposedly, and had the deformed hand—where they found the gun in the deformed hand? He was there that night, taking movies.

Gunn: Did you actually see him taking movies?

Custer: Yes, I did.

Gunn: What kind of movie camera was he using?

Custer: I would imagine, a simple 8 millimeter.

Gunn: Was he wearing a uniform?

Custer: Yes, he was.

Gunn: And what was his rank?

Custer: Chief [meaning "Chief Petty Officer," or an E-7, in the Navy].

Gunn: Did you hear any discussion during the time of the autopsy about movies being taken?

Custer: Well, there was [sic] quite a few upset people from the gallery that were—didn't like the idea. But the chief just kept right on going. He said "I'm doing my job."

Gunn: In addition to the chief who was—do you remember the chief's name?

Custer: No, I don't.

Gunn: Does the name Pitzer mean anything to you?

Custer: Yes. Now it rings a bell, but I'm not quite sure. But that name "Pitzer" does ring a bell.

Gunn: Are you able to elaborate at all why you—

Custer: Not really. I'm not sure if it was—it could have been brought to my recollection that night that we had the get-together in Pittsburgh. [This referred to a videotaped joint interview session in Pittsburgh in which many of the former Navy enlisted men at the autopsy had been interviewed by GNC Communications in 1992.] I think it was Pittsburgh. Yes, it was. [Dennis David was at the Pittsburgh taped interview session.]

Gunn: But did you know that name at all the night of the—

Custer: No, I didn't know that name at that time. No, I didn't. Some of this stuff is starting to come back.

Gunn: Did you see any other photographers during the night of the autopsy?

Custer: No. The only ones I saw were the news photographers out in the rotunda and the ones that kept trying to get in there. And the—and the [Marine] guards kept keeping them out.

Gunn: Do you know the name John Stringer?

Custer: I've heard the name, but I don't recollect personally who he is.

Gunn: Okay. A few questions back, I asked you if you had seen the body of President Kennedy at any time after there had been reconstruction. We then went off to the apparatus that you talked about. Could we go back, and let me ask you again. Did you see the body at all after there had been any morticians reconstructing or sewing the body—

Custer: When I left, the mortician was coming in.

Gunn: At the time that you left when the mortician was coming in, is that the last time that you saw President Kennedy's body?

Custer: Absolutely. That's when I took my x-ray machine and all my cassettes with me.

Gunn: Prior to the time of the autopsy of President Kennedy, had you ever been present during an autopsy?

Custer: Once or twice. And that was, basically, because of the training that I had to go through—the entry training, just to see what the cadavers looked like.

Custer then explained that he had seen one gunshot wound autopsy of a Marine killed when playing

471

"quick draw" with another Marine. He stated that this particular autopsy, of a gunshot wound to the head, was quite efficient and done very methodically, and that the doctor on that occasion knew exactly what he was doing.

Custer: ...I could honestly say that night was a total disaster.

Gunn: When you say "that night," you're referring to November 22nd, 1963?

Custer: November—right.

Gunn: In what ways did the autopsy, as you observed it on November 22nd, differ from the previous gunshot autopsy that you had seen?

Custer: They would pull out an organ—a big organ, and be up there cutting it up like a piece of meat.

Gunn: This is on November 22nd?

Custer: Right; November 22nd. And then—their basic thing was, "we're looking for shells, bullets, fragments." They weren't looking to, what caused it? How was it done? What was the tracing—what was the path of the bullet?

Gunn: How is it that you came to the impression that what they were doing was looking for bullet fragments?

Custer: That was plain and simple. They come right out and said, "You're taking x-rays for bullets."

Gunn: Do you recall who it was that said that?

Custer: Both. Humes said this to Ebersole, and Ebersole said the same thing to me. And then he turned to me and said, "Take whatever films you feel necessary." And he's the radiologist. He's supposed to lead me, not me leading him. And I'm showing him the films. And I'm saying, "Well hey, Doc, don't you think this—" [and Ebersole replied] "Shut up. It's none of your business."

Gunn: Do you know whether Dr. Ebersole knew how to take x-rays himself?

Custer: Let me—let me specify something to you right now. He's a Lieutenant—well, no. He's not a Lieutenant Commander. He's a full Commander [O-5] in the United States Navy. If you know anything about ranking officers and enlisted men, ranking officers do not—do not—lower themselves and do an enlisted man's job. If they have a technician there, the technician takes the x-rays. The radiologist reads the x-rays. Plain and simple. It's an unwritten law.

Gunn: That said, do you know whether Dr. Ebersole knew how to take x-rays, if he had wanted to? And what I'm asking is not what you would guess, but just what you know.

Custer: I'm not trying to be facetious about this, but that's funny. Dr. Ebersole had a very high-falutin' attitude about such things. [such as] "I don't want to dirty my hands." And this was his opinion. "I am here." [gesturing, pointing up] You are here." [gesturing, pointing down] "That's fine. If you want to feel that way, that's fine. I'll do my job. Do my job to the best of my ability. But don't step on my toes, and say you're doing my job." And he had a bad habit of doing that. He was a gentleman that liked to bask in the glory. But when the heat came down, he was the first one that went out the door.

Gunn: When you say "the heat came down," are you referring to his behavior generally, or are you referring to something specifically on the night of the autopsy?

Custer: Well, he was not a leader. He was a person that could be led. He was told what to do, and he did it.

Gunn: Just with respect to the autopsy and what you observed that night, did you see Dr. Ebersole doing something different from what you thought he should be doing during the course of the autopsy?

Custer: Correct. Yes, absolutely. He should have been directing me, as he viewed the films. Each set of films I brought down to him, I put on a board. I had a certain amount of expertise that I felt should have been noticed. I tried to bring this up to him, and tried to suggest different things to him. And he wouldn't—wouldn't listen. He kept listening to the gallery. He was being led. Plain and simple. It was right there. You couldn't help but see it.

Gunn: When you say he was being led by the gallery, do you mean by particular people in the gallery?

Custer: At least two particular people. One, a high-ranking military official. There was a four—four star general in there. Plus, there was a *civilian gentleman,* which I took to be Kennedy's personal physician because of the way he talked, particularly pertaining to the myelogram dye in the back. He knew exactly what it was.[16] And

_____

[16]This is a significant indicator of Custer's veracity in regard to instructions from the gallery. Jeremy had not yet shown him any x-rays of the body, and Custer had not read the HSCA report; therefore, he could not have known about the dye near JFK's spinal canal except possibly from reading the Ebersole transcript the night prior to his deposition in his hotel room (which he indicated he did do). I am inclined to believe that this was an independent recollection on Custer's part from the autopsy, and not a fabrication invented by

the only person who would know situations like that would be the personal physician. [Author's emphasis]

I wondered here if Custer was talking about RADM Burkley, the Military Physician to the President, who did wear civilian clothes on November 22, 1963. Dr. Boswell told the HSCA staff in 1977 that Burkley controlled the autopsy, and there are numerous witnesses from the morgue who recalled that Burkley kept trying to limit the scope of the autopsy, first to the head only, then extending it only to the upper thorax (the chest), then finally allowing access to the abdomen. Some witnesses have described Burkley's only concern being the recovery of bullets from the cadaver. Apparently he invoked the name of the Kennedy family whenever he attempted to limit the scope of the autopsy, attributing the restrictions to their wishes. It is not known with any certainty whether this was *actually true,* simply because the grieving family wanted to "get it over with," and also hide evidence of President Kennedy's Addison's disease; or whether Burkley was attempting to carry out a medical cover-up (of a conspiracy) on the orders of Robert Kennedy; or whether "the wishes of the family" was a complete smokescreen used by Burkley because he was part of a conspiracy, an 'inside job.' But one thing is clear: Dr. Burkley was not interested in the 35th President getting a full and complete autopsy—he was only interested in recovering bullets and bullet fragments at Bethesda the night of November 22-23, 1963. Additionally, in support of what Custer was telling us here, autopsy medical technologists Paul O'Connor and James Jenkins, respectively, told the HSCA staff of apparent control over the autopsy by persons 'whispering' in the morgue and 'relaying suggestions from the gallery.' O'Connor and Jenkins both corroborate Custer in this regard. O'Connor spoke of this with some eloquence on film to British documentary producer Nigel Turner in the documentary "The Men Who Killed Kennedy." In doing so, O'Connor was simply confirming what he and Jenkins had both told the HSCA staff in August of 1977. Finally, the reader will recall that Dr. Karnei, the second year resident at Bethesda the night of the autopsy, told the ARRB staff that photography in the morgue was controlled by "the people controlling the autopsy," i.e., the Secret Service—like Dr. Burkley, 'men in suits,' persons of authority dressed in civilian clothes.

Gunn: And were this general and the person in civilian clothing giving instructions to Dr. Ebersole?

Custer: Correct. Absolutely.

Gunn: And what kinds of directions were they giving him?

Custer: In a sense that, "The Kennedy family would not allow—like you to pursue that path any further. We do not want you to go any more in this direction."

Gunn: Did you perceive those sorts of comments during the night of the autopsy to be

---

him after reading the Ebersole transcript. If an authentic and independent recollection, it would confirm that it was almost certainly Dr. Burkley in the gallery giving instructions, and that Custer was indeed involved in helping to interpret, or in attempting to help interpret, the x-rays—and that he was paying attention that night.

related to personal health problems and disfigurement of the body, or did you understand them to be pertaining to something else?

Custer: I understood them to be pertaining to something else.

Gunn: What was it that you understood them to be pertaining to?

Custer: Let me put it this way, plain and simple. The autopsy was something that had to be done. It didn't have to be done correctly. It had to be done for record purposes only. Finding out the facts, forget it. This is something that had to be done, but done in a way that it's not going to implicate. And this is, basically, the opinion I got, because I made that statement, and I was told to shut up.

Gunn: To whom did you make the statement?

Custer: Well, I made it to Dr. Ebersole. And Dr. Ebersole told me right away to shut my mouth. "Do your job." Now, it didn't take a person with a genius intelligence to figure it out. It was right there.

Gunn: Were there any other observations that you had that night that led you to draw the conclusions that you've been drawing?

Custer: The film being taken from Floyd—the photographs and—or the exposed photographs. The comments being made. Dr. Finck coming in and pushing him, Ebersole—or not Ebersole—Humes and Boswell out of the limelight, and taking over. [At this point I suddenly remembered Stringer revealing to me that Finck had "caused too much trouble at the autopsy," while waiting for his ride in the lobby of Archives II after his deposition had concluded.] Different phone calls being received during the autopsy. Now, you know as well as I do. When you're doing a forensic autopsy, you do not want to be disturbed. Your mind is following a train of thought. You're not receiving phone calls. He received phone calls from Dallas. I know for a fact that he received phone calls from downtown Washington.

Gunn: Let me go back to Dr. Finck, and talk about the phone calls.

Custer: Sure.

Gunn: In what way did the direction of the autopsy change after Dr. Finck arrived?

Custer: In the sense that he was more—how can I put it—cohesive [???] with directions from the gallery. When I lifted the body up to take films of the torso, and the lumbar spine, and the pelvis, *this is when a king-sized fragment—I'd say—estimate around three, four centimeters—fell from the back.* And this is when *Dr. Finck came over with a pair of forceps, picked it up,* and took—that's the last time I ever saw it. Now, it was big enough—that's about, I'd say, *an inch and a half.* My finger, my small

475

finger. First joints. [Author's emphasis]

At this point in Custer's testimony, I immediately thought of several "indicia" that were consistent with his recollection of a fragment falling from the lower part of President Kennedy's back:

1.   John Stringer testified to the ARRB that the pathologists had sat President Kennedy in the upright position so that he could photograph *"some openings in the back."* Was there a second back wound (other than the one recorded high in the back in the autopsy report)? Is this where the fragment came from?

2.   Robert Knudsen testified to the HSCA staff that he had *seen a probe going through the thorax and coming out the mid part of the back in a black-and-white negative.* If correct, this probe could have been tracing the bullet track associated with the fragment described by Custer.

3.   In the HSCA OCR of his August 25, 1977 interview, Paul O'Connor is reported to have told the HSCA staff that he was asked by either Humes or Boswell to leave the morgue during the evisceration of the body cavity, and was guarded by a Marine during the estimated 30 or 40 minutes while he was outside. He told the HSCA staff that when he re-entered the morgue, the body cavity had been sutured shut. He said an x-ray technician told him that x-rays had been taken of the eviscerated body while he was outside the morgue. Later, someone else told him *that he had missed probing of the body* when he was outside the morgue. He also told the HSCA staffers that he had later asked fellow autopsy technician James Jenkins what he had missed, and Jenkins had told him that *the pathologists had found a fragment of a bullet lodged in the intercostal muscle on the right rear side of the President's body.* O'Connor said that one of the corpsmen, possibly the photographer [Riebe?], told him that *a lot of blood had infiltrated the intercostal muscle.* [The intercostal muscle is the muscle in between the individual rib bones.]

4.   One receipt from the autopsy has never been satisfactorily explained: it is the 'receipt of a missile' dated November 22, 1963 and addressed from FBI agents Sibert and O'Neill to CAPT Stover, and signed by them. Since the only bullet fragments from the body mentioned in the autopsy report, or the telegram Sibert and O'Neill sent to FBI headquarters after they left the morgue, or their FD-302 report of 11/26/63 were incredibly tiny (7 x 2 mm and 3 x 1 mm), and since there were *two* of them and not just *one,* it has always been hard to believe that this receipt was for those *two tiny slivers* of metal. The language is wrong—the receipt says "a missile"—and those two tiny pieces of metal would have been described by a reasonable person as "two small metallic fragments," or "two bullet fragments of such-and-such dimensions." However, Custer was describing a substantial piece of metal which he said was probably an inch-and-a-half long, which would seem to equate to the major portion of a bullet: the perfect object that might be described in a receipt as 'a missile.' The actual wording of the receipt reads: "We hereby acknowledge receipt of a missile removed by Commander James J. Humes, MC, USN on this date." It was prepared by the Navy, so Humes' name may have been used simply because he was designated as the chief prosecutor at the autopsy. This rather mysterious and unexplained receipt could have been for the fragment that fell out of the body when Custer was either

placing or retrieving his x-ray cassette, and which he recalls was picked up by Dr. Finck with a pair of forceps. If this is the case, it would mean that not only have Humes, Boswell, Finck, and Ebersole been covering up existence of the intercostal fragment all these years, but so have Sibert and O'Neill. This possibility will be explored later.

All of the above "dots" were connected in my mind in a flash; their association with the fragment described by Custer had been instantaneous. It was a true "ah ha" moment—an epiphany, if you will. This is what comes from immersing yourself in a mass of interrelated evidence to the point where you can almost quote various citations verbatim; when you 'swim in that sea' on a regular basis, insights like this are possible. Jeremy continued:

Gunn: In addition to identifying that fragment or picking up that fragment, what else did Dr. Finck do that led you to believe that he was taking—or that he was directing the autopsy?

Custer: *Well, he would bark orders at Humes and Boswell.*   [Author's emphasis]

Gunn: What kinds of orders did he give?

Custer: "Stop that. Don't do that anymore." Where—"you take records" or "you take notes." "Yes."

Gunn: *Was it your impression that Dr. Finck was taking instructions from one or more persons in the gallery,* or he was—   [Author's emphasis]

Custer: *Absolutely.*   [Author's emphasis]

Gunn: And from whom was he taking instructions?

Custer: From the same two gentlemen that had kept rolling the situation all that night.

Gunn: You've previously referred to that person being a four-star general. Which service was that four-star general with; do you know?

Custer: I'll be honest with you. I can't recollect. All I saw was four big stars. And that was enough.

Gunn: But you're calling him a general. It's, presumably, not an Admiral. I guess that's fair.

Custer: Yes.

Gunn: Presumably, it would be *either Army or Air Force?* [Author's emphasis]

Custer:	*Oh, it has to be one of the two.* I know an Admiral when I see one. Absolutely. He's got gold halfway up to his elbow. [Author's emphasis]

Pages From the Past: A Possible Clue to Who Was Controlling the Autopsy is Pulled From the Trash 'in the Nick of Time'

I mention a possibility here—just a possibility, not proof. It is a clue to the possible identity of the four-star general Custer mentions as being one of the two VIPs in the gallery of the Bethesda morgue who were apparently controlling the autopsy. (I have already identified RADM Burkley as the probable identity of the person in civilian clothes.) The ARRB received an Air Force logbook literally rescued from the trash at Andrews Air Force Base by a civil servant named Chuck Holmes during an office clean-out. He had received an all-DOD message stimulated by one of the ARRB omnibus search requests sent to the DOD General Counsel, and was responding to that 'dragnet' military telegram. The assassination record was an old large-format green military logbook with a cloth cover (i.e., hardbound), with the word "RECORD" printed on the cover, and "authenticated" by real coffee rings from coffee cups that had been placed on the cover and had sloshed their contents. It had the identifier "1254th ATW [Air Transport Wing] Command Post" stamped on the cover, and hand-printed on two labels were the words "JFK Assassination" and "RFK Assassination 5 June 1968." It really was an incredible find. The question was, did it contain anything important of an evidentiary nature, or was it just an interesting historical curiosity with sentimental value? At the very least this digression is an interesting story; and yet, on the other hand, it may be a vital clue to what really happened inside the Bethesda morgue, and to the United States of America, on November 22, 1963.

The first 7 pages of the log are titled "Death of J.F.K. 22 Nov 63," and later in the mostly empty logbook were 2 additional pages titled "Death of R.F.K. 05 June 68." Presumably, someone had placed it aside after November 22nd, in the belief that it had historical significance and should not have routine entries placed alongside those of November 22, 1963—and then someone else, who had custody of the log and was still aware of its significance in June, 1968 when Robert Kennedy was assassinated, had put the logbook to use again, recording the details of official transportation associated with RFK's assassination. (I become very sad whenever I look at my personal photocopy of this record; it is a grim reminder of the overwhelming tragedy that befell both the Kennedy family and this nation during the 1960s.) The two logs contain the tail numbers of aircraft, and for the most part denote takeoff times, destinations, ETAs, and arrival times at destinations.

To familiarize the reader with the format of the log entries, we will first examine some of the more 'routine' or 'non-controversial' entries in the 7 pages devoted to air operations connected to the JFK assassination (all times are local, i.e., EST, as indicated in the log):

Local Time	Text Entry in Logbook (Verbatim)	Author's Explanation
1446 [2:46 PM]	"Received word from 86972—returning to HIK, min gnd time, direct Dallas"	86972 is the tail number of the aircraft that Secretary of State Dean Rusk and Press Secretary Pierre Salinger were aboard, enroute Japan, when they heard about the JFK assassination. This entry indicates the flight has turned around and is headed for Hickam AFB in Hawaii, will spend minimal time on the ground there (for refueling), and proceed directly to Dallas.
1450 [2:50 PM]	"Set up MSN # 1617 12490 to take Sen Kennedy to OTIS"	Senator Ted Kennedy was being flown to Otis AFB in Massachusetts so that he could notify his father of his brother's assassination in person.
1500 [3:00 PM]	"(C.F.)—WASH ARTC called with flight plan on AF1. ETD Dallas 22/1515 Hi ALT to ADW, 2 + 10 enroute"	The flight plan for Air Force One (tail number 26000) calls for the aircraft to leave Dallas at 1515 (2:15 Dallas Time), fly high altitude to Andrews AFB, and that the flight time would be 2 hours, 10 minutes.
1515 [3:15 PM]	"Change 12490 dest Otis to Barnstable"	Senator Kennedy's flight will no longer land at Otis AFB but at Barnstable instead.
1530 [3:30 PM]	"12490 Sen Kennedy departed for Barnstable. Crew abd acft when he arrived. Sgt Pashney AFCP stated that the S.S. will take care of body at ADW."	The Air Force Command Post has informed the 1254th ATW at Andrews that the Secret Service will take custody of President Kennedy's body upon arrival.

1545 [3:45 PM]	"6000 returning ADW, Mr. Johnson ABD ETA 1725 (returning as AF-1) Body and Mrs. Kennedy ABD"	Tail number 26000 (the brand-new, permanent Presidential Boeing 707 jet), delivered in 1962, has "Mr. Johnson" aboard, along with Mrs. Kennedy and the body of the deceased Commander-in-Chief. No one yet considers LBJ as their President, even though by law he is.
1547 [3:47 PM]	"AF1 Dept DAL, ETA ADW 1805"	The actual takeoff time of Air Force One was 3:47 PM EST, or 2:47 CST (Dallas Time). The ETA at Andrews is 6:05 PM.
1609 [4:09 PM]	"6972 Dept Hik ETA 0024"	The Dean Rusk/Pierre Salinger flight took off from Hickam AFB in Hawaii at 4:09 PM EST, and its ETA at Andrews AFB (now its next destination) is 24 minutes after midnight, EST.
1650 [4:50 PM]	"Call from 26000, need steps fwd door, fwd galley door & lift truck aft PAX door, body in rear"	Air Force One has called via radio and requested passenger steps at the forward passenger door on the left side of the aircraft; additional steps at the forward galley door on the right-hand side of the aircraft; and a lift truck (for the Dallas casket) at the aft passenger door on the left-hand side of the aircraft, near the tail.
1740 [5:40 PM]	"AF1 req four A.P.cars, 2 FWD & 2 AFT of acft on ramp—CONFIRMED"	Air Force One has requested four Air Police cars on the taxi ramp after the aircraft rolls to a stop: 2 forward of the aircraft, and 2 aft of the aircraft.

1800 [6:00 PM]	"AF1 ARR ADW, 12489 slowing down to ARR after ADW opens, 42816 still holding"	Air Force One landed at Andrews AFB at 6:00 PM on November 22, 1963.
1830 [6:30 PM]	"86970 ARR ADW"	Air Force Two (which had been LBJ's airplane for the Texas trip) landed at 6:30 PM
0037 [12:37 AM on November 23rd]	"86972 arrived ADW with Sec Rusk, etc."	Various cabinet members who had been enroute Japan when the President was assassinated land at Andrews AFB after a very long flight from Hickam AFB in Hawaii.

For those readers who have already listened to the edited "Air Force One" audiotapes of communications between Air Force One and the Rusk/Salinger flight, the White House situation room, and various Air Force commands, much of the above will be quite familiar.

Was Air Force Chief of Staff Curtis E. LeMay Present at Bethesda Naval Hospital During President Kennedy's Autopsy?

Next, in the chart below, I have excerpted the movements of **Air Force Chief of Staff General Curtis LeMay** (a four star general, and someone with a strong visceral dislike for President Kennedy), as recorded in the same logbook delivered to the ARRB by Chuck Holmes.

Local Time	Text Entry in Logbook (Verbatim)	Author's Explanation
1420 [2:20 PM]	"2488 and 2493 CANX. 4197 set-up to dept to P/U Gen LeMay at Toronto, Canada. Trip # 1602"	The Air Transport Wing at Andrews is arranging for the Air Force Chief of Staff to return to the United States.
1446 [2:46 PM]	"4197 Dept for Canada. ETA 1546"	LeMay's aircraft has taken off for Toronto.
1450 [2:50 PM]	"Change Gen LeMay's P/U from Toronto to Wairton Canada 44.45 N 81.06 W"	The pickup point for LeMay has changed from Toronto to Wairton, Canada.
1505 [3:05 PM]	"Contacted 24197 (UHF) to change destination to Wairton"	N/A

1625 [4:25]	"24197 Gen LeMay dept Wairton 1604 ETA DCA 1715, Driver and Aide at DCA ETA changed 1710, Secy Zuckert will meet LeMay at ADW. (Notified acft)	General LeMay is going to land at *Washington National Airport* (DCA), adjacent to downtown Washington D.C., **not** at Andrews AFB, which is well south of the nation's Capital. The Secretary of the Air Force (nominally his superior) wants to meet him at Andrews AFB instead. The Air Transport Wing has notified the aircraft that Secretary Zuckert wants LeMay to land at Andrews AFB, not National Airport.
1700 [5:00 PM]	"Gen LeMay will land DCA **not** ADW." [emphasis is <u>in original</u>]	LeMay has just disobeyed the wishes of the civilian who is supposed to be his boss, and has decided to land at DCA, Washington National Airport, anyway. (This speaks volumes.)
1712 [5:12 PM]	"4197 Gen LeMay ARR DCA"	The Air Force Chief of Staff lands at a crowded civilian aviation airport in a military aircraft, in spite of being asked by the Secretary of the Air Force to land at Andrews AFB.

This is all quite interesting, to say the least, since LeMay's selection of Washington National Airport placed him much closer to Bethesda NNMC than landing at Andrews AFB would have. Secretary of the Air Force Zuckert had probably assumed that LeMay would "do the right thing" and land at Andrews to honor the fallen Commander-in-Chief when his body arrived. Not likely.

Deep Background: The Rift Between President Kennedy and General LeMay

General LeMay and President Kennedy shared a barely concealed, mutual contempt for each other which was widely known in Washington, and John F. Kennedy had more than once walked out of a meeting with LeMay in a fit of pique. President Kennedy was so upset when first briefed in September 1961 by General Lyman Lemnitzer (Chairman of the Joint Chiefs of Staff) about America's inflexible plan for total, world-wide nuclear war, SIOP-62—the 'Single Integrated Operational Plan' for Fiscal Year 1962—that he spent most of the meeting tapping on his teeth with his thumbnail, a sign of great irritation in him, and said in disgust to Secretary of State Dean Rusk at the conclusion of the meeting, "And we call ourselves the human race." (Although the target list in the first SIOP had been developed in 1960—and was officially the brainchild of LeMay's protégé and replacement as head of SAC, General Power—it was at heart really LeMay's plan, even though briefed by Lemnitzer, for it reflected LeMay's personal philosophy of massive *and continuing* retaliation for several days, in the event of nuclear war.) At that time, the SIOP essentially called for the massive and overwhelming destruction of the *entire* Communist bloc[17]—both military bases and major civilian targets (cities)—in the event of a nuclear war with any one of its members.[18] It was overkill on a grand scale, and greatly upset President Kennedy, who was already preoccupied about the danger—even the likelihood—of accidental nuclear war through mistakes or miscalculation, to the point where after this briefing, he ordered the SIOP revised to allow a more flexible response by the Commander-in-Chief than the obligatory destruction of half of the planet in the event of nuclear conflict. The revised plan, called SIOP-63, went into effect just prior to the Cuban Missile Crisis. LeMay, for his part, considered Kennedy a 'weak sister,' and was angry with JFK for not immediately bombing, and then invading Cuba during the Missile Crisis in October of 1962. General Thomas Power, an 'extreme personality' who himself sometimes made General LeMay look like a reasonable man, commanded the Strategic Air Command (SAC) during the Cuban Missile Crisis. On Wednesday, November 24, 1962, General Power not only took the dangerous and provocative step of moving SAC from DEFCON-3 to DEFCON-2 (one step short of nuclear war) *without* Kennedy's permission during the crisis, but made *two* unencrypted radio transmissions about this change in status to all of SAC, undoubtedly to ensure that the USSR knew what the U.S. Air Force was doing. (There was a great nuclear weapons imbalance at this time *in favor of* the United States, and both the United States and the Soviet political and military leadership knew this.) Kennedy and his advisors were not only furious that this had happened, but actually horrified, because putting SAC at DEFCON-2 could have been interpreted by the Soviets as the prelude to a pre-emptive "first-strike" by the United States, and thereby increased the risk of general war. General LeMay, as Chief of Staff of the Air Force, was not only responsible for Power's actions, but he supported them after the fact, even though Power had acted independently. (Thomas Power, Curtis LeMay's former Chief of Staff when LeMay commanded SAC, was the handpicked replacement chosen to take over the powerful organization LeMay himself had succored and nurtured through its childhood and adolescence, into the maturity of adulthood.) LeMay, furthermore, had given what new Joint Chiefs of Staff Chairman General Maxwell Taylor later called "half-assed" recommendations during the Missile Crisis, including telling President Kennedy that the Soviet Union would not respond with military force anywhere in the world—not even in Berlin—if the U.S. attacked Cuba, destroyed its missiles, and killed large numbers of its troops and technicians.

---

[17]National Security Advisor McGeorge Bundy called SIOP-62 and its predecessors "a massive, total, comprehensive, obliterating strategic attack...on everything Red." It allowed for no flexibility once nuclear hostilities began.

[18]For example, in a war with the Soviet Union, *all* major strategic targets in Eastern Europe, China, North Korea, and North Vietnam would have been destroyed.

Shortly after the Missile Crisis ended, President Kennedy met with Secretary of Defense Robert McNamara, Deputy Secretary of Defense Roswell Gilpatric, and the Joint Chiefs of Staff in the Cabinet Room at the White House to thank them for their efforts, after achieving a negotiated settlement with the Soviet Union that *both* guaranteed removal of the Soviet missiles from Cuba *and* avoided war. President Kennedy tried to put a good face on what had been a difficult and stressful two weeks with his military leadership, saying that he wanted to tell them how much he admired them and had benefitted from their advice and counsel. President Kennedy said, "Gentlemen, we've won. I don't want you to ever say it, but you know we've won, and I know we've won." At this point the Chief of Naval Operations, Admiral George Anderson, exclaimed "We've been had!" LeMay's own emotional outburst followed immediately thereafter. LeMay—who was enraged that the United States had not bombed and invaded Cuba—pounded the table in the Cabinet room and blurted out, "Won, Hell! We Lost! We should go in and wipe them out today!" LeMay then proclaimed the resolution to the Missile Crisis to be "the greatest defeat in our history," and ejaculated, "Mr. President, we should invade today!"—leaving President Kennedy stunned and stammering in amazement.[19]

President Kennedy and General LeMay no doubt both considered themselves patriots, but they were very different kinds of patriots—the type of men who were so far apart in their respective views of the world that they could not help but despise each other. LeMay was crude, bull-headed, profane, inflexible, demanding, and used to getting his way; President Kennedy was, more than anything else, flexible and open to new ideas, and his World War II experiences had made him very skeptical of the so-called wisdom of senior military officers. The animus between Kennedy and LeMay was real, and quite serious.

LeMay, who had earned his stars in the European Theater during World War II as a B-17 bomber unit commander (in the European 'daylight precision bombing' campaign of the Eighth Air Force) before moving to the Pacific and initiating the firebombing campaign against Japanese cities with the high-tech B-29 Superfortresses,[20] was the ultimate Cold Warrior. He was a strong advocate of nuclear deterrence, and had spent 8 years, from 1949 to 1957, building up the Strategic Air Command (America's extremely efficient and formidable organization established for the purpose of delivering long range nuclear weapons) into the greatest fleet of destruction ever assembled. In doing so he had ushered into service the B-36, B-47, and B-52 bombers, and a huge fleet of tankers to support worldwide operations. Curtis LeMay was *the* pre-eminent symbol of America's nuclear warfighting capability, in the era before the advent of the Polaris ballistic missile submarine. He was

---

[19]Sources for slightly different versions of this charged encounter are the acclaimed documentary interview of Robert McNamara, "Fog of War;" and *The Crisis Years*, by Michael Beschloss.

[20]McNamara called the LeMay he worked for in World War II a man who, although courageous and a strong leader, was someone considered by many to be "extraordinarily belligerent and even brutal"—and that was a description of his relations with his own subordinates. During the firebombing campaign against Japan, LeMay's B-29s killed 50-90% of the Japanese residents of 67 different cities.

upset that JFK had decided the United States only needed a future projected total of 1000 ICBMs, instead of the 3000 nuclear-tipped missiles LeMay wanted. Some military historians actually believe that LeMay attempted to *provoke* a violent response from the Soviet Union during the mid-to-late 1950s—through repeated, provocative overflights by SAC aircraft—and that he wanted to use the hoped for Soviet knee-jerk response as a *pretext* for an annihilating "first strike" against the USSR. During the 1950s, LeMay was certain that a nuclear war with the Soviet Union was not only survivable, but easily winnable, and apparently believed that since nuclear war with the Soviets was inevitable, the U.S. should consider striking first, before the USSR developed effective long-range delivery systems in large numbers. Robert McNamara has said that "LeMay believed that ultimately we were going to confront these people [meaning the Soviet Union] in a conflict with nuclear weapons, and by God, we'd better do it when we have greater superiority than we will have in the future."[21] In 1962, the number of U.S. nuclear warheads outnumbered what the Soviets had by a ratio of 17 to 1, and the respective numbers and reliability of our long-range delivery systems was equally superior. LeMay knew all this, of course, and he knew President Kennedy was aware of it, and was convinced that during the Cuban Missile Crisis, President Kennedy had 'blown' his best political opportunity to launch a justifiable pre-emptive first strike against the Soviet Union, and "win" the nuclear conflict LeMay felt was inevitable.

President Kennedy was so upset with LeMay's unsophisticated, bellicose response to the Cuban Missile Crisis, and his failure to adequately control General Thomas Power and SAC during those events, that he wanted to fire LeMay afterwards, *along with* the Chief of Naval Operations, George Anderson, who had openly quarreled with McNamara in the Pentagon. Kennedy was dissuaded from replacing *both* men by his advisors, because it would have been a public admission of serious friction between President Kennedy and his military leadership, and in the end, he only got rid of George Anderson (by appointing him as Ambassador to Portugal), and hoped to keep Air Force Chief of Staff LeMay "inside the tent pissing out," rather than have him "outside the tent pissing in."[22] JFK made a final public jab at LeMay in his famous 'Peace Speech' at American University in June 1963, encouraging Americans to "re-evaluate our attitude towards the Soviet Union;" saying that if the two peoples could not agree on everything, that the world should at least be made "safe for diversity;" and publicly disavowing those who called for "a Pax Americana enforced on the world by American

---

[21]"Fog of War."

[22]Author Richard Reeves reported in *President Kennedy: Profile of Power* that JFK had "a kind of fit" every time someone mentioned LeMay's name, and once stated to an aide, "I don't want that man near me again," after another frustrating exchange with America's foremost Hawk. His extreme frustration was no doubt exacerbated by the fact that he himself had promoted LeMay from Air Force Vice Chief of Staff to Chief of Staff in June 1961. Kennedy felt obligated to do this for two reasons: first, he could not afford to have LeMay out of uniform making anti-administration speeches about how weak the President was; and second, if the U.S. did get into a major war, LeMay was clearly the kind of commander you wanted in charge of your Air Force. June 1961 was a period of extreme tension with the USSR over Berlin, and no doubt promoting LeMay to Air Force Chief of Staff was an intentional signal which the Soviet military leadership took note of.

weapons of war."[23] This was all a public slap at LeMay and other hard-line Cold Warriors—but primarily at Curtis LeMay. JFK had also ordered Secretary of Defense McNamara to begin installing 'permissive action links' (PALs) on nuclear weapons, to prevent unit or theater commanders from starting a nuclear war on their own initiative during a crisis when emotions were running high. The Nuclear Test Ban Treaty (preventing the testing of nuclear weapons in the atmosphere, under the sea, and in outer space), patiently engineered by the Kennedy Administration over a period of over 2 years, was initialed in July and formally signed in August of 1963. It cannot have made LeMay happy at all, particularly because of the skillful way in which President Kennedy had shepherded its subsequent ratification through an initially dubious U.S. Senate. First, McNamara beat down the Joint Chiefs' initially unanimous objections to the treaty during a 2-week period of intense lobbying within the Pentagon, by convincing them that the test ban would effectively freeze into place the existing American superiority in reduced weapons size and sophistication. Then President Kennedy ensured that *only* McNamara and Maxwell Taylor appeared in the Senate to testify—and that they appeared before the Senate Foreign Relations Committee (whose chairman, Senator Fulbright, was favorably disposed to the treaty) *before* they testified to the more conservative Senate Armed Services Committee. JFK also called in political chips with retired President Eisenhower and Senator Dirksen to ensure their public support, even if lukewarm.

In a tour of Western States in the autumn of 1963, JFK was starting to talk about the themes of world peace and disarmament in his speeches, and those themes were resonating with audiences, even in conservative venues such as Wyoming and Utah. Although Kennedy had spent more money on Defense than President Eisenhower, he clearly was much more flexible and discerning about world events than the senior military leadership that he had inherited, and had scolded them (in writing) for not thinking 'globally' or 'responsibly' in NSAM 55, issued on June 28, 1961.[24]

---

[23]As author Dino Brugioni states in *Eyeball to Eyeball*, LeMay loved to discuss how Roman strength had produced Pax Romana; how the British, through their naval and military strength, had achieved Pax Britannica; and with unabashed gall, how 'his bombers' had achieved 'Pax Atomica.' Once, during a lecture, LeMay resorted to the term 'Pax Americana,' and it was to this that JFK was responding in his commencement address at American University.

[24]National Security Action Memo No. 55, addressed from the President to the Chairman of the Joint Chiefs of Staff (Lyman Lemnitzer, with whom Kennedy agreed on almost nothing) and titled "Relations of the Joint Chiefs of Staff to the President in Cold War Operations," was unusual in its frankness and in the clarity of its criticism. Some key passages read as follows: "I look to the Chiefs to contribute dynamic and imaginative leadership in contributing to the success of the military and paramilitary aspects of Cold War programs...I expect the Joint Chiefs of Staff to present the military viewpoint in governmental councils in such a way as to assure that the military factors are clearly understood before decisions are reached...while I look to the Chiefs to present the military factor without reserve or hesitation, *I regard them to be more than military men and expect their help in fitting military requirements into the overall context of any situation,* recognizing that the most difficult problem in Government is to combine all assets in a unified, effective pattern."

Kennedy did not equate Laos with Vietnam, or Vietnam with Berlin in importance, and the Joint Chiefs of Staff and the civilian Hawks knew it. The President had abruptly 'demoted' or reassigned many of the civilian Hawks within his government into new positions in November 1961, in what came to be known as the "Thanksgiving Day Massacre" within the National Security Council and the State Department. Furthermore, the Cuban Missile Crisis had confirmed his previously held conviction that the risk of accidental nuclear war was a serious problem, and increased his already considerable friction with the Joint Chiefs of Staff, since he refused to implement their advice to bomb and invade Cuba. (No matter how popular President Kennedy may have been with the rank-and-file military man, he was not at all popular with most of the senior military leadership. He did not defer to them, and allow them to make policy the way Eisenhower had. His interaction with them was as an activist, not one of passivity, as they had been accustomed to for the previous 8 years. He rolled up his sleeves and got involved in their business on a regular basis, and made these 'sacred cows' extremely uncomfortable on numerous occasions by openly questioning their advice, and judgment.) Finally, JFK's then Top Secret order to withdraw completely from Vietnam by the end of 1965, passed on initially to the Joint Chiefs in Honolulu in May of 1963 by Secretary of Defense McNamara, and formalized by National Security Action Memo 263 on October 11, 1963, was anathema to military zealots who had been longing to defeat Communism *on the battlefield* ever since the Korean War ended in stalemate and frustration in 1953. These facts did not sit well with Cold War Hawks.

All of the above is prelude to what is admittedly an 'urban legend,' but at any rate is a believable one. Former Navy Hospital Corpsman Paul K. O'Connor, whom I have dubbed the 'original body bag and shipping casket' witness because of his historic interview with the HSCA staff in August of 1977, told an anecdote for many years about something he witnessed during the autopsy on President Kennedy at the Bethesda morgue. The anecdote's essentials are that Dr. Humes, smelling cigar smoke in the morgue, loudly ordered whoever was smoking a cigar to 'put the damn thing out,' and told O'Connor to 'see to it,' or words to that effect. According to O'Connor, while Humes had his back turned to the gallery and was busy conducting the autopsy on the President's body, he (O'Connor) went over to the gallery to enforce Humes' dictate, only to run into the Air Force Chief of Staff, Curtis LeMay, who arrogantly blew smoke in O'Connor's face. When O'Connor informed Dr. Humes of the identity of the culprit, so the story goes, Humes turned quite pale, stuck his tail between his legs, and that was the end of the matter. According to O'Connor, when he saw LeMay the General had removed the four-star insignia from his uniform, but O'Connor recognized him nevertheless.[25]

Kennedy was stimulated to issue this admonishment by the very bad advice he had received from the Joint Chiefs prior to and during the Bay of Pigs fiasco, and over the crisis in Laos, as well. It was LeMay's failure to think globally and geopolitically during the Cuban Missile Crisis—as Kennedy had demanded in this NSAM—that caused JFK to want to sack him.

[25]This is not at all a farfetched possibility. LeMay was an extremely well-known military man who had a very efficient public relations machine of his own, second only to J. Edgar Hoover's; for example, in 1955, he had been glorified in a Jimmy Stewart and June Allyson Cold War film called "Strategic Air Command," where he was appropriately

While O'Connor's anecdotal evidence certainly does not *prove* LeMay was present, the behavior described sounds very much like the real Curtis LeMay. The entries in the logbook rescued by Chuck Holmes prove that LeMay had more than enough time to get to Bethesda from National Airport before President Kennedy's body arrived from Andrews AFB; Lemay landed 48 minutes prior to Air Force One, and Washington National Airport is much closer to Bethesda than Andrews Air Force Base. Did LeMay go to Bethesda to gloat over the corpse of his nemesis, a man he considered dangerously misguided and weak? Was he the four-star general that Custer recollected giving orders, or instructions, from the gallery? And if so, was he doing more than just gloating—was he an integral player in a domestic conspiracy to remove the Chief Executive and replace him with a 'known quantity' who was going to 'play ball' with the Hawks in the government? After Custer's deposition was over, I asked him in private if the uniform shirt of the general in the gallery was green or blue—and he said he thought it was light blue. [Air Force personnel wore light blue shirts; Army personnel wore light green shirts.]

One final item of *possible* corroboration for Custer's claim is the testimony of Pierre Finck at the Shaw Trial in 1969 in New Orleans. The exchange went like this:

Finck: I will remind you that I was not in charge of this autopsy, that I was called—

Oser: You were a co-author of the report, though, weren't you, doctor?

Finck: Wait. I was called as a consultant to look at these wounds; that doesn't mean I am running the show.

Oser: Was Dr. Humes running the show?

Finck: *Well, I heard Dr. Humes stating that—he said, **"Who is in charge here?"** and I heard an Army General, I don't remember his name, stating **"I am."*** You must understand that in those circumstances, there were law enforcement officers, *military people with various ranks, and you have to coordinate the operation according to directions.* [Author's emphasis]

This sounds like the Dr. Finck described by Custer—following instructions from the gallery.

Oser: But you were one of the three qualified pathologists standing at that autopsy table, were you not, doctor?

Finck: Yes, I was.

---

portrayed as a character named "General Hawks" by actor Frank Lovejoy. Many Americans knew who the real Curtis LeMay was in 1963, and knew what he looked like. As Brugioni wrote, "his beetle brows, jutting jaw, sagging jowls, shock of slicked down black hair, and ubiquitous brown cigar" gave him the visage of a bulldog. He was a living icon to many in 1963, especially former and active members of the military.

Oser:	Was this Army general a qualified pathologist?
Finck:	No.
Oser:	Was he a doctor?
Finck:	No, not to my knowledge.
Oser:	Can you give me his name, Colonel?
Finck:	No, I can't. I don't remember.

Later in the Shaw Trial, Finck changed his mind about hearing the Army general say "I am" himself, and turned it into a story—hearsay—that Humes had told him after the fact. That is clearly contradicted by the testimony reproduced above. Some people who have reviewed the Shaw Trial transcript have twisted Finck's words (when he testified that he heard VADM Kenney tell Humes not to discuss the autopsy with anyone) and said it must have been Vice Admiral Kenney, the Surgeon General of the Navy, whom Dr. Finck thought was in charge of the autopsy. I do not find this credible. First, Finck never changed his mind about an Army general saying he was in charge; he only changed his mind about whether or not he heard the general say it himself. Second, Finck testified that he remembered that RADM Galloway and VADM Kenney were both in uniform; if he saw them in uniform and knew that they were Navy Admirals, then he could not possibly have confused them with an Army general. (Finck was in the Army himself and therefore would be most unlikely to confuse a Navy Admiral with an Army General.) In November, a Navy Vice Admiral would be wearing his Dress Blues—a double breasted black uniform blazer (with gold braid "halfway up to his elbows"), over a white shirt. That would have no resemblance whatsoever to an Army Officer's dark green single breasted uniform coat and light green shirt. However, someone from Europe, like Finck, who did not grow up in this country, who was under great stress that evening and perhaps distracted, may just possibly have confused an Air Force general (in a dark blue single breasted uniform coat and light blue shirt) for an Army general—or he may have lied about it to protect himself, if he knew the identity of the Air Force general was the dreaded Curtis LeMay.

The lame explanation Humes offered for the "I am" quote at his ARRB deposition was not at all credible, but it does strongly suggest that he had studied the Finck testimony from the Shaw Trial and had actually adopted the lame story that Shaw's defense team encouraged Finck to use to wiggle out of his predicament. Humes claimed during his ARRB testimony that the "I am" comment was a statement made by the Army General commanding the Military District of Washington (i.e., General Wehle). According to Humes, when he asked on the loading dock, *prior to the arrival of the body,* "who is in charge here?" in order to try to get rid of a newspaper photographer who was trying to get into the morgue area of the hospital, the Commanding General of MDW responded "I am," and then promptly took action to shoo away the offending photojournalist. This doesn't hold water for even one second, because Humes claims this conversation took place *before* the body arrived—whereas Finck did not arrive at the morgue until about 8:30 P.M., after the lungs, heart, and brain had been removed from President Kennedy's body. Finck, remember, was the source of the "I am" quotation; he *originally testified* that he heard it *himself* from the mouth of a general after he himself heard Humes ask "Who is in charge here?" If Finck was not yet present at Bethesda when the oral utterance from General Wehle supposedly came forth on the loading dock, then Humes' sworn testimony to the ARRB cannot possibly be true, and in fact constitutes perjury.

So, if Humes—who oddly enough, volunteered his strange information early in his deposition without even being asked about the incident—perjured himself to avoid questions about the general's real identity, and if Finck offered up a lame excuse later in the Clay Shaw trial because his defense counsel coached him to do so, then the four star general of whom Jerrol Custer spoke *just may have been* Curtis LeMay. The command post logbook of the Andrews Air Force Base Air Transport Wing proves that LeMay *could have been* at the Bethesda morgue, and a basic knowledge of the modern political history of the United States in the late 1950s and the early 1960s provides a strong motive for his possible involvement in a coup.

Before the reader dismisses this possibility, ask yourself two things: why would Humes use words like "hysterical" and "three ring circus" over the years to describe the atmosphere in the morgue, if he was really in charge of the autopsy, as he has always claimed; and why would the Air Force Chief of Staff ignore instructions from the Secretary of the Air Force to land at Andrews Air Force Base, where everyone in America knew the President's body was being flown?

The very fact that Jeremy Gunn asked Dr. Humes, during his deposition, whether General LeMay was at the autopsy, speaks, I think, for itself.

And now back to Custer's testimony before the ARRB.

Dr. Ebersole Destroys an Assassination Record

Jeremy next asked Custer whether he saw people taking notes, and Custer testified that he observed Humes and Boswell taking notes in small black notebooks, and that some people in the gallery were taking notes as well.

Gunn: Were there any other records that you know about that relate to the autopsy? And by that, I would use, for example, log books or any other sorts of documents that you—

Custer: There was a log book in the radiology department. If I'm not mistaken, I made a—I made an entry that I had—was dispatched to the morgue to take films. But I wasn't allowed to place any other identification in there pertaining to what I did, or who it was, or what—whatever.

Gunn: When you say a log book—

Custer: It was a duty log.

Gunn: Duty log. Is there any other name that that went by, other than "duty log?"

Custer: There might have been—the Duty Officer might have made his log. And maybe the

490

Chief—his log, too.

Gunn: Do you have any knowledge as to whether those duty logs are the kind of records that are kept permanently by the military?

Custer: I have no idea. I would basically say no.

Gunn: Were you, at any point, asked to expunge any entries—

Custer: Asked to what?

Gunn: To delete any references.

Custer: Yes, definitely.

Gunn: Could you describe that for me, please?

Custer: Well, I had made the statement on the one duty log, in the main x-ray department, that I was going to the morgue to x-ray President Kennedy. And I was told to eradicate it. In fact, I was told to tear the whole page out.

Gunn: Did you tear the whole page out?

Custer: Yeah. I gave it to Ebersole, and he destroyed it.

Gunn: Did you see him destroy it?

Custer: Yes. I saw him destroy it.

Gunn: Did he give you any explanation as to why he wanted it destroyed?

Custer: "None of my business." That's exactly what he said. I asked him, I said, "What are you burning that up for? That's official government property." And he says, "It's none of your business." And burned it up. That is why I kept saying Dr. Ebersole was not a leader. Dr. Ebersole was a follower. He did what he was told to do.

Gunn: Did you notice anyone else taking notes at the autopsy?

Custer: The only people that I had stated to you: Humes, Boswell, a few of the gallery people. And that's about it, really.

Gunn: Did you see any FBI or Secret Service agents taking notes?

Custer: Oh, that's right. Sibert and O'Neill. I could swear they were writing a book that night. Everything that happened, writing it down.

Gunn:	Had you known Sibert and O'Neill from—
Custer:	Never.
Gunn:	—any other time?
Custer:	And truthfully, I'm not even sure which one followed me. I know it was one of the two of them. It was—I know I said the Secret Service, but I meant FBI. Let me correct that right now. It was the FBI agent that followed me up to the fourth floor. In fact, he was the gentleman who wanted to come into the darkroom with me and watch me develop the films. And I pushed him out, I said, "You can't come in here."
Gunn:	And that was either Mr. Sibert or Mr. O'Neill?
Custer:	One of the two.

More Timeline Questions

Jeremy was still trying to establish how long the various delays were between different events in which the x-ray technologists were involved.

Gunn:	Okay. Just to make sure that I'm understanding. The body [immediately following its arrival] then is taken out [of a casket] and put on the table.
Custer:	Right.
Gunn:	At that point, you were asked to leave.
Custer:	Leave.
Gunn:	Okay.
Custer:	So, from there on, whatever occurred, I was not there.
Gunn:	And so, at this point, you did not take any x-rays yourself?
Custer:	None.
Gunn:	Now, when you left the morgue, where did you go at this point?
Custer:	Back upstairs to the x-ray department, waiting for—
Gunn:	Through the rotunda?
Custer:	Right.

Gunn: And on that trip is not the time that you saw—

Custer: No.

Gunn: —the Presidential entourage?

Custer: No.

Gunn: That was later; is that right?

Custer: Later.

Gunn: And previously you've said that—in this deposition, if I understand it correctly—that you were out of the morgue for—the way that I'm understanding is, you said about an hour. Maybe more, maybe less.

Custer: Right.

Gunn: But approximately an hour.

Custer: Right.

Gunn: Were you with Mr. Reed at that time during that hour, or approximately an hour?

Custer: To the best of my recollections, yes, I do believe so.

Gunn: Was anyone else with you at that time?

Custer: There was a—one of the FBI agents were with us.

Gunn: But at his time, you were not developing any x-rays; is that right?

Custer: No. [meaning you are right, we were not developing any x-rays while waiting]

Gunn: Did you talk at all about what you had just seen?

Custer: No. We were told not to.

I'm personally very skeptical that either one of the FBI agents ever accompanied the x-ray technicians to the main x-ray laboratory on the fourth floor. There were only 2 FBI agents at the autopsy, and their job was simple: it was to accompany the body to Bethesda, to stay with the body, and to retrieve any bullets or bullet fragments removed from the body. A collateral duty was to observe the proceedings at the autopsy and record, to the best of their ability, its findings and conclusions. They would not have been able to do this very well if one of them had spent half the night outside the morgue escorting x-ray technologists back and forth to the main laboratory on the fourth floor. Furthermore, as David Lifton makes clear in *Best Evidence,* or rather, as Chief Layton Ledbetter, duty Chief for the Medical Schools Command, made clear to David Lifton in Lifton's 09/25/79 interview, three Secret Service agents met him in his office about 10 minutes prior to him assuming "the duty" at 4:30 PM, told him there were already 26 Secret Service agents on the compound, and made clear to him that all events henceforth that evening were going to be coordinated by the Secret Service. Furthermore, it was Secret Service agents who confiscated all film in the morgue immediately after it was exposed, per Stringer and Riebe. Likewise, it logically would follow that the Secret Service would take an equally high interest in x-ray images as they did in photographic images. And the Secret Service signed a receipt for x-ray film that night, not the FBI. I doubt that anyone under the circumstances Custer was under would learn the name, much less remember the name, of the Federal agent who accompanied him to and from the x-ray laboratory all night long. No doubt Custer obtained the names Sibert and O'Neill from Lifton's book, since they play such a prominent role in writing a report about that evening, and later convinced himself that one of these men had accompanied him upstairs. None of this means that Jerrol Custer was lying or fabricating a story; it simply means that he was wrong about the identity of his escort. In researcher interviews in previous years, he had always referred to his escorts as Secret Service agents. Furthermore, we know from Lifton's interviews of Navy corpsman James Metzler that some members of the Secret Service were taking copious notes, meticulously recording the names of the personnel entering and leaving the morgue; therefore, just because Custer recalls that the agent who accompanied him was taking notes that night, it does not mean that this agent was either Sibert or O'Neill. Some Secret Service agents took notes, too.

Gunn: What circumstances led to your going back to the morgue?

Custer: We were summoned.

Gunn: Did you get a telephone call?

Custer: Right.

Gunn: Do you remember who the call was from?

Custer: Ebersole.

Gunn: When you went back to the morgue, did you take any film cassettes with you?

Custer: Yes, definitely; because we didn't have enough with us.

Gunn: If I can go out of order chronologically, when did you take the portable x-ray equipment to the morgue?

Custer: Oh, this was at the beginning. This is when we first found out that we were going to be using the machine. And that was down there—placed there before anything had come through. Anything.

Gunn: Could you describe the x-ray—portable x-ray machine that you took to the morgue?

Custer: It was an old G.E. unit that weighed anywhere from 1500 to 2000 pounds. I mean, it was a bulky, old unit.

Gunn: About how big was it? If you can just describe the dimensions—

Custer: All right. I'm about five [feet] eleven [inches tall]. The main tower was pretty close to six foot. [sic] The table—the base unit was approximately three foot by three foot. [sic] And it was about three foot [sic] high. And it had a bunch of knobs on it. It had a door in the front, where all the cassettes would go. And the tube was able to swing 360 degrees, and tilt 90—or 360 either way.

Gunn: Was it on wheels?

Custer: Yes.

Gunn: So, you could push it down the hallway?

Custer: Yes, with great difficulty, of course. This was an old machine that was heavy.

Gunn: Okay. If we can go back now to—

Custer: Sure.

Gunn: —back to the chronology. You have now come back to the morgue after having been summoned by Dr. Ebersole. What do you observe on the body of President Kennedy? What was the condition at that point?

Custer: All right. The body was completely nude. The Y-incision had been made. And the skull literally was a mess.

Gunn: The Y-incision, you say, had been made. Had any of the organs been removed at this time?

Custer: I'm not sure, truthfully. I would safely say yes, because I remember—When I come, I remember Dr. Boswell there, sauteing the liver and—Yeah, it has to be. It has to be. I can't say all of them were removed. I know a good portion of them were removed.

Gunn: What was the first series of x-rays that you took?

Custer: Definitely, skull films.

Gunn: How many skull films did you take?

Custer: Well, I took a modified Waters. And, basically, the only reason why I took a modified Waters is, because rigor mortis had already set in. And the head was placed in a—the head was [in] a position already with a 30-degree up tilt due to the rigor mortis being set in. And the head, like I had stated before, was in such a[n] unstable—unstable situation, because—due to all the fractures. I could only place so much steadying apparatus around it, to get a halfway decent film. So, what you saw [on the resulting A-P x-ray] was an elongation of the orbits, which showed you, right there, there was a 30-degree up-tilt. Now, when the orbits are the other direction and become smaller, you're going—tilting towards the feet.

Gunn: Can you explain what you mean by "orbits?"

Custer: Orbits are your eye sockets, where your eyes and your optic nerves fit in.

Gunn: And so, when you're referring to the degrees, it is how far the head has been either tilted back or tilted forward—

Custer: That's correct.

Gunn: —in relationship to the neck?

Custer: Correct.

Gunn: When you referred to a "modified Waters," is that a particular angle?

Custer: A full Waters is 45 degrees. All right? And that's taken at a posterior-anterior. When you're in the—regular radiological positioning, anterior is your front. Posterior is your back, Okay? All the films [of President Kennedy] were taken in an anterior-posterior position. There's no way in God's creation we could have turned this body over on the stomach, and done the films the way they should have been done. So, we had to do them to the best possible way, and get the best possible films in that predicament.

Gunn: Let me go back to the earlier question, and ask you: how many exposures did you take of the skull?

Custer: [I] Took an anterior-posterior, both laterals, and I took two oblique films. And the only reason I took the two oblique films were to show any depth in bullet fragments.

Gunn: Is there a particular name or particular type of oblique films that you took?

Custer: No. I just took them to show fragments and to show the gaping holes.

Gunn: No. What I'm thinking of is a term such as "Townes" or "tangential" for the oblique—

496

Custer: Okay. Well, you could call them tangential views. But you wouldn't call them Townes. Townes is a complete—where you bring the chin all the way down to the chest, and you bring it in. You're diverging your central ray through the forehead, and it comes down through the occipital opening. It shows the foramen magnum. That's [the hole in the skull] where the spine comes through.

Gunn: And did you take a Townes—

Custer: To my best recollection, no. There's no way to take it, because of the rigor mortis, the way the head was positioned. You couldn't get a real good Townes, so I totally eliminated it because of that.

Custer had just contradicted his 1979 and 1989 interviews with David Lifton, in which he said he *did* take a "Townes" head x-ray, which he indeed described on those occasions as pointing the beam downward through the forehead through the foramen magnum, to show the occipital damage. However, he was 100 per cent *consistent* in both Lifton interviews, and before the ARRB staff, in saying that he exposed five (5) x-rays of President Kennedy's head.

Custer's Descriptions of the Wounds

Gunn: Was there any brain inside the cranium at the time that you took the first series of x-rays?

Custer: To the best of my recollection, no.

Gunn: Were you present at any time while brain tissue was being removed?

Custer: No, I wasn't.

Gunn: Did you ever see a wound on the front of President Kennedy's throat or the anterior of the throat [I believe Jeremy meant to say "anterior neck"]?

Custer: Yes, I did.

Gunn: Could you describe the wound that you observed?

Custer: A typical bullet hole.

Gunn: How large was it?

Custer: I would estimate, a little bit bigger than my little finger in dimension, across circumference—or diameter.

Gunn: Okay. So there was not a long incision or cut on the throat that you observed, is that correct?

497

Custer: Not at that time, I didn't.

When interviewed by Lifton in 1979, Custer said he saw a large tracheostomy incision in the neck with 'torn skin;' in his 1989 Lifton interview, and here, before the ARRB in 1997, he recalled what he interpreted as a round bullet hole in the anterior neck, instead of a ragged tracheostomy.

Gunn: And the first time that you saw this wound on the throat was when? At the time you were taking x-rays or before?

Custer: This was at the time I was taking the x-rays.

Gunn: Did you ever see a wound on the back of President Kennedy?

Custer: *That's when I picked him up, and the bullet dropped out of there.* There was a small wound. [Author's emphasis]

Gunn: Where was that wound located?

Custer: I would have to estimate in [the] mid-thoracic [region], somewhere around there—or upper thoracic.

Custer did *not* mention a bullet fragment falling from the body to Lifton in 1979. However, this 1997 ARRB testimony about the metal fragment falling from the President's back when the cadaver was lifted was consistent with Custer's 1989 Lifton interview (on video), and the *mid-to-upper thoracic location for the accompanying wound* (from which the fragment presumably dropped) is consistent with Robert Knudsen's HSCA testimony about where he saw *a metal probe exiting the back of the body* in the black-and-white negative that he developed and inspected on 11/23/63.

Gunn: And what kind of wound did that appear to be to you?

Custer: Another small bullet hole.

Gunn: And other than the Y-incision, did you observe any other wounds on President Kennedy's body, other than those you've described?

Custer: Let's see. I'm trying to think now. Well, there was a gaping hole in the right parietal region. The right eyeball was protruding. And truthfully, if you know anything about basic physics—when you have a force, you have an equal and opposite force in the other direction. So, that kind of—At that time, it didn't come to my recollection what it was. But later on, I realized that had to be an entrance wound of some sort there. Because if you read in that—the transcription that I brought in, that that's brought out—[Custer was referring to a transcript of his interview by researcher Tom Wilson of Pennsylvania]

Accurate word pictures were not forthcoming from Custer much of the time, so Jeremy decided to ask him to execute wound diagrams. Gunn accordingly produced three anatomical drawings, or 'templates' of the human skull and asked Custer to draw his best recollections of the head wounds he saw on President Kennedy on one or more of these templates (i.e., photocopies of skull diagrams) from *Grant's Anatomy*. Custer ended up drawing on two of the three templates, the right lateral view of the skull (Exhibit no. 206) and the rear, or posterior view of the skull (Exhibit no.207). [The template Custer chose not to draw on was the frontal, or anterior view of the skull.] Jeremy asked Custer to denote areas of missing bone with "hash marks," or parallel lines, on his two skull diagrams. (See Figures 34 and 33.) The questions and answers exchanged between Jeremy and the witness on the damage Custer remembered seeing to the skull are particularly frustrating to read in the transcript, because Custer's language was so imprecise. I will only reproduce below the few excerpts from Custer's testimony that help to clarify, or expand upon, his two diagrams—ARRB Exhibits no. 206 and 207.

Custer: ...I mean, it was a king-size[d] hole. I have extremely large hands. And to estimate the size of the hole, I could [have] put my hands together and place[d] my hands in the skull.

Gunn: Now, on the drawing you have made [Exhibit 207, or Figure 33], and with the bones as they're identified here, none of the principal part of the missing wound goes into the occipital bone; is that correct?

Custer: The hole doesn't, but this [indicating the back of his own head] is all unstable. *A lot of this bone was out. It would flap out.* [Author's emphasis]

Gunn: And when you say "this bone," you're referring to the—

Custer: The occipital region.

Gunn: —the parietal—

Custer: Right. And part of the lamboidal [sic], and down through the posterior of [sic] the occipital protruberance. This was all unstable material. I mean, completely.

Custer's diagram of Exhibit 206 (Figure 34) showed the right parietal bone completely missing above the lamboid suture, and he was telling us that the occipital bone was fractured and unstable from its edge at the right lamboid suture down to the external occipital protruberance.

Custer next testified that there was a flap of bone in the right temporal area that flapped out (or hinged), and that *it looked like it had been sawed.*

Gunn: You're referring—when you say "this here," it's not going to be clear on the transcript.

Custer: The temporal bone area.

499

Gunn:	Okay. What you're referring to is the suture [in the bone] between the temporal bone and parietal bone?
Custer:	Right.
Gunn:	Okay.
Custer:	This flapped out. *It looked as if they had sawed it.* But this was all missing here. [Author's emphasis]
Gunn:	And when you say "this," you're referring to the hash marks?
Custer:	The hash marks. And the parietal bone.

_____

Was Custer providing more evidence for "surgery of the head area?" I didn't know what to think of this testimony, because in his 1989 interview with Lifton, Custer specifically remarked that he *never saw* the temporal bone flap that is so prominent in the bootleg autopsy photographs, and yet now he was telling the ARRB under oath that he *did* remember it, but that it looked like the damage in that area was man-made, caused by a saw.

No doubt at this point the reader shares my frustration. Do not despair. Later in this chapter, I will present a chart showing the evolution of Jerrol Custer's recollections, over time, regarding the condition of the body; this chart will serve as an aid for subsequently determining which of his recollections may be judged more reliable than others, based upon either *consistency,* or upon the earliest recollections he had *when first asked* a question.

Custer:	[discussing the general damage to the skull, and the pattern of large fractures he was attempting to describe]...you had to have a king-size [sic] force coming anterior to posterior. Everything seemed like it was just pushed backwards. This whole area blew out. [indicating the right side and upper rear of the head]
Gunn:	And you're referring again to the part where you have the hash marks.
Custer:	Temporal area. Temporal bone—or the parietal bone.
Gunn:	Okay.
Custer:	And this has flopped.
Gunn:	Okay. Now, you've referred to portions of the skull being missing. Can you tell me whether the scalp was missing, too?
Custer:	It was shredded. The scalp was shredded.

Gunn: And—

Custer: And it was loose. When I—I remember, when I first came in and saw the face, everything had been drooped, like somebody had pulled the scalp and pulled it down. I had to look twice at it.

Gunn: Now, this time when you see this, this is when you have been out of the morgue for approximately an hour.

Custer: Right.

Gunn: And you've come back.

Custer: Right.

Gunn: But you see it that way.

Custer: Right.

_____

If the reader will examine Exhibit 207 (Figure 33), it is clear that Custer's annotation of the diagram of the posterior skull shows that the bone missing in the posterior skull is *right parietal,* i.e., "up high" in the back of the skull, and depicts large fractures in the *left parietal* bone. In this diagram, Custer did *not* indicate any of the occipital bone was *missing:*

Custer: [pointing to the occipital bone in his diagram] But again, all of this was unstable.

Gunn: And you're referring now to the occipital bone.

Custer: The occipital bone. And you had fractures. I mean, through here, through here. And near the sagittal suture, you had that portion of the bone that protruded upward.

_____

In his 1979 Lifton interview, Custer had said that there was a "king-sized hole in the occipital region;" in his 1989 Lifton interview the description had changed just a little, to "massive damage to the back-of-the-head," which could have meant either occipital, or occipital-parietal. Now, based upon Custer's two diagrams and his testimony *combined,* a paraphrased description of the wound description he was providing to the ARRB staff would have read: 'most, if not all, of the right temporal bone; the entire right parietal bone; and part of the right frontal bone was missing, and the occipital bone was badly fractured and extremely unstable.' When one examines Exhibit 207 (Figure33), Custer's annotations made upon the posterior skull diagram from *Grant's Anatomy,* it is clear that this *could* be described as 'massive damage to the back of the head,' but that the missing bone is *high* in the rear of the head, in the right parietal region, directly *above* the occipital bone. Interestingly, when one looks at both drawings—Figures 33 and 34—in conjunction with each other, one is reminded somewhat of the description of the head wound written by Dr. Finck in the

Blumberg report: "fronto-parietal-occipital." Although Custer did not say the occipital bone was *missing,* he did say that it was unstable (i.e., mobile), and could "flap out," i.e., hinge outward so as to appear to be missing when it "flapped." At least, this is my interpretation of his remarks.

President Kennedy's X-Rays: Who Did What?

Gunn: When you took the x-rays, did you have any kind of markers or tags that would identify, for example, who the subject of the x-ray was, or some unique identifier?

Custer: Nothing that would identify the subject. I had my—my own little measuring device on it.

Gunn: What kind of measuring device was that?

Custer: Well, it showed if a—the position was too far to the left, too far to the right, or the chin was up too high, or the chin was on—they had like little holes in it, and you could see the—it would either elongate, or you could see the little dot.

Gunn: Was there a name for that measuring device?

Custer: It was my own personal device.

This was virtually identical to Ed Reed's testimony about the lead marker with the hole in it that he placed on the left jaw of the decedent. There was no way for Custer to know about this from reading any of the assassination literature or official reports.

Gunn: Were there any other identifiers that would appear on the film that would help say when the—

Custer: Maybe. I'm not sure now. It could have had the hospital identification on the film. That's possible. I'm not sure.

This was probably another authentic, independent recollection by Custer: the hospital identification, the UIC code of 21296, *is visible* on most of the x-rays. This marker was *not* visible in the cropped photos of the x-rays published by the HSCA in its report; furthermore, Custer was honest enough to admit that he had not read the HSCA report. (While it is *possible* that Custer borrowed this information from the transcript of Dr. Ebersole's HSCA testimony, which he told us he had looked at the night before his deposition, I tend to doubt it, because he does not use the precise language, or the number assigned to the hospital, that Dr. Baden used when questioning Dr. Ebersole.)

Gunn: Is there any other way that you can think of that—if we were to show you the x-rays, that you would be—would help you identify whether they are x-rays that you, yourself, took on the night of November 22nd?

Custer: Well, there's one in particular. *One of the laterals—where Dr. Ebersole put it too close to the hot light, and he burned the emulsion.*[26]   [Author's emphasis]

This was interesting. It was actually the *A-P skull x-ray* in the collection that had two burn marks on the emulsion, *not* one of the laterals[27]; but Custer, here, remembered burn marks on an x-ray independently. If he had been borrowing information from Ebersole's HSCA deposition prior to his ARRB testimony to make himself look smarter, he would have known that the x-ray with the burn marks was the A-P head x-ray. He seems to have remembered this on his own, and even remembered it correctly as a *skull* x-ray, but simply as a *different* skull x-ray.

Gunn: Mr. Custer, is there any other identifying information that would help you be able to determine whether an x-ray that you took that night was in—let me withdraw that. Is there any other type of identifier that you can think of that would help you determine whether an x-ray is one that you took on the night of November 22nd and 23rd?

Custer: Well, there's one I know for a fact of the lumbar spinal region. He had myelogram dye in—it's contrast media dye. Because, you must remember, Kennedy had a back problem, which he had come to Bethesda to get films and treatment for, anyway. And this is one time that I had met him prior. Basically, that's it really.

Did Custer glean this from the Ebersole deposition or the Military Inventory of 11/1/66; or did he remember it independently? There is no way to be sure. However, he does use his own terminology, "lumbar spinal region," rather than the language in the Military Inventory (which reads "view of the pelvis," and mentions dye in the "sacral canal," rather than the region of the "lumbar spine").

The Skull X-Rays: The First Series Taken

Gunn: Okay. Who was involved in the setting up of the x-rays on the skull, in addition to—

---

[26]Apparently my earlier speculation that there was no hot light in the morgue was incorrect; I must defer to Custer on this point.

[27]The fact that the A-P skull x-ray in the collection has two burn marks on the emulsion does not necessarily mitigate against it being a forged composite copy film, as Dr. Mantik believes it is. If the original A-P head x-ray had burn marks on it, then anyone clever enough to make a forged composite copy film would also be clever enough to reproduce these burn artifacts on the emulsion, so that the x-ray would retain its original, damaged appearance *if examined at a later date by the radiologist,* for example. And in fact, that is what happened—Dr. Ebersole testified to the HSCA staff that he was called to the White House within about a month of the assassination to view the head x-rays with a Dr. Young. The circumstances of this visit relayed to the HSCA panel during his deposition were rather peculiar, and hard to believe. The non-credible particulars, and implications of this visit, will be discussed later in this chapter.

Custer: I was.

Gunn: Anyone besides yourself?

Custer: No. I was.

Gunn: You did all the work?

Custer: I did all of the work.

Here is the "illusion of centrality" rearing its ugly head again.

Gunn: What was Mr. Reed's role at that time?

Custer: Just assisting me, and handing me films, and basically, taking the cassettes out of the dirty coverings.

Gunn: Did Dr. Ebersole play any role in the technical part of taking the x-rays?

Custer: None whatsoever. I had total control. In fact, like I had stated to you before, I was guiding him, instead of him guiding me.

Gunn: After you had finished taking the x-rays of the skull, what did you do?

Custer: They were taken upstairs to the department, run through, brought back—this is the thing. Dr. Ebersole waited, like a man that was starving for a meal. As soon as I brought them in, he grabbed them, and threw them up there, and examined them. And then they went into their big conference. Da, da-da, da-da, da-da. And then he would say, "Okay, take the next set."

Gunn: Approximately how much time was there between the time that you left the morgue and you returned with the developed x-rays?

Custer: Around—now, this is an estimation. I'd have to say half an hour, at the most. Because I had to get on the elevator, go up to the first floor, walk down the corridor, go down to the other—past the rotunda, down to the other elevator, and go up to the fourth floor, take the films—processing at that time was 5 minutes [per x-ray]. Now, it's a matter of a minute and a half. But at that time, it was an old Payco unit, where it was about six foot [sic]—or I'd say 10 foot [sic] long. And it took a lot longer to develop.

Gunn: *Were all of the five skull x-rays taken at that first time,* or was there—those are actually two different series? [Author's emphasis]

Custer: No. *All of them were taken at that time.* [Author's emphasis]

504

This recollection of Custer's is entirely consistent with Dr. Finck's recollection before the HSCA panel that Dr. Humes had called him on the telephone and said that he already had a good set of head x-rays. Custer is saying here that all of the head x-rays were taken at one time, and were taken *first, before any others.* In terms of timeline analysis, since we know from the reports Finck wrote to General Blumberg in early 1965 that he arrived at the morgue about 2030 hours military time (i.e., 8:30 PM), we can deduce the skull x-rays were taken early enough that evening to allow approximately 30 minutes for their developing, then viewing and discussion in the morgue by Ebersole and the pathologists, then a phone call to Dr. Finck, then time for Finck to travel to Bethesda and gain admittance to the morgue at 8:30 PM. This allows us a *relative* placement in time in-between the arrival of the body and Finck's arrival. The conflicting evidence concerning when the body arrived will be addressed in detail in Chapter 6 and Chapter 8.

Gunn: By the time that you left the morgue on the time with the x-rays in your hand, had you seen any photographers taking pictures by that time?

Custer: No, not really. You mean photographers outside the morgue?

Gunn: Totally inside the morgue. Just—

Custer: Oh, like I stated before, they were taking pictures all the time.

Gunn: So, it's—

Custer: Even when I walked away, Floyd would come over and take films.

Gunn: Okay.

Custer: And then come—back off, and come in, take films; back off. It was a constant thing.

Gunn: Okay. When you came back, were you asked for any for any opinions on the results of the skull x-rays?

Custer: On the contrary. I was told to keep my mouth shut. I gave my opinions, and I was told it's not my job. "You're here to take x-rays only."

Gunn: Do the x-rays of the skull show any significant amount of brain tissue?

Custer: To the best of my recollection, I don't remember seeing any.

Later in this chapter I will discuss the professional opinion of two board-certified radiologists about this question, Dr. John Fitzpatrick and Dr. David Mantik. Their professional judgments on this question will assume primacy over anything Custer said here in response to Jeremy's question.

Gunn: What were you next asked to do?

Custer: Take pictures of the neck, and take pictures of the—the shoulder areas, the chest area—thoracic areas, the thoracic spine, the lumbar spine, the pelvis.

Custer's recollections here are "spot-on" with the x-rays in the Military Inventory.

Gunn: What was the—how many exposures were in the neck series that you took?

Custer: Oh, I'd have to estimate.

Gunn: Approximately.

Custer: There—one, two, three, four, five. Say five or six, maybe more. *There was a total of about anywhere from 14 to 20 films.* [Author's emphasis]

Gunn: That's total for—

Custer: Yeah, total for the whole night.

This recollection was also very consistent with the inventory taken on 11-1-66: if Custer is right about *5 head x-rays being taken,* instead of the 3 presently in the collection, that would boost the total number taken from the present fourteen to sixteen (16). Sixteen lies within the range that Custer had just estimated for the total exposed the night of the autopsy.

Gunn: Okay. But your estimate would be, on the second series, there were approximately four or five?

Custer: Normally.

Gunn: Is that right? How—

Custer: He—He wanted to not go too far. Just to shoot some films, run them up, bring them back, examine them. Shoot some more films, run them up, bring them back. And you['ve] got to remember, I was limited to what I had. I only had a certain amount of films there.

Gunn: So, approximately how much time passed between the time that you returned with the first series of skull x-rays and you then began taking the second series of neck and torso—

Custer: Well, long enough for them to discuss the films that they had, which—15, 20 minutes, half-hour. Somewhere around there.

Gunn: And then—

Custer: And that's a crude estimate.

Gunn: Sure, understood. Then approximately how long until you returned with the developed second series of x-rays?

Custer: Approximately about the same time.

Gunn: Okay. And then what was the next series of x-rays that you took?

Custer: Well, like I said, I took some spine films: thoracic spine, lumbar spine. And then I ran them up, brought them back. Then I took some pictures of the pelvis and a few of the lower extremities. And that's when I stopped them. I said "it's ridiculous to go any further. He's not going to be shot in his leg." And he agreed with me. And I stood there. But you got to remember. At this time, each one of these trips, there was a lot more conversation going on. There was a lot more interference going on. So, it stretched out. I was there for a good while.

Gunn: Okay. *Did you and Mr. Reed ever go develop film separately, or were you together?* [Author's emphasis]

Custer: *Always together.* [Author's emphasis]

Gunn: Okay.

I found this much more credible than Reed's testimony that he *ran up stairs* to the fourth floor main x-ray laboratory *several times by himself* to develop x-rays, *without any Federal agent accompanying him,* while his supervisor (Custer) *sat by himself in the gallery* inside the morgue. To put it bluntly, Reed's testimony in this regard sounded preposterous, and not worthy of belief.

Gunn: I'd like to show you another Exhibit, marked no. 208, that has another photograph. I'd like you to look at the one on the right.

Jeremy was showing Custer a photocopy of the photograph that appeared to show him and Reed walking down a hallway outside the morgue at Bethesda NNMC on November 22, 1963; it had been published in Lifton's *Best Evidence* as photograph no. 40, and was attributed by Lifton to *Life* magazine photographer Bob Phillips.

Custer: This is the one that I forgot to bring.

Gunn: Okay.

Custer: All right. This was what I told you was taken through the keyhole.

507

Not literally, of course. The photo caption in Best Evidence says that Phillips took the photograph from a stairwell, shooting through a glass window in a door that was blocked by a military guard.

Gunn: Okay. Could—

Custer: See who's carrying the aprons, don't you?

Gunn: Why don't you tell us, for the record?

Custer: The student.

Gunn: That's Mr. Reed?

Custer: That's Mr. Reed.

Gunn: And—

Custer: He's definitely carrying the aprons. That's—

Gunn: He's the one in the center; is that correct?

Custer: Correct. It's part of the military protocol. When I was a student, I did the work.

Gunn: Can you identify the person on the left?

Custer: That better be me.

_____

Gunn: I just had [sic] one follow-up question regarding you and Mr. Reed. Could you tell me what your rank was at that time?

Custer: ...E-4.

Gunn: E-4?

Custer: E-4.

Gunn: And what was the rank of Mr. Reed?

Custer: E-4, also.

An E-4 in the Navy is a Third Class Petty Officer, or the lowest form of non-commissioned officer. Custer and Reed were both hospital corpsmen, so the *rating* of each man was "HM3."

Custer Examines the A-P Skull X-Ray

Jeremy had done all he reasonably could with Jerrol Custer to "lay the foundation" for the ensuing testimony about the materials in the National Archives, just as he had with Ed Reed one week previously, before showing Reed the films.

Gunn: Mr. Custer, we're going to show you now x-ray no. 1, which has been identified in the 1966 Inspection as the "anterior-posterior view of the skull, slightly heat damaged." (See Figure 38.) My question to you, Mr. Custer, is whether you can identify that as an autopsy x-ray that you took—

Custer: Yes, this is definitely an autopsy film.

Gunn: If you could let me finish the question. Can you—

Custer: I'm sorry.

Gunn: Can you identify that as an autopsy x-ray that you took on the night of November 22nd/23rd, 1963?

Custer: Yes sir. Correct.

Gunn: How can you identify that as being one that you took?

Custer: Bullet fragment, right orbital ridge. [Later in the deposition it will become apparent what Custer was referring to here.] Fragments throughout the temporal region. Remember how I stated, it looked like somebody had sawed a portion over here.

Gunn: You're referring to the mid—

Custer: Midsagittal.

Gunn: —midline?

Custer: Midsagittal plane.

Gunn: Okay.

It's time to jump in here, and try to clarify for the reader what Custer has just said. Earlier in the deposition, Custer used "saw marks" to refer to the temporal bone flap present in some autopsy photographs. However, at this point, in discussing the A-P head x-ray, Custer is saying that he sees *evidence of sawing at the top of the head,* in the mid-sagittal plane. (See Figure 38, the HSCA enhancement of the A-P head x-ray.) This abrupt break in the bone in the A-P x-ray is anatomically just to the left of President Kennedy's centerline in the top of his head. There is a corresponding very straight line in the broken scalp in the autopsy photographs of the top of the head (view no. 3, photographs 7, 8, 9, 10, 32, 33, 34, 35, 36, and 37). (See Figure 61.) This could be what Humes was referring to when he made his famous oral utterance, recorded for history in the Sibert-O'Neill report, about "surgery of the head area, namely in the top of the skull."

Custer: See this?

Gunn: Yes. Now you're pointing to what looks like a—

Custer: Marker.

Gunn: —a marker.

Custer: That's my personal marker. See the opening? That shows the plane the film was taken [in]. It's off to the side.

Gunn: Now, let me just say for the marker [Jeremy meant "the record"], that that is—appears—When we are looking at the x-ray from the front, that there is on the bottom right near the—what would be the left—

Custer: Bottom left. [Custer is talking about President Kennedy's anatomical left.]

Gunn: That's on the bottom right in the way that we are looking at it.

Custer: Right.

Gunn: It's to the left of the victim, is that correct?

Custer: This is correct...yes, you're correct.

This is the same marker that Ed Reed said he placed on the President's left jaw with tape. (It may very well have been Custer's own marker, placed there by Ed Reed, at Custer's direction.) What is important is not who put it there—Custer or Reed—but that both men's recollections are 100 per cent consistent here about what is shown on the x-ray, thus authenticating it as being of the body of John F. Kennedy, and not of someone else. The reader should *not* look for either this marker, or the Bethesda UIC code marker, discussed next in the testimony below, on the photographic images of the enhanced A-P and lateral head x-rays in this book. The HSCA cropped the images reproduced in its report by removing the lower portion of the image that showed the jaw.

Gunn: Is there anything else that you can identify with this x-ray that helps you determine that it's an x-ray that you took on the night of November 22nd?

Custer: I remember this marker [pointing to a different lead marker at the bottom of the x-ray].

Gunn: And when you say that marker, what are you referring to?

Custer:	It's a label, "U.S. Naval Hospital, Bethesda Maryland."
Gunn:	So, that's writing that appears—again, as we are looking at it from the front—along the right margin?
Custer:	Yes sir.
Gunn:	Is that correct?
Custer:	Correct.
Gunn:	Earlier in your deposition, you referred to some heat damage on one of the x-rays. Do you see any heat damage on this x-ray?
Custer:	It's right here. You can see it. This is where Dr. Ebersole got it too close to the heat lamp. I stated to him twice, "please do not put it too close." You can see where it started to—
Gunn:	To wrinkle?
Custer:	—curdle, literally. And here, it started to burn. And isn't it funny how where it started to burn is the area where I suggested was an entry wound.

The reader will notice that Jeremy wisely doesn't bite on this. Custer was not a trained radiologist, and had no formal training or experience interpreting gunshot wounds in skull x-rays. (Neither did Ebersole, for that matter, who was a radiation oncologist.) As Jeremy explained to Custer more than once during the deposition—both on the record and off-the-record—we were interested in what he remembered seeing, hearing, and doing the night of the autopsy, not his own theories.

Gunn:	Now, are you certain that the heat damage took place on this x-ray the night of November 22nd?
Custer:	Yes sir. I was there, and I saw him do it.

Remember, I will deal with this issue extensively, in regard to the authenticity of this x-ray, later in this chapter.

Gunn:	Can you identify in the x-ray any brain shadow?
Custer:	No. There's no brain shadow that I can see. Maybe portions—very small. But this is all empty. Anything—
Gunn:	Wait, let me just—if I can get this for the record.
Custer:	Fine.

Gunn: When you say this is empty, you're pointing to the left side as we are looking at it, which is the right hemisphere—

Custer: Correct.

Gunn: —anatomically.

Custer: This—that doesn't set right with me. And if you're going to put it in the record like that, it's base—the damage—it should be, the damage is on the right side.

Gunn: The anatomical right.

Custer: Anatomical right.

Gunn: That's fine. Let's just continue to refer to it anatomically. [This was the proper decision by Jeremy.]

Custer: Okay.

Gunn: Earlier you pointed to what I'm going to call the half-circle that appears to be at the lightest part of the film [Jeremy means it was the most radio-opaque object present, and therefore appears brighter than any other object in the x-ray], and you referred to that as a bullet fragment; is that right?

Custer: Yes sir.

Gunn: Where was that bullet fragment located [on the body]? Let me withdraw that question, and ask another question. Do you know where the bullet fragment was located on the body?

Custer: *Right orbital ridge, superior.*   [Author's emphasis]

Wrong answer. If Custer had been on a game show, the buzzer would have sounded at this point and he, too, like Ed Reed, would have been dismissed. Everyone I know of who is qualified to interpret the A-P x-ray—the Clark Panel, the HSCA Forensic Pathology Panel, and Dr. David Mantik—agrees that the large, bright 6.5 mm wide semi-circular fragment corresponds in *location* (if not in density and corresponding brightness) with a very small metallic fragment on the exterior surface of the rear of the skull about 100 mm above the external occipital protruberance (EOP).

Gunn: How do you know that it was in the right orbital ridge, rather than at the back of the skull?

Custer: Because of the protruding eyeball.

Gunn: ***Did you see the fragment removed?*** [Author's emphasis]

Custer: ***No, I did not.*** [Author's emphasis]

This is the key answer here. I want the reader to remember this answer later, when I cover the answers Drs. Humes, Boswell, and Finck provided to the ARRB General Counsel in response to this same question. Dr. Burkley's sole goal at the autopsy, the sole goal of Dr. Ebersole, and one of the primary goals of the pathologists was to locate and remove bullets and bullet fragments from the body for evidentiary purposes. It is my contention that if this large, 6.5 mm object had been seen on the A-P x-ray the night of the autopsy, that it most certainly *would have been removed*. Remember, per the autopsy report and the Sibert-O'Neill report, two fragments much less obvious on the head x-rays, and smaller than this (i.e., 7 x 2 mm and 3 x 1 mm), *were removed*.

Custer: [continuing the same answer] Can I interject something here?

Gunn: Sure.

Custer: This area, I pointed out to Dr. Ebersole as a fragment. And he called it an artifact. I said, "How about these fragments up here?" This is when he told me to mind my own business. You can see that the skull has been fractured...

The reader should set this aside, mentally, and read the remainder of this chapter before deciding whether or not to believe whether Custer really saw this object the night of the autopsy, and whether or not Dr. Ebersole really saw the object also, and told Custer it was "an artifact."

Gunn: Previously in the deposition, you said that there was—there were metal fragments in the cervical spine [the neck]. Are you able to identify any cervical spine [metal] fragments, or is the picture too high?

Custer: Not in this projection.

Gunn: Okay.

Custer: The only part of the cervical spine I can identify [in this A-P x-ray of the head] is C-2. That is the part that the skull rotates on. You want to get further down.

Gunn: No, I understand...are you able to identify what kind of x-ray film that is?

Custer: Well, it's a 10 x 12 cassette—radiographic cassette and film. I would say, it would be medium par speed.

Gunn: Can you identify any edge markings?

Custer: No, that's just illuminized. That's [caused by] the screens [in the cassettes].

Gunn: So that—

Custer: Then it has a serial number in there. That doesn't tell what type of film it is.

Gunn: That tells what kind of cassette—

Custer: Right.

Gunn: —the film was in; is that correct?

Custer: That's all.

Gunn: Do you know what kind of film was used in the Bethesda radiology lab at that time?

Custer: At that time, at that year, it has to be a par speed screen, because the technological advancements weren't for the faster speeds at that time.

Gunn: Is there any question in your mind whether the x-ray that's in front of you now is the original x-ray taken at the autopsy?

Custer: No question.

Gunn: And the answer is—

Custer: It's the original film.

Gunn: Is "par speed" the speed of the film, or a brand name?

Custer: The speed of film.

Gunn: And do you know a brand name for the—

Custer: Kodak, probably. More than likely, it was Kodak.

Gunn: Do you know whether Kodak marked its x-ray film with a brand name on the edges of the film?

Custer: During that early part of the year, no, they didn't. It's, basically, on the boxes that ship them to you. Now they do.

Gunn: Okay.

Custer Examines The Lateral Skull X-Rays

Gunn: Can [you] look at no. 2 now, please, which is identified in the 1966 Inventory as a right lateral view of the skull with two angle lines overdrawn on the film? The question is, Mr. Custer, can you identify the film that is in front of you now as having been taken by you on the night of the autopsy of President Kennedy? (See Figure 37.)

Custer: Correct. Yes sir, I do.

Gunn: And how are you able to identify that as being—

Custer: My marker in the lower mandibular joint.

Gunn: And that—could you describe the marker to me, please?

Custer: Actually, all it is, is a metal—piece of metal, about a centimeter [in] thickness. Less than that. And about two inches long with numerous dots going from left to right.

Gunn: Is that a standard device for radiologists, or was that your own device?

Custer: That was my device.

Gunn: So, it was unique, as far as you know?

Custer: Correct. And this, again—the only reason why I put that on there is for my own basic identification, plus to show the rotation.

Gunn: Are you able to identify, by looking at this, whether we are looking at the anatomical right side of the body—or that the right side of the body is closer to the x-ray equipment, or whether the left side of the body is?

Custer: I can identify it as being the right anatomical [side of the] body because of the enormous defect. When you have the defect closer to the film, it's more detailed. You can see the lines, as you go around, a lot better. See how clear it is here? And let me inject [sic] something else. Dr. Ebersole kept going back to the quality of the film [in his HSCA deposition transcript]. The quality of the film did not depend upon the portable film [sic—Custer meant portable x-ray machine here, I believe]—the portable x-rays being exposed at that time. The quality of the film depended upon the type of film speed you used. And at that time, in that year, this was the film speed that was used. And this was recognized, and people accepted it as such.

Gunn: When you say Dr.—when you're referring to something that Dr. Ebersole said, are

515

you referring to his testimony before the House Select Committee on Assassinations?

Custer: Yes sir, I am.

Gunn: Okay.

Custer: Remember, also, I had stated how a portion of the skull had lifted up and pushed backwards?

Gunn: Yes.

Custer: Showing that there had to be a impact this way, in that—Well, look. Let me inject something else. From the right side, you notice—you see the fragmentation, how it starts to get larger and larger and larger. You have equal and opposite force. Everything being pushed forward. The brain has been pushed back, and it pops the skull out.

Gunn: So, it's your opinion that the trauma to the head began at the front and moved towards the back of the head?

Custer: Yes sir. Absolutely.

Gunn: Okay. Is there anything else on this x-ray film that allows you to be certain that this was taken by you on the night of the autopsy?

Custer: Yes sir. Not only this marker here, U—United—U.S. Naval Hospital, Bethesda, Maryland, on the right side of the film, but also—remember how I had stated to you about the cella [sella] turcica, the keystone of the sphenoid bone—it holds the cranial vault? Well, look how prominent it is. And the only possible way you can see that—this is all gone. This is all defective in here on the right side. That makes that much more visible.

Gunn: Are you able to identify any brain shadow in this lateral x-ray?

Custer: There is no brain shadow in this lateral x-ray at all. Look at the dark portion here. Dark through here. Now, there may be a minute amount, but not enough to make any gross difference. You don't see any markings here, vascular markings. Where's your vascular markings? There is [sic] none. A normal brain has vascular markings that will show.

Gunn: I'd like to show you now Exhibit no. 206 that we identified earlier in this deposition. Can you now, by looking at the original x-ray, compare that with the drawing that you made...? And let me know whether you would now amend Exhibit 206, or does that roughly correspond with the x-ray?

Custer: Okay. I would amend this somewhat.

Gunn: How would you amend—

Custer: I would brig this down in—more into the temporal bone area.   Come down through—

Gunn: You would add hash marks to the temporal—

Custer: Right.

Gunn: —bone area?

Custer: Right.

Gunn: Okay.

Custer: Your pen—but, here—you got to remember, too—this is only minute fragments of tissue maybe that are in there...so, it's basically pretty close.

Gunn: That is, the x-ray to your drawing?

Custer: Right. It's basically pretty close, except that I would bring the temporal [damage] down a little bit more [in my drawing].

Gunn: Okay. What I'm going to—when we take that x-ray off, I'm going to ask you to draw onto [Exhibit] 206 where you would think that it would be.

Gunn: If you can draw the lines at perpendicular angles to the other, so it will be clear to the reader which lines—

Custer: Oh, like this?

Gunn: Yes.

Custer: That would come down through here. (See Figure 34.)

Gunn: Okay. So, now the perpendicular lines are the ones that you would add after examining the original x-rays?

Custer: Correct.

Gunn: Okay.

[Discussion off the record.]

Gunn: Mr. Custer, I'd like to draw your attention to what appear to be straight—very thin, straight lines that come at an angle on the x-ray, and ask you if you can identify what those are? This is, again, on x-ray no.2.

Custer: Okay. I know exactly what they are. This is Ebersole's little scratches.

Gunn: Did—

Custer: This is what he was trying to say was [an] entry wound, here. I remember that now. This is where he drew, in here.

Gunn: Did you see Mr. [sic] Ebersole draw those lines yourself?

Custer: On the first set of films I brought back, he put them up, and he had a ruler there, and he was penciling it in. And this is when he got a comment, "Don't do that." And this came from the gallery.

Gunn: So, did you hear Mr. [sic] Ebersole identify the fulcrum of those lines as being the entrance wound?

Custer: Yes.

Gunn: Did any other doctor there make any comment on what Mr. [sic] Ebersole had just said or done?

Custer: I can't remember, basically. I just remember that the comment was made from the gallery, and it shut everything down.

Gunn: So, as far as you are aware, those lines are made with a pencil?

Custer: As far as I'm aware.

———————

Later in the deposition Jeremy returned to this subject:

Gunn: Mr. Custer, could we go back to x-ray no. 2? [The right lateral x-ray of the skull.] Do you recall previously we were talking about two lines that are pointing towards a fulcrum?

Custer: Yes.

Gunn: Could you identify where those lines lead to, and what you—where you

518

understand that Dr. Ebersole was trying—the point Dr. Ebersole was trying to identify?

Custer: They led to the occipital region.

Gunn: Is there a way that you can identify it more specifically than that? That's a little bit hard with this film? Would it—

Custer: It's kind of hard to say, because here's the mastoid region, down near the external auditory meatus. All right? It would be, I'd have to say, just above and perpendicular to that region.

Gunn: But it looks as if the fulcrum is coming close to where the outer skull is.

Custer: Correct.

Gunn: So, it's—

Custer: Like we had said before, this is the occipital region.

Gunn: Are you able to identify the external occipital protruberance on this x-ray no. 2?

Custer: Well, it'd have to be down through here.

Gunn: So, this is far above the EOP, is that correct?

Custer: Yes. Correct.

When Ed Reed was asked by Jeremy Gunn what the lines on x-ray no. 2 represented, he had testified that he thought they were scratches made by the x-ray developing machine. The Military Inventory lists them as "two angle lines overdrawn on the film." They are clearly pencil lines, as Dr. Ebersole testified to the HSCA. We will review later in this chapter what Dr. Ebersole told the HSCA these pencil lines represented.

Gunn: Could we now examine no. 3, which is identified as the lateral view of the skull?

Custer: Okay. This is the skull that I took—that I had taken. Same marker on the left side.

Gunn: And you're referring to the—

Custer: Yeah, the "U.S. Naval Hospital."

Gunn: —the date and the—

Custer: The date. Remember I had stated to you, this is the way the table was against the gallery. I could only get so close. There's my marker again.

Gunn: And you're referring to the metal marker that's—

Custer: Metal apparatus, mandibular region.

Gunn: —by the jaw.

Custer: And I cut the bottom portion of the skull [image] off, because I couldn't get low enough. Every time I put blankets underneath the head, the head would actually get smaller.

Gunn: Because it would be crushed?

Custer: Crushed.

Gunn: By the weight?

Custer: Right. Due to the instability of the bones.

Gunn: The fractures in the head?

Custer: The fractures in the head. But again, you see the big defects. But you don't see the cella [sella] turcica. Not as good. You see the fractures.

Gunn: Are you able to identify any metal fractures in the head? [Jeremy meant to say 'fragments,' instead of 'fractures.']

Custer: Sure.

Gunn: And you're pointing toward the flecks?

Custer: Towards the black area. Towards the top of the skull. Here. Here. That had—that's the only way that can be, this fragment. There's no way an artifact will show up like that.

Gunn: Now, what is supporting these arti—supporting these metal fragments, if there is no brain in the cranium? Where are they resting?

Custer: They have to be resting on the bone itself somewhere. That's the only thing I can possibly think of, unless there's enough tissue there in that region to hold them. That's the only possible thing that I can think of. Because here you go again. There's no brain here. It wouldn't be that dark.

Gunn: You're referring to the dark patch?

Custer: The dark area.

Gunn: On the first x-ray we looked at, you identified a large metal fragment. Do you remember that, semi-circular?

Custer: Correct.

Gunn: Can you identify the location of that fragment on this—

Custer: Not on this film.

Gunn: What does that signify to you, if anything; the inability to identify the location of that metal fragment?

Custer: Could be too dark. This area is just too dark to identify it.

Gunn: Wouldn't the metal fragment still appear and even be—have greater contrast?

Custer: No.

Gunn: Why is that?

Custer: Because—you've got to remember, the central ray [of the x-ray beam is] going through the body. It's hitting the film a lot faster. It's exposing it more. There were [sic] bone tissue on the A-P projection, which sort of backed off on the [x-ray] penetration. You had more penetration here. If you were to take a photo density [reading] of that picture, this photo density would be much greater.

Gunn: But wouldn't a metal fragment still appear white on this?

Custer: If it is dark enough to burn it out, it'll burn it out. That's why, when you take an abdomen film and you're looking for stones, stones will be burned out. And that's bone.

Nothing Custer said here was persuasive to me—nor was it to Jeremy, apparently. As David Mantik has verified, an object as radio-opaque as the 6.5 mm diameter fragment in the A-P head x-ray should definitely appear virtually equally as bright on the lateral x-rays, as well, if it is a *real object* on the A-P x-ray, *and not an artifact*. Furthermore, kidney stones, gall stones, and bladder stones are not made of bone, they are mineral accretions. The fact that stones in the body—mineral accretions—may be difficult to pick up on abdominal x-rays has nothing to do with whether a metal bullet fragment should or should not be visible in a lateral skull x-ray, because the real-life densities of those two objects are so dissimilar. Custer was clearly out of his element whenever he tried to interpret x-ray content, whether he was discussing how much brain tissue was present, where the 6.5 mm fragment seen on the A-P x-ray was likely located on the body, or why that same fragment was not visible (where he thought it should be) on the lateral x-rays.

Gunn: ...Do you have an opinion as to whether that [x-ray no. 3] is a right lateral or left lateral [of the head]?

Custer: That's a left lateral.

Gunn: And what's the basis of that opinion?

Custer: What is the basis of that opinion? Because I couldn't get close enough—

Gunn: No.

Custer: —to take a halfway decent film. And I knew that was the bad film—was the left lateral, due to my recollection.

Gunn: So, it's based upon recollection—

Custer: Correct.

Gunn: —rather than observation of the x-ray? Which is fine. Just—

Custer: Sure.

Gunn: Just on the basis of what you're saying?

Custer: Right.

Gunn: And so, it is from recollection?

Custer: Absolutely.

Gunn: Now, one thing I'd like to ask, just to make sure we're clear here, is that—is where you are locating the largest part of the wound. And now, if one were to think that either the occipital region towards the back or the parietal region towards the front—as between those two, where are you identifying the larger wound?

Custer: The larger wound would have to be further back. This one wasn't as bad, towards the temporal region. It was open. But the more you went further back, the more destruction you had.

Gunn: When you say "the more destruction," is that consistent with what you were seeing with the x-ray films, where—by what I have been understanding you to say—most of the destruction is towards the front, where it's darker and where there's an absence—apparent absence of bone?

Custer: No. Let me reiterate again. Most of the destruction was towards the occipital area. This area [indicating the front of the skull] wasn't as bad. You still had the orbital ridge. The frontal forehead was still here. But the further back you got, the worse the destruction became. And the more gaping the hole became.

Gunn: And so, why is it that on the x-rays—and I'm saying this from my perspective as a layman—the film appears to be darker more towards the front and lighter towards the back?

Custer: In other words, you're telling me, why is this lighter here?

Gunn: Why is it lighter with the more apparent bone in the occipital region, and why is there apparently less bone in the frontal and parietal region?

Custer: If you look at your diagram that you have of the occipital area—

Gunn: Let me get—let me get that out. You're referring to Exhibit 207?

Custer: Look how far the occipital region comes out. Okay. This whole area, right back through here, this was all gone.

Gunn: Okay.

Custer: This is all gone, here, from—

Gunn: Okay. Now you're pointing to the x-ray [no. 3]---

Custer: I see what—I see what we're—I'm getting confused here myself now. The occipital region is all down here, where my hands are—the portion that's all cut off [in the image—not present in the image frame of x-ray no. 3]. Straight through here. Here—let me see that other one.

Gunn: You're looking now at Exhibit 206.

Custer: No. 206. From the temporal region just behind the right orbit, you can see this defect. All right?

Gunn:	And that is in the temporal bone, is that correct?

Custer:	Temporal bone. But it also comes out of the temporal bone, and into the parietal. And you start to infringe just a little bit. The occipital region is right through here. And you start to infringe on it, right here. So, this is all gone.

Gunn:	But you're still pointing to the parietal region—parietal and temporal region?

Custer:	See where the temporal stops? This is occipital, back here. See? The occipital comes back to here.

Gunn:	Sure.

Custer:	See how far up it comes?

Gunn:	Sure.

Custer was pointing out here what any basic anatomy textbook diagram of the posterior skull shows: that directly behind the ears on either side of the skull, the temporal bone is adjacent to the widest part of the base of the occipital bone.

Custer:	That's what I'm trying to say. You still have damage that starts to some into the occipital region. It may not go all the way down, but it's coming down into that area.

Gunn:	Sure. My question is not whether there is damage in the occipital region, but where is the majority of the bone missing? And is the majority of the—

Custer:	Okay. The majority of the [missing] bone is in the—it has to be the [right] parietal [bone]. This is the parietal area, right here.

Gunn:	So, you see this x-ray as showing an absence of bone in the parietal region and showing damage, but presence of bone, in the occipital region?

Custer:	Correct.

Gunn:	Okay.

Custer:	Plus, you have absence of bone in this region, right here.

Gunn:	In the temporal region?

Custer:	Temporal region. Only a portion of the temporal region, behind the right occipital—or the right orbital area.

Gunn: Okay.

I think that this frustrating exchange was caused by the cognitive dissonance Jerrol Custer was experiencing between *his very vivid memories from the autopsy* of the skull damage getting worse toward the rear of the skull, and the two-dimensional picture represented by the lateral x-rays in the Archives, which to any viewer *who was not present in the morgue,* make it appear that the damage to the front of the skull was worse than to the rear of the skull. *If Dr. Mantik is correct that a dense patch is present behind the right ear* in x-rays 2 and 3—and that x-rays 2 and 3 are not originals, but instead are *forged composite copy films of the real laterals,* with a patch or large artifact covering up a blow-out behind the right ear superimposed, then this could account for the differences in perception between the many autopsy witnesses who recall the back of the head missing, or blown out, at autopsy, and who believed that night that President Kennedy had been shot from the front; and the perceptions of the Clark Panel, the HSCA panel, and most people who view x-rays no. 2 and 3 today, who see apparent evidence of an exit wound in the right-front of the skull.

Gunn: Previously in the deposition, you had said that the skull x-rays were all taken in the first series; is that correct?

Custer: Correct.

Gunn: And would it be fair to say, then, that x-rays 1 through 3 are those that you took in the first series?

Custer: You're missing two.

Gunn: Just—

Custer: Yes.

Gunn: Just as for that one.

Custer: Correct.

Gunn: Now, I can tell you that those are the only—the three that you have just looked at are the only skull X-rays present in the Archives. Are you aware of any other skull x-rays?

Custer: There should be at least two more.

Gunn: And you described those both as oblique x-rays; is that correct?

Custer: Or, like you had stated, tangential views.

Gunn:	Tangential. And are you certain that you took those other two x-rays on the night of the autopsy?

Custer:	Absolutely.

Custer Examines the Three X-Rays of Loose Skull Fragments

Jeremy next proceeded to show Custer x-rays no. 4, 5, and 6, which Ed Reed said he had never seen before. (See Figure 39.)

Gunn:	Okay. Could we go to no. 4?

Custer:	I know exactly what this is.

Gunn:	This is described in the 1966 Inspection as "x-ray of three fragments of bone with larger fragment containing metallic fragments." Mr. Custer, have you previously seen x-ray no. 4?

Gunn:	When did you first see those x-rays? [X-rays 5 and 6 were also laying on the table, in plain view.]

Custer:	The next morning. I took them.

Gunn:	And where did you take those x-rays?

Custer:	In the main department, in a private room, with a portable x-ray unit.

Gunn:	Was it the same x-ray unit that was used to take the autopsy—

Custer:	Yes sir. The same distance.

Gunn:	And what was the purpose of taking these x-rays?

Custer:	I was told by Dr. Ebersole that they were to be taken to make measurements, to make a bust of President Kennedy.

Gunn:	 What did you do when you took the x-rays? What were the procedures? How did you go about taking them?

Custer:	All I did was place the bone fragments on the film, and *I made different exposures at different distances.* [Author's emphasis]

This could possibly explain why Dr. Ebersole noted before the HSCA panel that *x-ray no. 6 appeared to be a much sharper image than x-rays no. 4 and 5.* This tends to lend credence to what otherwise sounds below like an outlandish story by Jerrol Custer.

Gunn: Did Mr. [sic] Ebersole—or Dr. Ebersole say anything to you about metal fragments?

Custer: He gave me three or four different metal fragments, varying in size. And he asked me to tape them to the bones.

Gunn: Did you tape metal fragments to the bones?

Custer: Yes sir.

Gunn: What was the purpose that you understood taping metal fragments to the bones to be?

Custer: That was a good question, because I didn't understand it at the time, either.

Gunn: Is there any question in your mind whether you, in fact, taped metal fragments to the bones?

Custer: Absolutely no question at all in my mind.

Gunn: Do you see the results of those metal fragments appearing on x-ray no. 4?

Custer: Only a few, here.

Gunn: And you're pointing to the largest fragment in—

Custer: The largest fragment. The superior portion of it.

Gunn: Approximately what time did you take the x-rays on the 23rd?

Custer: I have to guesstimate. Early morning, early afternoon—no, late morning, early afternoon.

Gunn: Did Dr. Ebersole ever subsequently explain to you the purpose for taping metal fragments to the bones to be—

Custer: No, he didn't. He just stated to me, when he brought the film—the bone fragments and the metal fragments to me, that he had just come back from the White House after being debriefed.

Gunn: And what did he say about that debriefing?

Custer: Well, he just said that he was debriefed by the Secret Service. And that was it. High-ranking people had talked to him. And he suggested to me that everything that I

[had] see[n] from now on, I should forget.

Gunn:	Did he say that to you at approximately the same time that you were working on x-raying the skull fragments?

Custer:	Absolutely.

Gunn:	Do you know where the skull fragments came from?

Custer:	They arrived, supposedly, that evening from Dallas.

Gunn:	When did you first hear that fragments had arrived from Dallas?

Custer:	The night of the autopsy.

Gunn:	Did you see the fragments on the night of the autopsy?

Custer:	No, I did not see the fragments. I just heard the conversation.

———————————

Gunn:	...With regard to taking the x-rays of the bone fragments that you have in front of you—

Custer:	No.

Gunn:	—were there any metal fragments that were in the bone, outside of this—the taped fragments?

Custer:	No.

Gunn:	So, in other words, the x-ray is—appears as if there are metal fragments in the bone. Whereas, in fact, that is all a construct of the way that the x-ray was taken; is that correct?

Custer:	Absolutely correct.

Gunn:	Okay, could you look at—I'd like you to take a quick look at x-rays no. 5 and 6 which are similar x-rays, in terms of showing the bone fragments. Let me try asking you one question, just to make sure that the record is clear on this. Did Dr. Ebersole ask you to tape the metal fragments to the bone after he had returned from the White House? Are you able to say with certainty?

Custer:	Absolutely. As soon as he walked in, that's the first thing he said. "I want these bone fragments x-rayed with metal fragments taped"...all I did was move them

528

	around, that's all. Different exposures. See the difference?
Gunn:	Yes.
Custer:	Darker. Lighter. Darker. Lighter. [Custer was comparing x-rays no. 4 and 5.]
Gunn:	And so, you would say that x-ray no. 5 was taken roughly at the same time as x-ray no. 4?
Custer:	Absolutely.
Gunn:	Can you look at no. 6, please? I'll ask a similar question.
Custer:	Okay. That's a better quality film. Absolutely.
Gunn:	Are you the person who took the x-ray of no. 6?
Custer:	Yes sir.
Gunn:	Is there any marking on the film, other than the fragments themselves, that helps you identify that as being an x-ray that you, yourself, took?
Custer:	No sir.
Gunn:	Is there a reason you did not use your metal marker?
Custer:	I was told not to.
Gunn:	Did Dr.—let me finish the question. Then—
Custer:	Go ahead.
Gunn:	—you can answer it. Was there any reason that you did not use the metal marker that you had used in previous x-rays?
Custer:	Yes, because he saw it that night, and he knew it belonged to me. And he stated, "I better not see it on these films."
Gunn:	And that was Dr. Ebersole who said it?
Custer:	Absolutely. Correct.
Gunn:	Did anyone else hear Dr. Ebersole say that?

Custer:	No.

Gunn:	When—

Custer:	It was said only in my presence.

Gunn:	On the 23rd when you took the x-rays of the skull fragments, was there any other person, besides you and Dr. Ebersole, present?

Custer:	No.

There was one serious problem with Custer's story; it appeared to be disproved by both the autopsy report, and the Sibert-O'Neill report in particular, from the timeline standpoint. *Both* of these documents state that the 3 bone fragments were x-rayed late at night *during the autopsy,* and both reports mention minute particles of metal in one of the corners of the largest bone fragment, the same corner of this fragment that exhibited beveling. While Humes testified to the HSCA in 1978 that he did not write the autopsy report until late Saturday night/early Sunday morning, and he certainly would have had an opportunity to collude with his Navy colleague Ebersole if desired, one cannot say that about FBI agents Sibert and O'Neill. The report they signed on Tuesday, November 26, 1963 *was written based upon the notes they took at the Bethesda autopsy;* at the very latest, they left Bethesda NNMC between 12:00 and 12:30 AM on November 23rd, 1963. They had no opportunity to learn of any x-rays taken by Jerrol Custer late on Saturday morning, November 23rd, after Dr. Ebersole returned from a White House briefing by the Secret Service. There are only two reasonable possibilities here: either Custer really *did* do what he described at Dr. Ebersole's behest, but it was simply a 'test run' of how to create x-rays showing bullet fragments which would incriminate the accused assassin—a test run that proved technically unsatisfactory and was therefore never utilized; or his story is a complete fabrication. There are many things about the assassination of President John F. Kennedy that will never be known with certainty this many years later; this is one of them.

Custer Examines the X-Rays of the Body

The noteworthy highlights of Custer's review of the x-rays of the body was Jeremy's attempt to see whether Custer could identify metal fragments near any of the cervical vertebrae, which Custer had mentioned earlier in the deposition.

Jeremy showed Custer x-ray no. 9, a view of the chest prior to removal of the lungs, and the exchange went as follows:

Gunn:	Previously, you referred to there being metal fragments in the cervical area. Are you able to identify any metal fragments in this x-ray?

Custer:	Not in this film.

Gunn:	Does this film include a view or an exposure that would have included such metal

fragments?

Custer: No sir.

Gunn: Where would the metal fragments be located?

Custer: Further up in there. This region.

Gunn: Can you—and you're pointing to?

Custer: Up into the, I'd say, C3/C4 region.

Jeremy asked Custer to review x-rays no. 8 and 10, of the right shoulder and chest, and left shoulder and chest, respectively—both are images following the removal of the heart and lungs. Custer could not identify metal fragments in either x-ray.

Later, Jeremy asked Custer the following questions:

Gunn: Now, you had raised, previously in the deposition...the possibility of some metal fragments in the C3/C4 range.

Custer: I noticed I didn't see that.

Gunn: You didn't see any x-rays that would be in—that would include the C3/C4 area?

Custer: No sir.

Gunn: Are you certain that you took x-rays that included the—included C3 and C4?

Custer: Yes, sir. Absolutely.

Gunn: How many x-rays did you take that would have included that?

Custer: Just one. And that was all that was necessary, because it showed—right there.

Gunn: And what, as best you recall, did it show?

Custer: A fragmentation of a shell in and around that circular exit—that area. Let me rephrase that. I don't want to say "exit," because I don't know whether it was exit or entrance. But all I can say, there was bullet fragmentations [sic] around that area—that opening.

Gunn: Around C3/C4?

Custer: Right.

Gunn: And do you recall how many fragments there were?

Custer: Not really. There was enough. It was very prevalent.

Gunn: Did anyone make any observations about metal fragments in the C3/C4 area?

Custer: I did. And I was told to mind my own business. That's where I was shut down again.

Gunn: You have, during the course of this deposition, identified three x-rays that you are quite certain that you took, but don't appear in this collection. Are there any others that you can identify as not being included?

Custer: That's the only three that come to my mind right now; the two tangential views, and the A-P cervical spine.

Gunn: Okay.

Custer: Can I add something to that?

Gunn: Sure.

Custer: In my own opinion, I do believe, basically, the reason why they are not here is because they showed massive amounts of bullet fragments.

Gunn: Did you ever hear of anyone connected with the autopsy making any attempts to remove, destroy any of the x-ray material?

Custer: Let me put it this way. Gossip is cheap. Everybody has some. I heard some. And sometimes you have to take it with a hill of beans—where it comes from. But I did hear that in a—in a conversation.

Gunn: When did you hear it in a conversation?

Custer: The next day.

Gunn: What did you hear?

Custer: That certain pertinent things were taken care of.

Gunn: Who told you that?

Custer:	I was afraid you were going to ask that. Nobody told me. I heard it between two officers. High-ranking officers.
Gunn:	Who were the officers?
Custer:	One was Ebersole. And one was another radiologist that—right now, his name just doesn't—can't come to my memory.
Gunn:	To the best of your recollection, who was it who made the statement, Ebersole or the other doctor?
Custer:	Ebersole.
Gunn:	And to the best of your recollection, what did Ebersole say?
Custer:	Just what I had said.
Gunn:	Are you acquainted with the name of Dr. Loy Brown?
Custer:	Yes, I am.
Gunn:	Who is Loy Brown?
Custer:	He was the Captain [O-6] in charge of the radiology department.
Gunn:	Is he the other officer whom you heard speaking with Dr. Ebersole?
Custer:	Yes, he was.
Gunn:	Did you hear discussion about disposition of any other autopsy materials, in addition to x-rays?
Custer:	No, I didn't.
Gunn:	So, for example, they did not talk about autopsy photographs?
Custer:	No, I didn't. And the funny part about it was, this was on—I just happened to be walking down the hall behind them, and the conversation was going on. And I was noticed, and everything shut down.

Custer Examines Selected Autopsy Photographs

Jeremy showed Custer view no. 2, specifically, color photos no. 26, 27, and 28, titled "right side of head and right shoulder."

Gunn: Do you see any differences between that photograph and what you observed on President Kennedy, such that it would lead you to question the authenticity of the photograph?

Custer: Not really. I notice one difference. The incision on the neck is a lot bigger than what I saw. But that could be due to probing.

Gunn: You're referring to the anterior neck wound; is that correct?

The next series of photographs viewed by Custer was view no. 3, corresponding to color photos 32, 33, 34, 35, 36, and 37, titled: "superior view of the head."

Gunn: Is there any question in your mind about the authenticity of that photo [no. 33]?

Custer: Not really.

Gunn: You're shaking your head—

_____

Custer: Wait, hold on one second.

Gunn: Sure.

Custer: Let me put this in the record. Do you notice the apparatus that is holding the head? You can see—

Gunn: Yes, metal apparatus. [referring to the metal stirrup or headrest]

Custer: It's like a metal half-moon. When I took my x-rays, that wasn't there.

_____

Gunn: ...Is it possible for you to determine, based upon this photograph alone, whether the x-rays of the cranium were taken before or after the photographs?

Custer: No sir, it's not possible.

Gunn: Okay. Mr. Custer, in the photograph, there was a picture of a—there was—a towel was included. Do you remember seeing a towel of that sort on the—

Custer: Mm-hmm.

Gunn: You did see a towel on the night of the autopsy that would correspond to what's shown in that photograph?

Custer: Not at that time, I didn't. When I took the x-rays, there was no towel there.

Gunn: Was there anything there at the time that you took the x-rays?

Custer: Just a sheet over the—the film.

Gunn: Okay.

Custer: Over that area where the skull was, to collect any body fluids.

Jeremy now showed Custer view no. 6, color photos no. 42 and 43, titled "wound of entrance in right posterior occipital region," what I have repeatedly referred to as the intact back-of-the-head photos drawn for the HSCA by medical illustrator Ida Dox.

Gunn: Mr. Custer, does that photograph correspond to what you observed on the night of the autopsy?

Custer: Truthfully and honestly, I cannot remember seeing that.

Gunn: Is that because you didn't have that view, or it does not appear the way that it appeared to you on the night of the autopsy?

Custer: Because it did not appear to me the way that appeared to me.

Gunn: In what respect is that photograph different from what you recall?

Custer: I did not see the back of the skull or the lower occipital region during the time I took the x-rays.

I was astounded at this response, given that Custer *had impugned the authenticity* of the intact back-of-the-head bootleg autopsy photos in his videotaped interview by David Lifton in 1989. Furthermore, this response contradicted, or at least called into serious doubt, his earlier response during the deposition that the *occipital bone, although unstable, was not missing.* How could he tell us it was not missing, and draw two skull diagrams showing the occipital bone to be present, if he "did not see the back of the skull or the lower occipital region" while he was taking x-rays?

Gunn: Does that mean that you didn't have a chance to observe that angle, or that the bone was not there?

Custer: I didn't have a chance to observe that angle, because the head was not picked up like that—

Then how, I asked myself, could Custer have described a huge occipital defect in the head on the audiotape of his 1979 Lifton interview, and how could he impugn the bootleg autopsy photos of the

535

intact back-of-the-head in his 1989 videotaped interview with Lifton? What was going on here? Was Custer simply a liar, a spinner of tales? Or was something more subtle going on here—were the autopsy photographs subtly changing his recollections of the autopsy? I didn't have an answer in 1997 when we took his deposition, and I don't have an answer today, almost 10 years later, as I struggle with his deposition transcript.

Gunn: Okay.

Custer: —where I could see behind it. All I lifted it was enough to place the cassette underneath.

Gunn: So, for practical purposes, you have—you had insufficient opportunity to view, to either authenticate or not authenticate this photograph. Would that be correct?

Custer: That's correct.

Gunn: Okay.

Custer: The only—let me add something to this. The only thing that I could authenticate is this flap, right there, on the right anterior portion of the skull.

Gunn: That looks as if it's over the top of the ear?

Custer: Right. Correct.

Gunn: And you remember the flap being there?

Custer: Oh, absolutely.

Jeremy brought out view no. 4, color photos 38 and 39, titled "posterior view of wound of entrance of missile high in shoulder."

Gunn: Mr. Custer, during the deposition, you said that you had—you had been able to see a wound that was on the back of President Kennedy. Does this photograph correspond to what you were able to view?

Custer: Yes sir, it does.

Gunn: And can you identify where on the photograph the wound was?

Custer: It would be on the right scapula region.

Gunn: And that's the larger marking that's just to the right of the ruler; is that correct?

Custer: Correct.

Custer Comments Upon Dr. Ebersole's 1978 HSCA Deposition

Custer had brought with him to the ARRB deposition his own annotated copy of Dr. Ebersole's HSCA deposition transcript. Jeremy decided to give him an opportunity to make comments on testimony by Ebersole that he felt required correction or comment.

Gunn: ...any important things that you have specific knowledge of yourself that you would like to either confirm what Dr. Ebersole said or dispute what Dr. Ebersole said, I would appreciate it. I would like you to identify the page number and the line number—

Custer: Okay.

Gunn: —if you could.

Custer: All right.

Gunn: Okay?

Custer: Ready?

Gunn: Yes.

Custer: Page two, line 23, 24, and 25...he states that he was acting chief radiologist at the National Naval Medical Center in Bethesda. Baloney. He was the radiologist on call. There was a lot more people higher ranking than him that were staff radiologists. They all took call. He was a resident radiologist studying for his board certification, which he did not receive until the end of that year. That's one thing that I have a problem with...and this is what is fantastic, where he states—Okay. Page three, lines seven and eight. He "personally carried the cassettes containing the x-rays to the x-ray department, which was on the fourth floor." Baloney. Dr. Ebersole never left the morgue. Reed and I personally carried the x-rays. There's pictorial evidence of that, that you have...at all times, Dr. Ebersole stayed within the morgue. Dr. Ebersole examined the films as I brought them back, made interpretations that contradicted many times throughout the evening. I suggested to Dr. Ebersole what films should be taken...why couldn't he see the displacement of the...the posterior portion of the skull, and realize there had to be force coming from the anterior portion of the skull. He knew that. Now, he's an educated man. He has to know that. Also, in the statements he made that he couldn't recollect certain things; how many people were in the morgue at that time. Oh, come on. It was pure mayhem. The gallery was completely full...there was definitely more than 15 people in the morgue at that time. The commotion was astronomical...and he [says he] took x-rays at 3:00 in the morning. That's crazy...and I was woke [sic] up at 5:00 o'clock in the morning by Captain Brown and Dr. Ebersole, commending me on my performance. And I just looked at them, and shook my head. And I said thank you, rolled over, and went to sleep...he was questioned [by the HSCA panel] to the fact, were there any controlling facet—or factors in the gallery that controlled the morgue—the morgue procedure at that time? "No, there were not." Come on. There were two men that constantly stood up, directed which way things would go.

Gunn: That's the general that you referred to and the other person—the civilian?

Custer: The general and the plain clothes. Which, by deduction, I assumed was President Kennedy's personal physician.

Gunn: Admiral Burkley?

Custer: Admiral Burkley.

_____

Gunn: If you look at page five...starting on line 19.

Custer: All right.

Custer: Where he says he may have drawn lines on the film [well after the autopsy, when visiting a Dr. Young at the White House]. Does that help refresh your recollection or change your mind at all about whether you saw him actually make lines on the films during—

Custer: He did draw lines.

Gunn: —lines during the time of the autopsy?

Custer: He—he did draw lines during the autopsy.

Gunn: And you saw those?

Custer: I saw those.

Gunn: Okay.

And so ended the strange, and mentally exhausting deposition of Jerrol Custer. The aspects of his testimony surrounding the taking of x-rays seemed reasonably credible—more than Ed Reed's testimony had seemed—while Custer seemed 'shaky' on many timeline questions. His testimony also included some modifications, and some outright reversals, of earlier responses in previous researcher interviews; some important new information about directions coming from the gallery (which expanded upon the recollections of O'Connor and Jenkins to the HSCA), and the behavior of Dr. Finck; information about a mangled bullet fragment that fell from the body which was consistent with his two most recent researcher interviews; and some tales that seemed not really worthy of belief. Custer was a complicated individual, and I do not feel it appropriate to affix any one "label," or characterization, to his credibility. What the researcher *can* do is attempt to assess his answers to specific questions based first on *consistency;* and where consistency is lacking, rely upon the *earliest documented answer* he gave to that question. The table below may help:

QUESTION/ ISSUE	LIFTON—1979	LIFTON—1989	ARRB—1997
How Many (and Which) Skull X-Rays Were Taken?	Five (5) skull x-rays; 1 A-P; 2 Laterals; 1 Townes; 1 Tangential	Five (5) skull x-rays; 1 A-P; 2 Laterals; 1 Townes; 1 Tangential	Five (5) skull x-rays; 1 A-P; 2 Laterals; 2 Tangential, or "Oblique" views
Cervical A-P X-Ray Showing Metal Fragments in Neck at the Level of C3/C4	Not mentioned.	Not mentioned.	Repeatedly mentioned.
Location of Large Skull Defect	An occipital "blowout."	Massive damage to the back of the head.	Fronto-temporal-parietal; occipital bone is unstable, but is not missing.
Temporal Bone Flap Seen in Autopsy Photographs	Not mentioned.	Did *not* see this damage at the autopsy.	Repeatedly affirmed that he *did see* this damage at the autopsy.
Bullet Fragment Falling from the President's Back When Positioning an X-Ray Film Cassette	Not mentioned.	*Did* mention; said Dr. *Ebersole* recovered fragment.	*Did* mention; said Dr. *Finck* recovered fragment.
Anterior Neck Wound	Looked like a *ragged tracheostomy,* with 'torn skin.'	*Round hole;* did *not* recall a tracheostomy incision.	*Round hole;* did *not* recall a tracheostomy incision.

SOME TENTATIVE CONCLUSIONS ABOUT THE AUTOPSY X-RAYS

I have reached the following conclusions about the taking of x-rays at President Kennedy's autopsy, taking into account the 'big picture' after reviewing the depositions of Ebersole and Finck before the HSCA; the Lifton interviews of Reed and Custer; and the depositions of Ed Reed and Jerrol Custer before the ARRB:

- Custer and Reed exposed the x-rays together as a team, and together took all of the x-rays up to the fourth floor x-ray laboratory for developing; a Secret Service agent accompanied them on each trip.

- Dr. Ebersole never left the morgue to take any x-rays to the main x-ray department.

- The skull x-rays were taken *as one series,* were taken *first,* and were taken *very early after the arrival of the President's body,* since Humes mentioned that he had a 'good set of head x-rays' to Dr. Finck on the telephone when he invited him to participate in the autopsy.

- At least *one* x-ray of the body—of the chest with the lungs and heart still present—was taken prior to Finck's arrival at the autopsy at 8:30 PM. Some of the abdominal and pelvic x-rays *may have been* taken prior to Finck's arrival.

- The sequence and timing of many of the body x-rays, after the exposure of the chest x-ray with lungs/heart present, is uncertain, and will remain so.

- Three x-rays of the body in the present collection were taken after evisceration.

- *Five (5) skull x-rays were taken*; **two (2) of them are now missing.**

- There *may be* **one** missing A-P cervical spine x-ray, showing metal fragments in the area of C3/C4, per Jerrol Custer.

- There *may be* **one** missing lateral x-ray of the cervical spine, per Ed Reed.

- The origin of the 3 x-rays of loose skull fragments is uncertain.

- The authenticity of the 6.5 mm diameter semi-circular object on the A-P head x-ray is uncertain; it may be an optical artifact intentionally superimposed upon a composite copy film of the real A-P x-ray. [See the section immediately below for further discussion and resolution of this issue.] Although Custer and Reed expressed interpretive, diagnostic opinions about this 'object' in the A-P x-ray to the ARRB, they were not qualified by education or training to *interpret* x-rays.

- The authenticity of the two lateral skull x-rays is uncertain, given that they are inconsistent with so many autopsy eyewitness claims of a blowout in the back of the head (such as the Reed/HSCA, Custer/1979 and 1989, Roy Kellerman/HSCA, Sibert/HSCA, O'Neill/HSCA), as well as reliable 1963 Dallas witnesses (Clint Hill, and Drs. Jenkins, Clark, Perry, McClelland, and Carrico). [See section immediately below for further discussion and resolution of this issue.]

THE CRUCIAL, GROUND-BREAKING WORK OF DR. DAVID MANTIK WITH THE AUTOPSY X-RAYS IN THE NATIONAL ARCHIVES, USING OPTICAL DENSITY (OD) MEASUREMENTS AS AN ANALYTICAL TOOL

David W. Mantik, who lives today in Rancho Mirage, California and at this writing in 2009, was still a practicing radiation oncologist, has contributed more to the study of the autopsy materials in the Archives than any person to date. I say this because he examined the original autopsy skull x-rays in the National Archives extensively (in 1993 and 1994), and did so by taking an extremely large number of *empirical measurements* with an optical densitometer—empirical measurements represented by numbers, which can be checked by others who might wish to replicate his experiments and check on his findings. The renowned British physicist Sir Arthur Eddington once said that all true scientific evaluations are based upon numbers (i.e., empirical data acquired from precise measurement of the natural world), and that if you are not dealing with numbers, you are not doing science. Well, for those critics who may disparage the large extent to which the many controversies and conclusions in the JFK medical evidence debate depend upon eyewitness testimony and eyewitness recollections, I can emphatically say this: Dr. Mantik's work and conclusions are based 100 per cent upon meticulously recorded numerical empirical data that are repeatable, and therefore subject to thoroughgoing outside peer review. It is true assassination science, in the very best sense of the word.

David Mantik received his M.D. from the University of Michigan, and a Ph.D. in Physics from the University of Wisconsin. The information that I will present in this section is derived from 6 different sources, listed below:

1. November 1993 videotaped lecture at the "ASK" JFK research symposium in Dallas, Texas.
2. October, 1994 videotaped lecture at the first annual "COPA" JFK research symposium in Washington, D.C.
3. October, 1995 videotaped lecture at the second annual "COPA" JFK research symposium in Washington, D.C.
4. Mantik's two articles in the anthology *Assassination Science,* edited by James H. Fetzer, Ph.D., Catfeet Press, published 1998, fourth printing (2000, with corrections). The articles are titled "The JFK Assassination: Cause for Doubt;" and "Postscript: The President John F. Kennedy Skull X-Rays," pages 93-139.
5. Mantik's long, comprehensive article in the anthology *Murder in Dealey Plaza,* edited by James H. Fetzer, Ph.D., Catfeet Press, published in 2000, fifth printing (2002, with corrections). The article is titled "Paradoxes of the JFK Assassination: The Medical Evidence Decoded," and appears on pages 219-297.

6.   Research notes provided to the ARRB by Dr. Mantik regarding certain control experiments he had conducted to test his conclusions about missing brain tissue in the JFK skull x-rays.

Introduction to X-Ray Films and the Science of Optical Densitometry

Any discussion of Mantik's work must begin with an explanation of *how an x-ray is taken*. Many lay persons may not realize that in all x-ray images, the image on the x-ray film is caused primarily *not* by the x-rays themselves, but by *light emitted from the two illuminator screens inside the x-ray cassette* that holds the film. The x-ray beam that creates the image passes through the body tissues being x-rayed and then impacts the illuminator screens inside the cassette. The residual intensity at any point on the screens depends on how much the x-ray beam has been reduced by absorption in the intervening tissue. The screens then emit light in a visible wavelength that exposes the film. (The film is sandwiched between the two illuminator screens.) The x-ray film is next developed, quite like ordinary photographic film. However, an x-ray image is always a black and white image.

The *x-ray film* at issue here, from 1963, consisted of a relatively thick, transparent plastic film base as the central layer in each film, coated on both sides with a very thin layer of emulsion, consisting largely of silver bromide (that is, silver ions very sensitive to light), whose properties change when exposed to light. When the silver bromide ions in the emulsion are exposed to great amounts of light from the illuminator screens, the ions are converted to metallic silver in large numbers, and the resulting image on the developed film appears relatively dark, since the passage of light through the developed film is impeded by the metallic silver. When relatively *less light* from the illuminator screens impacts the film emulsion, the silver bromide coating is washed away in great quantities during developing, since the ions were *not* converted to elemental silver in great numbers. Thus, the resulting images from those body tissues that were relatively dense (such as bone) appear lighter, or more white, on the developed x-ray film image; and the resulting images from materials that were not very dense (such as soft body tissues, or in the absence of tissue, air) appear darker, or blacker, on the developed x-ray image. On a developed x-ray image, very bright white areas usually represent bone, and the "whiter" the image, the denser the bone being portrayed. On a developed x-ray image, darker areas represent either soft tissue, or sometimes air inside a body cavity (such as air inside a large, open skull wound, or inside a sinus if the orbit of the eye is cracked, for example). The darker the image, the less material was present to impede the x-ray beam; the brighter the image, the more material was present to impede the x-ray beam.

Optical densitometry, in the application discussed here, is a scientific analytical tool that measures numerically the transmission of ordinary light through the developed x-ray film. (Interested readers may reference Mantik's articles in *Assassination Science* for the exact logarithmic formulas from which the OD measurement readings are derived.) The optical densitometry ("OD") measurements are expressed numerically in fractions of whole numbers; an explanatory table of different whole number OD values is presented below:

"OD" Numerical Reading	Per Cent of Light Transmitted Through Film in the Area Being Measured	Remarks
0	100 %	All light passes through film
1	10%	Only ten percent as much light passes through film as for a reading of zero
2	1%	Only ten per cent as much light passes through film as for a reading of 1
3	.1%	Only ten percent as much light passes through film as for a reading of 2; only one per cent as much as for a reading of 1
4	.01%	Only ten percent as much light passes through film as for a reading of 3; only one percent as much as for a reading of 2; only .1 per cent as much as for a reading of 1

In summary, the differences between each whole number on the OD scale is **one whole order of magnitude, i.e., a factor of ten.** As long as the same light source is used for a series of measurements, the intensity of the light source is irrelevant. With the equipment Dr. Mantik took with him to the Archives, he was able to take OD readings of the skull x-rays at intervals of one tenth of a millimeter (that is, 0.1 mm apart from each other). Dr. Mantik said that <u>on most clinical x-ray films</u>, the normal range of most OD measurements is between:

0.5 (for the lightest areas)   and   **2.0** (for the darkest areas)

Anomalous Aspects of the JFK Skull X-Rays

Photographs of two of the three extant JFK skull x-rays (the A-P skull and right lateral skull) were published by the HSCA, as well as photos of the HSCA's computer-aided enhancements of those two x-rays, *and* a *pre mortem* lateral skull x-ray of President Kennedy, taken when he was living. Any lay person can compare the pre mortem lateral skull x-ray (Figure 36) with the enhanced post mortem A-P and right lateral skull x-rays (Figures 38 and 37), and immediately see how "strange-looking" the autopsy skull x-rays are: how very much *brighter* *and* *darker* they are than the ranges of gray-scale present in JFK's *pre* mortem lateral skull x-ray published by the HSCA. According to Dr. Mantik, JFK's pre mortem lateral skull x-ray is typical of the average range of gray-scale present in clinical x-rays of the skull when viewed by the human eye. In his November 1993 lecture in Dallas, Mantik said that in his entire career, *he had never seen* an x-ray in real life that even approximated the extreme whiteness and darkness present in the A-P and lateral JFK skull x-rays in the National Archives. He has pointed out that the very fact that the HSCA decided enhancements were necessary at all, speaks to the very unusual nature of the JFK head x-rays. Unfortunately, he was not able to take OD measurements of the *pre* mortem JFK skull x-ray while examining the autopsy materials in the National Archives; the pre mortem lateral skull x-ray is located at the JFK Library in Boston, and is not among the autopsy materials that Dr. Mantik had been granted access to, in accordance with the Kennedy family's Deed-of-Gift provisions. For this reason, Dr. Mantik was limited to making visual, subjective human-eye comparisons between the pre and post mortem JFK lateral skull x-rays. The reader can easily make those comparisons as well, using either the illustrations in this book, or by accessing volume 7 of the HSCA's 1979 report. The difference is remarkable and cries out for an explanation.

The Lateral Skull X-Rays

Most noteworthy about any diagnostic analysis of the right and left lateral JFK skull x-rays is the fact that ***neither one shows a blowout of skull and brain tissue in the right rear of the skull, such as was noted by the treatment staff at Parkland hospital, and by many autopsy witnesses.*** The obvious question is, why? Were all of these eyewitnesses wrong, and *consistently* in error (rather than exhibiting *random* error in their recollections); or is there something wrong with the lateral skull x-rays from President Kennedy's autopsy? Was there really a blowout in the head in the right rear of the skull behind the ear, and if so, was it somehow obscured in the lateral x-rays? Furthermore, the *very dark region in the forward part of the skull* seen in these two x-rays implies a forward cranial vault ***devoid of brain tissue,*** which is greatly at variance with the brain photographs in the National Archives, as well as the rather robust brain weight of 1500 grams recorded in the supplemental autopsy report.

The A-P Skull X-Ray

Furthermore, the most prominent feature on the anterior-posterior (A-P) skull x-ray from President Kennedy's autopsy is the very bright, nearly circular 6.5 mm wide image of an apparent metal fragment that appears to be located, at first examination, in the area of the orbit of the right eye. Despite the immediate appearance to the layman of where it is located on the A-P skull x-ray, it really is *not* in the orbit of the right eye. An examination of the *right lateral* skull x-ray reveals only 2 significant fragments near the front of the skull, near the sinuses: what are universally agreed by all competent authorities (i.e., radiologists) to be the 7 x 2 mm and 3 x 1 mm fragments removed at autopsy, and documented in both the autopsy report and the Sibert-O'Neill report. There is also a *very small* metallic fragment present in the right lateral skull x-ray high on the back of the cranium, on the *outside* of the skull just below some large dislocated fragments of posterior parietal bone (which appear to have been dislocated <u>toward the rear from the front</u>). The small fragment on the right lateral x-ray corresponds ***in location*** (but <u>*not*</u> in ***brightness or implied density,*** or ***size***) with the large, apparently metallic 'fragment' on the A-P x-ray. This small fragment on the right lateral x-ray was mentioned in a rather imprecise manner in the Sibert-O'Neill report, and not mentioned at all in the autopsy report, or in Humes' Warren Commission testimony.

All of the above is of obvious interest because ***no one present at the autopsy*** testified to either the Warren Commission or the HSCA about removing the large 6.5 mm nearly-circular 'fragment' seen today on the A-P head x-ray from the body of the President; nor was the removal of such a fragment ever mentioned in either the 1963 Navy autopsy report, the 1963 FBI Sibert-O'Neill report, or the January 1967 Military Review report. X-ray technologist Jerrol Custer *did* testify that he recollected its presence on the A-P x-ray at his ARRB deposition, but the ***autopsy pathologists*** *did not recollect seeing it on the A-P x-ray* when specifically asked by the ARRB General Counsel, as we shall see later in this chapter. Their uniform testimony, *and* the absence of any mention of removal of this fragment from the body in any contemporaneous documents or testimony *from the time of the autopsy,* trumps Custer's testimony and makes it statistically insignificant, and indeed, not worthy of belief in regard to this specific question. Besides, when Jeremy Gunn asked Custer if he ever saw a fragment of that size *removed at autopsy*, he said "no." Surely, if it had been present on the A-P x-ray at the autopsy, it would have been removed by the pathologists. After all, they removed two smaller fragments that appear less dense, and therefore less luminous, on the skull x-rays. The sole concern of RADM Burkley, who apparently attempted to control the general direction of the autopsy and the restrictions imposed upon the pathologists, appears to have been the removal of bullets and bullet fragments from the cadaver for use as evidence. It is a **fact** that ***no such fragment was removed*** at autopsy—one of the very few undisputable facts in the Kennedy assassination. Since it was not removed from the body, it likely was not present on the A-P x-ray that night. This is the question that Dr. Mantik hoped to answer with his research: Is the large 'metallic fragment' on the A-P head x-ray authentic, or is it an *artifact* imposed in the deliberate creation of a forgery designed to incriminate Lee Harvey Oswald by linking the A-P x-ray—after-the-fact—to the supposed murder weapon?

A Common Mistake In Interpretation Should Be Avoided

One final point about apparent anomalies in the JFK head x-rays is in order. To the lay person who first examines the images of both the A-P and lateral skull x-rays published by the HSCA, it appears as if the frontal bone on the right side of the forehead, and the orbit of the right eye, are both missing. If true, this would present the grossest kind of disparity with the autopsy photographs, which show the forehead and the orbit of the right eye *to be present*. Examination of the A-P and right lateral x-rays by radiologists, however, reveals (when they are properly examined using a hot light) that the bone constituting the right orbit and the forehead is all present. Missing frontal bone is first detected on the right lateral x-ray *just behind* where President Kenney's hairline was located, which is entirely consistent with the autopsy photographs that show the forehead intact, and the skull and scalp severely disrupted *just behind the hairline in the front of the head.* Dr. Mantik is in full accord with these interpretations, and like other radiologists, attributes the extremely black or dark appearance of portions of the A-P and lateral skull x-rays to the presence of large amounts of air in the cranium. (More on the implications of this in a moment—for they are significant.)

What Mantik's OD Measurements Reveal About the JFK Skull X-Rays

I will present below the most basic findings of Dr. Mantik regarding whether or not the 3 JFK skull x-rays are authentic x-ray films, or are altered images. Before embarking upon these summations of his findings, I want to make very clear that David Mantik *is in full accord* with the HSCA's experts that the body depicted in the JFK x-rays is indeed the body of John F. Kennedy. Mantik paid special attention to the head x-rays, and agrees that the teeth (and fillings, or "amalgams"), the sinuses, and certain bone sutures in the skull that can be identified all agree with those features on the pre mortem lateral skull x-ray.

The Right Lateral Skull X-Ray: Evidence of Forgery Is Revealed by the OD Measurements

As a scientific "control," Mantik and his research partner Dr. Doug DeSalles took OD measurements of lateral skull x-rays from 9 coroner's cases to obtain a *range* of numerical measurements *between the brightest and darkest areas* on these skull x-rays. In general, the brightest areas of the 9 coroner's cases transmitted *about two or three times as much light* as the darkest areas. Furthermore, subjective, visual examination of the lateral x-rays of these 9 skulls did not reveal the extreme contrast between very bright and very dark areas that is seen in the JFK lateral skull x-rays. The subjective visual evidence was consistent with the OD measurements, and vice-a-versa.[28]

On the right lateral JFK skull x-ray, Dr. Mantik took many OD measurements of two specific areas. The optical density measurements for one extremely bright area located anatomically behind the ear, which he labeled area "P" (for posterior) in a diagram at his lectures, was compared with the optical densitometry measurements for a very dark area in the front of the cranium labeled area "F" (for front). (See Figure 67.)

Amazingly, on the JFK right lateral skull x-ray, OD measurements revealed that area "P" (in the rear of the skull behind the ear) transmitted ***about 1100 times more light*** than area "F" (in the forward part of the skull which appears so dark in the x-ray image). That's worth repeating. The "great white area" in the rear of the skull behind the ear in the JFK right lateral skull x-ray transmitted about 1100 times more light than the dark area in the front of the cranium, whereas on the "control" x-rays the ratio was only about 2 or 3 to 1 between the brightest area and the darkest area on each lateral x-ray. The specific OD measurements cited in Mantik's lecture in October 1994 are reproduced below, and refer to area "P" and area "F" in Figure 67:

---

[28]As an aside, it is worth mentioning that Dr. Mantik reported in his October 1994 lecture that whereas in the JFK lateral skull x-rays, the posterior part of the skull appears extremely white (implying great density of bone in that region) and the anterior portion of the skull appears quite dark, that in the 9 coroner's cases, *on four of the nine lateral skull x-rays,* the front (or anterior) part of the skull appears <u>whiter</u> than the rear (or posterior) part of the skull.

546

Area in JFK Lateral Skull X-Rays	Range of Optical Density Measurements	Remarks
Area "P" (posterior skull)	0.5 to 0.6	Implies tremendous bone density; an impossibility in nature
Area "F" (anterior skull)	3.5 to 3.9	Implies an absence of much bone and almost all brain tissue

As Dr. Mantik stated in his November 1993 lectures, only a posterior skull filled completely with bone (instead of brain tissue) could exhibit the OD numbers for area "P" above. Why does he say this? Because Dr. Mantik compared the OD readings from the petrous bone on JFK's lateral skull x-ray (where the ear canals are located) with area "P," and area "P" was *almost* equally as dense in terms of optical density measurements as was the area of the petrous bone on JFK's lateral skull x-ray. (The petrous bone is a region of almost solid bone running from left-to-right laterally through the human skull, and is the densest bone in the human body.) Mantik believes that the "great white area" in the posterior skull (the occipital-parietal region, to be precise) on the lateral x-rays is an optical "patch" (i.e., a "light-blasted" area) superimposed on top of the authentic x-ray image when a forged composite copy film was created sometime during the month following the autopsy. [How this was done will be discussed later in this chapter.]

The data table below provides the mean readings Mantik took on both of the JFK lateral skull x-rays, in which he compared area "P" and the petrous bone on each lateral x-ray:

	ODs for Area "P"	ODs for Petrous Bone	Difference Between ODs for Area "P" and Petrous Bone	Ratio of Transmission ("P" over Petrous Bone)
Left Lateral Skull X-Ray	.99	.73	.26	.55
Right Lateral Skull X-Ray	.625	.53	.095	.80

For each JFK lateral skull x-ray, area "P" (the "white patch") is almost as dense as the petrous bone, as revealed by the ratio of transmission of light, the right hand column in the data table above. For the left lateral, area "P" transmits 55 % of the light transmitted by the area around the ear canal; for the right lateral (see Figure 37), area "P" transmits 80% as much light as is transmitted by the area around the ear canal. These figures reflect mean values, also. In the localized *posterior-superior region of area "P" on the two x-rays,* the transmission ratios are even more disparate: 93% for the right lateral x-ray, and 63% for the left lateral x-ray. Since there should be no difference at all between these *ratios* when comparing the right to the left lateral x-ray, the disparities noted above are therefore 'problematic' in terms of what they say about x-ray authenticity. In other words, how can two different lateral x-rays of the same human skull show a different transmission ratio between area "P" (or any other area) and the bone around the ear canal? *The answer is that in real life, they could not.* The transmission ratios between area "P" and the ear canal are different on the JFK lateral skull x-rays because the forged composite copy films created after the autopsy were *imperfectly created*—that is, the right lateral was "light blasted" *more* than the left lateral was during the copying process, when the occipital-parietal blowout was obliterated by exposing the copy film to extra light in that region. The human eye cannot detect the difference, but the optical densitometer can, and the numerical readings it provided cannot be denied.

Additionally, area "P" on each of the two lateral x-rays is of a different size and shape—providing additional evidence that the "white patch" on each lateral skull x-ray is the result of forgery. Mantik reports that the overall size of area "P" on the left lateral is <u>larger</u> than on the right lateral, meaning that *if this white area represented a real object,* it would be closer to the right side of the skull. When the A-P x-ray is viewed—the anterior-posterior, or front-to-back view of the skull—the physically dense object seen on the lateral x-rays should be seen *closer to the anatomical right side of the skull than the left.* However, no correspondingly dense object is seen <u>anywhere</u> on the A-P skull x-ray, let alone closer to the right side. Therefore, both laterals are also revealed to be forgeries by simply comparing them to the A-P x-ray, and noting the total absence of any "hyperdense" area in the skull, to use Dr. Mantik's terminology.

It is noteworthy that no lamboid suture—the suture that knits together the occipital and parietal bones—can be seen in area "P" on either lateral x-ray, and that this area is devoid of the skull fractures that are present throughout other areas of the lateral skull x-rays. (See Figures 37 and 67.)

A Significant Amount of Missing Brain Tissue Is Confirmed by Comparing OD Measurements of "Control" X-Rays With the JFK Autopsy Skull X-Rays

Mantik believes that the peculiar appearance of the very dark area on the right lateral skull x-ray is *not* any indication of forgery, but rather, reflects *an almost total absence of brain tissue from the forward part of the cranium.* The near-total absence in the right lateral skull x-ray of brain tissue from the right and left cerebral hemispheres in the *forward cranial vault* is <u>completely inconsistent</u> with **both** the photographs of the brain in the autopsy collection (see Figure 35 for the sketch made by Ida Dox for the HSCA), **as well as** with the brain weight of 1500 grams (which exceeds the average weight of 1480 grams for a normal male brain) recorded in the supplementary autopsy report. To test his hypothesis that the dark void primarily represents missing brain, Dr. Mantik conducted "control" experiments on A-P and lateral skull x-rays (that he exposed himself) of cadaver skulls filled with different quantities of biological material, and compared the empirical data from these "controls" with his OD readings from the JFK A-P and lateral skull x-rays.[29] His experiments

---

[29]Mantik's notes on these experiments were sent to Jeremy Gunn and me. They were deposited in the National Archives after the ARRB staff shut down its operations. For anyone

with the control skulls confirmed that OD readings from the JFK right lateral skull x-ray are consistent with large amounts of brain tissue missing from the forward part of the cranium, and also that *more* brain tissue was missing from the *right side* of President Kennedy's brain than from the left side of the brain. This was based on OD data from the left and right sides of the A-P skull x-ray. The density of the skull bone imaged on the lower portions of the A-P skull x-ray, and the angle in which the x-ray beam was traveling through the skull (from lower front to upper rear), precluded direct longitudinal measurement of the skull at the site of the cerebellum, but Mantik *was* able to take meaningful OD measurements directly *above* the area of the cerebellum, and his OD readings of the JFK A-P skull x-ray in this area implied significantly *more* tissue present directly above the *left* cerebellum than was present directly above the right cerebellum. (Mantik estimated, based upon comparison of his control data with the data from the autopsy A-P skull x-ray, that there was approximately 5 cm *less* brain material directly above the right cerebellum in JFK's brain—as measured front-to-back through the A-P x-ray—than above the left cerebellum.) This result suggests significant brain tissue missing directly above the area of the *right* cerebellum—consistent with the observations of the medically trained professionals at Parkland hospital of a blowout in the right-rear of the head, and of severe damage and loss of tissue from both the right cerebellum, and the occipital lobe of the right cerebral cortex.

The A-P Skull X-Ray: Evidence of Forgery Is Revealed by the OD Measurements

To the human eye, the 6.5 mm wide object on the A-P skull x-ray (see Figure 38) is the brightest object in the x-ray image, and is therefore presumably a very dense metal fragment. (It even seems brighter to the human eye than the President's dental amalgams, or fillings, when they are viewed *collectively* from front to back on the A-P head x-ray.) However, it is not nearly as large or as bright on the *right lateral* skull x-ray as it appears to be on the *A-P* skull x-ray, which presents a paradox.[30] Dr. Mantik suspected, therefore, that the 6.5 mm "fragment" depicted on the A-P skull x-ray did not represent a real object present on the body at the autopsy. He set out to explore this hypothesis by taking OD measurements of the object on both the A-P and right lateral skull x-rays, as well as the dental amalgams. The apparent bullet fragment is *widest at the center when measured horizontally* on the A-P skull x-ray, since there is a small bite taken out of the fragment in its lower right hand corner (from 4 to 6 o'clock), as seen by the viewer when examining the x-ray. Mantik therefore took very careful OD measurements of the same object on the right lateral x-ray; if the large 6.5 mm object depicted on the A-P x-ray had been authentic, then OD measurements of the same object on the right lateral x-ray *should have shown it to be denser in the middle than at the bottom* of the

---

who wishes to examine them, they would be located either in my own collection of working papers in the JFK Collection, or possibly in those working papers associated with the preparations for the Humes deposition.

[30]The small fragment representing the 6.5 mm A-P object seen on the back of the skull in the *right* lateral x-ray cannot be seen in the *left* lateral x-ray because the entire image on one side—specifically, the image of the posterior skull—is "cropped," or truncated, based upon the way the x-ray cassette was placed under the skull at the autopsy.

fragment. This did not happen; the opposite happened. As Mantik said in November of 1993 in Dallas, this is "a gross violation of physical reality."

The data becomes more and more suspect when one compares the OD measurements and physical dimensions of the 6.5 mm fragment, the 7 x 2 mm fragment removed by Dr. Humes, and the dental amalgams. Those respective comparisons for both the right lateral skull x-ray, and the A-P skull x-ray, are reproduced below in data tables:

Data Table for Right Lateral Skull X-Ray (from article in *Assassination Science*)

Object	OD Measurement	Apparent Width (from right to left)	Actual Width (as seen on the A-P view)	Remarks
6.5 mm	1.5	Thin	2-3 mm	Inside the 6.5 mm diameter "bright fragment" image on the A-P, the actual fragment (which is smaller) can also be seen, and is only 2-3 mm wide, not 6.5 mm
Amalgams	1.0	Wider	10 mm	The dental fillings, as expected, are denser than the 6.5 mm fragment
7 x 2 mm	1.6	Thin	2 mm	Less dense than either the amalgams or the 6.5 mm as seen on the right lateral x-ray

<u>Data Table for the A-P Skull X-Ray</u> (from article in *Assassination Science*)

Object	OD Measurement	Apparent Length (from front to back)	Actual Length (as seen on the lateral view)	Remarks
6.5 mm	0.60	Very long	3-4 mm	*More dense* than all of the dental amalgams, *combined*
Amalgams	0.74, 0.78	Long	30-40 mm	*Less dense* than the 6.5 mm fragment, even though the amalgams range from <u>30-40</u> mm in length
7 x 2 mm	1.44	Short	2 mm	Less dense on the A-P x-ray than *either* the amalgams *or* the 6.5 mm fragment

There is one more way to view the data; the table below is taken from Dr. Mantik's October 1995 lecture in Washington, D.C.:

<u>OD Measurements, 6.5 mm Object vs. Dental Amalgams</u>

X-Ray	6.5 mm object	Amalgams	Remarks
A-P Skull	0.55	0.79	6.5 mm object *more dense* than <u>all</u> dental amalgams combined, viewed longitudinally through jaw
Right Lateral Skull	1.45	0.86	6.5 mm object *much less dense* than dental amalgams viewed crosswise through jaw

As Dr. Mantik stated in his lecture, the conclusion here is that the 6.5 mm object is remarkably *thick* on the A-P skull x-ray, and remarkably *thin* on the right lateral skull x-ray. This, of course, is also a gross violation of reality.

His conclusion: the extremely lucent A-P fragment seen on the A-P skull x-ray is an artifact, and the x-ray in evidence today is a forged composite copy film. The actual fragment is depicted on the right lateral skull x-ray, and is much smaller in dimensions, and less dense, than what is seen on the A-P x-ray. In fact, the large 6.5 mm object on the A-P skull x-ray is *so translucent* that the *actual fragment* <u>over which it was superimposed</u> can be seen inside the 6.5 mm image, and is only about

2-3 mm wide.

How Were the Fraudulent Skull X-Rays Created?

Although x-ray copy films today are made on films with emulsion on only one side, in 1963 technicians who made copies of x-ray films routinely used two-sided films that were identical to the two-sided films used for original exposures inside the x-ray cassettes.

During 1994 and 1995 Dr. Mantik did a considerable amount of research into the chemistry of x-ray films and the physics involved in copying images, by talking to Kodak film experts, x-ray technologists who had worked in the 1960s, and by reading the literature from the mid-1960s. In one publication from 1965, Dr. Mantik discovered a recipe for how much exposure time was required in order to convert standard x-ray films into copy films using a simple light box.

1965 Recipe for Making X-Ray Copy Films

Type of Image Desired on Copy Film	Pre-Exposure Time of Film to Ordinary Room Light	Time of Exposure of Film to Illuminator Light
High Contrast	15 seconds	15 seconds
Medium Contrast	30 seconds	30 seconds
Low Contrast	45 seconds	45 seconds

How the forged composite copy films were made is described by Dr. Mantik in his article in *Assassination Science,* on page 135. At that time, the literature from the period states, a good copy film was virtually indistinguishable from an original x-ray. The text quoted below explains how the 6.5 mm "fragment" was placed on the copy film made from the real A-P skull x-ray, but the technique applies equally to how the "great white patch" was superimposed over the blowout in the right rear of the skull in the lateral x-rays:

> So now, at last, we can explain what happened. Sometime after the autopsy the original x-ray films were taken to the darkroom for copying...a simple piece of cardboard (or whatever you wish to imagine) was cut out in the shape of a 6.5 mm fragment; it is anyone's guess as to why the bite was taken out (most likely, though, a perfect circle would have looked too suspicious to be shrapnel). Then the film was duplicated in the usual fashion, using light in the darkroom. But before the duplicate film was developed it was exposed one more time. This time the cardboard template was placed over the duplicate film so that light could only pass through this 6.5 mm hole. That area on the duplicate film then, when developed, would look very transparent, just like the autopsy 6.5 mm object...the entrepreneur who did this had to be clever, however. If he had simply placed a counterfeit image over the A-P view willy-nilly, most likely it would not have been spatially consistent on the two views. But, by using

something that was already there, Mother Nature solved the problem for him. He did not bother to alter the lateral—there was no need to. All he had to do was add the fake image right over the pre-existing shrapnel that the FBI had reported. Mother Nature had already located this image on both films consistent with reality, so he had no decisions to make. In fact, a small army of expert radiologists have noticed no problems at all with the A-P film—which is not a discredit to them. These issues are only accessible through OD measurements. Of course, in retrospect, it would be interesting now to ask the radiologists [who have reviewed the JFK x-rays in the past] about the "phantom image"—i.e., being able to see the original shrapnel through the 6.5 mm object.

Dr. Mantik has created his own forged composite copy films using test skulls, simulating both the 6.5 mm "fragment" superimposed on an A-P skull x-ray, and also simulating a "dense white patch" superimposed upon a lateral skull x-ray. They both looked virtually identical to the JFK autopsy skull x-rays.

OD Measurements Reveal <u>No</u> Entry Wound in the A-P Skull X-Ray Where the Clark Panel and the HSCA Panel Said it Was Located

The Clark Panel wrote in 1968 (with apparent certainty) that there was an entry wound on the right lateral skull x-ray slightly above the small metal fragment, approximately 100 mm above the EOP. What is almost certain is that this conclusion was that of one individual on the Clark Panel, its radiologist—Dr. Russell Morgan—and that the other three members just signed on to that finding of his, 'deferring to the expert.' The HSCA Forensic Pathology Panel concurred in his finding, and decided the sole entry wound in the skull was located one centimeter above the small metal fragment on the back of the head in the right lateral skull x-ray. In contrast, *none* of the 3 ARRB independent medical consultants, when evaluating the right lateral skull x-ray all by itself and without reference to any of the autopsy photographs, could find an entry wound anywhere on the x-ray; and none of these men seemed familiar with the JFK assassination medical evidence, or had a predisposition to believe there was a conspiracy. Even after viewing the autopsy photographs, none of them changed their minds and suddenly decided that they saw an entry wound that corresponded with any of the apparent wounds on the back of the head in the autopsy photos. Dr. Mantik conducted extensive searches for OD evidence of an entry wound 6 mm wide on the A-P skull x-ray, in the area 1 centimeter above the so-called '6.5 mm fragment,' where it should have been found using his analytical technique, if the HSCA panel had been correct about its location. There is no OD evidence supporting an entry wound of any size, anywhere in the neighborhood of 1 cm above the 6.5 mm object; therefore, Dr. Mantik concludes that the Clark Panel and the HSCA were wrong in their assessment of the right lateral x-ray, and that the entry wound in the rear of the head was almost certainly located exactly where the 3 pathologists said it was, about 2.5 cm directly to the right of, and slightly above the EOP. I suspect that Mantik is correct, and that the Clark Panel and HSCA panel were mislead into believing what they wanted to believe about the right lateral x-ray because of what they saw in the autopsy photographs of the back-of-the-head. Simply put, they saw a "red spot" up high in color photos 42 and 43, decided it was an entry wound, and looked for a corresponding defect in the lateral skull x-ray. They saw the large dislocation of the broken parietal bone high in the posterior skull in the right lateral skull x-ray, and interpreted it as what they wanted it to be—the 'entry wound' in the bone that corresponded to the "red spot" high in the scalp on the back of the head. (Providing one was willing to ignore the unanimous and unambiguous testimony of all three autopsy pathologists, this was a "neat solution" that made the photographic and x-ray evidence come together.) But the 3 ARRB consultants, and Dr. Mantik's negative search with the optical densitometer, have tipped the scales *against* an entry wound being in this location. The 3 autopsy pathologists were correct on this score, and the Clark Panel and the HSCA panel were wrong. David Mantik's OD search has been the referee that decided in favor of the autopsy pathologists. The opinions of the 3 ARRB consultants alone would not have tipped the scales, but they did certainly corroborate Mantik's definitive work in this area.

One Major Implication of A Low Entry Wound in the Back of the Head

Dr. Mantik believes that the apparent fragment trail seen in both lateral skull x-rays, high in the skull near the vertex, that appears to connect a point high in the forehead with the large displaced skull fragments high in the back of the head, *is real,* and is evidence of a bullet's passage through the skull, as it disintegrated. If his definitive finding that there is <u>no entry wound</u> 1 centimeter above the so-called 6.5 mm object on the A-P x-ray *is correct,* and if the 3 pathologists *are correct* that the entry wound in the skull <u>was really 4 inches lower</u> than where the Clark Panel and HSCA tried to place it, then as Dr. Mantik points out, the fragment trail near the vertex of the skull constitutes evidence of a *second shot to the head,* almost certainly entering high in the right front and exiting rather high in the rear of the skull, where the large, displaced bone fragments are located on the right lateral skull x-ray. There is much evidence to support this placement of the entry for the missile which caused this fragment trail in the right front, and its exit in the rear; it will all be detailed in Part II.

Mysterious Pencil Lines on the Right Lateral Skull X-Ray

Reproduced below is an excerpt of some provocative testimony by Dr. Ebersole from his 1978 HSCA deposition about the pencil lines he drew on the right lateral skull x-ray:

Baden: Now in fact on no. 2 [the right lateral skull x-ray] there are some pencilled lines.

Ebersole: Yes.

Baden: Are these the lines that you refer to as having—

Ebersole: Yes. On no. 2 specifically, this is a line that I made to identify definitely the lower line running from the naison [??? meaning unclear]. *There is a second line at the angle to that first one which I also made. <u>The attempt here was to get a line from the high point of the forehead back to the occipital.</u>* [Author's emphasis]

This is a terribly disingenuous statement by Ebersole: although the context is purportedly his discussion of lines he drew on the right lateral x-ray in order to allow him to later deduce magnification factors for the x-ray, so he could produce more precise dimensions for a sculptor's bust, I view that explanation as an unconvincing excuse for what Ebersole was *really doing* when he drew the line on the film connecting the "high point of the forehead back to the occipital." I believe that on the night of the autopsy, when Ebersole drew <u>one</u> pencil line from an area low in the occipital region to the large area of missing bone in the top of the head, and a <u>second</u> pencil line ***from the same point in the occiput*** to the right orbit, he was trying to account for *both* the missing skull bone in the fronto-parietal region, *and* the cracked orbit of the right eye, with two hypothetical fragments from one missile (see Figure 37). At this time, early in the autopsy, the pathologists had found a puncture wound low in the scalp in the occipital region. Although they had not yet been given the small fragment of bone by the Secret Service—which Boswell later explained to both the HSCA and the ARRB had completed the circumference of the entry wound in the back of the head—based upon the scalp perforation alone, they had presumably found a wound of entry, and were speculating about how one bullet might have caused such massive damage to the cranium. Dr. Ebersole was creating an unwelcome written record of this speculation by drawing pencil lines representing possible fragment trajectories, emanating from a single entrance wound very low in the skull. One pencil line connected the region of the posterior skull on the x-ray corresponding to the location of the scalp perforation on the body to the *presumed* exit site in the right-top of the skull; and the other pencil line connected *the same point on the posterior skull* to the cracked orbit of the right eye. Dr. Ebersole was making a written record of speculation during the early part of the autopsy—something which may not have set well with higher authority trying to control the autopsy's specific conclusions—which could account for why someone in a position of authority in the gallery ordered him to "stop that." The written results of an autopsy report could be "managed" through leverage and pressure, and even rewritten if necessary; but bullet trajectory lines drawn on an x-ray constituted a permanent record of the thought processes and tentative conclusions during the autopsy, unless that x-ray was to be destroyed. If Ebersole and the pathologists were discussing 'what they thought had happened' (i.e., a single head shot entering extremely low in the back of the skull) when he drew his hypothetical trajectory lines on the x-ray early in the autopsy, and someone in the gallery knew that such an entry, originating from high in the sixth floor of the Texas Book Depository was *inconsistent* with the pattern of damage observed on the body (i.e., the *top* of the head <u>missing</u>, but the *face* <u>intact</u>) it's no wonder that someone in authority in the gallery ordered "stop that," as Jerrol Custer recalled in his testimony. Dr. Ebersole's speculative trajectory lines for fragments from a hypothetical entering bullet low in the rear of the head had created a permanent record on an x-ray which implied that the shot could *not* have come from *high* behind the President, but instead *only low behind the President.* (If Dr. Ebersole's trajectory lines do pinpoint the precise location of an entry wound in the rear of the skull, this entry wound implies a shot from low in the Dal Tex Building, not from high in the TSBD; this will be explored further in Part II.)

Dr. Mantik is positive that the right lateral head x-ray is a copy film, and not an original. If it *is* a copy film (and was created simply to hide an occipital blow-out with a "white patch"), then the pencil lines drawn at the autopsy would have been transferred to the copy, however faint. The technician who performed this forgery would have had to *redraw* the pencil lines directly on top of the photographic image of those lines on the copy film; Dr. Ebersole would no doubt see the x-ray some day if it were ever introduced as evidence, and he would look for his pencil lines as evidence of the x-ray's authenticity. He would have to be psychologically tested by monitoring his reaction to the forged composite copy film of the right lateral x-ray; it would have his pencil lines overdrawn

555

on one side, thus implying that it was authentic, but would *no longer* show an occipital blow-out. How would Ebersole react to the forgery?

Dr. Ebersole's Testimony Provided Evidence As to When The X-Ray Forgery May Have Occurred, and Who May Have Been Involved

In his article in *Assassination Science,* and in his first lecture in Dallas in 1993, Dr. Mantik speculated that the HSCA testimony of Dr. Ebersole provided a clue as to *when* the forgery of the A-P and two lateral skull x-rays took place, and about the identity of at least *one* of the people who was likely involved. I have reproduced below the pertinent excerpt from Dr. Ebersole's HSCA deposition, and will follow with both Dr. Mantik's assessment, and my own, of what it means:

Ebersole: I must be a little vague on this but ***sometime within a month of the assassination*** I received a call from the White House medical staff—***a member of the White House medical staff, a [Navy] Captain James Young.*** *Dr. Young asked me if I could review the skull x-rays for the purpose of getting some measurements for a sculpture.* I said, yes, I thought that was feasible. I was driven to the White House Annex where I did see the skull films and took certain measurements and in taking those measurements *may well have drawn lines on the film.* It was then necessary for me to go back to Bethesda and determine some magnification or subtraction factors. I understand in the use of the portable x-ray equipment the structures depicted are not necessarily related to actual size and life. Now if one duplicates the conditions with the skull, you can establish a magnification factor or a subtraction factor. So after seeing the films at the White House Annex, going back to Bethesda and using a human skull to determine magnification factors, actually they were substantive factors. The image on the film was larger than in life one would expect from the physical setup. *I then phoned Dr. Young on open telephone using the expression like, something to the effect that "Aunt Margaret's skirts needed the following change,"* and gave him the numbers to multiply the numbers I had previously provided from examining the x-rays at the White House Annex...[Author's emphasis]

Weston: I would like to go back to the conversation you had with Dr. James Young in which you indicated that you went back to Bethesda and when back there you had reason to correct your measurements. What was the basis for that correction?

Ebersole: X-ray beams are divergent on an x-ray tube.

Weston: Yes, I understand that.

Ebersole: All x-ray beams from a tube diverge. An object placed here with a film underneath it is going to be distorted unless that object is placed at least six feet away from the tube. At that point the divergence has become almost non-existent. This is why in x-raying the chest and measuring the heart size we want a distance of at least six feet.

We can measure the heart reasonably accurately. In the use of portable x-ray equipment the source of radiation is very close to the object; therefore, there is a good deal of distortion. Second, there are two diversions. Now all one has to do is to duplicate that setup with a known steel ruler, what have you.

Weston: I see.

Ebersole: A known distance. Repeat the performance, measure it on the new x-ray and you have a factor. Perhaps your diameter from the liaison [sic] to the occipital bone might have been 12 centimeters. As a result of the calibration of the setup you might have to multiply this by something like .9 to have greater accuracy, or .8. It was that number that I had to go back and determine and then phone to the White House to apply to the numbers that I had furnished Dr. Young.

Weston: Do you have any independent recollection or do you have any record that would indicate what that factor was as you related?

Ebersole: No. I remember that one of the key measurements what we wanted to make was from on [sic] the base of the nose to the estimated point of the exit. The measurement I made was through the middle of the orbitals.

Weston: When you do this do you take a mean distance of thickness? In other words, above the cassette would you take, for example, like in the middle of the head as an average or do you take the closest point?

Ebersole: You try to take some anatomical that would be constant.

Weston: I am thinking about where you put your ruler.

Ebersole: On the film or some mean distance from the film.

Weston: In other words, you do recall what you did in that instance?

Ebersole: I used a skull.

Weston: Oh, you used a skull.

Ebersole: I said ruler here for this example but I used a skull, a human skull when I went back to Bethesda. You know, an anatomic specimen that we had in the department.

Weston: And you set the portable—the portable moves up and down, doesn't it?

Ebersole: Yes.

Weston: How do you know you set it [at] exactly the same distance?

Ebersole: We had a distance that we used the night of the autopsy. We used that distance, we used that machine.

Weston: I see.

Ebersole: And a human skull.

Weston: So you did make a record somewhere of how far above the body the x-ray—

Ebersole: Yes. That is the standard distance of a portable x-ray. While it may be varied, it is a standard.

At this point Dr. Baden, the head of the panel, unaccountably interrupted Dr. Weston's persistent questioning to begin asking Dr. Ebersole routine questions about his Curriculum Vitae; that ended Dr. Weston's pursuit of the matter. At least Dr. Weston demonstrated a healthy curiosity, and even apparent skepticism, about the strange tale spun by Dr. Ebersole, of his own accord, very early in his deposition.

To paraphrase Shakespeare, "methinks Dr. Ebersole doth explain too much," in an apparent attempt to make an excuse for why there are pencil lines on the right lateral x-ray. But there is probably more going on here than that. I now quote from Dr. Mantik's article in *Assassination Science:* "The strange episode about 'Aunt Margaret's skirts' suggests that Ebersole was being tested on his reaction to the altered films. (The official excuse of needing his help for a Kennedy bust makes no sense. If x-ray films were really useful for this purpose, then those taken during life would have been much more appropriate than the badly fragmented skull seen at the autopsy.) Ebersole, however, is either very tongue-in-cheek about all of this or else astonishingly naive."

As I see it, two principal opportunities present themselves here, and either one of them is more likely than the ridiculous story about taking measurements from the x-ray of a shattered and distorted skull for the purpose of 'making a sculpture' which, by the way, no one has ever seen. And since when did any artist ever worry about whether or not his bust was *exactly the correct size,* down to the precise centimeter? Artists are worried about correct *proportions* (which can be obtained from photographs); engineers and architects who build airplanes and bridges and buildings are worried about *exact measurements,* not artists. So, if the cock-and-bull story about obtaining magnification factors to apply to the head x-rays for the making of an accurate bust of President Kennedy is indeed false, what was really going on here? This is very important, and is a prime example of what Professor John Newman has called the 'principle of the adjacent square.' Whenever a lie is told, we must pay great attention to what was being covered up, and why.

Possibility One: If Jerrol Custer was *correct* about Dr. Ebersole using a pencil to mark estimated bullet fragment trajectories on a lateral skull x-ray the night of the autopsy, then those two pencil lines would have had to be redrawn after the forged composite copy film was created in order to

558

"authenticate" the x-ray in the eyes of Dr. Ebersole, were he ever to be called before the Warren Commission to testify about the x-rays. Those involved in creating the copy film of the right lateral which obscured the blowout in the right rear of the head would have *had to* re-draw (actually, overdraw) the images on the copy film of the pencil lines found on the original x-ray, and then "run it by Ebersole" to see if he raised any doubts about its authenticity. If he did have any doubts—i.e., if he did notice that the occipital-parietal blowout was now obscured in the x-ray—he would *also* have noticed the pencil lines redrawn exactly where he had originally drawn them, and would have seen 'the handwriting on the wall.' Years later a nervous Ebersole, under this scenario, would have invented the unlikely story about 'Aunt Margaret's skirts' out of whole cloth, simply to avoid admitting that he had been estimating bullet trajectories the night of the autopsy, as well as to avoid admitting that he had been manipulated, and compromised—that he had knowingly been an accessory-after-the-fact to a medical coverup. The Dr. Ebersole in this scenario is a man who would 'go along, to get along,' as they say in Texas.

Possibility Two: If Jerrol Custer was *incorrect* about Ebersole using a pencil to mark estimated bullet fragment trajectories on an x-ray the night of the autopsy, then Custer's memory (or his imagination) may have been influenced by reading the Ebersole transcript the night before his ARRB deposition. If his testimony about this purported event at the autopsy did not reflect reality, then when the coverup architects trotted out the forged composite copy film of the right lateral skull x-ray and "ran it by Ebersole" to gauge his reaction, he bought their story about a bust of the President hook, line, and sinker, and naively drew his pencil lines on the forged version of the right lateral x-ray in the White House Annex, and then went back to Bethesda and performed his experiment with the skull and the steel ruler with the portable x-ray machine, just as he testified to before the HSCA panel. If so, Dr. Young and his fellow conspirators must have had a good laugh when Ebersole proved how naive he truly was by calling back and relaying his magnification factors in 'code language' on an 'open telephone line.'

My own predisposition favors this possible variant of scenario number one above: If Dr. Ebersole privately protested when Dr. Young showed him the lateral x-rays with a radio-opaque patch now obscuring the occipital-parietal blowout, but was persuaded to go along with the coverup for "national security reasons," he may have asked Dr. Young what he was supposed to say about the pencil lines on the x-ray, in the event it was introduced into evidence. Under this hypothesis, the pencil lines would not have fooled him into believing the x-ray was authentic, but they were now nevertheless blatantly obvious on the x-ray and needed to be explained. At this point, the fairy tale about determining magnification factors for a bust of the President would have been invented in order to explain away the pencil lines. Exactly why this was necessary—why they could not be explained as bullet fragment trajectories—will be detailed in Part II.

One more thing is almost certain: when Ebersole went to the White House Annex he obviously had to be shown the forged composite copy film of the A-P x-ray as well, to see if he would object to the extremely prominent 6.5 mm fragment now present in the x-ray. He did use the plural expression, "skull films," when describing what he viewed at the White House Annex. Once again, there are two possibilities here:

Possibility One: If Custer was *correct* about Ebersole burning the emulsion on an x-ray the night of the autopsy through carelessness with a hot light, then those burn marks, like the pencil marks, would have been <u>photographically copied</u> onto the copy film, and would have had to be *recreated* in order to "authenticate" the copy film as the 'original' in the eyes of Ebersole, were he ever to be called to testify before the Warren Commission. <u>Recreating</u> the two burn marks on the emulsion where the real burn marks had been photographically copied would have obliterated the copied anomalies, and would also have ensured that their location was in exactly the right place on the film so as to be consistent with Ebersole's memory. Similar to possibility one above, if Ebersole had noticed that a large 'metallic fragment' was suddenly present where there had been *none* at autopsy, he would *also* have noticed the same two burn marks he remembered putting on the film himself, and would no doubt have been impressed with the hidden message being transmitted—namely, "you had better go along with this one, pal; we are giving you every reason to say that this A-P film is authentic...it even has your own burn marks on it."

Possibility Two: If Custer was *incorrect* about witnessing Dr. Ebersole burning the emulsion on the A-P film, and his testimony on this matter did not reflect reality, but was instead the product of an altered memory or a vivid imagination, then the burn marks could have been put there at almost anytime by anyone, prior to the November 1, 1966 Military Inventory.

I lean toward possibility one above, because Dr. Ebersole testified before the HSCA panel that *he* may have been responsible for burning the emulsion (and the film base itself) on the A-P x-ray; he did *not* say, for example, "the first time I saw that damage was when we conducted the 1966 inventory." One of the ARRB's outside medical consultants, forensic radiologist Dr. John Kirkpatrick, told the ARRB staff that he had "never seen" burn marks like the two artifacts on the JFK A-P skull x-ray, and commented that someone had been very careless with a hot light.

Summation: What the Ebersole Testimony Means

The Ebersole testimony before the HSCA about being called to the White House Annex to view the skull films is really most peculiar. It has never sounded "right" to anyone with an open mind (and any common sense) who has read his transcript, and in light of Dr. Mantik's ground-breaking work proving that altered x-ray images of the skull were created, it is obvious to me that Mantik's evaluation of his testimony is correct: Ebersole was being tested psychologically to see whether or not he would object to the forged composite copy films of the 3 skull x-rays. If Custer is correct that there were at least 5 skull films taken, Ebersole was also being tested to see whether he would object to *not seeing* the two missing films. (Presumably, the missing films—either two tangential views, or one tangential view and one Townes view—showed the large occipital defect so prominently that they could *not* be successfully altered to obscure that wound, so they had to be culled from the collection.) Whether Ebersole was really called to the White House Annex on the pretext of helping to obtain measurements for a sculptor's bust, or on the basis of some other excuse, is unclear; the significant thing is *where* he went, and *when*: to the White House Annex, and within a month of the assassination. It seems fairly obvious at this point in our research that the Secret Service and Dr. Burkley were controlling everything that was happening with autopsy photographs and x-rays out of their offices in the Old Executive Office Building (across the street from the White House).

Furthermore, this was the same time frame that the 'processing events' surrounding the autopsy photographs were occurring, according to the 1967 internal Secret Service reports—late November and into mid-December of 1963—within "one month of the assassination," as Ebersole put it. Anyone implementing a medical coverup would have to complete all photographic and x-ray work as soon as possible, in case those materials were called into evidence by a government investigation.

It is a shame that the HSCA did not see fit to interview or depose Dr. James Young. In retrospect, it seems almost certain that Young was testing Ebersole on RADM Burkley's behalf. If Young was a member of the White House medical staff as Dr. Ebersole testified, then he was working for RADM Burkley, the Military Physician to the President—the same person who, according to Robert Knudsen, had been controlling the developing of autopsy photographs (in concert with certain members of the Secret Service White House Detail). Of course, it's even more unfortunate that the HSCA panel did not take the deposition of George Burkley—but then that would have required not only an open mind to the possibility of a medical coverup—the ability to "think outside the box"—but a certain amount of courage as well, something the HSCA staff leadership did not posses in overabundance.[31]

One Additional Proof that the Left Lateral Skull X-Ray is a Copy Film, and <u>Not An Original</u>

After the ARRB concluded its work, Dr. Mantik made one final discovery (in April of 2001) about the President's left lateral skull x-ray that removes all doubt whatsoever *that it is a copy film, and not an original.* He discussed this finding during his presentation at Cyril Wecht's conference in Pittsburgh in November of 2003, titled: "The JFK Autopsy Materials: 20 Conclusions After 9 Visits;" published it in an on-line reproduction of this same Pittsburgh lecture material; and mentioned it again on page 16 of his review of Vincent Bugliosi's book *Reclaiming History,* titled: "*Reclaiming History* by Vincent Bugliosi: A Not-Entirely-Positive Review."

As Mantik pointed out in his November 2003 lecture, he had examined the JFK autopsy materials (the autopsy x-rays; autopsy photographs; the clothing; the 'magic bullet,' CE 399; and the two small metal fragments purportedly removed from the skull at autopsy) over the course of nine visits to the National Archives: four (4) in 1993; two (2) in1994; two (2) more in 1995; and one final visit on April 12, 2001. It was during this final visit that Dr. Mantik discovered simple, easy-to-understand, incontrovertible evidence—evidence not related to optical densitometry at all—that the left lateral x-ray of President Kennedy's skull is not an original, but is a copy film. I will summarize below the oral presentation he made at Cyril Wecht's 40th Anniversary JFK Assassination Conference in Pittsburgh in 2003.

---

[31] The HSCA staff contacted Dr. Burkley again, shortly after being briefed by David Lifton about the different Dallas and Bethesda accounts of the wounds on the body, since Dr. Burkley had been the only physician to see the body both at Parkland hospital and at the Bethesda autopsy. The staff then prepared an affidavit for Burkley to sign which they believed effectively debunked Lifton's hypothesis; but Burkley was not deposed. The affidavit (Appendix 73) will be discussed in detail in Part II.

On the left lateral skull x-ray of President Kennedy (the one in which the rear of the skull is not fully imaged because of the imperfect placement of the film by the technician), there is what appears to be a hand-drawn symbol shaped like a capital letter "T" resting on its side, which appears on the skull x-ray in front of the cervical spine and directly underneath the jaw. A great amount of light is able to pass through this hand-drawn capital "T," in what is otherwise a field of black emulsion. To Mantik, this man-made inscription appeared to be an area where someone had (for reasons unknown) inscribed a capital "T" on the x-ray by scratching off the emulsion on one side of the skull x-ray. Near the edge of the same x-ray, Mantik reported that he found an area where the emulsion had actually been scraped off on one side; it exhibited a much higher transmission of light also, and he could actually see the shiny, transparent film base underneath on the side where the emulsion had been scraped off. The damage to the emulsion on one side of the film's edge was easily noted when he viewed the surface of the film at a nearly horizontal angle. (This x-ray has never been published.)

Now, normally a very lucent region on a skull x-ray would denote an area on the body consisting of dense, radio-opaque material (such as bone or metal fragments); however, the "T" appeared *below the jaw and in front of the neck,* <u>outside the body of the President,</u> and was furthermore a letter of the Roman alphabet, so it could ***not*** have been human bone or bullet fragments. Clearly, it appeared to have been placed on the x-ray by scratching off the emulsion on one side of the x-ray with a sharp object. However, when Mantik closely examined the surfaces of the emulsion on either side of the lucent "T," he found ***no disruption or damage whatsoever*** to the emulsion on both sides of the x-ray film. Mantik said in his lecture that the emulsion on both sides of the film in this area was as smooth as new ice in a hockey rink. This had profound, immediate, and undeniable implications.

Dr. Mantik himself said during his Pittsburgh presentation: "There can only be one explanation. The left lateral skull x-ray is a copy. The reason, of course, is that the emulsion of a copy film would be fully intact, as it is here, but it still would record faithfully any areas of increased transmission or missing emulsion from the original. A simpler or more straightforward proof of film copying is unimaginable. ***This film is a copy.***"

In other words, someone inscribed his initial, perhaps, on the original film with a sharp instrument—did the forger leave a clue for future generations of researchers to uncover?—and that area of increased transmission of light was faithfully replicated on the copy film, but without the telltale damage to the emulsion that would have verified that the skull x-ray was an original. The absence of any damage to the emulsion above the "T" shaped inscription is proof that the left lateral skull x-ray in the Archives *is a copy film.* <u>There is no other explanation.</u>

Mantik summarized the magnitude of this discovery in Pittsburgh when he said: ***"This is the most important piece of evidence to emerge from my 9 visits."*** It is not only *consistent with* his findings, based on optical densitometry, that the two lateral skull x-rays and the A-P skull x-ray are copy films, but **confirms** <u>that the left lateral skull film is a copy</u> through a very simple and elegant proof *unrelated* to any inferences drawn from the data acquired through optical densitometry. And if the left lateral skull x-ray is confirmed to be a copy film, it increases the chances that the other two are also copies, to a virtual certainty.

As Mantik pointed out, the two other oddities about the left lateral skull x-ray are that there are no Kodak film numbers visible anywhere on that piece of film; and unfortunately, it was never published by the HSCA, which means that it appears nowhere in the public record. If an American citizen wanted to see for himself this proof that the left lateral skull x-ray of President Kennedy is a copy and not an original, he would have to first obtain the permission of the Kennedy family's legal representative before being allowed to see it—and even then, that researcher would *not* be allowed to photograph this important evidence or publish it.

And yet its importance is such that Mantik himself said that if he were asked whether he believed that there was a conspiracy to murder JFK and coverup the crime, he would respond: "I do not believe there was a conspiracy—*I KNOW there was a conspiracy.*"

Personally, I cannot overemphasize the importance of this April 2001 discovery by Dr. Mantik at Archives II in College Park, Maryland. This independent proof that the left lateral skull x-ray is a copy film is *strongly corroborative* of Mantik's interpretation of the optical densitometry measurements he took of the 3 skull films from 1993 to 1995. Even in the eyes of the most hard-headed skeptic, this elegant proof uncovered in 2001 that the left lateral skull film is not an original, *and is a copy film,* lends great credence to Mantik's conclusions—reached independently through a completely different methodology—that all three skull x-rays are forged composite copy films made from the (now missing) originals.

Let us now review what the three autopsy pathologists had to say about the skull x-rays when questioned about them by Jeremy Gunn during their ARRB depositions. Keep in mind that many of the questions that were posed to them by Jeremy Gunn were suggested by David Mantik himself, in consultation with the ARRB staff (Jeremy and me) prior to their depositions.

DR. HUMES TESTIFIES TO THE ARRB ABOUT THE SKULL X-RAYS

Toward the end of a long and tiring day of questions and answers with Dr. Humes, Jeremy Gunn produced the HSCA enhancement of x-ray no. 1, the A-P skull x-ray. It was time to test Dr. Mantik's hypothesis that the 6.5 mm object on this x-ray was an artifact superimposed on a copy film by persons involved in a frame-up of Lee Harvey Oswald, and that it did not reflect reality at the time of the autopsy—that no such bullet fragment was x-rayed on the body of the 35th President. As the afternoon had worn on and some of the questions had gotten a lot tougher, Dr. Humes had either feigned fatigue and confusion, or had demonstrated a genuine decline in his ability to give straight answers to questions; I wasn't sure what would happen with this round. I wondered if we had waited too late in the day to commence this important round.

Gunn: Dr. Humes, you're now looking at x-ray 5-B no. 1. [The HSCA enhancement.] I'd like to ask you whether you have previously seen that x-ray. [See Figure 38.]

Humes: I probably have. It's [an] antero-posterior view of the skull and the jaw. It shows the large bony defect in the right side of the skull, and some white material, which I presume may be metallic fragments, in the right side of the photograph.

Gunn: [Do you mean] The left side of the photograph but the right side of the skull?

Humes: Right side of the skull, yeah.

Gunn: And that appears to be, at least in height, in the orbital range?

Humes: Yes, somewheres. Yeah, I would guess.

Humes was visibly starting to relax, now that we had gotten off the touchy subjects of the Military Review from 1967; the extremely disorienting and discomforting subject of the autopsy photographs of the back-of-the-head; and the brain photographs. My impression during those rounds of questioning was that he pretended to be confused—that he had played the "tired old man" game—during his testimony on those subjects. He had been quite uptight, and many of his answers to those questions were either nonsensical, or combative. But his body language now showed that he was beginning to relax, and you could hear that in his tone of voice, too.

Gunn: Did you notice that [sic] what at least appears to be a radio-opaque fragment during the autopsy?

Humes: Well, I told you we received one—we retrieved one or two, and—of course, you get distortion in the x-ray as far as size goes. *The ones we retrieved I didn't think were of the same size as this would lead you to believe.* [Author's emphasis]

Gunn: Did you think they were larger or smaller?

Humes: *Smaller. Smaller, considerably smaller.* [Humes' interest was clearly aroused.] I mean, these other little things would be about the size of what [we retrieved] —I'm not sure what that is or whether that's a defect [in the x-ray]. I'm not enough of a radiologist to be able to tell you. *But I don't remember retrieving anything of that size.* [Author's emphasis]

Gunn: Well, that was going to be the question, whether you had identified that as a possible fragment and then removed it.

Humes: *Truthfully, I don't remember anything that size when I looked at these films.* They were all more the size of these others. [Author's emphasis]

This was a major breakthrough in our quasi-investigation of the medical evidence. Humes had just provided corroboration for an already "robust" scientific hypothesis, based upon persuasive empirical data, that the 6.5 mm object in the AP head x-ray was a man-made artifact, and that the x-ray in question was not an original, but a forged composite copy film.

Gunn: What we're referring to is a fragment that appears to be semi-circular.

Humes: Yeah. I don't know. [Humes was truly perplexed at this point.]

Gunn: Looking at the x-ray, could you correlate any damage that you see on the right hemisphere of the skull with the photograph that's to your left now, which is color photograph—

Humes: Oh, sure. The skull defect is obvious. Now, not the brain. You can't tell much about the brain from here. The brain doesn't—in plain films it doesn't, you know, it's not well imaged at all.

Gunn: To the lay eye—and I mean this to not have any presumption of being accurate—there is a large gap in the top right quadrant of the skull [in the A-P skull x-ray]. That's on the left side of the x-ray [as it is viewed on the light box], the right quadrant [of the skull, anatomically speaking].

Humes: Right.

Gunn: What does that signify, as best you recall, having been present at the autopsy?

Humes: That's the bone that was removed by the path of the missile.

Gunn: Was the frontal bone present on—was the frontal bone still intact on the President?

Anatomically the frontal bone begins at the top of the skull where the coronal suture crosses the cranium from left to right, and then curves downwards to connect with the orbits of the eyes. Anatomically speaking, it includes much more bone than the forehead, and I already knew that a considerable amount of frontal bone was shown to be missing on the skull x-rays from an area directly behind the hairline, in a posterior direction; I also knew that all radiologists who had interpreted the JFK skull x-rays agreed that the region of frontal bone that we call the 'forehead,' although difficult to see on the radiographs, was present. Jeremy may not have understood this; he was really asking Humes whether the *forehead* was present because he could not see it in the A-P skull x-ray.

Humes: It was intact, yes. I can't even make it out here, really.

Gunn: You can't see it there, but it was present?

Humes: No [I can't see it in the x-ray]. It was present, yes sir.

Gunn: Could we look at the second x-ray, please? This will be a right lateral view of the skull, 5B no. 2 [the HSCA enhancement of the right lateral skull x-ray]. Dr. Humes, can you identify 5-B no. 2 as being an autopsy x-ray taken on November 22, 1963? [See Figure 37.]

Humes: *I guess so. That's really—it's got some very—it's a peculiar exposure.* These are the spines of the vertebrae here, of course, and these are the bodies of the vertebrae. And these lines are some of the fractures that were present in the skull.   [Author's emphasis]

Gunn: You're referring to the lines that are in the top of the parietal bone—

Humes: Right.

Gunn: —and into the occipital bone; would that be correct?

Humes: Right. Those were the fracture lines, and it's difficult—*I don't know why this is so radio-opaque, this whole area.* [Humes misspoke here; he was referring to the very dark area in the front part of the cranium, not to an area of dense bone that was very lucent on the x-ray film. He should have said "so dark," instead of "so radio-opaque."] [Author's emphasis]

Gunn: You're referring to the right frontal area.

Humes: What seems to be the frontal portion of it. *I don't understand why that is. You'd have to have some radiologist tell me about that. I can't make that out.* [Author's emphasis]

Gunn: I'd like you to see if you could identify where you understand the entrance wound to have been on the skull, looking at this lateral x-ray.

Humes: Well, back in this area.

Gunn: You're referring to the very low back of the cranium—

Humes: Cranium.

Gunn: —very near to the vertebrae; is that correct?

Humes: Well, fairly near, yeah. You can't see it here. I can't see it.

Gunn: Do you see any fragments...that would be consistent with an entry wound in that point?

Humes: Well, there's no fragments there. There's fragments or what appear to be fragments up higher towards the vertex in this picture. Maybe one right in the middle of the picture. And this may be—do you see where this increased density is here? There may be two pieces—it may be overlapped. This piece of bone may overlap that one so it looks more dense there.

Humes was describing what was obvious even to a layman who had only briefly studied the autopsy photos and the right lateral skull x-ray: there is a loose bone flap in the temporal region that overlaps some intact skull bone in the same region, and looks more radio-opaque than other parts of the x-ray.

Gunn: Okay.

Humes: That's about as much as I can make out.

Gunn: What I'd like you to do is look at Exhibit no. 73, which is a drawing from *Grant's Anatomy,* and see if you could make a marking on *Grant's Anatomy*—these are both laterals with the posterior portion of the cranium on the left of the drawings. If you could make a mark with the pen at approximately where you understood the entry wound to have been?

Humes: No, because it would be down here and you wouldn't be able to see it on this lateral view, I don't think.

Gunn: You're referring to the Grant's Anatomy—

Humes: Whatever it is. [Humes was getting flippant again.]

Gunn: —drawing?

Humes: Yeah. See, but it was not that far from the midline, and this is really somewhat lateral to the midline, this depiction. But in general, it would be back in this area some place.

Gunn: You're making a blue marking approximately—

Humes: Right.

Gunn: —where the entry wound was. Of course, that's not showing it in relationship to the midline. [See Figure 16 for Humes' marking of the location of the entry wound on the lateral skull diagram.]

Humes: No, it does not show it. No. [Suddenly Humes changed the subject of his own volition, from the site of the entry wound, to the strange appearance of the x-ray.] *I don't understand this great big void there. I don't know what that's all about.* [Author's emphasis]

I do not know to this day whether Humes was simply reacting to the very strange contrast in the right lateral skull x-ray between very dark and very visibly transparent areas,[32] or whether he was worried about the great inconsistency between seeing no brain tissue in the forward part of the cranium in the right lateral, and the brain photographs he had just viewed, which showed great amounts of tissue present in the forebrain. He may have been afraid that Jeremy was about to pounce on this obvious discrepancy, and may have simply been setting up a defense ahead of time.

As the reader will see in Part II, I found persuasive evidence throughout the record while working on the ARRB staff that the brain photographs in the Archives are of a brain of someone other than President Kennedy, and that Dr. Humes and Dr. Boswell both knew this, and were in fact instrumental in carrying out this medico-legal shell game back in 1963. However, I had not yet reached this conclusion, nor had Jeremy, so he did not pursue what seems today to be an obvious, direct question for Humes: "If the brain photographs are authentic, why does the forward part of the cranium appear empty in the A-P and right lateral skull x-rays?" The answer today seems obvious: the brain *appears* to be missing from the forward cranial vault because it *was* largely missing: it had been partially blown out by a frontal shot, and it had been partially removed during post mortem surgery of the head area, hurriedly and crudely performed to remove evidence of multiple shooters prior to the autopsy. The dark void *did* signify substantially missing brain, and Humes was probably astounded that we did not ask him about this apparent discrepancy between the head x-rays and the brain photographs. It's easy to kick myself now, but the "epiphany" of my two-brain hypothesis did not occur until about 3 months after the Humes deposition; at the time of the Humes deposition, I believe Jeremy and I were bamboozled by his statement that the brain does not often show up too well in cranial x-rays. ARRB Executive Director David Marwell, who is Dr. Michael Baden's cousin, had more than once reminded Jeremy and me, when examining the x-rays at the Archives, that the presence of air in the cranium, not missing brain, probably accounted for why it appeared to be so dark.

Gunn: Excuse me for a moment.   [Pause]

Gunn: Dr. Humes, I had another question for you about the lateral x-ray.

Humes: Mm-hmm.

Gunn: And that is whether you can identify the particles that you made reference to before and where they appear in this photograph.

---

[32]Although David Mantik stated in a lecture that he does not believe the "high" OD numbers in the forward cranial area (readings of 3.5 to 3.9) are indicators of forgery, I nevertheless sometimes wonder whether the extremely high contrast in the JFK skull x-rays can be partially attributed to the exposure times used by the forgers when they created the copy films. The "recipe" chart reproduced earlier in this chapter clearly indicates that the lower the exposure time used in making a copy film, the higher the resulting contrast will be. Perhaps this accounts for why Dr. Mantik said he had never seen x-rays showing such extreme contrast in his entire career as a radiologist.

Humes:	Well, you see, *there's nothing in this projection that appears to be of the size of the one that appeared to be above and behind the eye on the other one* [the A-P skull x-ray]. But that could be positional *or the other thing is an artifact.* [Truer words were never spoken.] I don't know what. But here, above where I talk about this double density that you see here, there's a fragment. There seems to be one up here in the frontal region and a couple further up by the vertex. [Humes is describing the very obvious apparent fragment trail high in the skull, that connects the high forehead area with the upper back of the skull.] [Author's emphasis]
Gunn:	Do those metal fragments—or do those radio-opaque objects help you in any way identify entrance or exit wounds?
Humes:	No. No, they really don't.
Gunn:	Is there any relationship or correlation between those metal fragments and the bullet wound?

Humes was in great danger here—about to be hoisted on his own petard—and he apparently didn't even realize it.

Humes:	Not that I can make out at all, no. They seem to be random.
Gunn:	Okay. Dr. Humes, I'd like to show you Exhibit no. 3, which again, for the record, is the autopsy protocol, and ask you if you could read the paragraph on page 4 that starts with "Received."
Humes:	This would reinforce my opinion that that *one photograph was part of the margin of the exit wound.* [Humes had said in his Warren Commission testimony that there was *no* evidence of exit in the margin of the large skull defect. He was contradicting himself here.] [Author's emphasis]
Gunn:	You're referring to view no. 7 [photos 17, 18, 44, and 45] that showed the inside of the cranium? Is that—

By this time Humes was no doubt saying "oops!" to himself, because he had described that photograph in November 1966 as being of *the rear of the skull,* and yet had written in January 1967 in the Military Review that this photo *depicted part of the margin of the wound of exit.* Humes was on the verge of committing a major *faux pas*—of saying that there was an exit wound in the back of the head. He quickly backed off.

| Humes: | Well, it didn't really—I don't know what it showed, my problem is, but in one of the bone fragments there was a semicircular defect that was not complete, only part of it. And then when we got these fragments, at one margin of it there's something that seemed to match up with that [bone] fragment that was still in the skull. My |

memory's pretty good. I said we had three. That's what we have, I guess. *I described several metallic fragments along the line joining the occipital wound with the right supraorbital ridge.* [Author's emphasis]

Humes had just fallen into Jeremy's trap. This is what Jeremy was getting at: the apparent fragment trail in the right lateral head x-ray did *not* go from an occipital entry wound to the right supraorbital ridge. There was a major discrepancy here between what was shown in the lateral skull x-rays and what Humes had written in the autopsy report. The fragment trail in the lateral skull x-rays extended from an area high in the forehead to the upper rear of the skull.

Gunn: The above-described small occipital wound and the right supra-orbital ridge.

Humes made a lame attempt to obfuscate and get Jeremy off the subject by continuing to read his own autopsy report, and by changing his mind about having removed the large 6.5 mm object on the A-P x-ray from the body.

Humes: "Two small irregularly shaped fragments of metal are recovered. They measure 7 by 2 and 3 by 1." Well, that large one that you saw in that first A-P view of the skull could be the 7 by 2 millimeter one that we handed over to the FBI.

Nonsense. The 7 by 2 mm fragment was long and skinny, and the 6.5 mm fragment, if it had existed in nature, would have looked like a small nearly-circular disc of metal. Jeremy was not going to be distracted; he was undeterred.

Gunn: Could you point out for me on x-ray no. 2 [the right lateral skull] where the minute particles of metal in the bone are in relationship to the small occipital wound and the right supraorbital ridge?

Humes: *Well, they don't relate at all in this picture, as far as I'm concerned.* [Author's emphasis]

Humes looked quite sheepish at this point. Jeremy had just exposed either gross incompetence, or a bald-faced lie in the autopsy report written by Humes.

Gunn: "This picture" being x-ray no. 2? [See Figure 37.]

Humes: *Yeah. They don't. I don't know where I got that,* but there's—the occipital wound would never be up that high anywheres up there. [Humes was pointing to the posterior terminus of the fragment trail, in the region where there was a major dislocation of skull fragments high in the rear of the head.] There's nothing up there. [Author's emphasis]

I don't agree that there's nothing up there; I am convinced there is an exit wound in the rear of the skull "up there." I will lay all of this out in detail in Part II.

Gunn: You're pointing to the top left portion of the brain [Jeremy meant skull] slightly above—

Jeremy, who preferred to talk about photographs and x-rays in terms of reference related to the left or right of the picture, was confusing Humes, who as a physician thought in anatomical terms. But Jeremy was referring to the fragment trail which appeared to lead to the upper left portion of the skull image on the x-ray (i.e., the upper posterior skull); he was not referring to anatomical left or right on JFK's body.

Humes: Well, I don't know whether it's left or right. You can't tell that from this. Don't say that because there's no way of telling that it's left. An x-ray doesn't tell you whether it's left or right. These fragments here.

Gunn: *Do you see any fragments that correspond with a small occipital wound?* [Author's emphasis]

Humes: *No.* [Author's emphasis]

Gunn: *Do you recall having seen an x-ray previously that had fragments corresponding to a small occipital wound?* [Author's emphasis]

Humes: *Well, I reported that I did, so I must have. But I don't see it now.* [Author's emphasis]

I doubt that. I believe Humes blatantly lied about the fragment trail in his autopsy report, and I will explain why in Part II when I attempt to explain what I think really happened at the autopsy.

Gunn: Did you have x-rays available for your use while you were preparing the autopsy protocol?

Humes: No.

Gunn: Are you reasonably certain that there was an x-ray that showed metallic fragments going from a small occipital wound?

Humes: All I know is I wrote it down. I didn't write it down out of whole cloth. I wrote down what I saw.

Gunn: *Does that raise any question in your mind about the authenticity of the x-ray that you're looking at now in terms of being an x-ray of President Kennedy?* [Author's emphasis]

Humes: *Well, there's aspects of it I don't understand. I don't understand this big void up—maybe a radiologist could explain it. I don't know what this big—* [Author's

571

emphasis]

Gunn: You're referring to—

Humes: *—non-opaque area that takes up half of the skull here, I don't understand that.* [Author's emphasis]

Gunn: *Do you remember that on the night of the autopsy?*   [Author's emphasis]

Humes: *No, I don't.* That doesn't mean it wasn't there, but I don't remember it. [Author's emphasis]

———————

Gunn: ...Do you recall any photograph or x-ray that was taken with a probe inserted into the posterior thorax?

Humes: No, absolutely not. I do not have a recollection of such.

Gunn: Do you recall any x-rays that were taken that would have the extremities, including the hands and feet?

Humes: Yes, we had them. I thought we did, at least. Or maybe—whether we went as far as the feet and hands—we simply went down the arms. Whether or not the hands and feet were there or not, I can't remember.

This concludes my recapitulation of the testimony of Dr. Humes regarding the skull x-rays of President Kennedy. I knew at the time that Dr. Mantik would be most interested in reading this testimony.

DR. BOSWELL TESTIFIES TO THE ARRB ABOUT THE SKULL X-RAYS

Two weeks later it was Dr. Boswell's turn to be grilled about the skull x-rays, and the 6.5 mm object in the A-P skull film, in particular. (See Figure 38.)

Gunn: We're back on the record. We're now going to be looking at x-ray no. 1, anterior-posterior view of the skull. I think that is inverted left to right, if we can switch. Dr. Boswell, are you able to determine with any degree of certainty whether the x-ray that you're looking at now is an x-ray of President Kennedy?

Boswell: I have not seen this in an awful long time, but it certainly looks like what I remember.

Gunn: Let me draw your attention to a white semi-circular marking in what appears to be in the right orbit, and I'll say that it's on the left side of the x-ray as we're looking at it now. *Do you see that white apparently radio-opaque object?*   [Author's emphasis]

Boswell: Yes.

Gunn: *Do you know what that object is?*   [Author's emphasis]

Boswell: *No.*   [Author's emphasis]

Gunn: Do you know whether that is an artifact that is just there as part of either that developing process or whether that is a missile fragment?

Boswell: No, I can't tell you that. I don't remember the interpretations. I see a lot of metallic-looking debris, x-ray opaque material, at the site of the injury. And I remember that there were a lot of fragments around the right eye, and the rest of these could be from bullet fragments as well. I'm not sure—we found a couple of very minute metal fragments, but I do not relate them to the x-ray.

Gunn: *Can you relate that, again, apparently large object to any of the fragments that you removed?*   [Author's emphasis]

Boswell: *No. We did not find one that large. I'm sure of that.*   [Author's emphasis]

_____

Thus, for the second time in two weeks, Dr. Mantik's hypothesis that the A-P x-ray was a forged composite copy film, with the 6.5 mm "fragment" superimposed over the original image, had been supported by the sworn testimony of an autopsy pathologist.

Gunn: Do you see anything about that x-ray—again, view no. 1—that would seem to be inconsistent with what you recall from the night of the autopsy?

Boswell: No. It's very consistent with the trauma to the head.

Gunn: Could we look at x-ray no. 2, a right lateral view of the skull, with two angle lines overdrawn on the film? Dr. Boswell, can you identify x-ray no. 2 as being an x-ray taken of President Kennedy on the night of the autopsy? [See Figure 37.]

Boswell: Yes.

Gunn: First, where on the x-ray that you're examining would you identify the bullet entrance wound?

Boswell: I don't think I can identify the entrance wound...I cannot identify the entrance wound here.

Gunn: Do you recall if on the night of the autopsy you were able to identify the entrance wound in any of the x-rays?

Boswell: No—well, the entrance wound, no. I thought there was a little bit of metallic material along one of the transverse processes down here near the entrance wound in the back, but I don't see that in this x-ray. But this [gesturing toward the apparent fragment trail on the right lateral head x-ray] is all scattered around the exit wound in the head. Mr. Gunn, I believe we dug this piece out right here, but I'm not sure.

Gunn: You're pointing to what looks like a sliver near the—

Boswell: Right eye.

Boswell was pointing toward the image of the elongated 7 x 2 mm fragment in the right lateral skull x-ray; it had indeed been removed.

Gunn: —front right above the eye?

Boswell: Right. Right supraorbital area. Because I think that's about the size, but I'm not sure.

Gunn: If you could point to where on the x-ray to where you understand the entrance to have been even though you don't see it appearing on the x-ray.

Boswell: It must be around here someplace.

Gunn: That would be—

Boswell: Has to be in this general area right here. The left, left side of the x-ray at the base of the skull, just a[n] inch or so behind the vertebra.

Gunn: I'd like to draw your attention to what appears to be, in my term[s], sort of a shelf-like disruption of the skull. Do you recall seeing that on the night of the autopsy? I will say, in a very inexpert way, it's near the cowlick area, although that's not a medical term, I understand. But do you understand? Did you observe anything in that area on the night of the autopsy?

Boswell: No.

Gunn: Do you have any understanding as to what that shelf or plate is there?

Boswell: You're talking about—I don't know what any of this is. But you're talking about this fracture line right here?

Gunn: In the first instance, just right on the periphery.

574

Boswell: Right here?

Gunn: Yes.

Jeremy was pointing at the large break in the bone high up on the posterior skull, which the Clark Panel and the HSCA had equated with the entry wound in the back of the head, relocating it to a point 10 cm above where the pathologists had reported it was in the autopsy report. (Both Humes and Boswell had denied that this spot was an entry wound when they appeared before the HSCA panel in 1977.)

Boswell: Okay. Well, I recognize what that is. That's a depressed fracture.

Gunn: Does that depressed fracture correlate in any way to the entrance wound that you observed on the night of the autopsy?

Boswell: I think it's a long way from it. I think that's quite a ways from the entrance wound.

Gunn: Do you see what appear[s] to be [a] radio-opaque trail, metal dust?

Boswell: Yes.

Gunn: Going across the very top, I'd say the sixth, the top eighth of the skull, left to right, without indicating anything. Do you know what that is, what those are?

Boswell: Those are metallic fragments that have really dispersed. At some point, maybe when it entered, those perforated and went up, or maybe when it exited, those fragmented and fell there.

Gunn: Do the fragments tell you anything about the direction or the course of the bullet through President Kennedy's brain or skull?

Boswell: Well, at first glance, that looks like a straight line. But then you've got fragments elsewhere in there, and I—that wouldn't be inconsistent with a track, but I think that those have fragmented off at some point where the bullet has hit something really hard and scattered. I don't think traveling through the soft tissue of the brain that tiny fragments are going to just spill off like that.

Gunn: Okay.

Boswell: I don't think that's a track even though the fact that it's a straight line might suggest that.

Gunn: To an untrained eye such as my own, there appears to be a large, dark space, almost as if it's a figure eight, in this frontal area, somewhat behind the eye and down into the cheek. Do you see that area that I'm referring to?

Boswell: Mm-hmm.

Gunn: Can you tell me what that represents?

Boswell: Well, it looks almost like a pneumo-encephalogram where you got air in and displaced tissue, but—I suspect that's what that is. I think that's a space with a lot of air in it.

Gunn: So though it is darker, that does not signify it is missing skull?

Boswell: Oh, I don't think—well, the missing skull is all over. Of course, the drawing we have there is sort of similar to that, isn't it? Do we have an A-P, one straight on?

Gunn: Yes.

Boswell: Was that the one I just—

Gunn: The first one.

Boswell: The first one? May I look at that one again? Yes, you're right. Here it is. See, this is what's missing here.

Gunn: So you're pointing at what I would describe as the temporal and parietal bone on the right hemisphere? Is that—

Boswell: I guess that would—actually, that looks like frontal bone there, doesn't it? Frontal, temporal, some parietal [all missing]. But that's where this space is here. Now, you see, this [pointing to a randomly scattered mass of tiny metallic fragments in the A-P skull x-ray] is not in a straight line that [sic] it is here [on the right lateral skull x-ray]. These [fragments on the A-P skull] are all scattered around.

Gunn: You're referring to the radio-opaque fragments.

Boswell: Right, and I think probably the bullet hit up here. That may very well be that piece right there [discussing the possible exit wound].

Gunn: You're referring to the large semi-circular piece [the 6.5 mm object] in the A-P view—

Boswell: Yes.

Gunn: —being the same as the one that appears to be in the frontal bone in the lateral; is that correct?

This is an incorrect interpretation, according to all radiologists who have reviewed the skull x-rays.

Boswell: Right, and it's in a different perspective. Here it's narrow, but around-about the same size.

Boswell here is speculating that the 6.5 mm object on the A-P skull x-ray equates to the 7 x 2 mm fragment near the right orbit on the right lateral skull x-ray. As I have said above, this is an incorrect interpretation. Boswell is grasping at straws to try to explain what that confounded 6.5 mm object is, just as Humes did late in his testimony. In actuality, the 7 x 2 mm fragment which was removed at autopsy—which is what Boswell is discussing—appears the same on both the A-P and right lateral skull x-rays—long, and skinny. On the right lateral it is just slightly above the right orbit, but on the A-P it appears to be *well above* the right orbit because the x-ray beam was passing through the skull at an angle from the low-front to the high-rear.

It was now Dr. Boswell's turn to be asked about the apparent fragment trail's location in the right lateral skull x-ray vis-a-vis its described location in the autopsy report that he had signed in 1963.

Gunn: Okay. If we could see the lateral one more time. I'd like to show you a portion from the autopsy protocol. Particularly make reference to the "multiple minute metallic fragments along the line corresponding with the line joining the above-described small occipital wound and the right supraorbital ridge."

Boswell: Okay. What's your question?

Gunn: Now, the question would be: are the minute metallic fragments referenced in the autopsy protocol those fragments that go along the top of the A-P [sic] [Jeremy meant the right lateral skull x-ray]?

Boswell: Right.

Gunn: And I would just note that it says that "They're aligned corresponding with the line joining the above-described small occipital wound"—the entrance wound—"and the right"—that doesn't say—when I said "entrance wound," that was my gloss to this.

Boswell: Uh-huh.

Gunn: —"and the right supraorbital ridge." To me, it appears as if the line does not correspond with an entrance wound, but would be elsewhere.

Boswell: Is that from the autopsy?

Gunn: This is the autopsy protocol.

Boswell: And this is—

Gunn:	Now, I don't know that what is being referred to on the autopsy protocol is what is being referred to on this x-ray, but the question for you is: is what you are seeing on the x-ray itself what is being referred to in the portion of the autopsy protocol that I just quoted?
Boswell:	Right. Although I interpret it differently now than whoever did that. I see the line here, but it doesn't connect with the wound of entry, although they say it does there. [They??? Why didn't Boswell say "we?"] And apparently we gave this to the cops, O'Neill and Sibert.
Gunn:	This is the autopsy protocol.
Boswell:	Yes. This is, too.
Gunn:	Yes, right. But when you say you gave it to the cops, I'm not sure. Sibert—
Boswell:	To the FBI guys.
Gunn:	You mean you gave the x-rays?
Boswell:	No. That fragment.
Gunn:	Oh, the fragment, okay. That's what wasn't clear, okay. Was there any other x-ray that you now recall having seen that showed a line of metallic fragments connecting to the small wound of entry?
Boswell:	Not of the head.
Gunn:	*Is the fragment trail that you see* on the A-P—excuse me, *on the lateral x-ray, no. 2 that's in your hand, does that correspond to what you saw on the night of the autopsy, as best you can recall?* [Author's emphasis]
Boswell:	*Yes.* [Author's emphasis]
Gunn:	Okay. I think that's it for the x-rays.

This, in my view, is a significant answer by Boswell. He has affirmed that the apparent fragment trail on the right lateral skull x-ray is indeed what he saw on the night of the autopsy, but says that the words in the autopsy report about the location of the fragment trail are something "they" wrote. He involuntarily distanced himself from the incorrect statement in the report *he signed* that says the fragment trail on the lateral x-ray connected the low entry wound in the occiput to the right supraorbital ridge. Is that a clue to the mind set of the pathologists the week or so after the autopsy? Were they willing to sign anything that "they" put in front of them to sign? Or was this all just an honest mistake by Dr. Humes and his two colleagues simply because they did not have access to the x-rays when the autopsy report was written? I tend to believe that the description of the fragment trail in the autopsy report was an intentional falsehood about its location, intended to hide evidence of an entry wound high in the front of the head at the hairline, that exited high in the back of the skull. If I am correct and it was a lie, it was a risky one, for if the x-rays had been introduced into evidence, even Arlen Specter (or Gerald Ford) would have noticed the glaring discrepancy between the actual location of the fragment trail, and its described location in the autopsy protocol. Perhaps the pathologists were assured early on that "the fix was in," and the photos and x-rays would not be introduced into evidence. In Part II I will address in detail the problems I believe the pathologists were faced with as they drafted, and wrote, and rewrote, the autopsy report during the week following the assassination.

DR. FINCK TESTIFIES TO THE ARRB ABOUT THE SKULL X-RAYS

Dr. Finck's testimony at his deposition was maddeningly unresponsive whenever he either wanted to avoid answering, or was unsure that he could honestly provide a precise answer. Therefore, the few occasions during his deposition when he *did* provide a definitive, clear answer were worthy of note. Our questions about the 6.5 mm fragment obtained a clear, unambiguous response.

Gunn: ...This x-ray has been described as "an anterior-posterior view of skull, slightly heat damaged." Do you recall having seen this x-ray at the time of the autopsy?

Finck: I remember seeing an x-ray film at the time of the autopsy, but I can't say that it is this very x-ray film.

Gunn: Are you able to determine yourself right now whether this x-ray is an x-ray of President Kennedy?

Finck: No.

Gunn: I would like to draw your attention to a portion, to an object that is on the right hemisphere that is circular in shape, reasonably prominent there [indicating for Dr. Finck's benefit]. Do you know what that object is? [See Figure 38.]

Finck: *I don't. It's a radio-opaque object, opaque to x-rays.* [Author's emphasis]

Gunn: Do you recall at the time of President Kennedy's autopsy being made aware of an object, radio-opaque object in his head that would be commensurate with the dimensions of that object as it appears in the x-ray?

Finck: Can you repeat the question?

Gunn: Sure. Do you remember during the time of President Kennedy's autopsy seeing an x-ray of an object of those dimensions?

Finck: X-ray of an object. Separate from this x-ray film?

Gunn: Within—

Finck: An x-ray of an object?

Gunn: Just putting aside whether its this x-ray or another x-ray, any object appearing in an x-ray film that was approximately that size?

Finck: *If I remember an object being of approximately that size?* [Author's emphasis]

Gunn: *Yes.* [Author's emphasis]

Finck: ***I don't.*** [Author's emphasis]

With this definitive answer, 3 out of 3 autopsy pathologists had testified under oath to the ARRB that they had not seen an object the size of the 6.5 mm object on any x-ray the night of the autopsy. This was remarkable; and in my view, constituted confirmation of Mantik's hypothesis that the A-P skull x-ray was a forged composite copy film designed to link Oswald's 6.5 mm rifle to Kennedy's assassination.

Gunn: Does that object as it appears seem to you to be larger or no different from the types of bullet fragments that were removed from President Kennedy?

Finck: I don't understand the question.

Gunn: All right.

Finck: I see fragments on that x-ray film and do they look like fragments I have seen removed from the body?

Gunn: The large one is what I am referring to. *Do you remember one of that dimension being removed from President Kennedy's body?* [Author's emphasis]

Finck: *I don't.* But that doesn't mean I didn't see it. It means I don't recall. [Author's emphasis]

Gunn: Okay. Could we see the final x-ray, no. 2? Dr. Finck, I would like you to take a look at x-ray Exhibit no. 2, which is a right lateral view of the skull with two angle lines overdrawn. First, do you recall this x-ray as having been an x-ray taken at the autopsy of President Kennedy? [See Figure 37.]

Finck: I don't.

Gunn: Do you recall in any x-rays of President Kennedy there being a radio-opaque snow trail that crossed the x-ray from left to right?

Finck: No, I don't recall.

Gunn: From this x-ray of President Kennedy, are you able to identify the approximate location of an entrance wound in the skull?

Finck: I don't.

Gunn: Is it surprising to you at all that you would not be able to identify an entrance wound in the skull?

Finck: No, because it is a different type of evidence. I have looked at wounds. I was able to identify entry and exit when looking at wounds. Now we're looking at this x-ray. I can't elaborate on this.

Gunn: So it wouldn't be unusual not to be able to identify and entrance wound from an x-ray of the skull?

Finck: It would depend upon the case. It is not always possible I would say.

———————

Gunn: Are you able to identify from this x-ray the external occipital protruberance?

Finck: Can it be moved a little bit to the right? To your side? I don't want to touch it. This is a lateral view and there are protruberances in the occipital area. There is a protruberance here [indicating], but on one x-ray film only, I can't say much.

Gunn: All right. Dr. Finck, if you would take one last look at the x-ray and tell me whether the snow trail of radio-opaque objects is in the location that you would expect it to be for a bullet entrance wound that is slightly above the external occipital protruberance?

Finck: Possible so [sic].

Gunn: When there is a snow trail of radio-opaque objects for a skull wound to the head [Jeremy meant "bullet" wound], would it be typical for the radio-opaque trail to track the direction of the bullet?

Finck: Yes.

Gunn: Wouldn't that be the ordinary—

Finck: Only on a case-by-case basis.

Gunn: Okay.

Unlike Dr. Boswell, Dr. Finck—a forensic pathologist—had testified above that a fragment trail in the body *does* track or follow the path of the bullet in the body.

WAS AN X-RAY TAKEN OF A PROBE INSERTED IN THE NECK ?

The first significant books critical of the Warren Report's findings hit the shelves in 1966 and 1967; the assassination of President Kennedy was a hot topic. *LIFE* magazine launched a critical re-examination of the assassination in November of 1966 which was openly skeptical about the 'single bullet theory' sold to the Warren Commission by Arlen Specter in an issue titled, "A Matter of Reasonable Doubt." (Subsequently, *LIFE* then abandoned its efforts for reasons unknown.) In 1967 the *Saturday Evening Post* published portions of Josiah Thompson's new scientific study, *Six Seconds in Dallas,* in an issue with a cover that read "Three Assassins Killed Kennedy." CBS News became a major player in 1967 with its 4-part television documentary, hosted by Walter Cronkite, strongly supporting the Warren Commission's findings. CBS devoted major resources in its news division to the series, and as a result followed up on many leads. One lead concerned the possibility that an x-ray had been taken at the autopsy showing a wire or metal probe through the neck—an x-ray which supposedly would confirm the Warren Commission's finding that a bullet had transited the President's body from back to front, if its existence could only be confirmed. CBS's "slant" on the story was to support the government's official findings, so the news division was quite interested in this lead.

Surprisingly, the source of the lead was purportedly Dr. Humes himself! In a CBS internal memorandum dated January 10, 1967 from Bob Richter[33] to Les Midgley, the source of the information was laid out in detail. Richter wrote that Jim Snyder of the CBS bureau in Washington D.C. was personally acquainted with Dr. Humes, and had spoken in confidence to Humes about the assassination. Snyder claimed that Humes told him that "one x-ray from the Kennedy autopsy" would answer many questions that had been raised about the path of the bullet that the pathologists concluded had passed from Kennedy's back through his throat. According to Snyder, Humes told him that one x-ray film clearly depicted the path of the bullet through Kennedy's body, from its entry in the back to its exit in the throat, "as it was apparently taken with a metal probe stick of some kind that was left in the body to show the wound's path." Purportedly the path of the missile first went "downwards, then upwards slightly, then downwards again exiting at the throat." Humes reportedly also told Snyder that the FBI men at the autopsy "were not in the autopsy room during the autopsy; they were kept in an anteroom, and their report is simply wrong," and that the x-ray taken of the probe in the body was exposed *when no FBI men were present.*[34] (See Appendix 37.)

---

[33]Robert Richter would later produce and script one of the most popular episodes of NOVA ever aired on PBS, an independent documentary titled "Who Shot Presidet Kennedy?" which aired in 1988 (on the 25th anniversary of the assassination), and again in 1992, because of the renewed interest in the assassination caused by Oliver Stone's film *JFK.*

[34]This reported allegation by Humes that the FBI agents were not present in the morgue during the autopsy is consistent with David Lifton's interpretation of their November 26, 1963 report, in which he found wording that strongly implies they were kept out of the

One day later, on January 11, 1967 Les Midgley, the CBS News executive to whom Richter had written his memo the day before, himself wrote a memo to former Warren Commissioner John J. McCloy, and said in part, "I have been told, by a man who is a personal friend of Dr. Humes, that he says one of the x-rays shows a wire left in the bullet path through the neck. If this is indeed true, publication of same would resolve forever the discussion about back versus neck wound and generally settle the dust about the autopsy." Midgley had changed 'metal probe stick' to 'wire,' and the word 'back' to 'neck' in just one day. The wording of his memo implies that he spoke with Jim Snyder personally after reading the Richter memo.

As intriguing as this hearsay is, there are problems here that prevent a strong belief in its accuracy. First, neither Ed Reed, nor Jerrol Custer, nor Dr. Ebersole ever mentioned such an x-ray being taken. Second, if it was taken, then Humes, Boswell, and Finck have maintained a solid front about its existence to this day: none of them has ever mentioned such an x-ray before any official body. Therefore, it seems unlikely that this really happened.

But is it possible? Yes. First, Robert Knudsen recalled personally developing at least one black-and-white negative showing probes in the body—and one of them was in the neck. If a photograph can be taken, then so can an x-ray of the same object while it is in the body. Gawler's funeral home technician Tom Robinson recalled seeing a probe placed through the neck at the autopsy. (This will be covered in more detail in Chapter 6, the forthcoming chapter on the morticians.)

This issue will never be resolved unless or until such an x-ray is produced and its authenticity is conclusively established; both eventualities seem extremely unlikely. I suspect this will forever remain one of the unresolved loose ends in the Kennedy assassination.

OUTSIDE EXPERTS ANALYZE THE SKULL X-RAYS

I'll begin this section by reminding the reader that Dr. Russell Morgan, the radiologist on the Clark Panel, claimed he detected a bullet entry wound in the right lateral x-ray. He wrote the following:

"On one of the lateral films of the skull (# 2), a hole measuring approximately 8 mm in diameter on the outer surface of the skull and as much as 20 mm on the internal surface can be seen in profile approximately 100 mm above the external occipital protruberance. The bone of the lower edge of this hole is depressed. Also, there is, embedded in the outer table of the skull, close to the lower edge of the hole, a large metallic fragment which on the antero-posterior film (#1) lies 25 mm to the right of the midline. This fragment as seen on the latter film is round and measures 6.5 mm in diameter. Immediately adjacent to the hole on the internal surface of the skull, there is localized elevation of the soft tissues. Small fragments of bone lie within portions of these tissues and within the hole itself. These changes are consistent with an entrance wound of the skull produced by a

---

morgue for some undetermined period of time. The implications of Sibert and O'Neill being barred initially from the morgue will first become clear in Chapter 6, and again in Chapter 8, when the autopsy timeline is examined.

bullet similar to that of CE 399."

This finding of the Clark Panel became the lynch-pin of the HSCA's argument for moving the entrance wound up 100 mm, or approximately 4 inches, on the skull from where the 3 autopsy pathologists who examined the body said it was. Even when the 3 pathologists disagreed with the Clark Panel's and HSCA panel's interpretation of the high "red spot" in color photos 42 and 43, the HSCA panel had this unambiguous radiological interpretation of Dr. Morgan's to fall back on. It is my opinion that Dr. Morgan's findings, quoted above, tipped the scale and was the deciding factor in causing the HSCA Forensic Pathology Panel to relocate the entrance wound.

The only problem is that no one I know of since the time of the HSCA agrees with Dr. Morgan's interpretation of the right lateral skull x-ray. Humes, Boswell, and Finck do not agree with him, and they examined the body personally and palpated the wounds with their fingers. Dr. Ebersole did not agree with him when he appeared before the HSCA panel. Dr. Mantik, another radiologist, does not see an entry wound on the right lateral skull x-ray, and more significantly, his optical densitometry readings of the site Dr. Morgan identified revealed *no entry wound at that location* on the A-P x-ray, where it should be visible, if it really existed on the body in 1963.

Interestingly, *none* of the three ARRB outside medical consultants saw an entry wound on the right lateral x-ray, either. Quoted below are other observations about the x-rays made by these three men that may be of general interest to the reader, in no particular order:

Source: Forensic Anthropologist Dr. Douglas Ubelaker

Right Lateral Skull X-Ray

- *No entry wound* to the head can be seen in the right lateral skull x-ray.
- One fracture line occurred prior to another, because the longer one stopped the shorter one; but this still does not necessary indicate either 1 or 2 bullets to the head.
- Overlapping bone fragments are noted in the temporal-parietal region.
- Ubelaker was puzzled by the very dark regions in the forward part of the skull for two reasons: first, because they look so *unusually dark* compared with normal x-rays; and second, *because he does not see bone in the frontal region where the forehead is located,* whereas the forehead appears intact on the autopsy photographs. Ubelaker wondered if there might have been some kind of processing defect when the x-ray had been developed.
- *He could not see any lamboid sutures in the x-ray, and was puzzled by this.*[35]

---

[35]Did the "white patch" superimposed on the copy films of the two original lateral x-rays *obliterate the lamboid sutures* when the copy films were created? The lamboid sutures lie on the right and left side of the occipital bone, and fuse that bone with the right and left parietal bones in the skull. The lamboid sutures should be visible on a normal lateral skull x-ray. This observation by Dr. Ubelaker is further support for Mantik's contention that the right and left laterals are forged composite copy films, altered to hide the blowout in the right

<u>Anterior-Posterior Skull X-Ray</u>

- Ubelaker *could not find* the bright, 6.5 mm object on this A-P x-ray *anywhere on either lateral skull x-ray.*
- *No entry wound* could be located anywhere on the A-P x-ray.
- The orbit of the right eye appears to be displaced.
- The nasal septum is deviated.

<u>X-Rays of Loose Skull Fragments</u>

- Ubelaker could not determine from where in the skull any of these fragments came. He did notice suture present on the largest fragment in all 3 x-rays, but based upon the x-rays alone he could not determine which suture he was looking at, nor could he determine from where in the skull the 3 fragments came.
- Fragments of metal were noted on the largest of the 3 fragments in each x-ray.

<u>Caveats</u>

- Dr. Ubelaker was briefed by Jeremy Gunn and me about the various controversies surrounding the medical evidence in the JFK assassination *after* he concluded the assessments recorded above. At this time he reminded us that he was neither a "soft tissue man" (i.e., a pathologist) nor a radiologist, and encouraged us to consult a forensic specialist from each of these areas.

Source: Forensic Pathologist Dr. Robert H. Kirschner

<u>Right and Left Lateral Skull X-Rays</u>

- Kirshner could locate *no entry wound* on either lateral skull x-ray, but was more than content to defer to the opinion of a qualified radiologist on the matter.

<u>Anterior-Posterior Skull X-Ray</u>

- Kirschner said that the pattern of disruption appeared to be outward, from posterior to anterior.
- The rear of the right orbit was observed to be missing.
- When the ARRB staff asked Kirschner his opinion about the 6.5 mm object, he

---

rear of the skull. The blowout of the posterior skull seen in Dallas was most commonly described as "occipital-parietal:" that is, bordering on both sides of the lamboid suture on the right side of the occipital bone. Any alteration that masked this exit defect would also have covered up the remaining lamboid suture, explaining Ubelaker's observation above.

speculated that it might be a plug of bone forced forward into the skull by an entering bullet. Once again, he said he would gladly defer to the opinion of a radiologist.

Source: Forensic Radiologist Dr. John J. Fitzpatrick

Right and Left Lateral Skull X-Rays

- *No entry wound* can be seen on either lateral skull x-ray.
- *No object* directly and clearly corresponding to the bright 6.5 mm object on the A-P x-ray could be located on either lateral skull film. Fitzpatrick did note the small metallic fragment high on the exterior surface of the rear of the skull, but he did not believe this object was anywhere near the density or brightness required for it to correspond to the 6.5 mm very dense radio-opaque object on the A-P x-ray.
- Most of the missing bone is parietal.
- The two laterals seem to show a possible exit wound in the right-front parietal region.
- Overlapping bone is clearly present in both laterals.
- There is a "snow trail" of bullet fragments near the vertex of the skull which probably corresponds to a bullet's track through the head, but Fitzpatrick stated that the direction of the bullet (whether back-to-front, or front-to-back) cannot be determined by anything about the snow trail itself.
- After comparing both laterals with the A-P skull x-ray, Fitzpatrick gave his professional opinion that most of the frontal bone was present, at least up to the level of where the hairline would start. This conclusion was arrived at by comparing sinuses present on both the laterals, and the A-P skull x-ray. He said much of the dark appearance of the skull in the forward cranial vault was due to air present in the open head wound; some of it is also due to missing bone (above the level of the hairline in the frontal bone, and much of the parietal bone).

Anterior-Posterior Skull X-Ray

- *No entry wound* was seen on the A-P x-ray.
- The orbit of the right eye is cracked and displaced.
- The 6.5 mm object was noted to be metallic because of its density.
- Some brain is in the cranium; the outline of the left cerebral hemisphere can be seen in the A-P x-ray. Left frontal brain is present; right frontal brain is missing. The extremely dark area in the forward cranial vault indicates both absence of brain tissue and air inside the cranium.
- Fitzpatrick said he had "never seen" burn marks like the two artifacts on the A-P x-ray; he said someone was very careless with a hot light.

X-Rays of Loose Skull Fragments

- Metallic fragments were noted in the largest of the 3 bone fragments in each of these 3 x-rays.
- Beveling appears to be present on the largest of the 3 fragments in each x-ray, but it

is impossible to tell from the x-rays alone (without being able to visually examine the fragments and hold them in one's hands) the nature and direction of the beveling.

- Suture, as well as an adjacent bone-break line, was noted on the largest of the 3 fragments in each x-ray, but the type of suture could not be determined from the x-rays alone.

- The origin of these fragments in the skull could not be determined from the x-rays alone.

X-Rays of Thorax and Neck

- The right transverse process at T-2 could be broken; or, air in the open wound could account for what is seen in these x-rays. Fitzpatrick was uncertain whether he was discussing T-1 or T-2 here.

FINAL CONCLUSIONS ABOUT THE AUTOPSY X-RAYS

- *At least five* (5) skull x-rays were taken; ***two (2) are definitely missing.*** (Confidence: high.)

- The skull x-rays were taken in *one series,* were taken *first,* and were taken *very early after the arrival of President Kennedy's body.* (Confidence: high.)

- Per Jerrol Custer, there *may be* one x-ray missing of the neck, an A-P cervical spine, showing metallic fragments in the area of C3/C4. (Confidence: low.)

- Per Ed Reed, there *may be* a second x-ray missing of the neck, a lateral cervical spine. (Confidence: low.)

- There *may be* one x-ray missing showing a metal probe passing through a wound track in either the neck, or connecting the posterior thorax to the throat. (Confidence: low.)

- It cannot be known *with any certainty* who took the 3 x-rays of loose skull fragments. However, Custer's recollection that they were taken late Saturday morning must be incorrect, for both the autopsy report and the Sibert-O'Neill report make clear that the x-rays of these fragments were made prior to the end of the autopsy. It is possible that Custer exposed them late Friday night, and is confused about the timing. It is also possible that someone else at Bethesda exposed these x-rays, since none of the 3 images contain the personal or hospital markings Custer and Reed were using that night.

- *The two (2) lateral skull x-rays* are ***forgeries:*** *composite copy films* in which an occipital-parietal blowout in the right rear of the skull was obliterated with a very dense optical patch superimposed over the authentic JFK image on the copy film, by 'light-blasting' the blow-out in the right rear of the skull. (Confidence: high.)

- *The anterior-posterior skull x-ray* is a ***forgery:*** *a composite copy film* in which an apparent 6.5 mm radio-opaque, circular 'bullet fragment' was optically superimposed on the copy film by 'light-blasting' the precise area on the A-P image where a much smaller, less dense fragment was already imaged. (Confidence: high.)

- *All* skull x-rays were taken prior to Dr. Finck's arrival at the morgue at 8:30 PM on November 22, 1963. (Confidence: high.)

- At least one body x-ray, of the chest, was exposed prior to the removal of the lungs and the heart, and therefore prior to Dr. Finck's arrival. (Confidence: high.)

- Three body x-rays were taken after evisceration. (Confidence: high.)

- The timing and sequence of all other body x-rays showing organs present in the thorax and pelvis, and the lower extremities, cannot be determined with any precision.

- Custer and Reed together took the x-rays as a team, under Custer's supervision. They took them upstairs together each trip (to the fourth floor main x-ray department at Bethesda) for developing, using two different elevators and accompanied by a Secret Service agent each time they made this journey. (Confidence: high.)

- Dr. Ebersole did not take any x-rays of the body of President Kennedy himself, nor was he involved in developing any of the x-rays, nor did he carry any of the cassettes to the fourth floor main x-ray department. (Confidence: high.)

- Dr. Ebersole was used as a "guinea pig" by persons involved in a medical coverup to see whether he would react adversely to the forged A-P skull and lateral skull x-rays. (Confidence: high.)

- Dr. Ebersole's 1978 HSCA deposition is a "gift to history," since it contradicts many things about the autopsy that Humes, Boswell, and Finck have maintained a more-or-less united front about for many years. His testimony provides evidence supporting an exit wound in the back of President Kennedy's head; supporting the creation of dishonest and misleading autopsy photographs; supporting detailed contact by Dr. Humes with 'Dallas' (almost certainly Dr. Perry) during the autopsy; and confirming Dr. Boswell's ARRB testimony that there was at least a tentative conclusion that there was an *exit wound* at the tracheostomy site in the anterior neck *during the autopsy,* rather than on Saturday morning, November 23, 1963.

Chapter 6: The Morticians

In 1963 (and for many decades prior to the 1960s), Joseph Gawler's Sons, Inc. (hereafter referred to as "Gawler's") was the most distinguished funeral home in Washington, D.C. On November 22, 1963 Gawler's was tasked by an Army Colonel representing the Military District of Washington (MDW) with performing all of the embalming services and restorative art on the body of the 35th President of the United States, John F. Kennedy. The four individuals directly involved with this task were Joseph E. Hagan (the team's supervisor), Ed Stroble, Thomas E. Robinson, and John VanHoesen (pronounced "VanHeusen"). At the time of the ARRB's work, the only member of this team who was deceased was Ed Stroble; the ARRB staff conducted unsworn interviews with the remaining three members of the team. One of the team members, Tom Robinson, had been interviewed previously, in 1977, by the staff of the HSCA (Andy Purdy and Jim Conzelman)—and the HSCA had prepared a transcript of the tape recording of that interview, which was 'liberated' in August of 1993 by the JFK Records Act. Presumably, Robert Blakey did not want its contents revealed any more than he did the Finck or Ebersole depositions, so he had it sealed in 1979 for 50 years, along with other interview reports of persons at the autopsy which contradicted the conclusions of his medical panel.

The interviews the ARRB staff conducted of the three surviving morticians are an almost classic example of the distortion and uncertainty that a long passage of time creates in human memories. It is not safe for the researcher to pick out any single statement or passage from any one of these interviews and treat it as "fact" without first comparing it with the statements of the other morticians (and indeed, other autopsy eyewitnesses and even documents). My approach in this chapter, therefore, in the interests of transparency, will be to first recount all of the recollections of each mortician *directly and completely,* as they were reported to the HSCA and the ARRB, including each witnesses' own uncertainties and changes of mind during his testimony. The reader will find no 'cherry-picking' here. (As always, I will also make editorial or contextual comments where appropriate.) Following this, I will build a timeline of what I will term "Gawler's activities" at the autopsy which will summarize my own interpretation of their sometimes conflicting testimony regarding "what happened when" at Bethesda Naval hospital, in relation to other key events. I will conclude this chapter by providing my conclusions: an analysis, if you will, about *what the most significant passages of their testimony may mean* within the larger context of the autopsy. The testimony of the Gawler's personnel is important not only because they worked with the body of President Kennedy after the autopsy was concluded and could comment upon the condition they found at that time, but because various members of the team were present in the Bethesda morgue during substantial portions of the autopsy, and had vivid recollections of different events during the autopsy itself.

JOSEPH E. HAGAN

Mr. Hagan, who in 1996—when contacted by the ARRB staff—was the President of Gawler's, was very hesitant to talk with us because he felt it might subject him to possible criticism in the future about 'breach of confidentiality' with the decedent's family. He was concerned that this might upset the Kennedy family, and also feared that it might reflect badly upon Gawler's reputation for maintaining confidentiality with all customers. Therefore, at his request, the ARRB issued him a subpoena *Deuces Tecum* to appear and provide documents and testimony. This subpoena provided Mr. Hagan with protection against any possible future criticism that he had breached the confidentiality normally expected of a funeral home: we had compelled him to appear, and he had no choice. Once engaged with us during the interview process, he proved most cordial, friendly, and appeared to be cooperative, within what he claimed were the limits of his memory. Although Mr. Hagan was subpoenaed to appear and provide documents and testimony, he was *not* asked by the ARRB staff to provide sworn testimony before a court reporter. Instead, Jeremy Gunn chose to take unsworn testimony and to tape record Mr. Hagan's recollections in our offices. I had no problem with this approach, since the interview was being tape recorded. The audiotape recording of his interview is available at Archives II to any American citizen who wishes to listen to it, or obtain a copy.

The ARRB interview was conducted on May 17, 1996 in the ARRB conference room, which was wired for sound. Present were Mr. Hagan; our Executive Director, David Marwell; our Director of Communications, Tom Samoluk; General Counsel Jeremy Gunn; the supervisor of the Military Records Team, Tim Wray; and myself. The interview was very ably conducted by Tim Wray. (Tim Wray, my immediate boss at the time, was a recently retired Army infantry Colonel, and Jeremy Gunn felt that his seniority and previous experience, as well as his engaging personality, might allow Tim to establish a closer rapport with this witness than would other staff members. It proved to be a good decision.) Mr. Hagan was fully aware that we were recording the interview, and was provided with a copy of the tape afterwards.

Selection of Gawler's by the U.S. Army, And Initial Instructions

In November 1963 Joe Hagan was an "Operations Manager," a Gawler's employee who had a supervisory role in regard to the duties of all funeral home employees involved in preparation of a decedent for burial. He said Gawler's was called on the phone about 4:25 PM on 11/22/63 by Colonel Paul Miller, Chief of Ceremonies and Special Events at MDW, and asked to prepare President Kennedy for burial. Immediately after receiving this call, Gawler's independently called Colonel Miller back to confirm the authenticity of this tasking. Hagan said Gawler's was told three things during this second telephone conversation:

1. Provide funeral services for President Kennedy.
2. Have a hearse at Andrews AFB for "wheels down" of Air Force One about 6 P.M.
3. The body of President Kennedy would be driven in the hearse[1] directly to Gawler's

---

[1] A hearse, of course, was originally (in the 18th and 19th centuries) a black funeral carriage designed to carry a coffin, which was traditionally drawn by black horses. In the age of automobiles, a hearse (in the United States) was a stretched type of extra-long station wagon built by General Motors, with an unusually high roof, designed specifically to transport a large coffin, and sometimes family members of the deceased. General Motors hearses were all black in those days, and their appearance was unique.

funeral home in N.W. Washington, D.C.

Orders then began changing, according to Hagan. After-the-fact, Colonel Miller told Hagan that this was due to orders received from Sergeant Shriver (the head of President Kennedy's Peace Corps, and the husband of JFK's sister Eunice), who had taken charge of funeral arrangements at the White House on behalf of the Kennedy family. Miller later told Hagan that there was great uncertainty the evening of 11/22/63 over where the President was to be buried, the type of ceremony to be arranged, etc.—that the situation was very fluid the night of the assassination.

Hagan told us that a "death watch," i.e., an honor guard (branch of service not specified), arrived at Gawler's and set up a "command post" prior to the arrival of Air Force One at Andrews AFB.

Hagan said that at the "last minute," Gawler's received a call from someone—probably Colonel Miller again, or possibly Jack Metzler, Superintendent of Arlington Cemetery—who directed Gawler's NOT to send the hearse to Andrews AFB, since a Navy ambulance would be used instead to transport the President's body. (At this time the destination of the body in the Navy ambulance was not specified.) At a later date, Colonel Miller told Hagan that at one point on 11/22/63, there had been a plan for a helicopter to take the President's body from Andrews to the Naval hospital in Bethesda, but that the helicopter transportation plan had been cancelled.[2]

Finally, Gawler's was instructed to send their embalming team to the Naval hospital in Bethesda,

---

[2]Audio and video recordings made on 11/22/63 actually record a helicopter *landing and then quickly taking off* on the right-hand side of Air Force One shortly after the plane rolled to a halt. (The TV cameras and floodlights were on the left-hand side of the aircraft; the right-hand side was largely obscured by the fuselage of the large Boeing 707 aircraft, and by darkness.) This is all discussed in detail in the Epilogue to the 1982 paperback edition of David Lifton's *Best Evidence*. For those readers who do not have a copy of his book, I will summarize this evidence briefly here: (1) an audio recording of the arrival of Air Force One revealed the sound of a helicopter taking off within 90 seconds of the arrival of Air Force One; (2) an entry in an NBC-TV log indicated that a helicopter could be seen hovering alongside Air Force One when it landed; (3) voice radio transmissions from Air Force One to the White House Situation Room while the aircraft was enroute Washington from Dallas—recorded on audiotape edited by the Army Signal Corps and available from the LBJ Library—reveal that helicopter transportation for the body was planned; and (4) most significant, unedited film footage (with a soundtrack) located in 1981 by the Canadian Broadcasting Company reveals not only the sound of the whirring rotor blades of a helicopter as the engines of Air Force One are shut down, but also shows quite plainly, underneath the belly of the Presidential aircraft, the helicopter's blinking lights under its own fuselage near the area of the forward starboard galley door of Air Force One, where a ramp had been requested by radio prior to landing—and the helo's belly lights slowly move away from Air Force One as it prepares to take off. This irrefutable evidence is the perfect example of why no one statement of any eyewitness can be taken as "fact" without comparing it with all other available evidence.

Maryland. Joe Hagan specified that they never drove to Andrews AFB.

When Did the Various Gawler's Personnel Arrive at the Bethesda Morgue?

Joe Hagan's memory seemed most subject to error when he was discussing timelines: which events occurred first, the exact times that events occurred, and the duration of specific events. We experienced that problem more with some witnesses than others; it was particularly acute with x-ray technicians Jerrol Custer and Ed Reed, as well.

Hagan first said that the embalming team went out to Bethesda "around 11:00 PM" on 11/22/63, and said that the autopsy on President Kennedy was still in progress when they all arrived. He recalled that the body was still on the autopsy table being examined when he arrived. Hagan then said that some members of the embalming team (other than himself) may have gone out to Bethesda earlier in the evening in a private automobile, vice the hearse. He then made a further correction, stating that other members of the embalming team may have gone to Bethesda about 11:00 PM after all, ahead of John Gawler and him, because he and John Gawler had met with Kennedy aides at the funeral home and assisted them with the selection of a solid plank mahogany casket for the state funeral. He recalled that he, along with John Gawler, had driven the mahogany casket out to Bethesda in a hearse, *arriving sometime near midnight, but no later than 12:30 AM.* on 11/23/63.

Hagan told us that the hearse transporting the mahogany casket arrived at the loading dock behind the morgue, and was directed to park there by Secret Service personnel. He said that he remembered Secret Service agent Roy Kellerman (the ASAIC of the entire Texas trip, and the agent sitting in the right front seat of the Presidential limousine during the assassination) being present at the autopsy, and that *Kellerman controlled the entrance of personnel into the morgue during the autopsy.* [Hagan explained that he knew Kellerman from previous professional association.]

At a later point in the interview, when reviewing an internal Gawler's document called a "First Call Sheet" (see Appendix 39) which recorded key details of the events associated with the embalming operations, we asked him about a "2 AM" notation entered in the portion of the form labeled "Casket Delivery Details." Upon review of this entry on the form, Hagan said *he felt obliged to agree that the actual delivery time of the mahogany casket must have been 2 AM.* Ultimately, his own assessment of the inconsistencies in his own responses to questions about the timeline of events was to honestly say "I can't put it all together."[3]

---

[3]The "First Call Sheet" identifies the mahogany casket as a "Marsellus 710" model and the burial vault (within which the casket would later be sealed) as a "Wilbert-Triune," with dimensions of 30" x 86". Other Gawler's documents provided to the ARRB staff revealed that the casket weighed 255 lbs., and that the Wilbert-Triune vault weighed approximately 3000 lbs., including the lid, which was sealed in place with hot tar at the burial site before the gravesite was covered.

Events Observed at President Kennedy's Autopsy

Hagan told us that the embalming team waited in the morgue, in the "bleachers" (i.e., the gallery) while the autopsy was still in progress. He said that about 25 people were present in the morgue. Roy Kellerman was controlling entry into the morgue. Hagan said the atmosphere in the morgue was tense, and there was a sense of panic in the air—by this he meant that people were acting "touchy." When asked to elaborate upon these remarks, he said he could remember no specifics, and simply spoke of the general situation; i.e., a young President had been assassinated, and the facts were unknown.

Hagan said that when he arrived with the mahogany casket, *the autopsy was almost over;* he only had to wait in the gallery about 20 minutes before the autopsy was concluded. The body of the President was being "cleaned up." Hagan said <u>photos were being taken</u>,[4] but could remember no details—he could not remember which views were shot, how many photographers there were, or any details about their equipment.

He could recall no specific remarks, conversation, or conclusions by the pathologists. Hagan said it was obvious a "full post" had been done, since the thoracic and abdominal cavities on the President's body were open. The brain was not in the cranium when he arrived. He said he could not remember whether he saw the brain that night or not. The head of the President was supported on a block.[5] Hagan did not recall whether or not he saw a wound on the posterior thorax of the President, saying that the Gawler's team, in the course of their work, left the body supine, and did not turn the body over. He said he did see the autopsy prosectors turn the body over so that it was lying face down, but he did not remember details about what he saw during that event. Hagan said that his vantage point in the gallery was perhaps 12-15 feet away from the President, but that it was sometimes difficult to see the President's body because of the people working around the morgue examination table. He said he did not recall seeing any probes used.

The ARRB staff had to press Mr. Hagan pretty hard to get him to describe the damage to President

---

[4]These photos almost certainly *cannot be* the photographs developed by Saundra Spencer and described in her ARRB testimony, for the Gawler's team had not yet performed embalming, or their reconstruction of the head and the sewing of what remained of the scalp back into place. Did Joe Hagan witness photographs being taken by Robert Knudsen (after the departure of Stringer and Riebe) of the autopsy pathologists manipulating the loose and reflected scalp of President Kennedy to cover the exit defect in the back of his head? If he arrived at about midnight or "no later than 12:30," it could have been *either* the Stringer/Riebe team *or* Robert Knudsen; if he arrived at 2 AM as the First Call Sheet indicates, he was almost certainly witnessing *photography by Robert Knudsen* of a charade that both Knudsen and he *both* thought was "the end of the autopsy."

[5]I believe it is significant that Hagan, who arrived rather late and witnessed post mortem photography, did *not* see the head supported by the metal stirrup or head rest seen in many autopsy photographs. I will explain what this means to me at the end of this chapter.

Kennedy's head. He stated many times that he was not qualified to determine how much of the damage he observed had resulted from gunshot injury, and how much had been caused by the autopsy prosectors in the course of their work. He declined to draw his recollections of the damage to the head on either anatomical skull diagrams or on a human skull model. However, he did state that "all of this was open in the back," while holding his two hands about 6 inches away from his *upper posterior skull,* gesturing to the area *between both of his own ears on the back of his head.* On another occasion during his interview, when discussing the head wound as it appeared during the reconstruction of the head by his team of technicians, Hagan said that the hole he observed was in the *upper left posterior skull.*[6]

Hagan Describes the Work Performed by Gawler's Personnel to Embalm and Reconstruct the President's Body

Mr. Hagan said that his team performed a standard arterial embalming, and that no problems were presented in the course of this standard procedure (which involves injecting formaldehyde into major arteries of the deceased, until the blood in the body is substantially replaced by formalin solution). Hagan said embalming began shortly after midnight, and concluded about 3 AM. Later in the interview, the ARRB staff discussed with Mr. Hagan the contents of an internal Gawler's document called the "Arrangements File," in which appeared the notations "11:45" and "3:30" in Hagan's own handwriting. Hagan told us that 11:45 could refer to Gawler's start time, and that 3:30 could refer to the time Gawler's finished its work. Just as in the case of the "First Call Sheet," which recorded an arrival time of 2 AM for the mahogany casket, the "Arrangements File" may be a more accurate record of when the Gawler's team began and ended their work. Both were contemporaneous records, and were much more likely to be accurate than a human memory almost 36 years later.

Reconstruction of the body and the head did not begin until the embalming work was completed. Hagan said plaster-of-Paris was used to fill the empty cranium and provide the support necessary to reconstruct the head after completion of the autopsy. After a hardening agent dried the plaster in the cranium, Hagan said the scalp was pulled together and sutured into place. A primary concern of the Gawler's team was the avoidance of leakage in the casket. He did not recall much bone missing from the cranium, and did not recall any scalp missing. The hole in the cranium (meaning missing bone) was noted during reconstruction to be *in the upper left posterior portion of the head.*[7]

---

[6]This is roughly consistent with the damage in sketches drawn by Roy Kellerman and James Sibert for the HSCA; with the recollections of Dr. Karnei to the ARRB; and would also be encompassed by the enormous area of damage drawn on the skull model by Dr. Boswell at his ARRB deposition. It is inconsistent with the Parkland hospital observations of an avulsed wound localized in the *right rear* of the skull, and with the huge area of bone missing in the *top* of the skull on Boswell's autopsy sketch, his ARRB skull markings, and by the autopsy photographs showing the entire *top* of the head badly broken and disrupted.

[7]Both Drs. Boswell and Dr. Karnei had expressed their opinion to the ARRB staff that *the pattern of damage to the skull traveled along an axis from the right front to the left rear.*

Gawler's closed the tracheostomy wound by "suturing it up."[8] Hagan said a small amount of dermal wax was used to seal the anterior throat wound after it was sutured. He does not recall whether the tracheostomy incision was above, or below, the collar line on a buttoned dress shirt. Restorative art cosmetics were used to prepare the President for a possible open casket funeral; they were cream-based, and were used to hide some bruising and discoloration on the face. President Kennedy was dressed by Gawler's in a blue pin-stripe suit and a white shirt; the clothing had been brought from the White House.

Mr. Hagan said Tom Robinson performed most of the repair to the head, and said he would try to locate both Tom Robinson and John VanHoesen on our behalf so we could conduct interviews. He said that as a supervisor, he was in-and-out of the morgue during the embalming and reconstruction process, discussing various arrangements with John Gawler and Navy personnel, and was not privy to every step of the work taken by his people. He said that the Gawler's team completed reconstruction work no later than 4:00 AM, and that the new mahogany casket containing the deceased Commander-in-Chief was then loaded into a Navy ambulance[9] by the Secret Service, i.e., "Kellerman and others," in what he interpreted as a last act of respect. At that point, he said there was nothing to do but pack up the equipment and head back to Gawler's funeral home.

In response to follow-up questioning, Mr. Hagan said that he could not recall any rubber or plastic sheeting used to cover an open defect in the head. He said there was no visible damage to the head or scalp following reconstruction which would in any way have been indicative of the nature of the head wounds.[10] He did not recall, one way or the other, whether any photographs were taken during Gawler's work on the President's body. He said that he personally closed the casket at Bethesda, and said the President was ready for an open-casket funeral, if one had been desired. He was asked whether there was any wrapping or bandage around the head after work was completed, and he said no.[11]

The Casket Controversy

Possibly the most confusing issue of all regarding what happened the night of the autopsy, from the

---

[8] When I heard this I wondered whether Dr. Ebersole, in his HSCA testimony, was remembering this suturing performed by the morticians, and that the time when he had seen it was simply confused in his memory. We will never know.

[9] The Navy ambulances used on the evening of November 22-23, 1963 all appear to have been hearses that were painted a light gray in color, and which appear almost white in black and white photographs.

[10] This was contradicted by both of his surviving colleagues, Tom Robinson and John VanHoesen.

[11] In his book *Palimpsest,* author Gore Vidal wrote that Lee Radziwill had viewed President Kennedy's body in the White House after a casket opening, and had told him that the President's head was covered by a "turban."

standpoint of eyewitness recollections, is the controversial issue of what type of casket President Kennedy arrived in. It is no small issue; it is of great import. It is a fact that President Kennedy was loaded onto Air Force One at Love Field in Dallas in a very heavy (400-plus lbs.) bronze ceremonial viewing casket. However, there are two casket descriptions given by two different sets of witnesses, or "audiences," at the Bethesda morgue. One audience recalls an early casket arrival in a gray or pinkish-gray colored, lightweight, unadorned, shipping casket; another audience recalls him arriving later that evening in a bronze, ceremonial viewing casket identical with the Dallas casket received at Parkland hospital from the O'Neal funeral home. The importance of the shipping casket witnesses is really "off-scale:" if JFK *did* arrive in a shipping casket, then the chain-of-custody of the body had been broken prior to its arrival at Bethesda, pointing to some kind of shenanigans with his wounds—probable evidence-tampering. As will be revealed in Part II of this book, the evidence for the early arrival of a cheap shipping casket is so strong that it is *not* a matter of "either-or," that is, of *either* the shipping casket witnesses *or* the bronze casket witnesses being correct. Clearly, *both* a shipping casket and the Dallas casket arrived that night at the Bethesda morgue. If the witnesses who recalled the heavy, ornate bronze casket's delivery were correct when they say that *they witnessed the President's body removed from the bronze casket,* then, as David Lifton put it in *Best Evidence,* an elaborate shell game was going on with the President's body shortly after its arrival so as to create unimpeachable "bronze casket" witnesses, in order to be able to counter any contrary evidence of the President having arrived earlier in a cheap shipping casket, were that to become an issue after the autopsy. Why? *Because any autopsy report for an autopsy conducted on a body in which the chain-of-custody had been broken, and the wounds had been tampered with and bullets or bullet fragments had been removed prior to the autopsy, was impeachable and would be thrown out of evidence.*

Whether he liked it or not—and he clearly did not like it—Joe Hagan and the Gawler's funeral home had been thrust squarely into the middle of this debate by an entry on one of Gawler's own internal documents. The entry in question on the "First Call Sheet" (see Figure 69) reads as follows:

> "Body removed from metal shipping casket at USNH at Bethesda."

When we asked Mr. Hagan about this, he said that the entry was indeed made in his handwriting, but that he never saw the casket in which the body was delivered—that he had made this entry based upon what someone had told him. Hagan told us he never saw any casket on the evening of November 22-23, 1963 other than the mahogany casket which Gawler's brought to the morgue in its own hearse.

He did, however, indicate certain knowledge that the bronze Dallas casket was damaged. We asked him how he knew this, if the only casket he saw on the night of the autopsy was the mahogany casket Gawler's delivered. He responded by saying that some time after the autopsy, someone delivered the bronze Dallas casket to Gawler's funeral home. He observed that it had a damaged handle, and some scratches on the exterior surface. He was told GSA (the General Services Administration, of which the National Archives was a part) would pick it up later, and in fact said that GSA had done just that in the Spring of 1964, taking it away in a government truck. In fact, an internal Gawler's receipt (see Appendix 41) dated March 19, 1964 documents that the GSA picked up the casket that date and that Joe Hagan helped load it on the truck. Interestingly, it was picked up not by menial laborers, but by Lewis M. Robeson, Chief Security Agent at the National Archives. Hagan told us "none of our people were at the Naval hospital early that evening, so I can't account for what happened to the [bronze] casket or how it was damaged."

Mr. Hagan indicated a full awareness of the controversies about possible wound alteration and different casket entries raised in *Best Evidence,* and made it very clear that this subject was "radioactive" to him, and was something he did not want to become embroiled in. But these remarks by him made me wonder whether he was really being fully forthcoming about whether or not he had seen a "shipping casket" at the Bethesda morgue the night of the autopsy. After all, the words "shipping casket" *were* on the Gawler's document filled out that night, and they *were* in his handwriting. To paraphrase Dr. Humes, I presumed that Mr. Hagan did not make up that terminology 'out of whole cloth.' Furthermore, while Hagan had brought with him the six-sided folding "Arrangements File" document, there were three documents he did ***not*** bring with him, and that we 'sprung on him,' specifically:

1. The "First Call Sheet," containing its entry about the "shipping casket;"
2. The Gawler's Receipt for the turnover of the bronze casket to GSA; and
3. The "coffin card" from the Texas Coffin Company which had been placed inside the bronze Dallas casket by the O'Neal funeral home, which reads: "Handley reg. solid bronze full top with double inner panels—twin sealing feature—no glass—amber brit. finish."

"Radioactive," indeed. Hagan claimed that these records had either been lost, or that they had been given away to JFK researchers by another Gawler's employee as part of an 'inside job.' He professed joy in seeing them again. (Unfortunately, I had tipped him off on the phone that we were going to do so, so it wasn't a total surprise to him.) I could not conceive of anyone at Gawler's having given away the originals of such historical records to anyone outside the 'family.' Copies, yes, but not the originals. I wondered then, and I wonder now, whether Joe Hagan had destroyed the originals, or hidden them away, hoping not to become embroiled in the two-casket controversy. In any case, a researcher had obtained copies, and had provided copies of his copies to David Lifton, who had provided them to the ARRB staff. *And Hagan authenticated all of them during his interview.* The words "shipping casket" had been written by him. I wasn't satisfied with his answer about why he wrote these words. I thought he was 'playing dumb.' Dr. Finck would do so repeatedly about a week later during his sworn testimony. Finck wasn't any more convincing than Joe Hagan was, when he pretended not to remember things.

I will return to the casket controversy in considerable detail in Part II of this book.

Joe Hagan's Follow-Up Telephone Calls of June 11th and June 18th, 1996

Mr. Hagan and I spoke by telephone on June 11th. He said he had contacted John VanHoesen and had asked him to speak with us. Mr. Hagan then expressed great interest in where we had obtained the 3 'missing' Gawler's business documents. I told him we had obtained them from David Lifton, but that I did not know from whom David Lifton had obtained them. (This was true; Lifton had told me, but I had forgotten by this time. It was a detail that was irrelevant to me; all that mattered to me was that Hagan had authenticated them.) Hagan asked me whether a Mr. Russo worked with Mr. Lifton, and I said I did not know.

Most important, Joe Hagan said that after talking with John VanHoesen about the events the night of the autopsy, that his recollection was now refreshed somewhat. He told me he now believed that the embalming team of Stroble, Robinson, and VanHoesen arrived at Bethesda at about 8 PM, vice midnight, and said that Van Hoesen remembered having to wait a very long time in the morgue gallery before beginning embalming work. Hagan was still sure, however, that he himself was present at the funeral home at about 11 PM when the Kennedy aides (O'Brien, O'Donnell, Powers, and O'Leary, according to the "Arrangements File" document) came to Gawler's to select a casket, and he was still sure that he personally delivered the mahogany casket to Bethesda, and that he joined his team for a short while in the gallery after he arrived before they began their work.

On June 18th Hagan called me again to tell me that he had just located Tom Robinson, and that Robinson was currently staying with some friends in Maryland, very close to our offices in downtown Washington; he thought Tom Robinson would be amenable to speaking with us. (Robinson *was* amenable, and we interviewed him in our offices three days later.)

Hagan told me that Robinson recalled going out to Bethesda with Hagan and the mahogany casket, well before the end of the autopsy, and that Robinson recalled sitting in the gallery for a considerable period of time and watching the autopsy in progress, prior to beginning the embalming work. Hagan quoted Robinson as saying that Ed Stroble and John VanHoesen had come to Bethesda later in the evening with the portable embalming equipment.

Mr. Hagan, still nervous about the "shipping casket" statement in the Gawler's "First Call Sheet," brought up this subject (again) of his own accord, and reminded me that this written statement did not reflect any observation made personally by anyone at Gawler's. I found this most peculiar; I thought he protested too much. I countered by asking him if the term "shipping casket" had a specific meaning within the funeral trade, and he confirmed that it did: namely, that the terms "accommodation case, shipping case, airtray, and/or shipping casket" were interchangeably used to refer to cheap, unadorned lightweight metal containers which were used to ship cadavers from one location to another by air (or sometimes, by train).

After this exchange, Joe Hagan never called me again.

THOMAS E. ROBINSON

Tom Robinson proved very cooperative and forthcoming, and submitted to an interview at the ARRB offices on June 21, 1996, three days after Joe Hagan was kind enough to locate him for us. As I best recall, I was adamant that we should tape record this unsworn interview also, just as we had with Joe Hagan's about a month earlier. Unaccountably, Jeremy said "no," I protested rather vehemently, and this was when Jeremy responded with the words "you never know what these people are going to say—it might get the research community too excited," or words to that effect. (I still do not know what internal doubts, or external pressures, caused Jeremy to make this decision.) As a result, I made extra sure that I took copious notes during the interview, and wrote a particularly detailed interview report that same day, while it was all still fresh in my memory. I would prefer that people today could listen to an audiotape, but since they cannot, I can at least assure the reader that the interview report I wrote later that day was as accurate as carefully written notes, and a fresh memory, could make it. But before I proceed to recount below the contents of that ARRB interview, let us review what Tom Robinson told the HSCA staff in1977.

Tom Robinson's HSCA Staff Interview

This interview was conducted and tape recorded on January 12, 1977, and my summaries below are extracted from the transcript the HSCA prepared from the tape. The questioning jumped around a bit during the interview, so I will summarize Robinson's statements below by subject, rather than chronologically, since different questions were revisited throughout the interview. (See Appendix 54.)

Head Wounds Observed by Tom Robinson

Tom Robinson recalled a large wound *in the back of the head,* between the ears. He drew a sketch of what he remembered at the end of his interview (see Figure 26). His recollections about this wound are summarized below in bullet format:

- The defect caused by "the bullets" was about the size of a small orange.
- A good amount of bone had been blown away.
- The defect was circular, and about three inches in diameter.
- It was ragged around the edges.
- It was in the back of the head, directly between the ears.

Robinson also spoke of a small hole in "the temple" near the hairline, which was so small it could be hidden by the hair.

- Purdy asked Robinson to clarify which side of the *forehead* it was on, which tells me that Robinson had *said* "temple" but had actually *pointed* to his own forehead rather than to his temple. Robinson responded to this question by saying "the right side," thus confirming that it was indeed in the right forehead near the hairline. [12]

---

[12]This is consistent with Dennis David's account of seeing Pitzer's photos of a small round wound high in the right forehead, and of Joe O'Donnell's account of Robert Knudsen showing him a photo depicting an entry wound high in the right forehead. That is also the same location where a rather ugly incision is seen in autopsy photographs of the head—an area that Dr. Boswell once called a "laceration," and at another time called "an incised wound" during his ARRB deposition. The obvious question here is whether or not a frontal entry wound seen early after the arrival of the body at Bethesda was *obliterated* shortly thereafter by *post-mortem surgery?* If so, it is the *incision*—the post-mortem surgery—that was preserved in the autopsy photographs placed in the Archives, and it is the *original condition* of the wound that was remembered by Robinson in his HSCA interview, and

599

- Robinson said this wound did not have to be hidden by make-up, and was simply plugged by him with some wax during the reconstruction.

- The small wound in the forehead was about a quarter of an inch in diameter.

Tom Robinson expressed his opinion during the HSCA interview that the large 3-inch defect in the back of the head was an *entry* wound, and that the small quarter-inch hole in the upper right forehead near the hairline was caused by the *exit* of a bullet fragment or a small piece of bone. His *opinion* of the relative sizes of wounds caused by entering and exiting bullets is clearly upside down, or backwards, from the basics in any forensic pathology text, but that should not concern us here. What should concern is here is the <u>wound locations and sizes</u> remembered so vividly by Tom Robinson in 1977. Tom Robinson was not qualified to interpret the forensic significance of what he saw, but he was certainly capable of telling the HSCA staff what he *remembered seeing* in terms of locations and sizes of wounds to the head.

As a further indicator of the size of the defect in the back of the head, Tom Robinson described the restorative work required to repair the damage:

- Once the body was embalmed arterially, a piece of heavy duty rubber was obtained to cover the defect in the back of the head between the ears.

- The inside of the cranium had to be dried out and packed with material, then the rubber was placed under the hair, the scalp was pulled back over it as much as possible, and the scalp was actually sewn into the sheet of rubber to hold it in place.

- Placing President Kennedy's head on the pillow in the casket hid the damage that could not be completely repaired by the reconstruction. (This verifies that the area of *both* missing *scalp and bone* to which Robinson was referring was *directly between the ears in the back of the head,* and not at the top of the head or in the right side. We know from Boswell's skull diagram and the head x-rays that *bone* was certainly missing in the <u>top</u> *and* <u>right side</u> of the skull, but as Boswell indicated in his testimony, the lacerated scalp folded back over these two areas and covered the missing bone in those locations.)

- Robinson said he worked on the left side of the body during the reconstruction, and said that although the head was not shaved, he thought he would have noticed if there had been any other wounds to the head.[13]

---

recorded in photographs seen by Dennis David and Joe O'Donnell.

[13]I am not so sure about this, given that Father Oscar Huber, Dr. Marion Jenkins, and Dr. Robert McClelland in Dallas all thought there was a wound in the left temporal area. If such a wound had been inside the hairline on the left side of the head, and any clotted blood

Multiple Bullet Fragments Were Removed from the Head: Not Just Two

Tom Robinson spoke of seeing 'many' bullet fragments removed from the cranium. (My interpretation: the manner in which Robinson spoke about these fragments indicates that he saw *more* than the two fragments that both Humes and FBI agents Sibert and O'Neill wrote about in their reports. He said that the small bullet fragments removed from the head had to be handled with forceps, and were placed in a small vial or test tube. Robinson estimated that the largest was a quarter of an inch in size, but seemed to imply that most were much smaller than this. Two exchanges went like this:

Robinson: They were literally picked out, little pieces of this bullet from all over his head.

_____

Purdy: Do you think that they pulled out a fairly many pieces of it?

Robinson: I think so.

[This was clarified considerably in his ARRB interview in 1996.]

Was a Bullet Fragment Removed from the Thorax?

The following exchange is found in the HSCA transcript:

Purdy: In your impression, where is the lowest point on the body that any metal fragments were found?

Robinson: Somehow I feel like there was something found *in the thorax*. [Author's emphasis]

Purdy: Is that what I normally call the chest?

Robinson: Yes.

Purdy: Do you remember it to be metallic or a piece of bone?

Robinson: I think that they found a piece of metal, a piece of bullet. [Author's emphasis]

I view this as a highly significant exchange. It is corroborated by *three* other items of evidence. Paul O'Connor told the HSCA staff that his colleague at the autopsy, James Jenkins, told him that a bullet fragment had been removed from intercostal muscle (that is, between the ribs) when O'Connor was absent from the morgue; in addition, Jerrol Custer told David Lifton in1989, and testified to the

_____

had been washed or wiped away from a left temporal wound by the time Robinson observed the body at least 12 hours later, I am not at all sure that he would have noticed a small entry wound in this area. President Kennedy had a very thick head of hair.

ARRB staff in 1997, that he witnessed a rather large bullet fragment fall from the mid-thorax area of the back when he lifted the cadaver to move an x-ray film cassette; and John Stringer testified before the ARRB that the pathologists 'sat up' the cadaver of the President by bending it at the waist, so that he could photograph a "couple of openings in the back." (The one follow-on question I wish Purdy had asked was whether the fragment was taken out of the back, or the front, of the thorax. The word 'chest' wasn't specific enough for me, and was also a leading question which reveals more about Purdy's assumption—that the fragment may have been removed after the Y-incision opened up the chest—than about Robinson's independent recollection. Jeremy Gunn, for example, would have asked Robinson "from where on the thorax did you see this fragment removed?")

Damage to the Cranium Appears to Exceed that Caused by a Fully Jacketed Military Missile

Fully jacketed military bullets were specifically designed to pass cleanly through the body without causing the massive and catastrophic damage caused by soft lead (unjacketed) bullets, such as hunting bullets, or the type of unjacketed lead ammunition used during the American Civil War. Some independent researchers have noted that the extensive damage to President Kennedy's skull described by Dr. Humes in the autopsy report, and in his Warren Commission testimony, seems inconsistent with what should have been caused by one medium-velocity, fully jacketed bullet (similar to CE 399).

Robinson said that the bones of the skull *and the face* were "badly shattered," and on another occasion used the phrase "badly smashed." He said that the broken facial bones were not visible from the front, when looking at the President's face, but were visible from inside the empty cranium. (This reminds me of the entry on Boswell's autopsy sketch that said "vomer crushed"—the vomer is the bone in the middle of the nasal cavity; and of Humes' description of fractures in the cranium as much as 19 cm in length.) Robinson's description here seems more consistent with damage caused by a frangible (i.e., exploding), or soft-nosed (i.e., unjacketed), or hollow-point bullet—or with hurried, brutal post mortem tampering to gain access to the brain to remove evidence—than it does with a medium velocity, fully-jacketed military round.

Were the Organs of the Throat Really Removed After All?

Although Humes and Finck have both testified over the years that the organs of the throat were not removed, and Boswell testified to the ARRB that he didn't think they were, Tom Robinson twice told the HSCA staff that they *were removed.* The pertinent exchanges follow:

Purdy: [Questioning Robinson about why he said the tracheostomy was "nasty looking"] Did you ever hear any discussions that would have indicated why that was the case or what might have caused that, caused [sic] obviously the tracheostomy occurred prior to the time the body came there?

Robinson: Yes, those things are done very quickly. By nature of the situation, but *it was examined very carefully. The throat was.* **All that was removed**. [Author's emphasis]

Purdy: Was it your understanding that that was just a tracheostomy, or was there some other cause that may have made it ragged or something else?

Robinson: There is something about the bullet exiting from there. A bullet exiting from there. I don't know whether I heard the physicians talking about it or whether I read it now.

——————————

Conzelman: In the region of the throat, when you were putting him back together, did you notice that [sic] any large holes other than what could have been through the autopsy?

Robinson: The tracheostomy.

Conzelman: Besides that?

Robinson: And if it was, a bullet wound. [Robinson was saying that the tracheostomy may have been made over a bullet wound.]

Purdy: Could you tell any kind of a path that the wound had taken from looking in there?

Robinson: No, not really. ***All that had been removed.***   [Author's emphasis]

If Robinson is correct about this—if the trachea and larynx were indeed removed—then Humes and Finck have perjured themselves on this issue.

Was Tom Robinson An Unknowing Witness to a "Shell Game" with President Kennedy's Body?

There is a particularly vague, but very intriguing statement by Robinson in the transcript that reads as follows:

Purdy: You said that later, when you read some things about the assassination or the autopsy, you heard or read some things which struck you as incorrect. What would those things be?

Robinson: *The time the people moved (autopsy). The body was taken....and the body never came....lots of little things like that.*   [Author's emphasis]

This is a bombshell, in view of the hypothesis published in *Best Evidence* four years later (without David Lifton ever having read this sealed transcript, or having interviewed Tom Robinson).

Context: In *Best Evidence,* David Lifton documented the early arrival of a cheap shipping casket at the Bethesda morgue at about 6:40 or 6:45 PM in a black hearse, escorted by Federal agents, *before* the arrival at the front of the hospital at 6:55 PM of the motorcade from Andrews AFB, carrying the bronze Dallas casket (which he is certain was empty by the time Air Force One took off from Love Field in Dallas). He also documented that the bronze casket in the light gray Navy ambulance was *not* driven away from the front of the hospital toward the morgue at the rear until about 7:07 PM, and that it entered the morgue shortly before or at 7:17 PM. Subsequently, the military Joint Service Casket Team, which had literally "lost" the President's casket while they were chasing an empty Navy ambulance in the darkness around the grounds of the Bethesda complex, were reunited with the bronze Dallas casket at the front of the hospital, followed that (second) Navy ambulance to the morgue loading dock, and carried the bronze casket into the morgue at 8:00 PM. Numerous persons witnessed the opening of the bronze casket from Dallas at about 8:00 PM inside the morgue, and saw President Kennedy's body inside the casket (wrapped in sheets). And yet, numerous persons in an *earlier* audience had seen the President's body removed from a cheap, gray metal shipping casket (in a body bag), *before* the Andrews motorcade arrived out in front of the hospital. As Lifton pointed out in his book, if both audiences were correct, then *President Kennedy's body must have been reintroduced into the bronze Dallas casket,* in order for the second audience to be able to see what transpired at 8:00 PM. [The reason for reintroducing it, of course, is that the military Joint Service Casket Team, whose job was to stay with the body at all times and carry the casket when it needed to be moved, had helped offload the heavy Dallas casket at Andrews AFB; they knew exactly what it looked like. Although they had temporarily "lost" the casket at the Bethesda compound when they tore off chasing after the wrong Navy ambulance, it was their duty to carry it into the morgue. They *had to be allowed to carry it into the morgue,* not only to perform their expected duties, *but to reestablish the chain of custody* that had in reality been broken when the body was stolen from the bronze casket during the swearing in of LBJ on Air Force One, and placed in the forward luggage compartment of the airplane, which was both air conditioned and pressurized.]

Tom Robinson's statement that **"the time the people [the Secret Service?] moved [the?] (autopsy). The body was taken....and the body never came...."** could be evidence that he witnessed President Kennedy's body removed from the morgue following initial examinations and/or manipulations, and the taking of the head x-rays, so that it could be reintroduced into the bronze Dallas casket. To readers of my book who have not yet read *Best Evidence* and may be a bit incredulous at this point, I wish to point out that there is a pattern of evidence that indicates the original morgue audience of what I call 'bit players,' or audience one—who witnessed the earliest arrival of President Kennedy's body in the shipping casket—as well as the 2 FBI agents, were kept out of the morgue until after the second casket entry at 8:00 P.M. That pattern of evidence is outlined below. It is essential that the reader now consult Figure 40, a diagram of the Bethesda morgue as it appeared in 1963, before tackling the next paragraph.

I quote below from the FBI Sibert-O'Neill report (see Appendix 16); explanatory comments, and speculation, are surrounded by brackets, as always:

> On arrival at the Medical Center, the ambulance stopped in front of the main entrance, at which time Mrs. Jacqueline Kennedy and Attorney General Robert Kennedy embarked from the ambulance and entered the building. The ambulance was thereafter driven around to the rear entrance where the President's body [i.e., the empty bronze casket from Dallas weighing over 400 pounds] was removed and taken into the autopsy room. Bureau agents assisted in the moving of the casket to the autopsy room. [I strongly suspect that it was only taken to the anteroom or "chill box" room outside the morgue; the President's body was probably inside the morgue at this time, lying on the examination table, and the empty Dallas casket was probably placed in the anteroom. If I am wrong and Sibert, O'Neill, Kellerman, and Greer

really *did* place the Dallas casket inside the morgue at 7:17 PM, then it simply means JFK's body was temporarily moved out of sight, either into a chill box, or into the shower room or chemical room behind the morgue.] *A tight security was immediately placed around the autopsy room by the Naval facility and the U.S. Secret Service.* *Bureau agents made contact with Mr. Roy Kellerman [who Joe Hagan told the ARRB was controlling entry to the morgue], the Assistant Secret Service [sic] Agent in Charge of the White House detail, and advised him of the Bureau's interest in this matter*. He advised that he had already received instructions from Director Rowley as to the presence of Bureau agents. [Author's emphasis]

In my opinion, David Lifton's interpretation of the passage above, namely, that Sibert and O'Neill were kept out of the morgue by the Secret Service and the Navy (i.e., United States Marines who were keeping a security watch outside the morgue with weapons at the ready), is the only reasonable explanation for this language. I suspect that they were not just kept out of the morgue, but also escorted out of the morgue anteroom, where they had likely deposited the Dallas casket.[14]

Although Frank O'Neill made a big point of denying Lifton's interpretation of the above passage at his ARRB deposition, his denial that he was barred from entering the morgue rings rather hollow in view of the following quotation from the text of the aforementioned CBS News memo dated January 10, 1967 from Bob Richter to Les Midgley (see Appendix 37):

> *Humes said FBI agents were not in the autopsy room during the autopsy; they were kept in an anteroom,* and their report [about there being no bullet track through the body from back to front] is simply wrong. Although initially in the autopsy procedure the back wound could only be penetrated to finger length, a probe later was made—*when no FBI men were present*—that traced the path of the bullet from the back going downwards, then upwards slightly, then downwards again exiting at the throat. [Author's emphasis]

These two conscientious FBI agents, whose assignment was 'to stay with the body and to obtain bullets reportedly in the President's body,' would have raised hell at a very high level if they had seen the Dallas casket opened with no body inside. They, as well as the Joint Service Casket Team, *had to be allowed to see JFK's body inside the Dallas Casket.* As James Sibert stated in his HSCA staff interview and subsequent HSCA affidavit, another one of their assignments was "*to maintain the chain of custody on the body."* Therefore, they had to be temporarily kept out of the morgue and the adjoining anteroom where they had almost certainly set down the casket, and were surely

---

[14]The HSCA staff interview of Frank O'Neill in January 1978 reveals that he and Sibert, along with Secret Service agents Kellerman and Greer (the driver of the President's limousine in Dallas), *alone,* moved the Dallas casket from the loading dock either to the vicinity of the morgue, or into the morgue itself, using a "roller" [most likely a dolly with wheels specifically designed for the funeral trade, called a "church truck"]. No one else was involved, according to O'Neill's recollections to the HSCA staff. His insistence later, during his ARRB deposition in 1997, that an "honor guard" assisted Sibert and him with the casket, does not ring true because of his earlier statements to the HSCA. Furthermore, Sibert also told the HSCA that *only those four agents* moved the casket to the morgue.

sequestered somewhere nearby. Meanwhile, the President's body was reintroduced into the Dallas casket; the bronze Dallas casket (with JFK's body now inside) was surreptitiously loaded into one of the two gray Navy ambulances in the Andrews motorcade; driven back to the front of the hospital where it was reunited with the Joint Service Casket Team; and brought into the morgue at exactly 8:00 PM, with appropriate ceremony and respect, by the multi-service honor guard. I conclude that *after* the Dallas casket was brought into the morgue by the casket team at 8:00 PM, and the honor guard had performed its duties, Sibert and O'Neill were immediately allowed back into the morgue *to witness the body of the President being removed from the bronze casket.* In his 1978 affidavit to the HSCA, O'Neill says he witnessed the President's body placed on the examination table in the morgue, but he *never said* he saw the casket opened, nor did he mention seeing the honor guard when he and Sibert delivered the Dallas casket to the Bethesda morgue. [He and Sibert, of course, *could not be permitted* to see the Joint Service Casket Team perform its function of <u>bringing the casket into the morgue</u>, since Sibert and O'Neill *knew* that <u>they</u> had taken the casket into the morgue *themselves.*] Members of the Joint Service Casket Team *did* see the casket opened, but *none* of them saw the body placed on the examination table; they left the morgue immediately. Their recollections dovetail perfectly with those of Sibert and O'Neill, who did *not* see them bring the Dallas casket into the morgue, but *did* see the President's body placed on the examination table. Someone—Roy Kellerman, apparently—was a very busy stage manager that night.

The need to clear the room of all personnel except those needed for the taking of x-rays—which is well documented that night, in both the Sibert-O'Neill report, and by Floyd Riebe in his 1989 Lifton interview—was no doubt a 'safety ploy' used to clear most of the *first* audience, whose members witnessed the early arrival of the shipping casket, out of the morgue *prior* to reintroducing JFK's body into the Dallas casket. Only the two Navy pathologists, the Secret Service, the controlling VIPs in the gallery (and perhaps Dr. Ebersole) need have known of this shell game. The x-ray technicians, who were members of audience one, were sent upstairs for a considerable period of time after they developed the head x-rays and returned them to Humes and Ebersole in the morgue, so they were prevented, by their absence, from knowing about this charade. After the Joint Service Casket Team brought the heavy, ornate bronze Dallas viewing coffin into the morgue, they witnessed the casket opening and saw the President's body inside, and immediately departed. Sibert and O'Neill witnessed the body placed on the examining table, but not its arrival in the Dallas casket immediately prior to that. The witnesses to the shipping casket's early arrival who had been asked to leave the morgue immediately after the shipping casket was opened—Paul O'Connor, James Jenkins, John Stringer, and Floyd Riebe—were allowed back into the morgue shortly after Sibert and O'Neill, perhaps right after the first round of pre-incision body x-rays were taken, and just prior to 8:15 PM, knowing nothing about the 'shell game' that had just transpired with the President's body during the previous 40 minutes.

Navy Corpsman James Metzler, who witnessed the delivery of the bronze casket by the Joint Service Casket Team and saw the President's body after the opening of the casket, recalled with some disquiet when interviewed by David Lifton, that the Secret Service was keeping a list of who was in the morgue, and that he became alarmed when the Federal agents ominously told him that he was "not on the list"—apparently a list of who had entered the morgue at a particular time, or of who was supposed to be in a particular audience. The Secret Service apparently became alarmed as well, for they physically prevented his departure from the morgue until they could record his name. He was subsequently issued an official gag order by the Navy, threatening him with court-martial if he ever spoke about the autopsy. Given the shell game underway with the President's body—the need to show it arriving in the Dallas casket to those who expected that to happen, and the need to shield this event from those who had seen it arrive earlier in a shipping casket—the atmosphere of paranoia which Metzler described to David Lifton, and the written threat subsequently issued to him by the Navy, are understandable.

As if all this was not disturbing enough, <u>the wording of the HSCA transcript during this one passage indicates that a portion of the conversation is likely missing from the transcript</u>. Note the ellipses in the following quotation from the Robinson transcript:

Robinson: The time that the people moved (autopsy). The body was taken....and the body never came....lots of little things like that.

The use of ellipses means that testimony is missing; it is a standard convention <u>for anyone typing a transcript or quoting another person</u>.

Furthermore, I do not know what the parenthesis around the word "autopsy" indicates, either. It is found in the HSCA transcript, and was not added by me.

But I do know one thing: when I asked my ARRB colleague, Eric Scheinkopf, to locate the audiotape of the HSCA staff interview of Tom Robinson, the tape he brought back with that label on it had something *entirely different recorded on it.* At the time, this seemed like a minor annoyance, and I grumbled about the suspected incompetence of the personnel in charge of copying the audiotape recordings at Archives II. I now wonder, in light of this epiphany years later, whether the original recording of Tom Robinson's interview still even exists. Some motivated JFK assassination researcher can perform a great service in clearing up this matter if he or she can find the actual Tom Robinson interview tape at the National Archives. This one sentence cries out for explanation and clarification.

When the ARRB interviewed Tom Robinson in June of 1996, we failed to ask about this statement of his; quite frankly, Jeremy and I missed its significance at the time. We were very much focused at the time on his description of the wound in the back of the head, and on the wound he described high in the right forehead, and the possible significance of the above passage escaped us completely. It only caught my attention at this writing, 10 years later in 2006, upon re-reading the Robinson transcript while writing this chapter.

Robinson's Recollections of Probes in the Body

Robinson was in the process of telling Purdy that he recalled the use of an 18 inch metal probe somewhere in the back of the body during the autopsy.

Purdy: Do you feel they probed the head or they probed the neck?

Robinson: *It was at the base of the head* where most of the damage was done, the things that we had to worry about. So it all runs together in my mind. [Author's emphasis]

Purdy: Did they probe with anything other than the 18 inch probe, either prior to or after the use of that probe? Did they use a shorter probe?

Robinson: I don't remember, I remember them probing.

Purdy: What is your impression as to either how far or in what direction they probed with that probe?

_____

Purdy: On this probe, do you remember if the probe went all the way through whatever they probed, do you remember—

Robinson: I don't recall.

The Back Wound

Tom Robinson gave his shakiest testimony to the HSCA staff about whether or not he remembered a back wound on the President's body, and whether or not that back wound was incised and opened up.

Purdy: Was there any other mark, hole or wound in [the] body [other than the tracheostomy and the head wounds Robinson had spoken of]?

Robinson: I saw the body turned over, it was turned over and examined on its side, rolled from each side. I saw nothing down below where the doctors had been working on the head.

Purdy: Did you see anything between the head wounds and the...on the back that could have been a wound? [Ellipse is in the HSCA transcript, and is not inserted by the author]

Robinson: No.

_____

Purdy: Specifically, when you say the body, you saw the back, I want to know specifically if either you know there was not a wound from the head down to the waist anywhere on the back, neck, or whatever, or that the autopsy work may have either obliterated it or made it not evident to you that there was such a wound?

Robinson: It might have done that, there was...but the back itself, there was no wound there, no. [Ellipse is in the HSCA transcript, and is not inserted by the author]

_____

Purdy: Let me just clear [up] one thing about the back. To what extent if any was that back area opened up? Or was that just all intact?

Robinson: No, it was opened up. The brain had to come out.

Purdy: I mean below that wound. *In other words the neck and the back.*   [Author's emphasis]

Robinson: It was well examined I recall.

Purdy: In the sense of being cut open or being looked at closely?

Robinson: *Yes, I mean looked at and cut.* [Author's emphasis]

Purdy: How big a cut? Where would the cut have gone from and to?

Robinson: I don't remember if it went off in many angles. It was not a nice clean cut.

Purdy: So there was a cut open in the neck to look in there?

Robinson: They had this all cut out. [Apparently referring to the enlarged tracheostomy incision seen in autopsy photographs.]

Purdy: How far down on the back of the neck did they cut open?

Robinson: That's what's bothering me*. I can't recall whether you would say they went into the back or not.* I remember seeing the back. [Author's emphasis]

Purdy: So you had to close up the work they did on the neck. You had to close that up?

Robinson: Yes, it seems to me that Ed [Stroble] did that.

Purdy: [Very skeptical by this point] So you don't recall anything.

Robinson: You can't have three needles in the same area, somebody is going to get it.

_____

Purdy: Do you remember any discussion of the possibility that there was a wound in that area? Is it your impression now that there was a wound in that area, *or was the only wound present on the back of the President was in [sic] the back of his head?* [Author's emphasis]

Robinson: No, I wouldn't say that.

Shortly after this exchange Purdy threw in the towel and terminated the interview.

Of course, if Robinson is correct that the wound high in the back was incised, was laid open by post mortem surgery at the autopsy in order to try to find a wound track, then all three pathologists have lied about this for years. But I just don't have a lot of confidence about Robinson's testimony in this one area.

Did the Pathologists Perform a Partial Craniotomy?

Twice during his interview Robinson stated he saw the pathologists opening up the back of the skull with a saw. This contradicted their consistent testimony over the years that they did not have to perform a standard craniotomy to get to the brain, and in fact did only a minimum of cutting to gain access to what was left of that organ.

Purdy: Where on his face were they shattered, which of the bones?

Robinson: You cannot see that on the outside. *This is looking through the opening that the physicians had made at the back of the skull.* [Author's emphasis]

Purdy: How big is that opening? Was it an official [?] opening?

Robinson: Well, there, of course, was an opening from the bullets, *but then they had enlarged that.* [Author's emphasis]

_____

Purdy: [asking about the posterior thorax]...to what extent if any was that back area opened up? Or was that just all intact?

Robinson: [misunderstanding] *No, it was opened up* [talking about the rear of the skull]. *The brain had to come out.* [Author's emphasis]

Tom Robinson would revisit this issue, and indicate what he meant with a diagram, during his ARRB interview.

The ARRB Staff Interviews Tom Robinson

This interview was conducted on June 21, 1996, just three days after Joe Hagan had led us to Tom Robinson, who had left Kentucky where he had formerly lived and was temporarily staying with friends in Maryland. Present were David Marwell, Jeremy Gunn, Tim Wray, and myself. Jeremy conducted most of the questioning, while I wrote as fast as I possibly could, to compensate for the fact that the interview was not being tape recorded.

Timeline Chronology

At our request, Mr. Robinson provided a chronology of events, to the best of his ability to remember, of the events of November 22-23, 1963 in which he was involved.

610

- He came to work about 4 PM on 11/22/63.
- Everyone at Gawler's thought President Kennedy's body would be coming to Gawler's; MDW had sent a military contingent to Gawler's funeral home, and military guards were posted at every door.
- About suppertime, the plans were changed. Joe Hagan told Robinson to "get the house grips—you're going to Navy." ("House grips" were defined by Robinson as portable embalming equipment.)
- He and Joe Hagan drove from Gawler's to Bethesda at extremely high speed in the Gawler's hearse. They transported in the hearse the new casket selected by Kennedy aides who had visited Gawler's, a Marcellus 710 model, made of plank mahogany. It was covered with an American flag when transported to Bethesda.
- Mr. Stroble and Mr. VanHoesen drove out to Bethesda in another vehicle, with the portable embalming equipment ("house grips"); they may have arrived subsequent to Hagan and Robinson.
- Robinson said he and Hagan arrived "early" in the autopsy, *before* the Y-incision had been made in the chest, and just as the gross examination of the head was starting.
- Work by the Gawler's team started "after midnight."
- He saw President Kennedy's body (in the mahogany Marcellus casket) leave Bethesda in the gray Navy ambulance before he left the premises himself.

Observations Regarding the Autopsy on President Kennedy

- Robinson told us he had seen approximately 50 autopsies prior to observing President Kennedy's.
- When asked by the ARRB staff, Robinson said he did see one other casket sometime that night aside from the Marcellus mahogany casket brought from Gawler's: he said it was a metallic, bronze casket which was copper-colored. He said this casket had a dent or break in the handle, where it was attached to the casket by lugs. (He had no recollection of what time of night he saw this casket or the damage to its handle.)
- He and Joe Hagan arrived "early in the autopsy,"meaning that he knew it had not been underway long because the chest incision had not been made yet, and the gross examination of the head was just beginning.
- Robinson said he had a "50 yard line seat" at the autopsy, and was leaning on the rail with his arms, from his seat in the gallery. He said the President's head was to his right, which means that he was on the anatomical left of the President during the autopsy. He said that most of the pathologists and their assistants were opposite him, on the anatomical right of the President during the autopsy. The gallery observers were behind him in the gallery; he had a seat in the front row.
- Robinson said the gallery was practically filled—that there were way too many people in the morgue. At one point in the interview, he said the atmosphere was like a "cocktail party," and at another point he said the atmosphere in the morgue was like a "circus." When asked to specify what he meant by those descriptions, he said that there were people there who clearly had no business being there, and that there was continuous and loud discussion from the gallery which he thought was both improper, and distracting. He said that a Federal agent (either Secret Service or FBI)

took him aside during the autopsy (after the head examination was well underway) and offered to get him some coffee, knowing that he was upset. Robinson said the agent told him that "it had to be this way" (in regard to having so many observers in the morgue), since there had to be "creditable witnesses" to the wounds observed and procedures performed during the autopsy, because "the world was watching."

- Robinson said the same agent claimed to be a ballistics expert, and showed him a glass vial, similar to a test tube (which may have had a cork stopper on it), containing several pieces of tiny bullet fragments which had been removed from President Kennedy's head by the pathologists, and that it contained "quite a few" fragments of shrapnel. Robinson said that these bullet fragments were very small. When asked by the ARRB staff whether the number of fragments was closer to 2, 5, 10, or 15 fragments, he said that the total number was close to 10 fragments.

- Robinson said that one man was definitely in charge of the autopsy, and that there was no doubt about that, but that he didn't know his name. When asked by the ARRB staff, he said he did not recall anyone trying to rush the pathologists.

- Robinson said that he saw the brain removed from President Kennedy's body, and that a large percentage of it was gone "in the back," from the "medulla," and that the portion of the brain that was missing was about the size of a closed fist. He described the condition of the brain in this damaged area as the consistency of "soup." He said the brain was not "cut up" at the autopsy. When he was asked whether the brain was weighed at the autopsy, he said "he was sure they did," but had no independent recollection of that happening.

- Robinson recalled the following visible damage to the skull which he interpreted as being caused by bullets (and not by the pathologists):

    - He saw two or three perforations or holes in the right cheek during embalming, when formaldehyde seeped through these small wounds and slight discoloration began to occur (and executed a drawing of this damage on the frontal portrait of President Kennedy taken by Robert Knudsen).[15]

    - He described a "blow-out" which consisted of a flap of skin in the right temple of the President's head, which he believed to be an exit wound based on conversations he heard in the morgue amongst the pathologists. (Robinson executed a drawing of this "blow-out" on an anatomical template of a right lateral view of a human skull from *Grant's Anatomy*—see Figure 27.)

    - He described a large, open head wound in the back of the President's head, centrally located right between the ears, where the bone was gone, as well as some scalp. He related his opinion that this large defect in the back of the President's head was an entry wound occurring from a bullet fired from behind, based upon conversations he heard in the morgue among the pathologists. Robinson annotated the approximate position and size of this

---

[15]Although not mentioned earlier in this chapter, this was consistent with his recollections to the HSCA staff in January of 1977.

large defect in the rear of the head on both the previously mentioned right lateral view of the human skull from *Grant's Anatomy* (see Figure 27), as well as on a *Grant's Anatomy* illustration of the posterior view of a human skull (see Figure 28). On the right lateral view of the skull (Figure 27), the posterior defect is much larger than the temporal defect that Robinson drew.

- Skull fractures: Robinson said that every bone in the President's face was broken, but that this could not be determined when viewing the body from the front. He also said that there were fractures all over the cranium, including the floor of the skull, saying on another occasion, "every bone in his head was broken." (It was unclear to me as a note-taker how much of this was observed by Robinson during the autopsy, and how much was observed during embalming and reconstruction.)
- When asked, Robinson said he had no recollection of any skull fragments being brought into the morgue during the autopsy.
- When asked, Robinson said he had no recollection of photography the night of the autopsy, one way or another—no recollection whatsoever.

- Removal of the President's brain: Robinson drew roughly horizontal dotted lines on the same posterior illustration of a human skull upon which he had drawn the large defect in the rear of the head (Figure 28). When asked what the dotted lines represented, he said "saw cuts." He explained that some sawing was done to remove some bone before the brain could be removed, and then went on to describe what is a normal craniotomy procedure, saying that this procedure was performed on JFK. He seemed to remember the use of a saw, and the scalp being reflected forward.
- Tracheostomy: Robinson remembered the tracheostomy wound in the anterior neck. In his opinion that wound represented the exit wound of a bullet.
- Use of Probes: Robinson had vivid recollections of a very long, malleable probe being used during the autopsy. *His most vivid recollection of this probe was seeing it inserted near the base of the brain in the back of the head (after removal of the brain), and seeing the tip of the probe come out of the tracheostomy incision in the anterior neck.* He was adamant about this recollection. He also remembers seeing the wound high in the back probed unsuccessfully, meaning that the probe inserted into the back wound did not exit anywhere. When asked, Robinson said he could not recall anything about the angle at which the probe went into the back wound (i.e., whether it was a steep angle or shallow angle).[16]

---

[16]This is more detail about the use of probes than Robinson recalled, or was willing to divulge, to the HSCA staff. The reader will have to keep this in mind when assessing Robinson's credibility. Did the process of being interviewed—and knowing for three days that he was going to be interviewed—refresh his recollections, or was he "remembering" things in his ARRB interview that never happened? There is significant corroboration for this recollection of his in the HSCA OCR of the staff interview with Richard Lipsey, which I will discuss in detail in Part II. (See Appendix 51.) Based upon the Lipsey recollections to the HSCA staff, I have concluded that all of Robinson's recollections to the ARRB staff about the

- Mr. Robinson said that he worked right over the President for over 3 hours, but that he was ***not*** the person who reconstructed the President's head; he said this was done by John VanHoesen.
- Embalming was done before reconstruction.
- The President suffered from some very slight blue discoloration under his eyes, but this area was not "black and blue" by any means; to Robinson this was evidence that President Kennedy "died instantly" after being shot. He based this opinion on his previous observations of autopsies and cadavers during embalming.
- Robinson said that Ed Stroble (now deceased) had cut out a piece of rubber to cover the open wound in the back of the head, so that the embalming fluid would not leak inside the casket; the piece of rubber was slightly larger than the hole in the back of the head, and Robinson estimated that the rubber sheet was a circular patch about the size of a large orange (demonstrating this with a circular motion, joining the index fingers and thumbs of his two hands).
- He said that the cranium was packed with material during reconstruction, but that he did not believe it was plaster-of-Paris; rather, he believed it was either cotton or kapok material used in conjunction with a hardening compound. The rubber sheet was used outside this material to close the wound in the area of the missing bone. The scalp was sutured together, and also into the rubber sheet to the maximum extent possible, and the damage to the back of the head was obscured by the pillow in the casket when the body lay in repose, so that upon completion of embalming and the application of restorative art, President Kennedy's body was ready for an open casket funeral, if one had been desired. No damage to the head could be seen once the Gawler's crew had finished their work and the President was lying in repose in the Marcellus casket; in this condition, President Kennedy's head was lying on a pillow in the casket, *turned slightly to the right.*[17]
- Robinson described in considerable detail the embalming procedures employed in regard to infusion of the thoracic region and the head with formaldehyde solution.
- He said that there was considerable pressure on the Gawler's crew to finish their work as soon as possible, and that it was coming from an Admiral. He recalled becoming upset by this, and being calmed down by Joe Hagan; he remembered responding to one impatient query about when they would be finished by saying, "You can't put on make-up with a barn brush!" He remembered with pride that

---

use of probes are credible, and *are* worthy of belief. I assessed Tom Robinson as a person who would likely have had no familiarity whatsoever with the HSCA OCR document releases (such as the Lipsey interview) that had occurred since August of 1993.

[17]This is significant to me. If the goal was to hide any damage to the head, the head would *have* to be turned "slightly to the right" on the pillow in the casket if the area of missing bone and scalp that could not be completely closed *was in the right rear of the skull behind the right ear,* where the treatment staff at Parkland hospital said it was located.

someone else in the morgue said that the President "looked good" when they had finished their work, and Robinson reiterated at this point that an open casket funeral could have been held if the Kennedy family had desired one.

- When asked whether the pathologists stayed in the morgue during the embalming and reconstructive work, he said they did not.

Robinson Comments On the "Fox Set" of Bootleg Autopsy Photographs

- After he completed his sketches of the President's head wounds on the anatomy illustrations, we showed Robinson my collection of what is alleged to be the "Fox Set" of bootleg autopsy photographs, which are all black-and-white 8" x 10" prints. Our goal was to see whether they were consistent with what he remembered seeing in the morgue at Bethesda. His comments follow, related to various photographs that he viewed:

  - Photos 5 and 6 ("right side of head and right shoulder"): Regarding this image of the so-called 'right superior profile,' he does not see the small shrapnel holes he noted in the right cheek, but he assumes this is because of the photo's poor quality. (See Figure 62.)
  - Photos 15 and 16 ("wound of entrance in right posterior occipital region"): Regarding this image of the 'intact back-of-the-head,' Robinson said "You see, this is the flap of skin, the blow-out in the right temple that I told you about, and which I drew in my drawing." When asked why this photograph does not show the hole in the back of the head that he had drawn on the posterior skull illustration (Figure 28), he put his finger just above the so-called "white spot" near the hairline in this photograph and said, "The hole was right here, where I said it was in my drawing, but it just doesn't show in this photo."[18] (See Figure 64.)

---

[18]The matter-of-fact way in which Robinson made this remark astonished all of us; he was so confident that his recollection of a large occipital wound was correct, that the fact that the photograph showed no hole in the rear of the head did not really bother him that much. He considered this a minor problem of no great concern, so confident was he in his recollection of a large occipital defect in the bone and scalp. Unlike Stringer and Riebe—who would later recant, under oath, about their earlier recollections of an occipital defect—Tom Robinson was *not* willing to disregard his memories, to modify his recollections of the President's wounds, just because they were contradicted by a set of photographs. I now wonder if perhaps the reason Robinson was not that disturbed by the image we showed him of the intact back of the head was because he was a member of the embalming team that performed the *reconstruction of President Kennedy's skull,* and applied restorative art to the body? He saw the damage to the skull repaired by Mr. Stroble, and helped prepare the body for an open casket funeral, so rather than viewing the photograph as a 'contradiction' of the damage he saw at the autopsy, he may have viewed it as simply a *confirmation* of the restorative efforts of his own team later that evening. If this explanation of mine is correct, it has major implications for what the

- Photos 7, 8, 9, and 10 ("superior view of head"): Robinson frowned when he looked at these views of the top of the head, and said in disagreement, "This makes it look like the wound was in the top of the head." He explained that the damage in this photograph was "what the doctors did," and explained that they cut his scalp open and reflected it back in order to remove bullet fragments—the fragments he observed in a glass vial. ARRB staff members asked Robinson whether there was damage to the top of the head when he arrived at the morgue and before the brain was removed; he replied by saying that this area was "all broken," but it was not open like the wound in the back of the head. (See Figure 61.)
  - Photos 13 and 14 ("right anterior view of head and upper torso, including tracheostomy wound"): Robinson examined the so-called "stare-of-death" photo and said that the tracheostomy in this photograph was consistent with what he saw in the morgue. (See Figure 60.)

Gawler's Documents

- First Call Sheet: Robinson said he had seen this document previously; upon closer examination, he recognized some of the handwriting as his own, specifically, the sections labeled "Dressing" and "Remarks" at the top of the page. We asked him to explain what the entry "2 AM" meant on the bottom third of the page in the section called "Casket Delivery Details." He said that the time "2 AM" is "not right," i.e., is incorrect, since he knows he and Joe Hagan arrived with the Marcellus casket early in the autopsy.
  - Arrangements File: Robinson said the times of "11:45" and "3:30" looked like they were written in Joe Hagan's handwriting. He said the body chart on the page entitled "Embalmer's Report" would normally have been filled in by Gawler's personnel, and he did not know why it had not been filled in for President Kennedy. (There are no wounds of any kind annotated on the body chart in the Gawler's Arrangements File.)

Tom Robinson's recollections in 1996 were remarkably consistent with his recollections when he was interviewed by the HSCA staff in 1977, nineteen and one-half years previously. I would assess his overall credibility, and the reliability of his recollections, as very high. As I write this chapter today, I am puzzled that none of us on the ARRB staff asked Mr. Robinson about the small wound in the upper right forehead which he told the HSCA staff had been obscured by the hair, and which he had probably filled with wax during the application of restorative art. Clearly, we forgot to cover this—and yet his words from more than 19 years previously, when his memory was presumably much better, are preserved on the HSCA transcript, since their staff made a tape recording of his interview. In this one respect—in their decision to tape record the interview—they outperformed the ARRB staff when they interviewed Mr. Robinson.

---

pictures of the back of the head *really portray,* and for when they were created.

616

JOHN VAN HOESEN

Jeremy Gunn and I drove down to a remote, "country" location in Maryland called Cobb Island on September 25, 1996 to interview the third surviving member of the Gawler's team, John VanHoesen. Once again, I found myself taking copious notes, since Jeremy claimed to have forgotten the office's portable tape recorder; only this time it was more difficult, since I was also conducting the interview, with only occasional assistance from Jeremy.

Mr. VanHoesen was most cordial, and welcomed us with great hospitality to his somewhat rustic cabin on Cobb Island, on Chesapeake Bay. His memories of the events of November 22-23, 1963 were generally not sharp, and perhaps the least firm, of the three Gawler's personnel we interviewed. Nevertheless, he was firm about some recollections, as noted below, and the interview yielded valuable evidence.

Mr. VanHoesen (who pronounced his name "VanHeusen") stated that he worked for Gawler's from 1950-1987, when he retired at the age of 62 to care for his ailing wife. He described his duties at Gawler's in 1963 as those of a "service man," meaning that although he would assist with embalming when required, his primary duties were to ensure that the bodies of the deceased were properly dressed prior to funerals, and that the details of each funeral service were arranged as desired by the customer.

He first heard about the assassination of President Kennedy on television, and went home to eat his dinner. At the time he went home to eat he suspected he would be involved with President Kennedy's funeral preparations, but he was not sure. He said that only when he came back to work about 6 PM on 11/22/63, did he realize that Gawler's had been officially tasked to prepare President Kennedy for burial. He said that he went to Bethesda Naval hospital in a vehicle with Joe Gawler, and that they carried part of the portable embalming equipment with them in their vehicle. When asked whether Tom Robinson was in his vehicle, he said he did not think so. He verified that part of the portable equipment was in another vehicle. He said that he would estimate he and Joe Gawler arrived at Bethesda about 7:30 PM on November 22nd. He described a scene of confusion in and around the morgue, with many people running around, "like a Chinese fire drill," as he so colorfully put it. He said that there were too many people in the morgue during the autopsy, and that access to the morgue seemed to him to be virtually unrestricted. He repeated this observation twice more during the interview, and each time stated that in this respect—overcrowding and easy access—it was unlike any other autopsy he ever attended. *Initially, upon arrival, he said that he and Mr. Gawler had to wait in the anteroom (where the chill boxes were)* because initially, no one knew who they were, or why they were there. (See Figure 40.)

I wonder today whether he and Mr. Gawler were kept out of the morgue while the President's body was being reintroduced into the bronze Dallas casket. The arrival time he recalled, about 7:30 PM, is during the period *after* Sibert, O'Neill, Kellerman, and Greer unloaded the Dallas casket and first brought it into the hospital on a dolly, and *before* the Joint Service Casket Team brought it into the Morgue at 8:00 PM, per the MDW summary report of the casket team's activities. His statement that they were not admitted into the morgue initially is at odds with his recollection of almost unrestricted access that night; I therefore conclude that he and Mr. Gawler were kept out for a good reason. Once the body of the President had been reintroduced into the Dallas casket and publicly brought in by the Casket Team for audience two to witness, access to the morgue may very well have opened up considerably, for by then the illusion of the proper "chain of custody" had been restored by the 8:00 PM casket entry in the bronze casket.

Mr. VanHoesen said he and Joe Gawler went into the morgue proper about 8 o'clock, before any of the normal autopsy procedures had begun. He said that there were three tiers of benches in the morgue gallery, and that he sat on the back bench. When asked whether he sat with Tom Robinson, he said he did not think so. When specifically asked whether any incisions had been made yet, he said "no." His recollection on this was quite firm. He said that initially, several people were crowded around the autopsy table examining the body, and in this connection he vaguely recalled discussions about whether or not a full autopsy was really necessary. He said he could not recall the appearance of President Kennedy's head wounds at the beginning of the autopsy, and had a hard time seeing what was happening during the course of the autopsy, because of the number of people crowded around the examination table and directly involved in the autopsy procedures. VanHoesen was positive that he was present when the autopsy proper—the incisions—actually began. (Presumably he was referring to the y-incision in the chest, which was made at 8:15 PM.)

Mr. VanHoesen independently recalled that the President's body had arrived in a black, zippered, "plastic pouch" inside a casket. Initially, when he recounted this memory, he said he actually saw the President's body removed from this black, plastic pouch and placed on the autopsy table. During subsequent questioning about this recollection, **he confirmed that what he saw was a body bag,** and that it was made of plastic, not cloth. Upon further discussion, he said he was not sure whether he actually saw the body removed from the body bag, or saw the body on the table immediately after it had been removed; in any case, **he was firm about his recollection of seeing a black, zippered body bag inside the President's casket,** and was of the definite opinion that President Kennedy's body had been inside the body bag. When asked whether the body was nude when removed, or wrapped in sheets, he said he thought it was wrapped in sheets, or partially wrapped in sheets, but was much less sure of this recollection than he was of the presence of a black body bag, which he confidently recalled.

Mr. VanHoesen independently recalled that some lugs were broken on one of the handles of the President's casket.

When asked what he recalled about the autopsy beyond the President's wrappings and the condition of the casket, he could recall very little. When asked, he had a vague recollection of photography during the autopsy, but could not recall why he remembered photography, not any details such as how many photographers, types of photos taken, types of cameras, or numbers of photos taken. He could not remember anything about use of probes during the autopsy, or about the condition of the President's head, or the size and location of the head wounds prior to the commencement of autopsy incisions or procedures, nor could he remember anything about statements made or conclusions reached by the autopsy pathologists. He could remember no details about autopsy procedures.

He recalled that the Gawler's team—Mr. Hagan, Mr. Stroble, Mr. Robinson, and himself—began its work about midnight. He could not remember anything about the condition of the President's head at the beginning of the embalming process, nor could he remember anything, one way or the other, about any wounds on the back of the President's body. In response to this question, he said, "I'm not sure we turned the body over." He could not remember whether photographs were taken during the embalming and reconstruction process. When asked what his role was on the Gawler's team, he said that he worked on the body cavity and the legs, and did not touch anything above the neck. VanHoesen said that the work on the body included the removal of all organs from the thoracic and abdominal cavity, preserving them in a bucket of formaldehyde, placing them in a plastic bag, and returning them to the body cavity inside the plastic bag. He said that he stitched up the body cavity following completion of this process. *He said that Mr. Stroble (now deceased) performed the reconstruction of the President's head, not him.* VanHoesen described Joe Hagan as the Services Manager, described himself as the Assistant Services Manager, described Tom Robinson as an Arrangements Man, and described Mr. Stroble as a full-time embalmer. The persons who directly participated in hands on work—embalming, reconstruction, and preparation for burial—were Stroble, Robinson, and himself.

When asked to recall the condition of the President's head at the *completion* of the embalming and reconstruction process, Mr. Van Hoesen recalled that there was a section of material missing from the skull—either scalp, or bone, he was just not sure which, this many years later. *He described the size and location of the missing skull material as follows:* **it was roughly the size of a small orange** *(as he demonstrated by gesturing with his hands),* **located in the center of the back of the head, and its elevation was in the upper posterior part of the skull** *(which he demonstrated by placing the palm of his right hand on the upper rear portion of his own head, just at or below the so-called "cowlick" area).* He independently recalled one of the doctors at Bethesda bringing back what he described as a sheet of plastic for the Gawler's team to use in covering the area of missing material to prevent leakage.

At the conclusion of the embalming and reconstruction process, the President's body was wrapped in plastic, and then dressed in clothes which had been brought to the morgue from elsewhere. *He said that the damaged area on the back of the President's head was not visible as the President lay supine in the casket with his head on the pillow; the pillow obscured the remaining defect in the back of the head.*[19]

As the entourage left Bethesda, he said he and John Gawler were in the lead car, and the hearse which the President's new casket was in [i.e., a gray Navy ambulance] followed his car all the way to the White House. He said the pace was very slow and stately (the speed of a walking horse, he was told), and that there were policemen on every corner.

Mr. VanHoesen's most vivid recollections seemed to be of opening the mahogany casket in the East Room of the White House so that Jacqueline Kennedy could view the body. He said he recalled that she came back down the stairs after the casket was in place on the bier in the East Room, and that he was quite surprised that she was still wearing the same pink suit she had worn during the assassination. He said he personally opened the casket, and it was quickly closed after a brief

---

[19]This observation was 100 per cent consistent with Tom Robinson's recollection.

viewing. Persons he recalled as present during this viewing included Mrs. Kennedy, Joe Gawler, himself, "some artist" (meaning a commercial artist—someone had told him it was Andy Warhol), and possibly a priest. When asked whether Robert Kennedy was present during this viewing, he said "no." When asked whether there was any locking device on the casket, he said there was not.

At our request Mr. VanHoesen reviewed the Gawler's business documents. He said that the term "shipping casket" on the first call sheet probably meant whatever casket the body was transported from Dallas in.[20]

A TENTATIVE, COMBINED GAWLER'S/AUTOPSY TIMELINE

Below I have listed my best attempt to make coherent sense out of both "Gawler's events" and other key events known to have occurred at the autopsy; it will be followed by a discussion of how I resolved certain conflicts within the testimony of the three surviving members of the Gawler's team sent to Bethesda NNMC on the evening of November 22-23, 1963. This is the first introduction of the reader of this work to an autopsy timeline analysis. A much more detailed timeline analysis of autopsy events will be revisited in Part II of this book, when I will make a comprehensive attempt to explain and reconstruct *all* critical events the night of the autopsy. The reader's patience is solicited here, for I have listed below as "facts" certain conclusions of mine which will be justified in detail at a later point in the text; this was necessary in order to place certain Gawler's testimony in the proper context and render the proper significance to these Gawler's recollections.

Time	Event
4:25 PM (11/22/63)	Colonel Miller of MDW calls the Gawler's funeral home and tasks them with all embalming and restorative art necessary for a funeral, and with having a hearse at Andrews AFB for "wheels down" of Air Force One; the plan at that time was to drive the body directly to Gawler's funeral home.[21]
About 5:30 PM	The "Death Watch," a contingent of the U.S. Army's Old Guard from Fort Myer, arrives at Gawler's, establishes a "command post," a

---

[20]The reader should remember here that it was Joe Hagan, to whom the subject of caskets was "radioactive," who had located VanHoesen by telephone, before passing on his location to the ARRB staff. As Joe Hagan told me on the phone the previous June, they had compared their respective memories of events the weekend of the assassination. It would not surprise me if Hagan had steered VanHoesen away from any possible casket controversy.

[21]The time is listed on the First Call Sheet, and is the same time Joe Hagan gave us in his interview; it was no doubt part of his standard 'Kennedy presentation' that he gave when requested to speak of those events, and he undoubtedly took this time from the same document.

security perimeter, and begins rehearsing for its ceremonial tasks.[22]

Undetermined	Colonel Miller countermands his order to send a hearse to Andrews AFB "at the last minute," explaining that a Navy ambulance will be used instead. It is unclear whether Gawler's actually sent a hearse to Andrews or not.
About 6:40 PM	A shipping casket with JFK's body inside (wrapped in a body bag, nude except for the head, which is wrapped in a sheet[23]) is taken inside the morgue from a black hearse which arrives at the loading dock filled with "men in suits" who observe while the Navy sailors supervised by HM1 Dennis David transport the casket to the anteroom outside the morgue. The sailors and supervisor Dennis David then depart.[24]
Undetermined	The series of skull x-rays must have been taken approximately 30-45 minutes after the body's arrival (and no later) in order to allow time for their development and viewing, and to permit time for Dr. Humes to call Pierre Finck on the phone and ask him to participate in the autopsy—telling him, in the process, that he had a 'good set of skull films.'
About 6:55 PM	Jerrol Custer, possibly carrying the x-ray cassettes for 5 skull x-rays—or possibly after being dismissed from the morgue for about 15 minutes *prior* to the exposure of the skull films—sees Jackie Kennedy in the Bethesda lobby (while on his way upstairs to the x-ray department, accompanied by a Secret Service agent) as she enters the hospital, enroute the 17th floor VIP suite. Custer has already seen the body of President Kennedy in the morgue; this proves that the Dallas casket, which remains out in front of the main entrance, sitting in the

---

[22]Sources for this entry are both Joe Hagan's interview, and *Death of a President,* by William Manchester.

[23]Paul O'Connor has consistently recalled that when removed from the body bag, the President's body was nude and his head was wrapped in a sheet. Like his colleague Dennis David, O'Connor also consistently recalled, over the years, seeing the President arrive in a shipping casket.

[24]Dennis David provided this information and the approximate time to David Lifton in 1979, and to the ARRB in 1997. The exact time of this event will later be pinpointed as 6:35 PM, based upon a key document provided to the ARRB by the Marine Corps sergeant in charge of the Marine Barracks security detail, which will be discussed in detail in Chapter 8. (See Figure 68.)

gray Navy ambulance just vacated by JBK, must be empty.[25]

About 6:55 PM	Dennis David, in an office on the second floor, also sees JBK enter the lobby at the same time Custer does down in the lobby. This also proves that the Dallas casket is empty, since David's sailors have already unloaded the shipping casket (with the body bag inside) at the morgue loading dock in the rear of the hospital.
Undetermined	Tom Robinson and Joe Hagan arrive at the morgue (without the mahogany casket, which was chosen later in the evening); they arrive before VanHoesen and Joe Gawler, but how much earlier is unclear.
About 7:07 PM	Secret Service agent Greer, the driver of the Navy ambulance with the empty Dallas casket inside, follows Sibert and O'Neill back to the morgue loading dock.[26]
7:10-7:17 PM	Sibert, O'Neill, Kellerman, and Greer place the empty casket on a dolly and wheel it either *into the morgue,* or *into the morgue anteroom.* (See Figure 40, a diagram of the Bethesda morgue in 1963, prepared by Paul O'Connor in 1992.) The empty bronze casket is not immediately opened. If the Dallas casket was really taken into the morgue proper, as O'Neill testified to the ARRB, then it means President Kennedy's body was simply temporarily removed from sight; there was ample opportunity for this, given that a shower room and chemical room were adjacent to the morgue. A tight security is placed around the morgue area, and Sibert and O'Neill, under protest, are forced to stay outside by the Secret Service and the Marine Corps security detail. They have lost sight of the body, and its chain of custody has been broken, something they implied rather obliquely in their report 4 days later, but to which they would not openly admit, to

---

[25]Whether he had x-rays in his arms or not is irrelevant. If Custer had already seen the President's body when he went upstairs, then the Dallas casket which had just arrived with Mrs. Kennedy had to be empty. Ed Reed said that he and Custer were dismissed early in the autopsy for about 15 minutes, then called back down to the morgue. Custer might have seen JBK *after* being dismissed and *before* taking x-rays, *or* he might have seen her *after* taking the series of skull x-rays while carrying the films upstairs to be developed. The import is the same, because *he did not go upstairs until after he had seen President Kennedy's body arrive*.

[26]Secret Service agent Clint Hill wrote in his report that the Andrews motorcade arrived in front of Bethesda NNMC at 6:55 PM, and a local newspaper recorded that the ambulance sat out front and was not driven around to the rear of the hospital until twelve minutes later. The time of 7:07 PM is twelve minutes later.

either the HSCA or the ARRB.[27]

After 7:17 PM — While Sibert, O'Neill, and the early shipping casket/body bag audience (O'Connor, Jenkins, Riebe, Reed, and Custer) are outside the morgue, the President's body is reintroduced into the Dallas casket. The body bag has been discarded and the body has been rewrapped in two sheets, reproducing the same condition it was in when it left Dallas.[28]

About 7:30 PM — John VanHoesen and Joseph H. Gawler ("Joe"), the owner of the funeral home,[29] arrive at Bethesda and are kept waiting in the anteroom where the chill boxes are located.

After 7:30 PM — The Dallas casket, now reunited with the body of President Kennedy, is either hurriedly wheeled on a dolly, or carelessly carried, out to a clandestine rendezvous with one of the two Navy ambulances in use that night, damaging it in the process. (In the process its sides become badly scratched, are dented, and one of the handles is broken completely off of the coffin—and later becomes item # 1 on the Burkley inventory dated April 26, 1965.) Numerous people at the autopsy vividly remember seeing the damage to the casket when they saw it in the morgue that evening.[30]

---

[27]Admiral Galloway confirmed to David Lifton, per *Best Evidence,* that the FBI agents *were* kept outside the morgue for a period of time. Similarly, Dr. Humes, per the CBS News memo from Richter to Midgley in 1967, told his neighbor that the FBI agents were absent from the morgue *throughout the autopsy;* this is clearly an exaggeration, but it does indicate to me that there was a period of time that they were *not* present.

[28]The time of 7:17 PM is obtained from a March 12, 1964 internal FBI document in which Sibert and O'Neill recounted to their superiors Arlen Specter's questions to them, and their answers to him, in an interview earlier that day. They described 7:17 as the time of "preparations for the autopsy." By inference, this is the approximate time they were barred from entering the morgue. (See Appendix 18.)

[29]Joe Gawler, the owner and proprietor of the funeral home that bore his name, should not be confused with his son, John P. Gawler, who signed the receipt for the bronze Dallas casket when GSA picked it up from the funeral home on March 19, 1964.

[30]William Manchester incorrectly reports in *Death of a President* that the casket was damaged when it was taken aboard Air Force One at Love Field. David Lifton exhaustively documented in *Best Evidence* that the damage to the bronze casket was *first observed* as it was taken from a Navy ambulance into the Bethesda morgue at 8:00 PM by the Joint Service Casket Team. (The bronze casket was *not* observed to be damaged when taken off of Air Force One earlier in the evening.) It seems obvious today that the casket was dropped—with

8:00 PM	The Joint Service Casket Team carries the Dallas casket into the morgue, presumably through the morgue door that opens onto the hallway (see Figure 40). Sibert and O'Neill are either being held in the anteroom with the chill boxes (along with VanHoesen and Gawler), or are sequestered in an office nearby, awaiting permission to enter the morgue and observe the autopsy. One member of the casket team (Sergeant Felder) and HM3 James Metzler have both recalled witnessing the Dallas casket being opened, and seeing JFK's body inside, wrapped in sheets. Metzler assists other Navy personnel in placing the President's body on the autopsy examination table.
About 8:02 PM	Sibert and O'Neill are admitted to the morgue *after* the casket team brings the Dallas casket into the morgue; they do not see the honor guard bring in the casket, but they do see the bronze casket sitting on the floor with the lid open. They see Navy personnel place President Kennedy's body on the examination table, and like HM3 Metzler, see the wrappings (two sheets) removed. They do not realize the heavy bronze casket was empty when they brought it into the morgue shortly before 7:17 PM, and do not know that it has just been reintroduced into the morgue by the Joint Service Casket Team. They later attribute the apparent delay in the casket opening to "preparations for the autopsy," which is evidence that they were given a cover story about why they could not enter the morgue and stay with the body initially.
About 8:05 PM	VanHoesen and Joe Gawler are first admitted to the morgue, and the early shipping casket/body bag audience (O'Connor, Jenkins, Riebe, and Stringer) are readmitted to the morgue. The President's body is on the examining table. VanHoesen sees a zippered body bag inside the morgue—either inside the shipping casket, if the conspirators were so careless as to not remove that item—or perhaps inside the bronze Dallas casket, placed there intentionally to confuse the memories of those who had earlier seen a body bag inside the shipping casket. VanHoesen assumes that the President, who is lying nude upon the examination table, had just been removed from the body bag.
8:15 PM	The 'first incision'—the y-incision in the chest—is made on the body,

the President's body inside—when it was hurriedly being loaded into the second Navy ambulance in use that night, prior to being driven back around to the front of the Naval hospital so that it could be "found" by the Casket Team. The Joint Service Casket Team had lost track of it earlier in the evening while chasing an empty 'decoy ambulance' in the dark in a pickup truck. (For details of the 'ambulance chase,' see David Lifton's *Best Evidence.*)

per Sibert and O'Neill. (It is the first incision they witness, but not necessarily the first incision made on the body that night.) They consider this time of 8:15 PM to be the start of the autopsy.

8:30 PM   Dr. Finck arrives; the lungs, heart, and brain have all been removed prior to his arrival, per his 1965 report to General Blumberg.

Undetermined   Joe Hagan likely returns to Gawler's funeral home to deal with the selection of a casket by the four Kennedy aides, the "Irish Mafia." (Tom Robinson may have accompanied him on this return trip, which could explain why Robinson has no recollection of seeing skull bone fragments brought to the morgue late that evening by the Secret Service.)

Between 11-12 PM   A large fragment of skull bone, measuring 10 x 6.5 cm, with beveling on the exterior surface, is brought to the morgue by the Secret Service. It is considered crucial evidence of a bullet's exit, and features prominently in both the autopsy report, and in the FBI agents' report about the autopsy.

About 12:00 PM   Kennedy aides Larry O'Brien, Dave Powers, Kenny O'Donnell, and Muggsy O'Leary arrive at Gawler's funeral home and select the Marcellus 710 model hand-rubbed, plank mahogany casket.[31]

Undetermined   Joe Hagan and John Gawler (Joe's son) race back to the Bethesda morgue in a hearse at high speed, with the mahogany casket. (Tom Robinson may be with them.) Hagan witnesses the last 20 minutes or so of the autopsy; he sees the head of President Kennedy supported on a block—not by the metal stirrup or headrest seen in many of the post mortem photographs.

NLT 12:30 AM   Sibert and O'Neill depart and the morticians commence their work.

3:30-3:45 AM   The Gawler's team finishes its work.[32]

---

[31] In *Death of a President,* Manchester makes clear that Dave Powers wrote down the time that the new casket was selected—"about midnight"—in his diary.

[32] A Joe Hagan entry in the Arrangements File reads "3:30" but is not explained. The Gawler's internal history of that weekend says that they finished their work at 4:00 AM, but that cannot be accurate because the precise time the motorcade left Bethesda was at 3:56 AM. The Kennedy entourage needed time to come downstairs after completion of the work, so 3:30 to 3:45 AM is the most likely estimate of when the Gawler's team finished its work.

| 3:56 AM | Jacqueline Kennedy and her husband's body depart Bethesda Naval hospital for the White House in a light gray Navy ambulance. |

Timeline Discussion

First, Tom Robinson is probably *correct* in remembering that he went to Bethesda early with Joe Hagan, since Hagan was the supervisor; but he is almost certainly *incorrect* in his recollection that they had the Marcellus casket with them when they arrived at the morgue. Both Joe Hagan (in his recollections to the ARRB) and Dave Powers (in his diary) indicated that the new casket was selected very late in the evening. This also means that Hagan must have returned to Gawler's to be present when the Kennedy aides made their selection; he simply doesn't remember going back, that's all. Furthermore, he only remembers his *return trip* with the new casket—not his *first trip* much earlier that evening with Tom Robinson.

Second, Tom Robinson may very well have accompanied Joe Hagan when Mr. Hagan went back to Gawler's to assist the Kennedy aides. Not only are almost all of his recollections of the autopsy from very early during that examination, but he has a vivid memory of driving to Bethesda with *both* Joe Hagan *and* the Marcellus casket. If Robinson was indeed with Hagan on his return trip with the mahogany casket, Hagan does not remember Robinson; instead, he remembers John Gawler being with him. Remembering that John Gawler was with him does not necessarily mean that Robinson was *not* in the hearse also.

Third, the "2 AM" entry on the First Call Sheet would normally trump a human recollection, but not in this case. Both Joe Hagan and Dave Powers recollected the casket selection taking place near midnight; and both Joe Hagan and Tom Robinson were convinced that the "2 AM" entry was wrong. Late in his ARRB interview, Mr. Hagan noted that not only did several persons make different entries on the First Call Sheet, but that some entries were made 2 or 3 days later. This probably explains the erroneous "2 AM" entry in the section titled "Casket Delivery Details."

Finally, we can be sure that Tom Robinson was present in the morgue quite early for two reasons:

1. He was present before any incisions were made.

2. He told the HSCA staff that he had some memories that "the body was taken," and then said that "it never came." This strongly implies he was present in the morgue *before* about 7:10 PM, when the empty Dallas casket was first brought to the morgue to be reunited with the body. The whole purpose of that exercise was to take the casket (with the body now back inside) outside the morgue and allow the Casket Team to "find it," so they could carry it into the morgue with the proper ceremony, as was their duty. Unfortunately for the plotters, this meant that the body of the President would be absent from the morgue for a good many minutes, and ran the risk of the wrong people noticing, if the morgue audiences and the movements of the body were not stage-managed properly. Robinson must have been aware that the President's body had been taken away from the morgue; must have wondered where it was being taken and why; and the amount of time it was missing—probably 30 or

35 minutes—must have seemed an eternity to him, amplifying his anxiety considerably. No wonder he told the HSCA staff over 13 years later that he knew some things he had read were incorrect, saying "...the time the people moved [the?] (autopsy)...the body was taken...and the body never came...lots of little things like that."

A final implication of Robinson's awareness that something was amiss is that the person who accompanied him to Bethesda—his supervisor, Joe Hagan—was probably just as aware of all this as he was, unless he was in conference elsewhere with Secret Service or Navy officials. Even if Hagan did not directly witness the temporary disappearance of the body from the examination table as Robinson apparently did, no doubt Robinson shared his apprehensions with Hagan, his supervisor, later that evening, and likely asked him what was afoot. Whether Hagan was directly aware of a shell game with the body, or only indirectly aware through Robinson's queries, this could explain his extreme reluctance to discuss any casket issues with the ARRB staff, and his feeble and unconvincing attempts to belittle the significance of the "shipping casket" entry on the First Call Sheet. I am reasonably convinced that Joe Hagan either saw the shipping casket himself early that evening, or Tom Robinson did, and told him about it. Since Tom Robinson only described the bronze Dallas casket to the ARRB staff, it seems even more likely that Hagan saw the shipping casket *himself,* which would explain why the entry is in *his handwriting.* Hagan's admitted familiarity with Lifton's book *Best Evidence* tells me that he fully understood the implications of having seen a shipping casket, and why he was reluctant to discuss it: he just didn't want to get involved in an assassination controversy at his advanced age, and knew he was "trapped" by his own words, written down on a Gawler's document over 35 years previously. Hence, his reluctance to speak to us unless we issued him a subpoena. Even then, in spite of the legal requirement to bring all records related to the assassination with him, he did *not* bring the First Call Sheet with the "shipping casket" entry, or the two other items related to the bronze Dallas casket. In the final analysis, Mr. Hagan's claim to have "lost" these documents is not really credible, nor are his attempts to distance himself from the "shipping casket" entry that he placed himself on the Gawler's First Call Sheet.

THE SIGNIFICANCE OF THE KEY GAWLER'S TESTIMONY

The recollections of the three surviving Gawler's employees interviewed by the ARRB staff (1) provide confirmation of a posterior skull defect; (2) provide explosive new evidence about the possibility of post-mortem tampering with President Kennedy's wounds at Bethesda Naval hospital *prior to* the formal commencement of the autopsy; and (3) provide additional support to the existing pattern of evidence that President Kennedy's body did not make an uninterrupted journey from Parkland hospital to the Bethesda morgue.

Confirmation of a Posterior Head Wound

One undeniable effect of the testimony of the surviving Gawler's personnel is its corroboration that there *really was* a large defect at the rear of President Kennedy's head, thus reinforcing both the collective observations of the Parkland hospital treatment personnel, and the recollections of Navy photographer's mate Saundra Spencer. The recollections of a posterior head wound by the Dallas physicians and nurses were a "before autopsy" lens, and the recollections of Saundra Spencer of a posterior head wound that could not be closed were an "after autopsy lens," since her testimony reveals that she clearly developed images of the cleaned-up body of the President, taken after embalming and reconstruction were completed. The recollections of the Gawler's personnel reinforce both of these lenses, as explained below.

Tom Robinson's recollections are a "before autopsy" lens, in the sense that he described the appearance of the President's head wounds *prior to* the time Dr. Humes made any incisions on the head. John VanHoesen provided a "post autopsy" lens, since he recalled the pattern of damage *still present* after the embalming and reconstruction was completed. The recollections of both men—that there was a large defect in the posterior skull—confirm that the autopsy photographs showing the back of the head to be intact are an attempt to conceal, rather than reveal: that they are evidence of a medical coverup.

Was Post Mortem Surgery of the Head Area Performed at Bethesda Naval Hospital to Obtain Access to the Brain and Alter the Appearance of the Exit Wound in the Skull Prior to the Start of the Autopsy?

Both x-ray technician Ed Reed *and* Gawler's mortician Tom Robinson witnessed autopsy pathologists using a saw on President Kennedy's cranium, in the apparent performance of a craniotomy, and vividly described this to the ARRB staff. (This is highly significant because Drs. Humes and Boswell have uniformly testified for years that it was *not necessary* to perform a craniotomy to remove President Kennedy's brain; furthermore, Navy autopsy technicians Paul O'Connor and James Jenkins, who normally performed the craniotomy themselves at Navy autopsies, told the HSCA staff that they could not remember seeing one performed at the autopsy.) If Reed and Robinson are correct in their recollections, it means that O'Connor and Jenkins had been excluded from the morgue when this took place, and Humes and Boswell committed perjury, in order to hide the fact that they may have gained access to the brain early in the evening before the autopsy officially began.

The Surgery Witnessed by Ed Reed

Ed Reed testified at his ARRB deposition (see pages 57-58 of the transcript) that at one point during the evening of November 22, 1963 he witnessed Dr. Humes make an incision across the "forehead" near the hairline, and then employ a circular mechanical saw to the cranium in this same area—and that shortly after this procedure had begun, he and his instructor, Jerrol Custer, were abruptly ordered to leave the morgue. Since extant autopsy photographs *do not* show that the "forehead" *per se* was opened up, but *do* show an enormous head wound in the top of the head beginning *just behind the hairline,* in the *frontal bone,* in an area directly *above* what laymen call "the forehead"—and since the extant skull x-rays *do* show considerable skull bone missing from the top of the head commencing just behind the hairline *in the frontal bone*—it seems clear that Ed Reed's recollections of seeing Humes use a saw on the forward part of the cranium are accurate. The next consideration is timing: when did this occur?

Since Reed did *not* recall seeing the y-incision in the chest, but *did* recall seeing Dr. Humes commencing post mortem surgery on the President's skull before he and Custer were summarily dismissed from the morgue, I conclude that he was describing an event he witnessed *very early in the evening,* shortly after the arrival of the body. I believe his testimony to the ARRB that this occurred later in the evening is simply temporal distortion of his memory of *when* this happened that night; the key marker for this event, in my view, is that it occurred *before* the y-incision.

We know that the x-rays of the skull were taken before any other x-rays, and well before Dr. Finck arrived at 8:30 PM, and that the 3 surviving skull x-rays in evidence today show considerable bone to be missing from the top of the skull. Therefore, I conclude that <u>Reed observed post mortem surgery to the skull **prior** to the taking of *any* skull x-rays.</u> Both Jerrol Custer and Ed Reed testified to the ARRB that they were ordered to leave the morgue early in the evening shortly after the body arrived and before any x-rays were taken, and Ed Reed testified to the ARRB (see page 32 of the transcript) that they were only gone approximately 15 minutes before they were recalled by a phone call from Dr. Ebersole. Based upon an arrival time for the body of 6:35 PM (per the Boyajian report—see Appendix 38), this short absence would have allowed the x-ray technicians plenty of time to return to the morgue (after the hurried craniotomy was performed), and take the series of 5 skull x-rays remembered by Custer, *prior* to the time President Kennedy's body was reintroduced into the Dallas casket—which occurred sometime between 7:17 PM (the latest possible time the Dallas casket was brought to the morgue by the FBI and Secret Service agents) and 8:00 PM (when we know it was reintroduced by the Joint Service Casket Team). After the skull x-rays were developed, they were viewed in the morgue by Ebersole, Humes, and Boswell; and Dr. Humes had sufficient time to call Dr. Finck on the telephone and request his assistance, while telling him that he already had a good set of head films. All of this happened in sufficient time for Dr. Finck to arrive at 8:30 PM, and to find that the brain, heart, and lungs had all been removed, facts that he later recorded for General Blumberg in 1965.

Succinctly put, if the skull x-rays in evidence today were taken *before* the post mortem surgery performed by Dr. Humes and remembered in 1997 by Reed, then why would Dr. Humes perform surgery on the frontal bone—on an area of the skull where the skull x-rays show bone was clearly *already missing?* As far as Dr. Humes is concerned, Reed's vivid recollection of exactly where the surgery was performed on the skull is quite damning, and suggests that Dr. Humes committed perjury when he said that a craniotomy was not necessary. The recollections of Tom Robinson, explored below, transform the likelihood that Dr. Humes committed perjury into a virtual certainty.

The Surgery Witnessed by Tom Robinson

Tom Robinson drew a diagram of a large hole in President Kennedy's posterior skull for both the HSCA staff and the ARRB staff almost twenty years apart, and the two sketches are virtually identical. On the diagram he executed for the ARRB, he also drew horizontal dotted lines, representing "saw cuts," both above and below the circular posterior skull defect. Robinson told both the HSCA staff and ARRB staff that the doctors opened up the back of the head to remove what was left of the brain. There can be no doubt about what he recalls seeing; he was quite consistent, and quite explicit in his two descriptions of this procedure, over 19 years apart. (Furthermore, Robinson told the ARRB that he had witnessed about 50 autopsies, so it seemed unlikely that he would mistake what he saw.) It seems obvious to me that he was witnessing the same procedure that

Ed Reed recalled—except that Ed Reed and Jerrol Custer were asked to leave the morgue, and Tom Robinson, unaccountably, was not. The only difference is that Ed Reed recalled seeing post mortem surgery just behind the hairline in the *forward top portion* of the skull, and Tom Robinson recalled seeing post mortem surgery *in the rear of the skull*, as well as the subsequent removal of the brain itself, which he noted was missing significant mass in the rear, in an area directly corresponding to where the hole in the head (the exit defect) was. The reader will also recall that when Tom Robinson was shown the extensive damage to the *top of the skull* in the "Fox Set" of autopsy photographs, he unambiguously stated to the ARRB staff that this was damage caused **by the doctors,** not by the bullet. He told the ARRB that this area was "broken" when the body arrived, but that the extensive damage to the top of the head in the autopsy photographs (see Figure 61) was caused by the pathologists.

AN EPIPHANY: THE POST MORTEM SURGERY TO THE HEAD WAS PERFORMED AT BETHESDA NAVAL HOSPITAL AFTER THE BODY ARRIVED, NOT ELSEWHERE PRIOR TO THE BODY'S ARRIVAL

It is clear to me, as I write this chapter in 2006, that Humes performed, and Boswell witnessed, a hurried, modified craniotomy, a surgical removal of large portions of the skull cap, immediately after the body of President Kennedy arrived at 6:35 PM (wrapped in a body bag inside a shipping casket), and while the bronze Dallas casket was still in transit from Andrews AFB in the Navy motorcade, or perhaps sitting in the parked Navy ambulance in front of Bethesda Naval hospital. During this procedure the large exit wound in the rear of the skull, a blowout resulting from a frontal shot, *was surgically enlarged to four or five times its original size,* and expanded in both a *lateral* and *superior* direction on the skull, in order to facilitate access to the brain, and the removal of evidence (see below), prior to the taking of skull x-rays by Custer and Reed. The purposes of this post mortem surgery would clearly have been threefold:

(1)   to remove bullets or bullet fragments from the brain that would have provided proof of a shot from the front, leading inevitably to a conclusion of crossfire, and therefore evidence of conspiracy; and to do so *prior* to the taking of x-rays, and *prior* to later removing what was left of the brain during the autopsy, after 8:00 PM;

(2)   to attempt to change the physical appearance of what was clearly noted to be an exit wound *in the back of the skull* when the body arrived at the morgue, to a much larger head defect that could later be represented as a 'blowout' or exit wound *chiefly in the top and right side of the skull,* caused by a hypothetical shot from behind; and

(3)   to remove any forensic evidence on the body of an entry wound in the front of the head, and also to remove any brain tissue that may have contained an obvious bullet track indicating a shot from the front.

In short, the post mortem surgery was a damage control exercise, performed by pathologists who had already been told that the President had been shot from both the front and behind, and that evidence of frontal shots had to be suppressed for reasons of national security.

This breakthrough in how to reinterpret the evidence of a head wound seen at Bethesda which was markedly larger than the one observed in Dallas came as a sudden insight; it was a true paradigm shift that I had been led to by "connecting the dots" of Robinson's testimony, Reed's testimony, and Boswell's skull diagram. This reassessment of <u>where the alteration of the head wound had taken place</u> immediately began to knock over several other dominoes: it caused me to completely reevaluate other patterns in the evidence which I had previously interpreted differently.

First, I am led to the inescapable conclusion that Boswell's autopsy sketch showing the top of the skull missing, and his corresponding annotations on the skull model at his ARRB deposition, are in reality describing *not* any damage caused by a gunshot wound in Dallas, <u>but damage inflicted by post mortem surgery performed by Dr. Humes as part of a coverup, and witnessed by Boswell, the author of the sketch.</u> By executing his sketch showing "10 x 17 cm missing" at the autopsy, Boswell was integrally involved in the coverup from the moment the body arrived, and was ***consciously and falsely representing the modified craniotomy Humes had performed as damage caused by an assassin's bullet.*** This conclusion implies that Drs. Humes and Boswell were ordered by higher authority to simply complete the post mortem tampering that had commenced elsewhere, and been badly bungled by someone else. Remember, Tom Robinson said the top of the head was "broken," but that the *doctors* <u>sawed it open</u> and *caused the damage in the autopsy photographs* of the superior view of the head. The gamble worked brilliantly; no one in the United States government ever suspected, until 1996 when Tom Robinson spoke so forthrightly and with such self assurance to the ARRB staff, that Boswell's diagram *represented post mortem surgery performed at Bethesda Naval hospital.* Humes and Boswell had to 'sell' to the establishment—including any future commissions or investigations—that the craniotomy Humes performed was *really* damage caused by an assassin's bullet, fired from behind. This explains to me why Humes did *not* destroy Boswell's autopsy drawing in his fireplace, even though it was covered by the blood of the President. The sketch could prove integral to selling the coverup, especially if the Dallas physicians were to make a lot of noise about having seen an exit wound *only in the <u>back of the head</u>* at Parkland hospital.

Second, this insight, in turn, causes a major reappraisal of Humes' oral utterance, noted by Sibert and O'Neill in their FD-302 report, that there had been *"surgery of the head area, namely, in the top of the skull."* Whereas David Lifton had interpreted this for years as a genuine exclamation of surprise by Humes, and evidence of post mortem surgery to the head area *prior* to arrival of the body at Bethesda, I interpret it today as a charade by Humes intended to mislead and deceive the two FBI agents and other autopsy witnesses, lest they become suspicious of the enormous size of the head wound. As it turned out this was unnecessary, but this "CYA" statement by Humes was then irretrievably placed into the official record in the Sibert-O'Neill report of 11/26/63. Humes had just inflicted this pattern of damage—the "surgery of the head area"—himself, and was probably in a high state of anxiety, and confusion, and may have even felt quite guilty at the time, so he erred in overdramatizing his "reaction" to the enormous cranial defect seen by the autopsy witnesses when the wrapping was removed from the skull following the 8:00 PM entry of the Dallas casket. Clearly, Humes *did make the statement about noticing surgery at the top of the skull,* which the FBI agents then dutifully recorded in their notes, and in their subsequent official report four days later; FBI documents from its own internal inquiry into this matter in 1966 (released long ago in response to FOIA requests) make it quite clear that the two FBI agents were directly quoting the chief pathologist, as Sibert and O'Neill confirmed to the ARRB staff during their depositions. There is no doubt in my mind that both Humes and Boswell deeply regretted this oral utterance from the moment it was made. They both denied seeing any evidence of surgery of the head area during their ARRB depositions. I conclude today that because they dared not admit the real reason for the statement recorded by the FBI agents, they simply stonewalled, and brazenly denied *ever* seeing evidence of 'surgery of the head area,' primarily because they were responsible for it themselves, and chose not to admit to being an integral part of a coverup. In *Best Evidence,* Lifton writes that author Josiah Thompson told him many years ago that when he interviewed Dr. Boswell in January 1967, "Boswell was very evasive...really very nervous indeed." Lifton wrote that Thompson said when he told Boswell he wished to discuss some aspects of the Sibert-O'Neill report with him, and reached into his briefcase for a copy of the document, "I think he turned five shades of white...I pulled the report out of the briefcase and showed it to him, and he physically blanched. I handed it to him and said: 'Look, read this paragraph;' and I could see the blood drain from his face." Lifton wrote that Thompson was baffled by Boswell's reaction, inasmuch as all he wanted to question him about was the by-then well publicized conflict between the Navy autopsy report, which said a bullet transited the body, and the FBI report of the events at the autopsy, which said the bullet entering the back did not transit the body. Like Lifton, I suspect that Boswell was afraid Thompson was going to raise the surgery issue; but unlike David Lifton, I interpret his "blanching," the blood draining from his face, and turning "five shades of white," as visible evidence of fear that his personal participation in a major coverup was about to be exposed by an investigative journalist. Twenty nine years later, before the ARRB General Counsel in 1996, and fifteen years after the publication of *Best Evidence,* Boswell was well prepared for the question, and laconically denied ever seeing any evidence of surgery of the head area. Humes denied it too, in a rather uptight manner, and with an edge to his voice that indicated he was not pleased with the question.

Third, it seems clear to me now, at this writing in 2006, that autopsy technician Paul O'Connor, who told both David Lifton (in 1980) and film maker Nigel Turner (in 1988) in filmed interviews that there was "no brain in the cranium" when the President's head was unwrapped in the morgue, was providing an honest recollection that a massive amount of the brain was missing, but that he was simply **conflating two events:** namely, *what* he saw (very little brain tissue in the cranium) *after he re-entered the morgue* shortly after 8:00 PM, and *when* he made this startling observation (i.e., 8 o'clock), with the *mode of transportation* of the body's initial arrival at 6:35 PM (namely, inside a shipping casket and wrapped in a body bag). The only thing "off" here in his recollection is his <u>time sense</u> of *when* he saw these different events; O'Connor always maintained that he saw the empty cranium as soon as the body was removed from the shipping casket, and that the shipping casket (with the body bag inside) arrived at 8:00 PM. My analysis is that his recollection of the President's body arriving in a shipping casket, wrapped in a body bag, is "spot on," and consistent with the first casket entry; I also believe his recollection of seeing "no brain in the cranium" is essentially accurate (even if an exaggeration), but I am now convinced he made this observation when the head was unwrapped following the *second casket opening* (the opening of the bronze Dallas casket), witnessed by Sibert, O'Neill, Metzler, and presumably VanHoesen, Joe Gawler, and others. The time of 8:00 PM that O'Connor so vividly recalls, and that he has associated with the arrival of the shipping casket and body bag, is likely the result of temporal disorientation and memory merge, and in my view really represents the actual time that night he was shocked by the sight of an unexpectedly large head wound, and a cranium that was more than half empty—in his words, that contained only "splattered brain matter." The audible "gasp" O'Connor recalled hearing in the morgue from others when they saw the enormous size of the (now enlarged) head wound, and the absence of much of the brain was, in my view, a genuine reaction of shock and disbelief that so much damage could have been caused by one bullet—and may have been what prompted Humes to engage in his prevarication, uttering mock surprise that there had been "surgery of the head area, namely in the top of the skull." Humes' handlers and superiors that night must have recoiled in horror when he made this statement; it was probably no more convincing than the Claude Rains character was in *Casablanca* when he professed surprise, and shock, that there was gambling going on in Rick's *Café Americain*—and it was certainly dangerous, because if Arlen Specter had shown any curiosity in 1964 about the surgery statement, and the contrary observations of the Dallas physicians about the size and location of the exit wound in the head, he may have exposed the coverup.

There is no doubt in my mind that O'Connor did see the nude body of President Kennedy, with the head wrapped in a sheet, removed from a zippered body bag from inside a shipping casket, and that he helped place it on the examination table earlier that evening immediately after it arrived at the morgue. I now conclude that the actual time he was ordered to leave the morgue was in reality *right after this event,* rather than later as he recalled to the HSCA staff, and that as a result he was completely unaware of the hurried craniotomy performed by Humes. (Both O'Connor and Jenkins said it was normally their job to remove the brain at Navy autopsies; if they had witnessed Humes performing one, they surely would have recalled it, because it was normally their function to do so.) The Bethesda alteration hypothesis explains why Humes would have ordered O'Connor out of the morgue—where he remained under Marine guard for about 40 minutes!—before commencing the modified craniotomy procedure. I infer that Humes was ordered to execute a coverup by enlarging the head wound and removing crucial evidence—of a frontal shot—from the brain, and O'Connor, whose job it normally was to perform all craniotomies at Bethesda, would have expressed undue curiosity if he had seen Humes doing an enlisted man's job.

I also conclude that O'Connor did not see President Kennedy's head *unwrapped* until following the opening of the bronze casket just after 8:00 PM—thus accounting for the time marker of 8 o'clock, which he so vividly remembered being associated with first seeing the enormous size of the head wound, and the 'empty' cranium. Those few autopsy witnesses who *did* see the head wound prior to the hurried, covert craniotomy performed by Humes and Boswell, such as Ebersole and Kellerman, committed a crucial error when they later honestly reported, under questioning, the true nature of what they had first seen—the Dallas head wound—when the President initially arrived in the shipping casket and body bag. In a sense, Ebersole "gave the store away" at his HSCA deposition by saying the back of the head was missing when the body was unwrapped, and by saying the autopsy photographs showing the back-of-the-head to be intact *did not look like what he remembered.* So did Kellerman, in his description of a head wound localized behind the ear that he gave to Arlen Specter when he was under oath in 1964, and in the sketch of the head wound he later made for the HSCA staff, showing a hole solely in the back-of-the-head, and not primarily in the top and right side of the head (see Figure 82).

How 'Flap Management' Affected the Descriptions of the Head Wound by Different Witnesses After Post Mortem Surgery

Dr. Boswell testified twice at his ARRB deposition that even though most of the bone was missing from the top of the cranium, that when the scalp flaps were folded over and into place on the top of the head, that this area looked essentially intact and the missing bone was not readily apparent. This is significant, because it explains how both Sibert and O'Neill could execute drawings for the HSCA staff that show a large defect in the back of the head, *but not in the top of the head*. They were recalling the head wound they first saw *when the scalp flaps in the top of the head were still in place* immediately after the head was unwrapped at 8:00 PM. They both recorded for the HSCA staff (and Sibert again for the ARRB) *their first impression of the head wound*. Jenkins, O'Connor, and Lipsey are recalling in their HSCA diagrams, and in their verbal descriptions, the way the head wound looked *after* the scalp flaps were reflected—that is, the area of *missing bone* after post mortem surgery, which was considerable, and much larger, than the area devoid of *both bone and scalp* in the rear of the head. O'Connor, understandably more than anyone else, was naturally attuned to the fact that much of the brain's mass was missing and that he subsequently did not have to perform a craniotomy, so this is his most vivid memory of that evening. He is clearly remembering what he saw *after* the scalp flaps—which in reality were created by incisions, and did not result from lacerations or tears caused by any bullet—were reflected shortly after the head was unwrapped. In contrast, Sibert and O'Neill remembered what they *first saw*—a posterior head wound devoid of scalp *and* bone—before reflection of the scalp flaps on the top of the head revealed the missing bone underneath.

How Much of the Brain Was Really Missing from the Cranium After Post Mortem Surgery?

The reader will recall that during his ARRB deposition, x-ray technician Jerrol Custer did not specifically recall a brain being in the cranium when he exposed the series of 5 skull x-rays. While I consider this an exaggeration of the true situation, the absence of a large percentage of brain mass *would be consistent* with Humes having performed a quick craniotomy and having removed a considerable amount of brain tissue (in order to dispose of bullet fragments, and perhaps even evidence of a bullet track from a frontal shot) while Custer and Reed were briefly upstairs on the fourth floor in the main x-ray department awaiting recall to the morgue. Custer also recalled some distortion of the President's visage—a sagging of the facial features—when he returned to the morgue to take the skull x-rays, causing him to believe that a craniotomy had already been performed, resulting in loose scalp and the corresponding alteration of facial features that always accompanies the removal of the skull cap and the reflection of the scalp. This recollection of Custer's during his ARRB testimony is consistent with my hypothesis that Humes had performed a quick, modified craniotomy and removed some superior and frontal brain tissue (to get the bullet fragments) before the skull x-rays were taken. The skull x-rays do show evidence of *some* brain tissue remaining in the cranium, but the x-rays reveal that much of the *forebrain* is missing from both hemispheres, and particularly from the right hemisphere.

Similarly, I view Paul O'Connor's recollection that there was "no brain in the cranium" as an understandable exaggeration, a snap judgment which *characterized the truth as he knew it when he first sighted the President's head wound*. Consider this: the right rear of the head was blown out in Dallas, along with about one third of the cerebral tissue and part of the right cerebellum, according to Dr. McClelland's 1964 Warren Commission testimony. Additionally, analysis of the three skull x-rays in the Archives by both Dr. Mantik (through optical densitometry) and Dr. Fitzpatrick (through visual observation) reveals that much of the forebrain was also missing when the skull x-rays were taken, particularly in the right hemisphere. Since the bone in the top of the skull was not missing in Dallas, and was removed surreptitiously by Dr. Humes prior to the start of the autopsy (per Robinson and Reed), I conclude that he did so primarily to gain access to the brain and to remove evidence from the body. Surely, in doing so as part of a hurried covert operation, he removed much of the forebrain, since this would have been the most efficient way of getting rid of the bullet fragments which were evidence of a frontal shot. (I also suspect that this is why no brain weight was recorded on the autopsy descriptive sheet: why bother to record brain weight, when you have already disposed of a significant portion of the brain's mass yourself, as part of a coverup? This failure, I believe, betrays the psychology of Dr, Humes that night: he was not accustomed to this kind of subterfuge, and so failed to record the weight of the remaining brain tissue after the brain was removed later in the autopsy, because he knew that the weight would constitute "meaningless" data.) Summarizing, when Paul O'Connor examined the President's head wound, he saw brain tissue missing *in each area where bone was missing* from the cranium—in the top of the skull on the right side (from post mortem surgery), and in the right rear of the skull (from the area of the exit wound observed in Dallas). Surely, he can be excused from deducing that the entire brain was missing, especially since he saw no craniotomy performed during the autopsy, either. While the x-rays reveal that there was more brain tissue present in the left cerebral hemisphere than on the right side, FBI agent Frank O'Neill still testified to the ARRB that *more than one half of the brain was missing* when he saw it outside the body. That description seems consistent with the recollections of Custer and O'Connor, providing shock and exaggeration are factored into their recollections.

Humes' testimony under oath to the Warren Commission and the ARRB that only minor cutting was necessary to remove what was left of the brain was probably only applicable to the actions he performed later, well after the skull x-rays were taken, in front of a public audience (i.e., the observers in the gallery and the FBI agents) after 8:00 PM. In other words, it is my contention that the craniotomy Robinson witnessed was performed to facilitate the clandestine removal of bullet fragments (and the associated brain tissue) from the cranium prior to the taking of x-rays, and that what remained of the brain—less than 50% of its mass, according to O'Neill—was removed well after the skull x-rays were taken, early in the autopsy, *after* the Dallas casket was opened at 8:00 PM, and *before* Finck's arrival at about 8:30 PM. When the remainder of the brain's mass was removed from the enlarged skull defect after 8:00 PM, a craniotomy was <u>not necessary</u> *because Humes had already performed one during clandestine, post mortem surgery earlier in the evening.* So, while I believe Tom Robinson when he says he saw the doctors saw away significant portions of the skull to get to the brain, I do not believe it was removed immediately, or in its entirety, at the same time as the craniotomy. I am of the opinion that Robinson saw *part* of the brain's mass removed immediately, in conjunction with the craniotomy, in order to remove evidence of a frontal shot (bullet fragments) from the cranium, which was the goal of the damage control operation. But I also believe that Humes had to leave the remainder of the organ in place for the taking of the (sanitized) skull x-rays. He certainly could not place skull x-rays in the record that depicted <u>no brain whatsoever in the cranium</u>, because that would blow the whistle on the coverup. Nor would Humes and his minders likely have presented an entire morgue full of witnesses with a body which had no brain at all remaining in the cranium when the Dallas casket was opened—especially after going to so much trouble to reintroduce the body into its original coffin in order to preserve the illusion that nothing was amiss, and that the chain of custody was intact. So it seems most likely, indeed almost certain, that the remaining portion of the brain—the portion of its mass not blown out by gunshot in Dallas, or removed earlier in the evening at the Bethesda morgue during the damage control operation—was removed from the enlarged cranial defect sometime between 8:00 PM and 8:30 PM. Since a craniotomy had already been performed in secret, this explains why no major incisions, or surgery, were necessary when the remainder of the organ was publicly removed. Sibert and O'Neill could therefore truthfully write in their report that the "first incision" they saw on the body was the y-incision, made at 8:15 PM, because they witnessed <u>no surgery on the skull cap</u> to remove what was left of the brain.

Why the Skullduggery?

The reader may now be wondering "why did the President's body have to arrive in a different casket, and inside a zippered body bag (instead of wrapped in sheets, as it was when it left Dallas), if the post mortem alteration of the head wound was to be performed at Bethesda, the site of the forthcoming autopsy?" In other words, why was such a convoluted shell game, with all its attendant risks, necessary? The answer comes in two parts.

The first part of the answer is that *the alterations were attempted elsewhere,* in a very hurried and inexpert manner—probably in the forward luggage compartment of Air Force One on the ground at Love Field, prior to takeoff—and there is evidence that *this initial attempt at evidence tampering was badly executed.*[33] I firmly believe that the small tracheostomy incision made at Parkland by Dr. Perry over the bullet wound in the throat—a bullet fired from in front of the motorcade—was likely tampered with prior to the body's arrival at Bethesda. I believe that someone grossly enlarged the tracheostomy incision—tearing the skin and damaging the tissues around the trachea in the process—expanding what had been a neatly closed, modest tracheostomy incision into a wound with widely gaping, irregular edges that no longer resembled a normal tracheostomy in either size or appearance. The individual who performed this tampering removed a small caliber bullet that had entered the front of the President's neck, had torn open the trachea, and had been deflected a short distance downward in his chest without exiting, where it had lodged atop the right lung where the large 5 cm bruise noted on both the pleural dome, and on the apical tip of the lung itself, was later noted at the autopsy. Dr. Charles Crenshaw expressed the opinion on national television, in 1992, that the tracheostomy incision shown in the autopsy photos was a least *twice* the length of the incision made by Dr. Perry at Parkland hospital, and that rather than looking like the neatly closed

---

[33]I agree with David Lifton that President Kennedy's body was removed from the bronze Dallas casket during, or prior to, the swearing-in of Lyndon Johnson in the center of the airplane, and that it was placed in a body bag and transported to Washington aboard Air Force One inside the forward luggage compartment, which was a pressurized, lighted, and air conditioned space. JFK's Air Force aide, Brigadier General Godfrey McHugh, was incensed at the delays in takeoff blamed on a "luggage transfer" from Lyndon Johnson's Vice Presidential jet, which made no sense to him at the time since both aircraft were going back to the same destination, Andrews AFB. I conclude that the 'luggage transfer' was a cover story for the delays involved in stowing the body safely in the forward luggage compartment of Air Force One, following its hurried removal from the Dallas casket before the heavy bronze coffin was secured for takeoff.

incision he had last seen following the President's death, it had become an open, gaping wound with no resemblance to Perry's incision. Dr. Humes described the 'tracheostomy' he encountered as a large, open, incised wound 7-8 centimeters long, with "widely gaping, irregular edges." He seemed genuinely perplexed by the ragged nature and large size of a supposed 'tracheostomy' during his testimony before both the Warren Commission, and the ARRB. (If only a *fragment* of the frontal shot to the neck was recovered by the plotters, or if *none* of it was recovered, then later intervention would have been necessary to complete the goal of removing evidence of a frontal shot to the anterior neck.) Furthermore, it appears that the cranium of the deceased President may have been subjected to brutal and extremely violent post mortem blunt force trauma in a botched, incomplete attempt to alter the appearance of the head wound, which was so obviously an *exit wound* in the rear of the head when observed at Parkland hospital. The reader will recall that Tom Robinson stated more than once that every bone in the President's face was broken; Jerrol Custer likened the crushed skull to the smashed shell of a hard boiled egg that had been rolled between one's hands while exerting too much pressure; Dr. Humes stated in his autopsy report that the extent and degree of the fractures to the skull taxed satisfactory verbal description, and that some fractures were as much as 19 centimeters in length. Humes also rather vividly described, on more than one occasion, that the severely fractured skull was essentially falling apart in his hands as he manipulated the scalp. Clearly this is more damage than would be caused by any single bullet, and is strongly suggestive of severe force applied to the skull after death in an attempt to gain access to the brain and alter the appearance of the wound. Yet this crude damage inflicted upon the cranium was apparently not sufficient to fool any observer into believing that the President had an exit wound in the top of his skull, nor did it enable access to the brain, and removal from the brain of bullets or bullet fragments. It is my contention that what David Lifton wrote about in Chapter 19 of *Best Evidence*—"certain preliminary examinations" (I prefer Lifton's term "pre-autopsy autopsy")—became necessary at Bethesda because the attempt by conspirators to alter the crime scene, the body of President Kennedy, had been so badly executed that the appearance of the head wound still made it obvious that he had been shot from the front. The alteration of the cranial wound to make it look less like an exit from a frontal shot, and the removal of forensic evidence of a frontal shot—bullet fragments—from the brain, had to be completed at Bethesda because these tasks had been mismanaged, in haste, earlier in the day. This realization no doubt led to mass confusion, improvisation, panic, and a literal host of unwanted witnesses to the interruption of the chain-of-custody of the body; luckily for the plotters, the body's arrival in the wrong casket, and in the incorrect wrappings, at an 'impossibly early' time, was only discovered years later. The problem the plotters had was that once the body was removed from the Dallas Casket onboard Air Force One and the aircraft took off from Dallas, it had to be *reintroduced* into the casket if the attempt at tampering was to go undetected.

This leads us to the second part of the answer: fate, and bad luck for the plotters, intervened in a way they could not have anticipated. If Jacqueline Kennedy had decided to return directly to the White House while the autopsy was performed at Bethesda Naval hospital, the plotters could have reunited the body of the President with the Dallas casket in private, prior to its arrival at the morgue, and thus avoided a whole host of problems that were encountered later that evening. Instead, she decided to stay with the Dallas casket herself all the way to Bethesda Naval hospital, making it impossible to place President Kennedy's body back into the bronze viewing coffin (in which it had left Trauma Room One) before that container reached the morgue. As a result, the plotters were forced to come up with an *ad hoc,* improvised, covert operation "on the fly," until they could reunite the body of President Kennedy with the casket in which it was known to have departed Parkland hospital. The result was literally almost a disaster, with numerous witnesses to the President's arrival at Bethesda in the wrong casket, in the wrong wrappings, and at an impossibly early time. Furthermore, when the plotters finally stage-managed a Dallas casket opening at 8:00 PM after President Kennedy had been reintroduced into the proper container, those persons who had witnessed his earlier arrival in the shipping casket, and the two FBI agents who had already carried the empty Dallas casket into the morgue earlier in the evening, had to be sequestered, and kept from witnessing the 8:00 PM entry. It appears to have been a narrow escape for those in charge of the coverup, and a virtual miracle that the shell game with the body and the two caskets was successfully executed. There were so many loose ends that inevitably, over time, the machinations of the plotters have been completely exposed, but they got away with their brazen tampering with the throat wound on November 22, 1963.

This major paradigm shift in my thinking about the autopsy—my changed assessment of the roles of Humes and Boswell, the "surgery of the head area" statement, and Boswell's autopsy sketch of 'damage' to the top of the head—all stemmed from the recollections of a mortician, Tom Robinson, and the subsequent marriage of his recollections with those of Navy x-ray technician Ed Reed. The clear and incontrovertible 'surgery of the head area' witnessed by these two men at the Bethesda morgue led me to deduce that Humes actually performed post mortem surgery on the President's head *himself,* and did so *early in the evening* immediately after the body arrived. Sometimes the "little people" on the stage of life make extremely valuable contributions to history with their observations. Such, I believe, is the case here. I no longer subscribe to David Lifton's 1981 hypothesis (published in *Best Evidence*) that Humes and Boswell (and the autopsy camera and x-ray machine) were "fooled by the body," i.e., deceived by *alteration and reconstruction* of the President's cranium by a skilled surgeon before the body arrived at the Bethesda morgue; I now believe they altered the crime scene *themselves* in the name of "national security." I believe they readily complied with the orders they received to do so because they were 'leaned on' by men of superior rank in a crisis situation; because they were scared; and because they found themselves in an impossible situation from which they could not escape. They were, after all, men in uniform who had been obeying orders all of their lives, in order to succeed and advance professionally. There can be no doubt that a very strong, intense, and completely convincing national security cover story was employed to get the two Navy pathologists to participate in a coverup from the moment the body arrived at the morgue. It probably involved the possibility of nuclear war, and was no doubt brutally and directly delivered to them by someone very high in their chain-of-command. It is no wonder that these two men of such different temperaments remained lifelong friends and bridge partners, for they shared a very big secret, and a searing experience. And it is no wonder that their testimony about what had happened at the autopsy began to diverge as soon as the ARRB separated them and questioned them separately; it wasn't possible to say "me too" anymore as they both had to the HSCA Forensic Pathology Panel in 1977, or "I have nothing to add," as Boswell had to the Warren Commission in 1964.

Gawler's Observations of a Body Bag and Shipping Casket Confirm a Broken Chain-of-Custody for President Kennedy's Body

John VanHoesen's independent recollection of a seeing a zippered body bag in the morgue, and his certain impression that the body had been transported in that body bag, is confirmation of the recollections throughout the years of other body bag witnesses: Paul O'Connor, Jerrol Custer, Floyd Riebe, and Captain Stover.

The "shipping casket" entry on the Gawler's funeral home "First Call Sheet" is stunning contemporaneous documentary corroboration of the recollections years later by Paul O'Connor, Floyd Riebe, Ed Reed, and Dennis David that the President's body arrived in an unadorned, simple, lightweight casket of the type normally used for shipping purposes, and not for ceremonial viewing or burial.

A bungled covert operation created numerous unwanted witnesses to the broken chain-of-custody of the President's body, and to the changing appearance of his wounds. Only desperate, on-the-fly improvisation by imperfect stage managers, and heavy-handed Cold War security measures—threatening the autopsy witnesses with court martial if they talked about the events they witnessed, and withholding the autopsy photographs and x-rays from public view—prevented the grossest possible tampering with the medical evidence from being exposed. The conspirators were lucky to have gotten away with their obstruction of justice. Only the extreme compartmentalization of the operation, and the more-or-less successful separation of the audiences witnessing different and mutually incompatible events—as well as the presumption of 'normalcy'—allowed the shell game with the body and the alteration of the wounds to go undetected in 1963 and 1964. Key to this was the suppression of the autopsy photos and x-rays by the Warren Commission, and the continued separation of the Dallas and Bethesda witnesses. The 'covert operation' on November 22-23, 1963 designed to secretly alter President Kennedy's wounds to suppress all evidence of shots from the front—which was really not that covert at all—has now completely unraveled and been revealed to the full light of day, but only after the passage of many years. In the mid 1960s the U.S. government controlled the flow of information about the event by suppressing evidence, and by either keeping witnesses separated, or silenced. The results of the HSCA investigation and the ARRB's 'under the radar' reinvestigation have been to expose how much the 'big picture' does not come together at all, and how problematic most of the medical evidence truly is. The observations of the Dallas treating physicians, the Gawler's morticians, and the autopsy witnesses, coupled with the leaking of the bootleg autopsy images, have together revealed the blatant and brazen nature of the medical coverup in the Kennedy assassination. It was not uncovered in 1964 because the Warren Commission chose to present a one-sided, prosecutorial brief based on medical illustrations made by an artist who was not present at the autopsy, rather than conduct an adversarial, fact-finding inquest using the autopsy photos and x-rays (which would have been subject to verification by Dallas and Bethesda witnesses). For the Warren Commission, controlling rumors and calming public fears took precedence over the truth; politics trumped forensic science.

Was Gawler's the Source of the Hearse That Delivered the Shipping Casket to the Bethesda Morgue?

In both his 1979 and 1980 interviews with David Lifton, and in his 1997 interview with me (see Appendix 61), Dennis David spoke of a black hearse delivering the lightweight shipping casket that his duty sailors carried into the morgue chill box anteroom. He also said that the hearse was filled with 'men in suits' (i.e., Federal agents of some kind), and that the two civilians who emerged from the front seat were dressed in white operating room smocks. I cannot help but wonder whether the hearse that delivered the shipping casket to the Bethesda morgue loading dock 20 minutes prior to the arrival at Bethesda of the gray Navy ambulance containing Robert and Jackie Kennedy—and the empty Dallas casket—was the hearse that Colonel Miller had originally requested Gawler's to send to Andrews Air Force Base. If Colonel Miller did not call in time to cancel the hearse *prior to its departure from Gawler's,* then the hearse Dennis David witnessed arriving with the body could very well have been the Gawler's vehicle sent to Andrews AFB. (This means that Hagan's claim that the hearse sent to Andrews was recalled, or cancelled by telephone could have been a lie, or that when it showed up unexpectedly at Andrews, it was nevertheless put to good use immediately.) I even have to wonder whether the two civilians Dennis David saw in white smocks were Joe Hagan and Tom Robinson. The white smocks do not necessarily mean that the two persons who emerged from the vehicle were engaged in tampering with the President's wounds—it seems more likely to me that those two people might have been morticians attired for their jobs, "ready to go to work," as it were. If it was a Gawler's hearse that delivered the shipping casket at 6:35 PM, then it was almost certainly Hagan and Robinson who emerged from the vehicle. This would nicely answer the so-far unanswered question of exactly when they did arrive at the Bethesda morgue. We know Tom Robinson was there early—early enough to witness the "Dallas wound" in the back of the head being enlarged by Humes with his saw so that the brain could be removed, and early enough for him to be certain years later that the damage to the *top* of the head in the autopsy photos was "caused by the doctors." This hypothesized early arrival of a Gawler's hearse with the shipping casket that contained the President's body would be consistent not only with Robinson being present in the gallery to witness early post mortem surgery on the deceased President's cranium, but could also explain why Joe Hagan's account of when he first arrived at Bethesda appeared to be so uncertain, and was so inconsistent during his interview—he might simply have been intentionally evasive in order not to reveal his role in a clandestine operation to which he might have sworn eternal secrecy in 1963, with the best of intentions. This is admittedly speculation, but this question needed to be openly raised. <u>*Someone* sent a black hearse with a shipping casket in it to the Bethesda morgue—and in my view, Gawler's is the prime candidate</u>. If Joe Hagan and Tom Robinson were in that hearse, it would explain Robinson's early presence in the morgue (prior to VanHoesen and Joe Gawler), and why the subject of caskets in general, and the "shipping casket" entry on the Gawler's "First Call Sheet" in particular, was so "radioactive" to Joe Hagan when he was interviewed by the ARRB staff. It would also mean, of course, that Joe Hagan had lied to the ARRB staff when he said he never saw any casket that night other than the mahogany model that Gawler's delivered to the morgue, *and* when he said that he only made the "shipping casket" entry on the "First Call Sheet" because of *what someone else had told him.*

In Part II of this book, the key events in the tentative "Gawler's/Autopsy Timeline' in this chapter, and the new insights about post mortem surgery at Bethesda Naval hospital, will be married with other key evidence about the autopsy photographs and x-rays, and the autopsy itself, to create an overview of what *really* happened at the Bethesda morgue on the evening of November 22-23, 1963 from the time the President's body arrived at about 6:35 PM on Friday evening, until the time it departed Bethesda for the White House just before dawn, at 3:56 AM on Saturday morning.

Chapter 7: A Short Trip to Texas

Calendar year 1996 was the year the ARRB staff deposed the three autopsy pathologists and the photographer of record, John Stringer. Jeremy Gunn knew that throughout this period I was quite anxious to interview or depose some of the Parkland hospital treating physicians. Furthermore, he was just as intrigued as I was about why the Dallas eyewitness testimony overwhelmingly supported the presence of an apparent exit wound in the right rear of President Kennedy's head, in contrast to the autopsy photographs. Jeremy's problem was that since the ARRB was not empowered to reinvestigate the assassination, he, as a member of the senior staff, had to come up with an appropriate justification for the expenditure of time and money that would be invested in any interviews of Dallas medical witnesses. Accordingly, Jeremy asked me to check the Warren Report and its accompanying 26 volumes of evidence, and the HSCA report, and determine whether there were any November 22, 1963 eyewitnesses from Trauma Room One at Parkland hospital who had been missed, or ignored by both the Warren Commission and the House Select Committee on Assassinations.

I came up with three candidates for potential interviews: Dr. Charles Crenshaw, Nurse Audrey Bell, and Dr. Robert Grossman. Dr. Crenshaw and Nurse Bell had been interviewed for television programs[1] (and in Crenshaw's case had published a book, *Conspiracy of Silence*), and Dr. Grossman had been interviewed circa 1981 by the Boston Globe newspaper—but none of these three people had been deposed or interviewed by either the Warren Commission or the HSCA. Since the two major government investigations into President Kennedy's assassination had not interviewed these three Trauma Room One witnesses, it was easy to justify the expenditure of scarce staff resources in this effort to 'clarify the record'—actually, in this case, we would be *completing* an <u>incomplete record</u>. I made all of the necessary contacts with these three witnesses after staff investigator Dave Montague located them, and they all agreed to meet with us in March of 1997.

In this chapter I will first describe the content of these three witness interviews during the short three and one half day trip to Texas Jeremy and I made from March 18-21, 1997. Following this, I will attempt to frame the results of our three interviews within the larger context of previously recorded recollections from other Parkland hospital witnesses over the years. All three of these interviews were recorded on audiotape using an inexpensive portable tape recorder purchased by the ARRB. The quality of each recording is not all that one would desire, since there is a high level of background hiss, but at least the recordings are available in the Archives for anyone who wishes to obtain copies and "clean them up" digitally. I also wrote ARRB meeting reports following the conclusion of our trip, and it is those meeting reports that are the source of most of the interview material in this chapter. Our three Texas witnesses were interviewed separately on successive days, and had not seen each other for many, many years.

---

[1] Audrey Bell had appeared in the 1988 *NOVA* documentary "Who Shot President Kennedy?" Charles Crenshaw had appeared in a major journalistic piece on ABC's "20/20" in 1992.

DR. CHARLES CRENSHAW

Dr. Crenshaw was a third year resident at Parkland hospital in 1963 who was present during the treatment of President Kennedy in Trauma Room One on November 22, 1963. He "went public" with his recollections of the events of that day in 1992 in his book *Conspiracy of Silence,* and on ABC's "20/20" television news magazine. He was subsequently attacked by some of his former colleagues at Parkland hospital in an article in the May 27, 1992 issue of *JAMA,* the *Journal of the American Medical Association.* His ethics were impugned in the article, and one former colleague questioned whether he was even present in Trauma Room One. Dr. Crenshaw subsequently sued *JAMA* for libel, and won an extremely large out-of-court monetary settlement. At the time the editor of *JAMA* was George Lundberg, a lifelong personal friend of Dr. Humes who published, in that same issue, an article strongly defending Drs. Humes and Boswell and the Warren Commission's findings. Following the monetary settlement of the libel lawsuit in Dr. Crenshaw's favor, *JAMA* fired Lundberg. The controversy garnered Crenshaw more attention and notoriety than he bargained for—he was even interviewed by the FBI regarding what he saw in Trauma Room One on November 22, 1963 following the publication of his book. I have reviewed the FBI report and his statements therein are very consistent with those in his ARRB interview.

We met with Dr. Crenshaw on March 19, 1997 at his home in Fort Worth.

Crenshaw's Summary of President Kennedy's Wounds

- He only saw one head wound.

- The head wound was *behind the right ear,* in the **occipital-parietal** region, in the right-rear quadrant of the head, and was *baseball-sized.*

- Brain matter was oozing from the wound as the President lay supine on the gurney, and had the consistency of oatmeal.

- He recalls seeing *cerebellum* extruding from the wound.

- *There was a complete absence of bone, hair, and scalp at the wound site.*

- There was a large blood clot high in the left forehead, above the left eye, but when the body was washed at Parkland after the President was declared dead, there was no wound there.

- He observed what he interpreted as a classic *bullet entrance wound* in the anterior neck, the size of the tip of one's little finger, just prior to Dr. Perry performing a tracheostomy.

- He observed **no damage** to the *right side* of the head, above the ear or forward of the ear; nor did he observe any damage to the *top* of the head.

642

Inaccuracies in Crenshaw's Book Were Unintended Journalistic Exaggeration

Dr. Crenshaw stated that he regretted certain inaccuracies in his book, which he described as embellishments by journalist and co-author Jens Hansen; he blamed these inaccuracies on a rushed and incomplete proofreading process. He told us the primary form of relating Parkland events he witnessed to Jens Hansen was via conversations which were tape recorded.[2]

Federal Agents Visited Parkland Hospital On Multiple Occasions

He recalled that Secret Service and FBI agents visited Parkland several times after the assassination. The one specific incident he recalled was a November 29, 1963 visit to Parkland by Secret Service agents who met with several Trauma Room One doctors; Crenshaw said he was not a part of this meeting. He said he was aware of no incidents in which either the FBI or Secret Service "forced changes" in testimony or observations of Parkland hospital personnel.

Crenshaw Saw No Damage to the Top or Right Side of the Head at Parkland Hospital

I vividly recall to this day that when I asked Dr. Crenshaw whether he had seen any damage to the *right side* of the President's head *above the ear,* or to the *top* of President Kennedy's head, he looked at me with a sense of astonishment that I would even ask such a question, and said "absolutely not."

Crenshaw Believed the Tracheostomy Incision Was Enlarged After President Kennedy Left Parkland Hospital

It is worth pointing out that in his ABC "20/20" interview in 1992, Dr. Crenshaw stated unambiguously that the size of the tracheostomy incision seen in the bootleg autopsy photographs was at least *twice as wide* as the small, neat incision he remembered Dr. Perry making at Parkland hospital, and that whereas the tracheostomy incision in the autopsy photographs was a gaping wound that was not closed, the incision made at Dallas in the anterior neck *closed completely after removal of the breathing tube* following the President's death.

Jeremy Gunn would not permit me to show or discuss any of the bootleg autopsy photos with Dr. Crenshaw.

Dr. Crenshaw Executes Drawings of President Kennedy's Head Wound

We took with us anatomic templates from *Grant's Anatomy* and asked Dr. Crenshaw to sketch on these diagrams his best recollection of President Kennedy's head wound. His three drawings are included in the illustration section of this book as Figures 17-19. He made no markings on the frontal view of the skull, "Crenshaw 1," so it has not been reproduced.

---

[2]As I recall, in his book the descriptions of the head wound are more consistent with the massive damage to the skull seen in the autopsy photographs, and not with the localized damage described above by Dr. Crenshaw.

NURSE AUDREY BELL

Nurse Audrey Bell was the Parkland hospital Supervisor of Operating and Recovery Rooms in 1963; she viewed President Kennedy's head wound, and then participated in the surgery on Governor Connally. We met with Audrey Bell on March 20, 1997 at her residence in Vernon, Texas.

Audrey Bell's Summary of President Kennedy's Wounds

- She did not see the throat wound herself; the tracheostomy had already been performed when she entered the room and the breathing tube had already been inserted in JFK's neck.

- Although only in Trauma Room One for 3 to 5 minutes, she did see the head wound. After asking Dr. Perry "where is the wound," she said he turned President Kennedy's head slightly to the President's anatomical left, so that she could see a *right rear posterior head wound,* which she described as *occipital* in both her oral remarks, and her drawings.

- Ms. Bell said she could see both brain and spinal fluid coming out of the wound, but could not tell what kind of brain tissue it was.

- She said it was her recollection that the right side of the President's head above the ear and forward of the ear, and the top of his head, were both intact, which is why she had to ask Dr. Perry where the wound was in the first place.

When I asked her whether the top or right side of President Kennedy's head was damaged, she too, just like Dr. Crenshaw the day before, registered on her face what I interpreted as amazement that I would even ask such a question.

Nurse Audrey Bell Executes Drawings of President Kennedy's Head Wound

Like Dr. Crenshaw, Audrey Bell made drawings of President Kennedy's head wound on three of the four anatomical templates from *Grant's Anatomy* that we presented to her, and these are reproduced in the illustration section of this book as Figures 20-22. She made no markings on the frontal view of the skull, "Bell 1," so it is not reproduced in this book.

A Major Revelation About Dr. Perry: Pressure from Bethesda Naval Hospital the Night of the Autopsy on President Kennedy

The following incident is not recorded in my meeting report of the interview, but is on the audiotape. I had read in a book written by assassination researcher Harrison Livingstone[3] that Dr. Perry (the surgeon who performed JFK's tracheostomy) had told Audrey Bell on the day following the

---

[3]See page 121 of *High Treason 2.*

assassination that he had been badgered all night on the telephone by people at Bethesda Naval hospital who attempted to get him to change his mind about having seen an *entry wound* in the front of the President's neck. I wanted to determine whether this account was true—whether or not Dr. Perry had really said this to Ms. Bell on November 23, 1963. While driving to Audrey Bell's home in Vernon, Texas Jeremy Gunn and I had a rather unpleasant disagreement in the car about whether or not I would be allowed to ask her this question. The dispute was finally resolved by Jeremy telling me that I was permitted to ask Ms. Bell if she had discussed the events of 11-22-63 with her co-workers that weekend, but that I was *not* permitted to ask her any leading questions about the event recounted in Harry Livingstone's book. (Jeremy did not trust Livingstone's research.)

Sure enough, at the end of the interview, I asked Ms. Bell is she had discussed the events of that weekend with her colleagues during the days immediately following the assassination. Just when I thought she was about to terminate the interview without addressing my true concern, she "made my day" by bringing up that very topic, almost as an afterthought, without me asking any leading questions. She told us that when she saw Dr. Perry Saturday morning, November 23, 1963 at Parkland hospital, she told him that he "looked like hell," or words to that effect. She said he responded by telling her that he had not gotten much sleep because people from Bethesda Naval hospital had been harassing him all night on the telephone, trying to get him to change his mind about the opinion he had expressed at the Parkland hospital press conference the day before, namely, that President Kennedy had an entry wound in the front of his neck. He told her that "his professional credibility was at stake here," and he did not know what he was going to do, or words to that effect.

There it was—"on the record" with a U.S. government agency—apparent attempts by members of the U.S. government the night of the autopsy to change history by altering the recollections and testimony of a key assassination witness. Of course it was hearsay, and would not have been admitted as evidence at a trial proceeding. But as Jeremy once pointed out to one of our own witnesses, hearsay *was allowed* at depositions. And this wasn't even a deposition; it was an unsworn witness interview. It didn't matter to me that it was hearsay, because the source of the hearsay, Audrey Bell, was an unimpeachable witness of sterling character with tremendous credibility. After all, she had been the Supervisor of Operating and Recovery Rooms at Parkland Hospital.

The Significance of the "Dr. Perry Controversy"

Following President Kennedy's death on November 22, 1963, a press conference was held in a classroom at Parkland hospital in which Dr. William Kemp Clark, the neurosurgeon who pronounced the President dead, and Dr. Malcolm Perry, the surgeon who had administered the tracheostomy and closed chest massage in an attempt to save his life, answered the questions of reporters. A document which provides a verbatim transcript of the questions and answers at that press conference, "White House Transcript 1327-C," has survived. (See Appendix 2.) The transcript reveals that in response to three different questions, Dr. Perry stated that President Kennedy had a bullet entry wound in the front of his neck. Those verbatim exchanges are reproduced below:

> Perry: The neck wound, as visible on the patient, revealed a bullet hole almost in the

mid line.

Q: What was that?

Perry: Bullet hole almost in the mid line.

Q: Would you demonstrate?

Perry: In the lower portion of the neck, in front.

Q: Can you demonstrate, doctor, on your own neck?

Perry: Approximately here (indicating).

Q: Below the Adam's apple?

Perry: Below the Adam's apple.

Q: Doctor, is it your assumption that it went through the head?

Perry: That would be conjecture on my part. There are two wounds, as Dr. Clark noted, one of the neck and one of the head. Whether they are directly related or related to two bullets, I cannot say.

Q: *Where was the entrance wound?* [Author's emphasis]

Perry: *There was an entrance wound in the neck.* As regards the one on the head, I cannot say.   [Author's emphasis]

Q: *Which way was the bullet coming on the neck wound? At him?*   [Author's emphasis]

Perry: *It appeared to be coming at him.*   [Author's emphasis]

_____

Q: *Doctor, describe the entrance wound. You think from the front in the throat?* [Author's emphasis]

Perry: *The wound appeared to be an entrance wound in the front of the throat; yes, that is correct...*[Author's emphasis]

The press conference was televised, as well as recorded by White House stenotypist Wayne Hawks. Without a doubt, high level officials were aware of Dr. Perry's statements by the time President Kennedy's autopsy began at Bethesda NNMC. The attempt by persons at Bethesda to pressure Perry to change his mind the night of November 22-23, 1963 about President Kennedy being shot from the front, is just one of many indicators that there was a concerted effort by members of the Federal government, immediately after the assassination, to implement a medical coverup. The government's seizure of the videotapes of the Parkland hospital press conference about the President's death, and its temporary suppression of the transcript of that press conference, is another.

Missing Videotape of Dr. Perry's Press Conference

David Lifton wrote in *Best Evidence* that "During the Warren Commission investigation, Arlen Specter requested the Secret Service to obtain videotapes and transcripts of the Parkland press conference." On March 25, 1964 James J. Rowley, Chief, U.S. Secret Service, wrote a letter to Warren Commission General Counsel J. Lee Rankin stating, in part, "The video tape and transcript of November 22, 1963, of the television interview of Doctor Malcolm Perry mentioned in your letter has not been located. After a review of the material and information available at the Dallas television and radio news stations, and the records of NBC, ABC, and CBS networks in New York City, no video tape or transcript could be found of a television interview with Dr. Malcolm Perry." Lifton also wrote that "Marvin Garson, a researcher assisting Mark Lane in preparing *Rush to Judgment,* was told by Dallas television executive Joe Long, of radio station KLIF, that the original recordings had been seized by Secret Service Agents."

A Government Lie

Secret Service Chief James J. Rowley, in the March 25, 1964 letter quoted above, twice stated that no transcripts of the Malcolm Perry press conference could be located. However, I have found unambiguous evidence that this is one of the "Big Lies" the U.S. government has perpetrated about the Kennedy assassination. On my copy of White House Transcript 1327-C, which ironically surfaced years later through the LBJ library, is stamped the following information with an automated U.S. government date/time stamp:

"RECEIVED
U. S. SECRET SERVICE

1963 NOV 26 AM 11 40

OFFICE OF THE CHIEF"

That's right: the transcript which Chief Rowley told the General Counsel of the Warren Commission could not be located was actually received by his own office on November 26, 1963, the day after President Kennedy's funeral. The Secret Service conducted its own investigation of the assassination for about one month, until it was forced to cease and desist by the FBI, so it would simply not be believable if an apologist were to speculate that the transcript got inadvertently "lost in the files." The information in the transcript would have been germane, and indeed central, to the Secret Service's own investigation. There is no possible benign excuse worthy of belief for the letter Chief Rowley signed out to J. Lee Rankin on March 25, 1964. The U.S. Secret Service was involved in the coverup of the true nature of President Kennedy's death, and Rowley's letter to

Rankin proves it. White House Transcript 1327-C, and Rowley's March 25, 1964 letter, together constitute "smoking gun" documents in the coverup of the Kennedy assassination.

Dr. Perry's Decision

History has shown how Dr. Perry reacted to the pressure he was subjected to the night of the autopsy by unknown persons at Bethesda. By March of 1964 Dr. Perry had changed his tune; the following exchange took place between Arlen Specter and him, under oath, on March 25th: (See Appendix 9.)

Specter: Were there sufficient facts available to you for you to reach a conclusion as to the cause of the wound on the front side of the President's neck?

Perry: No sir, there was not. I could not determine whether or how this was inflicted, per se, since it would require tracing the trajectory.

—————————

Specter: Well, what questions were asked of you and what responses did you give at the press conference? [Specter is referring to the press conference within one hour of President Kennedy's death managed by Wayne Hawks, and attended by Kemp Clark and Malcolm Perry—the same one that produced the verbatim White House Transcript 1327-C.]

Perry: Well, there were numerous questions asked, all the questions I cannot remember of course. Specifically, the thing that seemed to be of most interest at that point was actually trying to get me to speculate as to direction of the bullets, the number of bullets, and the exact cause of death. The first two questions I could not answer, and my reply to them was that I did not know, if there were one or two bullets, *and could not categorically state about the nature of the neck wound, whether it was an entrance or an exit wound,* not having examined the President further—I could not comment on any other injuries. [Author's emphasis]

Of course, the transcript of the press conference reveals that Dr. Perry did not testify accurately as to what he really said the day the President died. A short while later during the deposition, Specter asked Perry a number of leading, and hypothetical questions about whether or not the small wound in the anterior neck could have been an *exit wound:*

Perry: *It would be entirely compatible* [with the long, convoluted description Specter read to him about a hypothetical bullet transiting the neck from the rear to the front]. [Author's emphasis]

—————————

Specter: And would the hole that you observed on the President's throat then *be consistent with an exit wound?*   [Author's emphasis]

Perry: *It would.*   [Author's emphasis]

Specter: Has your recollection of the nature of the President's neck wound changed at any time from November 22 to the present time?

Perry: No sir. I recall describing it initially as being between 3 and 5 mm in size and roughly spherical in shape, not unlike a rather large puncture wound, I believe is the word I used initially.[4]

Specter: Have you changed your opinion on the possible alternatives as to what could have caused the President's wounds?

Perry: No sir. I have no knowledge even now of my own as to the cause of the wounds. All I can report on is what I saw, and the wound is that as I have described it. It could have been caused conceivably by any number of objects.

Specter: So, that the wound that you saw on the President's neck would be consistent with an *exit wound* under the factors that I described to you?   [Author's emphasis]

Perry: *Yes.*   [Author's emphasis]

Specter: Or, might it be consistent with an entry wound under a different set of factors?

Perry: That's correct, sir.

In other words, Perry is saying it "could have been either," although he did agree that it was consistent with an *exit wound* three different times in response to Specter's questioning. Specter only gave him a little wiggle room at the end of the exchange.

He was interviewed by the HSCA staff (Purdy and Flanagan) on January 11, 1978 and a transcript was made of the interview. The following exchange took place regarding the nature of the wound in the anterior neck:

Purdy/Flanagan: Do you have an opinion based on those two points [a tear on the right side of the trachea and slight bruising of the strap muscles] that you described as to the origin of the missile that caused the damage [to the anterior neck]?

Perry: No, I don't. The reason is that I didn't clearly identify either an entrance or an exit wound, and in the press conference I indicated that the neck wound appeared like an entrance wound. And I based this on its size and the fact

---

[4]In the Warren Report testimony, "cm" appears instead of "mm." However, we know from Dr. Humes' notes of his telephone conversation with Dr. Perry on 11-23-63 that the wound described by Dr. Perry was actually 3 to 5 *millimeters* in diameter, not centimeters.

that exit wounds in general tend to be somewhat ragged and somewhat different from entrance wounds...but in general, full[y]-jacketed bullets make pretty small entrance holes, and so, I don't really know. I thought it looked like an entrance wound because it was small, but I didn't look for any others, and so that was just a guess.

It appears to me that Dr. Perry must have become aware of White House Transcript 1327-C, because he is no longer denying that he said the throat wound was one of entrance, as he did under oath to Arlen Specter in 1964.

On August 27, 1998 Jeremy Gunn, who had resigned from the ARRB staff in July of 1998 but had been rehired as a consultant to perform a joint deposition of five of the Dallas treating physicians in Texas, had the following exchange with Dr. Perry during the ARRB deposition:

Gunn: Talk briefly about the neck wound, if we could. Dr. Perry, do you think that you were the one who probably had the best view of the neck wound?

Perry: I'm the one that stuck my foot in my mouth, but actually it looked like an entrance wound and the bullet appeared to be coming at him and I based that mainly on the fact it was a small wound to the neck and without any other information. I prefaced those comments at the press conference both before and after by saying that neither Dr. Clark nor I knew how many bullets there were or where they came from. Unfortunately, my comment said it's an entrance wound, and that was taken out of context of the others, but I did say that small wound.

Out of context? The transcript reveals he said unambiguously that it was an entrance wound, three times.

Perry: And I estimated, as I recall, about five millimeters [in diameter] like a pencil eraser I think I used as an example, something like that...

Baxter: I think you could sum up all of our comments on that wound that it would—it appeared to be an insignificant wound and—

Perry: Except for where it was.

Baxter: Yeah.

Perry: There's a lot of material in there.

Jones: When Dr. Perry and I went back upstairs into the OR after this had happened, I think we both—we were both talking in terms that this was an *entrance wound,* my impression when I saw it in the emergency room. *It never crossed my mind it was anything but an entrance wound.* Without having any history to go by, I thought it was an entrance wound. [Author's emphasis]

The Gochenaur HSCA Interview Transcript

The reader might well wonder, "what caused Dr. Malcolm Perry to change his certainty on November 22, 1963 about the presence of an entry wound in the President's throat, to an apparent willingness to please Arlen Specter and conclude that the wound he had observed was probably an exit wound, instead?" The material presented below offers one possible explanation.

In 1975 a former graduate student in the Seattle, Washington area named James Gochenaur contacted the "Church Committee" of the U.S. Senate (which was investigating past CIA and other intelligence agency activities in the United States) with disturbing allegations regarding Secret Service agent Elmer Moore. Gochenaur alleged, among other things, that Moore had pressured Dr. Perry in late 1963 to change his opinion about the nature of President Kennedy's throat wound from entry to exit before Perry testified to the Warren Commission. The Church Committee staff contacted Elmer Moore about the allegations. Although he admitted meeting with Dr. Perry on November 29, 1963 at Parkland hospital, Moore denied Gochenaur's claims that he pressured Perry to change his mind about the direction of the shot that caused the anterior neck wound; Moore told Senate investigator Patrick Shea that he had received a copy of the autopsy report while he was in Dallas and had simply asked Drs. Perry and Carrico, the two treating physicians who administered aid to the President, some questions about the report. Moore did admit, however, purchasing some photographs of demonstrators from a recent "riot" at a Seattle courthouse from Gochenaur, and confirmed that they had met three or four times, thus confirming that there was indeed a relationship between the two men.

Subsequently, the HSCA staff contacted Moore and received an angry, stonewalling response. Moore told the HSCA that the Schweiker subcommittee had already contacted him twice and that he had nothing more to say. He stated Schweiker's subcommittee was a waste of the taxpayer's money, and that a young lawyer on the subcommittee staff *had been ready to send him to jail for perjury* when he had told the staffer he could not remember all the details about questions that were asked him about past events. The HSCA staff member who wrote the OCR wrote, "Interview with kid gloves," and staff member Eileen Dineen wrote, "or boxing." Interesting.

On May 10, 1977 HSCA staff member Howard Gilbert interviewed Gochenaur on the telephone, and tape recorded the interview with Gochenaur's consent. The following exchanges are from that HSCA transcript of that recorded telephone interview:

Gochenaur: When I first talked to him...he was, you know, just completely and totally, ah, into the thing that I was trying to write him about the whole Kennedy thing, and all I really wanted to do is get information where I can get ahold [sic] of a photo [a JFK autopsy photo, according to the Church Committee records of its interviews with Gochenaur and Moore]...he says, hey, why don't you come on over to my office one day, we'll sit down and talk about it. I said—fine. Hey. So I went over there, and I talked with him for about five hours...

651

Gilbert: Now, what did your conversations with him [Moore] pertain to?

Gochenaur: Ah, basically, him venting anger at Kennedy, and ah...

Gilbert: What was the anger based on? Did he say?

Gochenaur: Well, *he said he was a traitor.* [Author's emphasis]

Gilbert: *He said Kennedy was a traitor?* [Author's emphasis]

Gochenaur: *Yeah.* [Author's emphasis]

Gilbert: This is what Elmer Moore said?

Gochenaur: Right.

Gilbert: Now, why [did] he say—how did he explain that? What did he mean?

Gochenaur: Well, he prefaced it by saying that ah, well, he said, you know, no matter how strange things get here, we've got it better than they do. But he was giving away everything to them. That's what he was saying.

Gilbert: *He was saying Kennedy was giving things away?* [Author's emphasis]

Gochenaur: *Yeah, to the Russians. OK?* [Author's emphasis]

Gilbert: All right.

Gochenaur: And, ah, he said ah, he says it's a shame that people have to die, but you know, maybe it was a good thing. A lot of people thought he was a traitor and sometimes I think that, too.

Gilbert: OK

Gochenaur: And, ah, then he went on to say that ah, well, ah, one of the things that was pretty impressive to me was the fact that when I was talking with him, he said that, ah, *we had to do what we were told, in regards to, you know, the way they were investigating the assassination, or we get our heads cut off.* [Author's emphasis]

Gilbert: Did he say who told, who gave them the orders?

Gochenaur: No.

Gilbert: Did he explain what he meant by getting his head cut off?

Gochenaur: No, but he certainly was shaking at the time, he was ah, he went fro—OK, let me explain that when I, when I talked to him it was on May—trying to think—it was May, May 7th—

Gilbert: What year?

Gochenaur: 1970, I believe. May 7, 1970, in the evening, I had come over there roughly around 4:30 or so, and I stayed until about 8 o'clock with him. And ah, as, as the evening wore along, he was scaring me. He was giving, you know, his speech mannerisms were getting pretty violent. OK?

Gilbert: Well, did you think it was odd that he was being this candid with you, a complete stranger?

Gochenaur: Completely. Ah, I—to tell you [the] truth, if I were to all put it down into words, I'm very amazed by the whole series of events.

Gilbert: Well, he, this was at the Secret Service office that you met him, right?

Gochenaur: Right.

Gilbert: OK. Was there anyone else present?

Gochenaur: No.

Gilbert: All right. What else did he have to say about Kennedy? Or anything that indicates to you that he may have had knowledge—ah, or may have done something wrong in the investigation?

Gochenaur: OK, what he told me was this, he said that *he badgered doctor Perry into changing his testimony,* he did not feel good about that. [Author's emphasis]

Gilbert: He—being Moore?

Gochenaur: Yes, Moore talked to Perry and, I guess, really laid it on to the poor guy.

Gilbert: In what respect, what areas did he badger Perry with respect to?

Gochenaur: Ah, what Perry had seen, as he was doing his emergency operation, apparently.

Gilbert: *Well, in what ways did he indicate to you that he had Perry distort the truth?* [Author's emphasis]

Gochenaur: In—I think that *what he was trying to say was [get] him to making a flat statement that there was no entry wound in the neck...*[Author's emphasis]

_____

Gilbert: Well, did he, did he indicate to you in any way, or can you recollect as best you can, the exact words or substance that he used with respect to what he did to Perry?

Gochenaur: ...from Washington, he got some marching orders to go down and talk with the doctors at Parkland hospital.

_____

Gochenaur: ...he immediately went to talk to the doctors, and he talked to Perry, and apparently he told me that there was one thing that he did during the whole thing that he didn't have a very good feeling about, was, the way he put it, badgering Perry.

_____

Gochenaur: ...when everything started to get heated was when I asked him—were you really in San Francisco that day [11-22-63], you know, then the guy really blew up.

Gilbert: What did he say?

Gochenaur: He started shouting, he said, he came out with that phrase I told you about—we were—I did everything I was told, we all did everything we were told, or we'd get our heads cut off. You better believe that, is the way he put it. Then he went in, launched into this ah, thing about—right, immediately after that launched into the thing that ah, you know, Kennedy was ah, you know, he had [sic] a traitor...

This has been a lengthy digression, but it shows the potential importance of even "one little statement" in an interview, providing one understands the context of that statement. Let's sum up here: Dr. Perry was apparently pressured the night of President Kennedy's autopsy by telephone calls from Bethesda, and was apparently badgered again by Secret Service agent Moore about two weeks after the assassination (on or about December 11th), and by the time he testified before Warren Commission staff attorney Arlen Specter in March of 1964, he had changed his mind about what he was once sure was an *entrance wound* in the President's throat, and testified to Arlen Specter three times, under the onerous influence of blatantly leading questioning, that the wound he had seen was consistent with an *exit wound.* And Dr. Perry has been 'tap dancing' ever since. I believe that Audrey Bell's recollections of Perry's troubled remarks the day after the assassination, and the excerpts above from the HSCA transcript of its interview of James Gochenaur, illustrate the mechanics of how a coverup is executed in this country. If you scare people a little bit, harass them, badger them, and possibly threaten them with ridicule (or worse), they will generally "go along to get along." And just to make sure, you confiscate the videotapes of what they said at the official press conference, and deny that a transcript exists, even though you have had one for four months. It's sad, but true. This is how the United States Secret Service and an ambitious and unscrupulous young staff attorney covered up evidence that President Kennedy was shot in the throat from the front.

DR. ROBERT G. GROSSMAN

On March 21, 1997 Jeremy and I interviewed Dr. Grossman in Houston at the Baylor University Medical School. Dr. Grossman told us that on November 22, 1963 he was a recently-hired instructor in neurosurgery at Parkland hospital, and that Dr. Kemp Clark was his supervisor.

Dr. Grossman's Recollections of President Kennedy's Wounds

- When he arrived in Trauma Room One with Dr. Clark, the tracheostomy had already been performed on President Kennedy.

- He said that he and Dr. Clark (Chairman of Neurosurgery at Parkland) together lifted President Kennedy's head so as to be able to observe the damage. It was Grossman's impression that no one in Trauma Room One even knew there was a head wound until he and Dr. Clark discovered that fact.

- Grossman said he observed two wounds to President Kennedy's head:

  - One was a circular puncture in the occipital region, which he characterized as an entry wound, approximately two centimeters in diameter, near the external occipital protruberance (EOP)—located approximately centerline, or just right of center, in the posterior skull. Through this wound he said he could see brain tissue which he believed was cerebellum.

  - The second wound was larger, was in the right parietal region, and was characterized by Grossman as an exit wound. He made clear to us that this wound was not an open hole in the cranium, but was a plate of bone, about 6 cm in longest dimension, lifted up from inside, which could only be seen when Dr. Clark lifted up some of President Kennedy's hair.

- Dr. Grossman indicated he believed one bullet caused both wounds, and entered through the tentorium (the membrane around the cerebellum) and traveled through the right cerebral hemisphere, exiting through the right parietal bone.

- Repeatedly throughout the interview, Dr. Grossman suggested we interview Dr. Kemp Clark, and said that he felt Dr. Clark's observations would be more accurate than his, since Dr. Clark had much more experience at that time than he with gunshot wounds to the head, and neurosurgery in general.

Dr. Grossman Executes Drawings of President Kennedy's Head Wounds

Dr. Grossman obliged us by annotating his recollections of President Kennedy's head wounds on the same anatomical templates from *Grant's Anatomy* that Dr. Crenshaw and Nurse Bell had drawn on. His three illustrations as reproduced as Figures 23-25. He did not annotate the frontal view of the skull, "Grossman 1," so it is not reproduced in this book.

An Oral Utterance from Dr. Grossman

After Jeremy Gunn turned off the tape recorder and indicated the formal interview was concluded, he asked me to produce the Ida Dox illustration of photographs 42 and 43 (Figure 54), showing the back of the head to be apparently intact, with the exception of a tiny wound of "entry" in the cowlick region. I was surprised, because Jeremy had been unwilling to produce this diagram, or any of the bootleg autopsy photographs, at the Crenshaw or Bell interviews. He was once again demonstrating inconsistent behavior that I did not then understand, and do not understand to this day. I believed at the time that all of our Trauma Room One witnesses should have been shown the same exhibits, and I still believe that today.

Dr. Grossman examined the Ida Dox illustration of the intact back-of-the-head at Jeremy's urging, and immediately opined, "that's completely incorrect." He insisted there had been a hole devoid of bone and scalp about 2 centimeters in diameter near the center of the occipital bone. Jeremy's eyes got rather large when Grossman made this forceful statement, and exchanged looks with me. He knew he had "blown it." This should have been on record—recorded on our cassette tape along with the remainder of the interview. And because of Jeremy's inexplicable reluctance, it was not. But Grossman said it; it will always be one of the most vivid memories that I have from all of our interviews and depositions.

Dr. Grossman's Recollections Constitute A Statistical Anomaly

Dr. Grossman recalled during his interview that Jackie Kennedy had worn a white dress; he is the only witness from Parkland hospital that I have ever heard describe Jackie Kennedy's striking pink Chanel suit worn on November 22, 1963 as a "white dress." But I do know one thing: Jackie Kennedy wore a white dress on November 21, 1963, the day prior to the assassination, in Houston. It was in all the filmed television coverage on the late evening news the night before the assassination.

Dr. Grossman is the only Parkland witness I am aware of—and I have studied the testimony of the Parkland staff since 1965 when I bought my abridged copy of the Warren Report—who says he saw an *entry wound* in the back of the President's head at Parkland hospital. I think more significant is the fact that if the reader examines his diagram of the back of the skull, Figure 24, it bears a truly striking resemblance to the drawing made by Navy photographer's mate Saundra Spencer at her ARRB deposition, Figure 32. The defect in the back of the head that he drew is almost identical to the one Spencer drew in terms of both placement and size.

Furthermore, what matters the most to me, as someone who looks for patterns in the evidence, is the fact that *he drew a hole in the rear of the head,* not the fact that he characterized it as an entry wound. Tom Robinson of Gawler's funeral home also characterized the hole he recalled in the back of the head as an entry wound, but its location was almost identical to the one Grossman drew. I believe that both Robinson had Grossman have been heavily influenced by the findings of the Warren Commission, specifically the drawings of H.A. Rydberg, the Navy illustrator. Thus they characterize the hole they each remember in the skull as an "entry wound."

Perhaps the most anomalous thing about Grossman's recollections is his statement that the hole in the posterior skull was a *puncture*. He is the only Dallas witness to describe the large defect in the posterior skull in this manner; many of those who saw it described it as an *avulsed wound*, and thought it was an *exit wound* as a result.

In the sense that Grossman believes he saw cerebellar brain tissue, his testimony is not so anomalous. This recollection corroborates those of Drs. Clark, Carrico, and Jenkins the weekend of the assassination that they saw cerebellar tissue extruding from the wound. Dr. McClelland testified to Arlen Specter in March of 1964 that he saw a large portion of cerebellum fall out of the posterior head wound onto the cart during the President's treatment.

I do not know what to make of Dr. Grossman's recollection of a parietal bone flap slightly lifted up from within, but still covered with hair. This makes me wonder whether he had been influenced by repeated viewings of the bootleg autopsy photographs.

Only one Parkland hospital employee who testified before the Warren Commission staff recalled seeing Dr. Grossman in Trauma Room One, and that was Dr. Kenneth Salyer, who stated that Dr. Grossman stayed only briefly; Dr. Clark, his companion and supervisor, did not even mention Grossman's presence in his Warren Commission testimony.

One final fact causes us to treat Dr. Grossman's recollections with extreme caution: he never wrote any contemporaneous reports at the time of the assassination, nor, of course, did he testify before the Warren Commission. It is true that Dr. Crenshaw did not write any contemporaneous reports or testify to the Warren Commission either, but we at least know that Crenshaw was in Trauma Room One for some time, since he was administering an IV to the President's right leg. Dr. Grossman was not interviewed by the media until 1981, and the Boston Globe newspaper story simply indicates that he saw two wounds to the head. By 1981, Grossman's recollections could well have been tainted by the Warren Commission's findings and its published medical illustrations.

Comparing Dr. Grossman's Recollections with Dr. Kemp Clark's

Grossman told us repeatedly during his ARRB staff interview *that Dr. Clark's recollections should be more accurate than his,* and deferred to Clark's greater experience in neurosurgery, and in observing and treating gunshot wounds in 1963.

I agree that Dr. Clark's immediate recollections should be more accurate than Dr. Grossman's in 1997, but not because I am willing to defer to authority—simply because they were written the weekend of the assassination, and were therefore more likely to be accurate, and *untainted* by any future investigative findings.

Dr. Clark's handwritten treatment report written on November 22, 1963 reads (in part) as follows:

"...a large wound beginning *in the right occiput extending into the parietal region.* Much of the skull appeared gone at first examination..." [most of Dr. Clark's handwritten treatment report is illegible, as published in the Warren Report] [Author's emphasis]

657

Fortunately, Dr. Clark also wrote a summary report that weekend consolidating the observations of all the primary players in Trauma Room One, and had it typed before signing it. It reads (in part) as follows:

"There was a large wound in the *right occipito-parietal region,* from which profuse bleeding was occurring. 1500 cc of blood was estimated on the drapes and floor of the emergency operating room. There was considerable loss of scalp and bone tissue. Both *cerebral and cerebellar tissue* were extruding from the wound." [Author's emphasis]

Dr. Clark's Warren Commission testimony to Arlen Specter on March 21, 1964 in Texas included the following exchanges: (See Appendix 3.)

Clark: ...I then examined the wound in the *back* of the President's head. This was a *large, gaping* wound in the *right posterior part,* with *cerebral and cerebellar tissue* being damaged and exposed." [Author's emphasis]

———————————

Specter: [referring to the Parkland press conference shortly following the President's death] At what time did the press conference occur?

Clark: Approximately 2:30.

———————————

Specter: What mechanical instruments were used, if any, by the press at the conference?

Clark: Tape recorders and television cameras, as well as the usual note pads and pencils, and so forth.

Specter: And who was interviewed during the course of the press conference?

Clark: Dr. Malcolm Perry and myself.

———————————

Specter: What, if anything, did you say in the course of that press conference?

Clark: I described the President's wound in his head in very much the same way as I have described it here. I was asked if this wound was an entrance wound, an exit wound, or what, and *I said it could be an exit wound, but I felt it was a tangential wound.* [Author's emphasis]

Specter: Which wound did you refer to at this time?

Clark: The wound in the head.

Specter: Did you describe at that time what you meant by "tangential?"

Clark: Yes sir, I did.

Specter: What definition of "tangential" did you make at that time?

Clark: As I remember, I defined the word "tangential" as being—striking an object obliquely, not squarely or head on.

Summarizing, *nowhere* does Dr. Clark state that the head wound he is describing is an *entry* wound; he only describes *one* head wound, not two; and the wound he recalls is characterized as "large" and "gaping,"and is therefore not consistent with the wound only about 2 cm in diameter described by Dr. Grossman. Clark characterized the head wound as either an *exit wound* or a *tangential wound,* not an entry wound. His written description of both cerebral *and cerebellar* tissue extruding from the head wound is consistent with Grossman's recollection of seeing *cerebellum.*

In conclusion, to the extent that Grossman's recollection is of a wound in the back of the head, and that he saw cerebellar tissue, it can be trusted. To the extent that he saw an *entry* wound in the back of the head, or that he saw *two* wounds to the head, it cannot be trusted, since it is so much at odds, statistically, with *all other* Parkland testimony. Coming in 1997 as it did, more than thirty-three years after the event, and being so inconsistent with all other Parkland recollections and testimony recorded shortly after the event in 1963 and 1964 when memories were fresh and less likely to be tainted and become modified, anyone who would use Dr. Grossman's testimony to contradict that of other Parkland physicians is skating on very thin ice.

A SIGNIFICANT SAMPLING OF PARKLAND HOSPITAL TESTIMONY CONFIRMS THE RECOLLECTIONS OF CRENSHAW AND BELL

To assist the reader in evaluating the unsworn testimony and wound diagrams provided by Dr. Crenshaw, Nurse Bell, and Dr. Grossman, I have set forth below the verbatim statements of those who assisted directly with the treatment of President Kennedy—that is, those who were standing right alongside the gurney in Trauma Room One administering treatment, and in a position to see the President's wounds up close. The reader will find that referring to the *Grant's Anatomy* templates in the illustration section (Figures 9 and 10) will help in understanding the word pictures painted by the physicians in both their written treatment reports and their subsequent Warren Commission testimony in March 1964.

Dr. Robert N. McClelland

Here is a pertinent excerpt from Dr. McClelland's March 21, 1964 Warren Commission testimony before Arlen Specter in Texas: (See Appendix 5.)

Specter: Before proceeding to describe what you did in connection with the tracheostomy, will you more fully describe your observation with respect to the head wound?

McClelland: As I took the position at the head of the table that I have already described, to help out with the tracheostomy, I was in such a position that I could very closely examine the head wound, and I noted that the *right posterior portion* of the skull had been extremely blasted. It had been shattered, apparently, by the force of the shot so that *the parietal bone was protruded up through the scalp and seemed to be fractured almost along its right posterior half, as well as some of the occipital bone being fractured in its lateral half, and this sprung open the bones that I mentioned in such a way that you could actually look down into the skull cavity* itself and see that probably *a third or so, at least, of the brain tissue, posterior cerebral tissue and some of the cerebellar tissue* had been blasted out. [Author's emphasis]

This description is very consistent with Dr. Crenshaw's drawing of the location of the posterior skull wound, particularly with regard to the area of damage being centered at the lamboid suture, where the occipital and parietal bones are joined.

Dr. Charles J. Carrico

The excerpt immediately below is taken from Dr. Carrico's handwritten treatment report prepared on November 22, 1963:

Two external wounds were noted. One small *penetrating* wound of the neck in the lower one third. The other wound had *avulsed* the calvarium and shredded brain tissue [was] present and profuse oozing...attempt[ed] to control slow oozing from [sic] *cerebral and cerebellar tissue* via packs instituted... [Author's emphasis]

An *avulsed* wound is one that is exploded outward, from inside to outside, and is consistent with an exit wound. This contradicts Grossman's recollection of a *puncture* in the back of the head. Incidentally, Carrico, who first saw the neck wound, describes it as a *penetrating wound,* which is <u>inconsistent</u> with the autopsy report's findings, and Arlen Specter's repeated attempts to characterize it as a wound of exit at the testimony of each Parkland treating physician.

This next excerpt is from Dr. Carrico's Warren Commission testimony before Arlen Specter in Texas on March 25,1964: (See Appendix 4.)

Carrico: ...The large skull and scalp wound had been previously observed and was inspected a little more closely. There seemed to be a *4 or 5 cm area of avulsion* of the scalp and the skull was fragmented and bleeding [oozing?] *cerebral and cerebellar tissue.* [Author's emphasis]

The mention again by Dr. Carrico of *cerebellar brain tissue* localizes the wound to the <u>posterior</u> skull, and makes certain that the head wound was *not* in the top or right side of the skull. If the head wound had been in the top and right side of the skull, as is shown in the extant autopsy photographs, there would not have been any *cerebellar tissue* extruding from the wound while the patient was lying supine on the gurney at Parkland hospital.

Later in the same deposition Carrico was asked to describe the head wound again:

Specter: Would you describe as precisely for me as possible the nature of the head wound which you observed on the President?

Carrico: The wound that I saw was a large gaping wound, located in the *right occipitoparietal area*. I would estimate [it] to be about *5 to 7 cm in size,* more or less circular, with *avulsions* of the calvarium and scalp tissue. As I stated before, I believe there was shredded macerated *cerebral and cerebellar tissues* both in the wounds and on the fragments of the skull attached to the dura. [Author's emphasis]

Dr. Carrico testified one more time, on March 30, 1964 before both Arlen Specter and the Warren Commissioners in Washington D.C.: (See Appendix 4.)

Specter: Will you describe as specifically as you can the head wound which you have already mentioned briefly?

Carrico: Sure. This was a *5 by 7 cm* defect[5] in the *posterior skull, the occipital region.* There was an absence of the calvarium or skull in this area, with shredded tissue, brain tissue present and initially considerable slow oozing...[Author's emphasis]

Specter: Was any other wound observed on the head in addition to this large opening where the skull was absent?

Carrico: No other wound on the head.

Dr. Paul Peters

The following excerpt is from the Warren Commission testimony of Dr. Peters in Texas before Arlen Specter on March 24, 1964: (See Appendix 6.)

Peters: ...I noticed there was a large defect in the *occiput.* [Author's emphasis]

Specter: What did you notice in the occiput?

Peters: It seemed to me that in the *right occipitalparietal* area that there was a large defect. There appeared to be *bone and brain loss* in the area. [Author's emphasis]

Specter: Did you notice any holes below the occiput, say, in this area below here?

Peters: No.

---

[5]The text on page 361 of volume III of the Warren Commission Hearings contains a typographical error: it reads "5- by 71-cm defect;" clearly, however, the intent was to say "5 by 7 cm defect."

Dr. Malcolm Perry

The excerpt below is from Dr. Perry's handwritten treatment report written on November 22, 1963:

> A large wound of the *right posterior cranium* was noted, exposing severely lacerated brain. Brain tissue was noted in the blood at the head of the carriage. [Author's emphasis]

Dr. Perry testified before Arlen Specter in Texas on March 25, 1964: (See Appendix 9.)

Perry: I noted there was a large wound of the *right posterior parietal area* in the head exposing lacerated brain. There was blood and brain tissue on the cart. [Author's emphasis]

Five days later, on March 30, 1964 Dr. Perry testified before both Arlen Specter and the Warren Commissioners in Washington, D.C.: (See Appendix 9.)

Perry: ...there was blood noted on the carriage and a large *avulsive* wound on the *right posterior cranium.* I cannot state the size, I did not examine it at all. I just noted the presence of lacerated brain tissue. [Author's emphasis]

Perry was concentrating upon the damage to the President's airway, performing a tracheostomy, and doing closed chest massage in an attempt to obtain a pulse—and yet he still noted that the skull wound was *posterior, and avulsive* in nature.

Dr. Ronald Coy Jones

Dr. Jones testified before Arlen Specter on March 24, 1964 in Texas: (See Appendix 8.)

Jones: ...he had a large wound in the *right posterior* side of the head. [Author's emphasis]

———————

Specter: Will you describe as precisely as you can the nature of the head wound?

Jones: There was a large defect *in the back of the head* as the President lay on the cart with what appeared to be *some brain hanging out of his wound* with multiple pieces of skull noted next [to the wound?] with the brain and with a tremendous amount of clot and blood. [Author's emphasis]

Dr. Marion T. Jenkins

Dr. Jenkins, the anesthesiologist in Trauma Room One, prepared a typewritten statement of his recollections on November 22, 1963. The excerpt below is from that document: (See Appendix 7.)

> There was a great laceration on the right side of the head (*temporal* and *occipital*), causing a great defect in the skull plate so that there was herniation and laceration of great areas of

the brain, even to the extent that *the cerebellum had protruded from the wound.* [Author's emphasis]

The reader will note by examining any anatomical diagram of the skull that the temporal and occipital bones join each other *behind the right ear.* In essence, this is simply a different use of words to describe the same location that others in Trauma Room One described with the words "occipital-parietal." Both descriptive phrases indicate a head wound localized in the right-rear quadrant of the head, behind the ear. Furthermore, Jenkins' use of the phrase "temporal and occipital" was corroborated by his recollection of *cerebellum* protruding from the wound: if he had meant "above the right ear" when he said "temporal," then the cerebellum could not have protruded at all.

Dr. Jenkins testified before Arlen Specter on March 25, 1964 in Texas:

Specter: Now, will you describe the wound which you observed in the head?

Jenkins: ...there was a great rush of blood from the skull wound. Part of the brain was herniated; I really think part of the *cerebellum,* as I recognized it, was herniated from the wound...[Author's emphasis]

Dr. Charles Rufus Baxter

Dr. Baxter wrote a handwritten treatment report on November 22, 1963, and the excerpt below is from that document:

On first observation of the [illegible] wounds *the right temporal and occipital bones were missing* and the brain was lying on the table, with extensive maceration and contusion. [Author's emphasis]

Dr. Baxter has described a wound in the *right rear quadrant of the skull* in the same manner that Dr. Jenkins did above; the "right temporal and occipital bones," to use Dr. Baxter's precise terminology, meet *behind the right ear.*

Dr. Baxter testified before Arlen Specter in Texas on March 24, 1964. The excerpt below is from that testimony:

Baxter: ...we had opportunity to look at his head wound then and saw that the damage was beyond hope, that this, in a word—literally *the right side of his head* had been blown off. With this and the observation that the *cerebellum* was present—a large quantity of brain was present on the cart, well—we felt that such an additional heroic attempt was not warranted...[Author's emphasis]

A very curious thing then happened. Arlen Specter asked Dr. Baxter to read his own handwritten treatment report from November 22, 1963, and the words spoken by Dr. Baxter, that described the location of the wound, **misreported** what he himself wrote the day the President died, as follows:

Baxter: On first observation of the remaining wounds, the temporal and parietal bones were missing and the brain was lying on the table with extensive lacerations and contusions.

Let us be clear here: Dr. Baxter *changed the content* of what he had written—"the right temporal and occipital bones were missing"—to "the temporal and parietal bones were missing," as he supposedly 'read' his own report aloud, under oath.[6] I can recall no other instance in which Specter asked a treating physician to read his own report aloud during his deposition. Furthermore, the change in content was significant. He had just testified to Specter that "the right side of his head had been blown off." His misreading of his own report—now saying "the temporal and parietal bones were missing," is entirely *consistent* with his other characterization in the same deposition, in which he said "the right side of his head had been blown off." What was going on here? Was it a simple error by Dr. Baxter? I suspect not. What I do suspect is that one of the Secret Service agents who visited Parkland hospital in late November and early December 1963 may have shown Dr. Baxter some autopsy photographs, either photographs 42 and 43, or perhaps photograph 26, and that this may have caused Dr. Baxter to doubt his own memory and then modify his own treatment report (and indeed, his recollections) accordingly.

What gives the lie to this redescription, and makes it not worthy of belief, is that in the same testimony before Specter, Baxter did note that he saw *cerebellum* present on the cart. If it was really only the *right side* of JFK's head that was gone—the temporal and parietal bones—then Dr. Baxter could not have seen *cerebellum* lying on the table in Trauma Room One on November 22, 1963. When Dr. Baxter testified to seeing **cerebellum,** he invalidated his own erroneous redescription of President Kennedy's head wound.

What the Parkland Testimony Does Not Say—And Why That Is So Important

The testimony I excerpted above covers *all* of the treatment physicians who were standing immediately around the gurney on which the President lay, and who assisted in a "hands-on" manner with efforts to resuscitate him. They, therefore, are the people who had the best view of the wounds.

The reader will note that **none** of these individuals described the *top* of the head as even *damaged,* nor did they describe significant portions of the *bone* in the top of the head to be missing, as Dr. Boswell did in his autopsy sketch on November 22, 1963 (see Figure 11), and on the ARRB skull model he annotated over 32 years later (see Figures 12-15). In this respect their testimony is greatly at odds not only with Boswell's consistent recollections, but with the autopsy photographs of the superior skull, ARRB view no. 3, photographs 7-10 and 33-37 (see Figure 61). Drs. Humes and Boswell both told the ARRB during their depositions that those photos were taken *prior to any incisions made by them.* I submit to the reader that if President Kennedy's head had looked at Parkland hospital the way it does in these autopsy photographs, the Dallas doctors would **not** have written the descriptions they did on November 22, 1963, or testified the way they did in March of

---

[6]I want to credit Dr. Gary Aguilar for making this discrepancy publicly known; it was a significant find.

1964.

Furthermore, the excerpts above from Parkland staff treatment reports, and from Parkland Warren Commission testimony, is entirely *consistent* with what Charles Crenshaw and Audrey Bell told the ARRB staff in March of 1997.

Some people study these conflicts—between the contemporaneous written reports and 1964 testimony of the Parkland physicians, and the autopsy photographs showing the back-of-the-head apparently intact, and the top of the head horribly disrupted and broken open—and conclude that the Dallas treatment staff was simply "wrong" in its collective observations because the focus was on treatment, and because the treatment staff was not performing an unhurried autopsy designed to explore with precision the patterns of damage to the body. I find this explanation unacceptable for four reasons:

First, as Dr. Clark indicated in the press conference following the President's death, his body lay upon the gurney in Trauma Room One for 40 minutes, so there was plenty of time to observe the head wound.

Second, if the Dallas treatment physicians have made mistakes in their descriptions of the head wound, *why is the error not random,* and why are their observations *so consistent with each other?*

Third, psychological studies show that when an event is extremely important, and the observations one is asked to recall are *salient* to what one was doing at the time (rather than, say, about irrelevant details), that the adrenalin in one's blood stream, combined with the intense focus on the issue at hand, together cause human memories about the salient details to be *remarkably accurate,* rather than inaccurate. It is irrelevant details that are remembered inaccurately by eyewitnesses, as is also the case for events that occur unexpectedly and end quickly, without giving the observer a chance to adequately focus on what is happening. The standard trick played on first year law students in which an impostor comes into the lecture hall and pretends to shoot the professor, and the students are subsequently asked to recall how many shots were fired and to describe the features and clothing of the assailant, is not at all analogous to the Parkland observations of President Kennedy's wounds. The recollections of the features and clothing of the assailant, and even of the number of shots fired, as remembered by the first year law students, usually vary widely, because: (1) it was an unexpected situation for which they received no warning, meaning their attention was not focused; (2) it happened and was over with very quickly, minimizing the opportunity for observation; and (3) the features and clothing of the assailant were irrelevant details compared to the fact that he fired a weapon—his features and clothing were not *salient* details. In contrast, the members of the treatment staff at Parkland hospital, many of whom were in Trauma Room One for 20 or 30 minutes, or even longer, had plenty of time to focus on what they were doing because the attempted resuscitation of the President went on for some considerable time. Since they were intent upon saving his life, the location and characteristics of his wounds were both *salient,* and within each observer's area of specialty—that is, anatomical details and locations they were well equipped to understand and describe.

Fourth, Parkland hospital was a teaching hospital and handled the majority of the violent trauma cases in Dallas. Its physicians were accustomed to seeing all manner of head injuries and gunshot wounds. Not only that, but these people had all been to medical school and had experience with both cadavers and with brain specimens used for teaching purposes. It is really highly unlikely that Dr. Kemp Clark (the Head of Neurosurgery), Dr. Jenkins, Dr. Carrico, and Dr. Baxter would *all* write and testify that they had seen *cerebellum* extruding from the President's head wound *in error*. A cursory examination of any anatomy textbook or atlas will reveal to the reader that cerebellar tissue looks very different from the brain tissue of the cerebral cortex. (See Figure 10.)

I believe that those such as Andy Purdy, Robert Blakey, Michael Baden, Gerald Posner, David Marwell (former Executive Director of the ARRB staff), and the members of the Review Board itself, who firmly defend the accuracy of the autopsy photographs, find it convenient, indeed even *necessary,* to believe that the Dallas treatment personnel were "simply all wrong," because to believe otherwise would upset their entire world view—their strong desire to believe that our government is basically good, that our institutions could not possibly have failed us so badly in 1963 and 1964, and that coverups of the magnitude of the JFK medical evidence suppression documented in this book do not happen in the world's greatest democracy. I believe that in view of the overwhelming evidence that the autopsy photographs present an inaccurate and intentionally dishonest portrayal of President Kennedy's wounds, that people of this mind set are burying their heads in the sand and engaging in psychological denial of the strongest kind, in order to preserve their own world view, so that they can literally "sleep well at night." This world view is *not* evidence-based; it is based on political mythology and on what they *want* to believe about their country's history. They have, in short, a psychological problem. The lens through which they view the Kennedy assassination is not based upon empirical observations, is not scientific, and is not rational; it is irrational, and is predicated upon emotional needs—an excessive identification of their own sense of well-being, and importance, with the wholesome reputation of their nation-state as a "good" nation, superior to all others. There are many people of this mind set who will deny whatever evidence is placed before them that President Kennedy's assassination was a large domestic conspiracy—an inside job—no matter how persuasive that evidence is, because it is psychologically necessary for them to do so. Fortunately, there also many in this country who are realists, and whose belief system about the natural world and the political universe they live in is empirically based—that is, based upon facts—and not upon mythology. I believe that our democracy becomes a better one, and a stronger one, when its citizens are informed by hard truth (no matter how unpleasant), rather than by lies, spun in support of the psychological imperatives of a self-centered political mythos.

In conclusion, the very consistent observations and testimony of the Parkland staff in 1963 and 1964 not only robustly support the wound diagrams made for the ARRB staff by Charles Crenshaw and Audrey Bell, but they further impugn the autopsy photographs showing President Kennedy's head damaged only on the top and the right side. In Part II of this book I will explain what I believe is the proper interpretation of the inconsistencies in the evidence between the Dallas observations, the autopsy photographs, and the testimony of Humes and Boswell. It will not be the same approach that the Clark Panel or the HSCA employed.

Made in the USA
Middletown, DE
13 December 2021

55565582R00234